Student Atlas of World Geography

Second Edition

John L. Allen
University of Wyoming

McGraw-Hill/Dushkin
A Division of The McGraw-Hill Companies

Book Team
Vice President & Publisher *Jeffrey L. Hahn*
Acquisition Editor *Theodore Knight*
Director of Production *Brenda S. Filley*
Designer *Charles Vitelli*
Graphics *Eldis Lima, Michael Campbell*
Typesetting Supervisor *Juliana Arbo*
Proofreader *Robin Charney*
Cover Design *Tom Goddard*
Cartography *Carto-Graphics, Eau Claire, WI*

We would like to thank Digital Wisdom Incorporated for allowing us to use their Mountain High Maps cartography software. This software was used to create maps 64, 65, 67, 68, 69, 70, 71, 72, 74, 75, 76, 77, 79, 80, 81, 82, 83, 85, 86, 87, 88, 90, 91, 92, 93, 94, 95, 96, 98, 99, 100

McGraw-Hill/Dushkin
A Division of The McGraw-Hill Companies

The credit section for this book begins on page 205 and is considered an extension of the copyright page.

ISBN 0-07-242547-4 ISSN: 1531-0221

Printed in the United States of America

123456789QPDQPD543210

A Note to the Student

The study of geography has become an increasingly important part of the curriculum in secondary schools and institutions of higher education over the last decade. This trend, a most welcome one from the standpoint of geographers, has begun to address the massive problem of "geographic illiteracy" that has characterized the United States, almost alone among the world's developed nations. When a number of international comparative studies on world geography were undertaken, beginning in the 1970s, it became apparent that most American students fell far short of their counterparts in Europe, Russia, Canada, Australia, and Japan in their abilities to recognize geographic location, to identify countries or regions on maps, or to explain the significance of such key geographic phenomena such as population distribution, economic or urban location, or the availability of natural resources. Indeed, many American students could not even locate the United States on world maps, let alone countries like France, or Indonesia, or Nigeria. This atlas, and the texts it is intended to accompany, is a small part of the process of attempting to increase the geographic literacy of American students. As the true meaning of "the global community" becomes more apparent, such an increase in geographic awareness is not only important but necessary.

The maps in the *Student Atlas of World Geography* are designed to introduce you to the patterns or "spatial distribution" of the wide variety of human and physical features of the earth's surface and to help you understand the relationships between these patterns. We call such relationships "spatial correlation" and whenever you compare the patterns made by two or more phenomena that exist at or near the earth's surface–the distribution of human population and the types of climate, for example–you are engaging in spatial correlation. Like the maps, the data sets in the atlas are intended to enable you to make comparisons between the distributions of different geographic features (for example, population growth and literacy rates) and to understand the character of the geographic variation in a single geographic feature. In many instances, the data in the tables of your atlas are the same data that have been used to produce the maps. At the very outset of your study of this atlas, you should be aware of some limitations of the data tables. In some instances, there may be data missing from a table. In such cases, the cause may represent the failure of a country to report information to a central international body (like the United Nations or the World Bank), or it may mean that the shifting of political boundaries and changed responsibility for reporting data have caused some countries (for example, those countries that made up the former Soviet Union or the former Yugoslavia) to delay their reports. It is always our aim to use the most up-to-date data that is possible. Subsequent editions of this atlas will have increased data on countries like Slovenia, Ukraine, or Uzbekistan when it becomes available. In the meantime, as events continue to restructure our world, it's an exciting time to be a student of world geography!

You will find your study of this atlas more productive if you study the maps and tables on the following pages in the context of the five distinct themes that have been developed as part of the increasing awareness of the importance of geographic education:

1. *Location: Where Is It?* This theme offers a starting point from which you discover the precise location of places in both absolute terms (the latitude and longitude of a place) and in relative terms (the location of a place in relation to the location of other places). When you think of location, you should automatically think of both forms. Knowing something about absolute location will help you to understand a variety of features of physical geography, since such key elements are so closely related to their position on the earth. But it is equally important to think of location in relative terms. The location of places in relation to other places is often more important as a determinant of social, economic, and cultural characteristics than the factors of physical geography.
2. *Place: What Is It Like?* This theme investigates the political, economic, cultural, environmental, and other characteristics that give a place its identity. You should seek to understand the similarities and differences of places by exploring their basic characteristics. Why are some places with similar environmental characteristics so very different in economic, cultural, social, and political ways? Why are other places with such different environmental characteristics so seemingly alike in terms of their institutions, their economies, and their cultures?
3. *Human/Environment Interactions: How Is the Landscape Shaped?* This theme illustrates the ways in which people respond to and modify their environments. Certainly the

environment is an important factor in influencing human activities and behavior. But the characteristics of the environment do not exert a controlling influence over human activities; they only provide a set of alternatives from which different cultures, in different times, make their choices. Observe the relationship between the basic elements of physical geography such as climate and terrain and the host of ways in which humans have used the land surfaces of the world.

4. *Movement: How Do People Stay in Touch?* This theme examines the transportation and communications systems that link people and places. Movement or "spatial interaction" is the chief mechanism for the spread of ideas and innovations from one place to another. It is spatial interaction that validates the old cliché, "the world is getting smaller." We find McDonald's restaurants in Tokyo and Honda automobiles in New York City because of spatial interaction. Advanced transportation and communications systems have transformed the world into which your parents were born. And the world your children will be born into will be very different from your world. None of this would happen without the force of movement or spatial interaction.
5. *Regions: Worlds Within a World.* This theme helps to organize knowledge about the land and its people. The world consists of a mosaic of "regions" or areas that are somehow different and distinctive from other areas. The region of Anglo-America (the United States and Canada) is, for example, different enough from the region of Western Europe that geographers clearly identify them as two unique and separate areas. Yet despite their differences, Anglo-Americans and Europeans share a number of similarities: common cultural backgrounds, comparable economic patterns, shared religious traditions, and even some shared physical environmental characteristics. Conversely, although the regions of Anglo-America and Eastern Asia are also easily distinguished as distinctive units of the earth's surface, they have a greater number of shared physical environmental characteristics. But those who live in Anglo-America and Eastern Asia have fewer similarities and more differences between them than is the case with Anglo-America and Western Europe: different cultural traditions, different institutions, different linguistic and religious patterns. An understanding of both the differences and similarities between regions like Anglo-America and Europe on the one hand, or Anglo-America and Eastern Asia on the other, will help you to understand the world around you. At the very least, an understanding of regional similarities and differences will help you to interpret what you read on the front page of your daily newspaper or view on the evening news report on your television set.

Not all of these themes will be immediately apparent on each of the maps and tables in this atlas. But if you study the contents of *Student Atlas of World Geography,* along with the reading of your text and think about the five themes, maps and tables and text will complement one another and improve your understanding of global geography.

John L. Allen

New to this Edition

The second edition of the *Student Atlas of World Geography* has several important changes and additions, making it even more useful than the first edition. A number of new world maps have been added, including a new double-page map showing major topographical and hydrographical features as well as sea-floor topography, a map of annual precipitation variability, and a map illustrating the distribution of globally-significant infectious diseases like AIDS and TB. We've also modified a number of existing maps to make them more readable: for example, adding the names of ocean currents to the map of temperature regions and ocean currents, splitting the map of mineral fuels and critical metals into two separate maps, and dividing the map of international alliances into separate maps showing current international alliances on one map and conflicts between nations on another. And, of course, the data-based choropleth maps on demographic, economic, and other conditions have been updated to reflect the most recent data avialable.

Perhaps the most significant change, however, and the one the users of the first edition recommended most, is an expansion of the number of regional maps in the final section of the atlas. In addition to the physical and political and thematic maps of general world regions, we've added larger-scale maps of subregions. For example, in addition to the general North American maps, we've added separate maps on Canada, the United States, Middle America, and the Caribbean. Each of the major regions now is accompanied by three or four larger-scale subregion maps, a change that should make using the atlas for reference purposes much easier. We've also added maps of the three major ocean basins as well as polar maps showing the Arctic and Antarctic. We hope you like these additions and changes. We've put a lot of thought and effort into making an atlas that you will think is even better than the first edition.

About the Author

John L. Allen is Professor and Chair of Geography at the University of Wyoming and Emeritus Professor of Geography at the University of Connecticut, where he taught from 1967 to 2000. He is a native of Wyoming and received his bachelor's degree in 1963 and his M.A. in 1964 from the University of Wyoming, and in 1969 he received his Ph.D. from Clark University. His special areas of interest are perceptions of the environment and the impact of human societies on environmental systems. Dr. Allen is the author and editor of many books and articles as well as several other student atlases, including the best-selling *Student Atlas of World Politics.*

Acknowledgments

The author wishes to recognize with gratitude the advice, suggestions, and general assistance of the following Advisory Board Members:

Nozar Alaolmolki
Hiram College

Barbara Batterson-Rossi
Palomar College

A. Steele Becker
University of Nebraska at Kearney

Koop Berry
Walsh University

Daniel A. Bunye
South Plains College

Winifred F. Caponigri
Holy Cross College

Femi Ferreira
Hutchinson Community College

Eric J. Fournier
Samford University

William J. Frazier
Columbus State College

Hari P. Garbharran
Middle Tennessee State University

Baher Gosheh
Edinboro University of Pennsylvania

Donald Hagan
Northwest Missouri State University

Robert Janiskee
University of South Carolina

David C. Johnson
University of Louisiana

Effie Jones
Crichton College

Cub Kahn
Marylhurst University

Artimus Keiffer
Franklin College

Leonard E. Lancette
Mercer University

Donald W. Lovejoy
Palm Beach Atlantic College

Mark Maschhoff
Harris-Stowe State College

Richard Matthews
University of South Carolina

Madolia Mills
University of Colorado–Colorado Springs

Robert Mulcahy
Providence College

Otto H. Muller
Alfred University

J. Henry Owusu
University of Connecticut

Steven Parkansky
Morehead State University

William Preston
California Polytechnic State University, San Luis Obispo

Neil Reid
The University of Toledo

A. L. Rydant
Keene State College

Deborah Berman Santana
Mills College

Steven Slakey
University of La Verne

Rolf Sternberg
Montclair State University

Richard Ulack
University of Kentucky

David Woo
California State University, Haywood

Donald J. Zeigler
Old Dominion University

Table of Contents

Part I. Global Physical Patterns 5

Part II. The Human Environment: Global Patterns 27

Part III. Global Demographic Patterns 35

Part VII. World Regions

Australasia

World Oceans, Arctic, and Antarctica

Part VIII. World Countries: Data Tables 133

Part IX. Geographic Index 187

Introduction: How to Read an Atlas

An atlas is a book containing maps which are "models" of the real world. By the term "model" we mean exactly what you think of when you think of a model: a representation of reality that is generalized, usually considerably smaller than the original, and with certain features emphasized, depending on the purpose of the model. A model of a car does not contain all of the parts of the original but it may contain enough parts that it is recognizable as a car and can be used to study principles of automotive design or maintenance. A car model designed for racing, on the other hand, may contain fewer parts but would have the mobility of a real automobile. Car models come in a wide variety of types containing almost anything you can think of relative to automobiles that doesn't require the presence of a full-size car. Since geographers deal with the real world, virtually all of the printed or published studies of that world require models. Unlike a mechanic in an automotive shop, we can't roll our study subject into the shop, take it apart, put it back together. We must use models. In other words, we must generalize our subject, and the way we do that is by using maps. Some maps are designed to show specific geographic phenomenae, such as the climates of the world or the relative rates of population growth for the world's countries. We call these maps "thematic maps" and Parts I through VI of this atlas contain maps of this type. Other maps are designed to show the geographic location of towns and cities and rivers and lakes and mountain ranges and so on. These are called "reference maps" and they make up many of the maps in Part VII. All of these maps, whether thematic or reference, are models of the real world that selectively emphasize the features that we want to show on the map.

In order to read maps effectively—in other words, in order to understand the models of the world presented in the following pages—it is important for you to know certain things about maps: how they are made using what are called *projections*; how the level of mathematical proportion of the map or what geographers call *scale* affects what you see; and how geographers use *generalization* techniques such as simplification and symbols where it would be impossible to draw a small version of the real world feature. In this brief introduction, then, we'll explain to you three of the most important elements of map interpretation: projection, scale, and generalization.

MAP PROJECTIONS

Perhaps the most basic problem in *cartography,* or the art and science of map-making, is the fact that the subject of maps—the earth's surface—is what is called by mathematicians "a non-developable surface." Since the world is a sphere (or nearly so—it's actually slightly flattened at the poles and bulges a tiny bit at the equator), it is impossible to flatten out the world or any part of its curved surface without producing some kind of distortion. This "near sphere" is represented by a geographic grid or coordinate system of lines of latitude or *parallels* that run east and west and are used to measure distance north and south on the globe, and lines of longitude or *meridians* that run north and south and are used to measure distance east and west. All the lines of longitude are half circles of equal length and they all converge at the poles. These meridians are numbered from 0 degrees (Prime or Greenwich Meridian) east and west to 180 degrees. The meridian of 0 degrees and the meridian of 180 degrees are halves of the same "great circle" or line representing a plane that bisects the globe into two equal hemispheres. All lines of longitude are halves of great circles. All the lines of latitude are complete circles that are parallel to one another and are spaced equidistant on the meridians. The circumference of these circles lessens as you move north or south from the equator. Parallels of latitude are numbered from 0 degrees at the equator north and south to 90 degrees at the North and South poles. The only line of latitude that is a great circle is the equator, which equally divides the world into a northern and southern hemisphere. In the real world, all these grid lines of latitude and longitude intersect at right angles. The problem for cartographers is to convert this spherical or curved grid into a geometrical shape that is "developable"; that is, it can be flattened (such as a cylinder or cone) or is already flat (a plane). The reason the results of the conversion process are called "projections" is that we imagine a world globe (or some part of it) that is made up of wires running north-south and east-west to represent the grid lines of latitude and longitude and other wires or even solid curved plates to represent the coastlines of continents or the continents themselves. We then imagine a light source at some location inside or outside the wire globe that can "project" or cast shadows of the wires representing grid lines onto a developable surface. Sometimes the basic geometric principles of projection may be modified by other mathematical principles to yield projections that are not truly geometric but have certain desirable features. We call these types of projections "arbitrary." The three most basic types of projections are named according to the type of developable surface: cylindrical, conic, or azimuthal (plane). Each type has certain characteristic features: they may be *equal area* projections in which the size of each area on the map is a direct proportional representation of that same area in the real world but shapes are distorted; they may be *conformal* projections in which area may be distorted but shapes are shown correctly; or they may be *compromise* projections in

The Coordinate System

which both shape and area are distorted but the overall picture presented is fairly close to reality. It is important to remember that all maps distort the geographic grid and continental outlines in characteristic ways. The only representation of the world that does not distort either shape or area is a globe. You can see why we must use projections–can you imagine an atlas that you would have to carry back and forth across campus that would be made up entirely of globes?

CYLINDRICAL PROJECTIONS

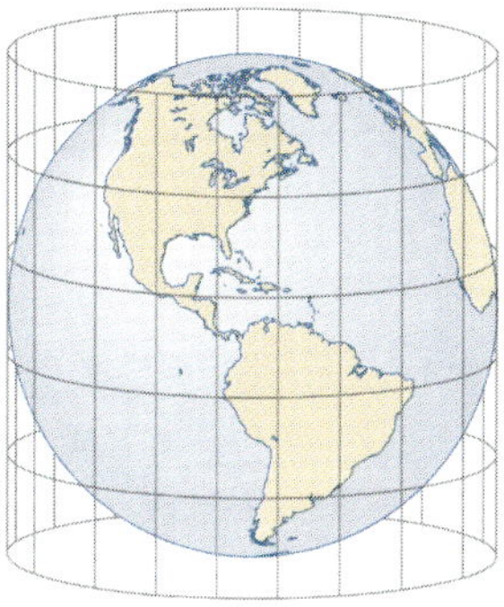

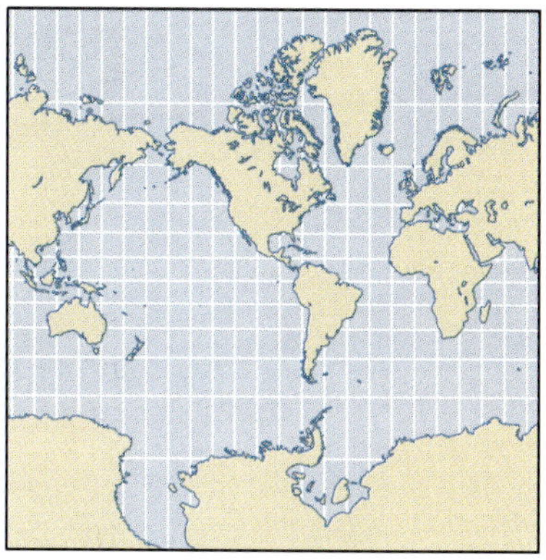

The Mercator Projection

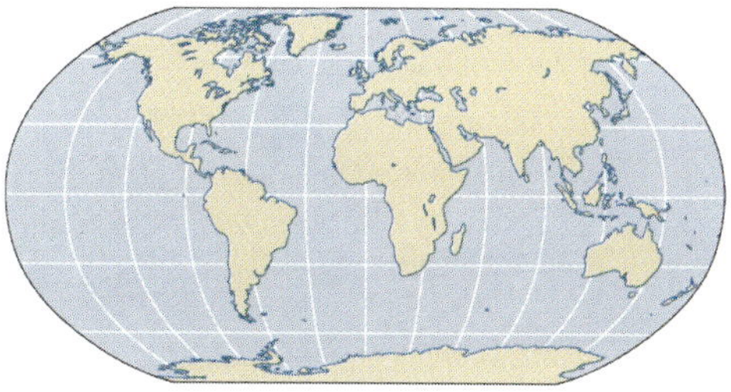

The Robinson Projection

Cylindrical projections are drawn as if the geographic grid were projected onto a cylinder. Cylindrical projections have the advantage of having all lines of latitude as true parallels or straight lines. This makes these projections quite useful for showing geographic relationships in which latitude or distance north-south is important (many physical features, such as climate, are influenced by latitude). Unfortunately, most cylindrical-type projections distort area significantly. One of the most famous is the Mercator projection shown above. This projection makes areas disproportionately large as you move toward the pole, making Greenland, which is actually about 1/7 the size of South America, appear to be as large as the southern continent. But the Mercator projection has the quality of conformality: landmasses on the map are true in shape and thus all coastlines on the map intersect lines of latitude and longitude at the proper angles. This makes the Mercator projection, named after its inventor, a 16th century Dutch cartographer, ideal for its original purpose as a tool for navigation–but not a good projection for attempting to show some geographical feature in which areal relationship is important. Unfortunately, the Mercator projection has often been used for wall maps for schoolrooms and the consequence is that generations of American school children have been "tricked" into thinking that Greenland is actually larger than South America. Much better cylindrical-type projections are those like the Robinson projection used in this atlas that is neither equal area nor conformal but a compromise that portrays the real world much as it actually looks, enough so that we can use it for areal comparisons.

CONIC PROJECTIONS

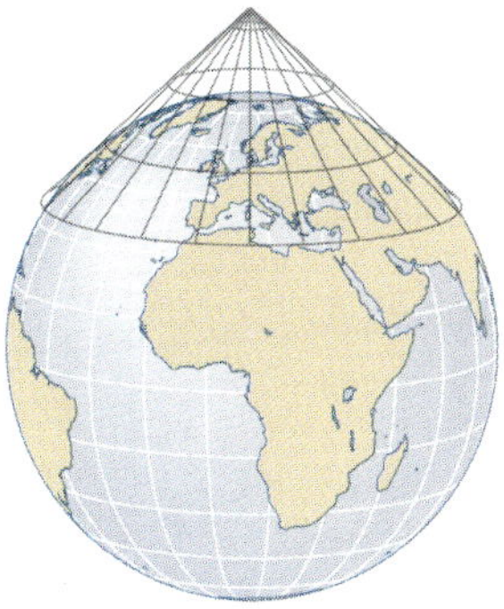

Conic projections are those that are imagined as being projected onto a cone that is tangent to the globe along a standard parallel, or a series of cones tangent along several parallels or even intersecting the globe. Conic projections usually show latitude as curved lines and longitude as straight lines. They are good projections for areas with north-south extent, like the map of Europe to the right, and may be either conformal, equal area, or compromise, depending on how they are constructed. Many of the regional maps in the last map section of this atlas are conic projections.

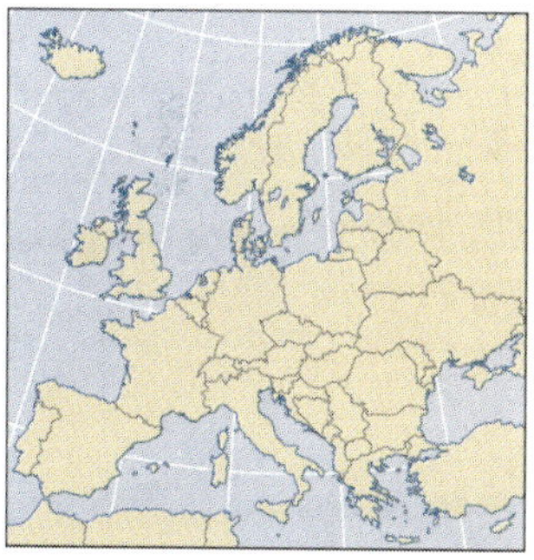

Conic Projection of Europe

AZIMUTHAL PROJECTIONS

Azimuthal projections are those that are imagined as being projected onto a plane or flat surface. They are named for one of their essential properties. An "azimuth" is a line of compass bearing and azimuthal projections have the property of yielding true compass directions from the center of the map. This makes azimuthal maps useful for navigation purposes, particularly air navigation. But, because they distort area and shape so greatly, they are seldom used for maps designed to show geographic relationships. When they are used as illustrative rather than navigation maps, it is often in the "polar case" projection shown below where the plane has been made tangent to the globe at the North Pole.

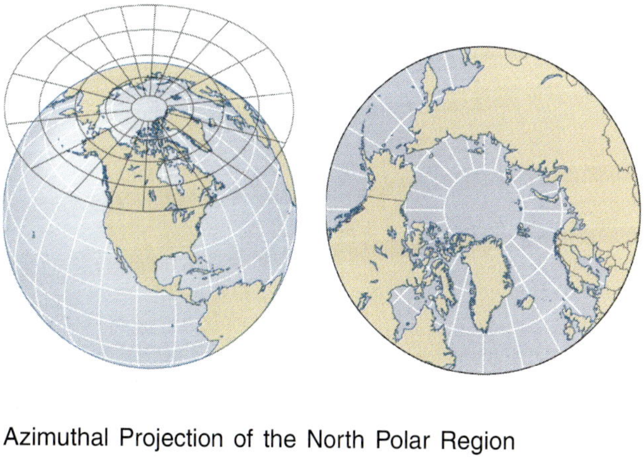

Azimuthal Projection of the North Polar Region

MAP SCALE

Since maps are models of the real world, it follows that they are not the same size as the real world or any portion of it. Every map, then, is subject to generalization, which is another way of saying that maps are drawn to certain scales. The term "scale" refers to the mathematical quality of *proportional representation,* and is expressed as a ratio between an area of the real world or the distance between places on the real world and the same area or distance on the map. We show map scale on maps in three different ways. Sometimes we simply use the proportion and write what is called a "natural scale" or representative fraction": for example, we might show on a map the mathematical proportion of 1:62,500. A map at this scale is one that is one sixty-two thousand five-hundredth the size of the same area in the real world. Other times we convert the proportion to a written description that approximates the relationship between distance on the map and distance in the real world. Since there are nearly 62,500 inches in a mile, we would refer to a map having a natural scale of 1:62,500 as having an "inch-mile" scale of "1 inch represents 1 mile." If we draw a line one inch long on this map, that line represents a distance of approximately one mile in the real world. Finally, we usually use a graphic or linear scale: a bar or line, often graduated into miles or kilometers, that shows graphically the proportional representation. A graphic scale for our 1:62,500 map might be about five inches long, divided into five equal units clearly labeled as "1 mile," "2 miles," and so on. Our examples below show all three kinds of scales.

The most important thing to keep in mind about scale, and the reason why knowing map scale is important to being able to read a map correctly, is the relationship between proportional representation and generalization. A map that fills a page but shows the whole world is much more highly generalized than a map that fills a page but shows a single city. On the world map, the city may appear as a dot. On the city map, streets and other features may be clearly seen. We call the first map, the world map, a "small scale" map because the proportional representation is a small number. A page-size map showing the whole world may be drawn at a scale of 1:150,000,000. That is a very small number indeed–hence the term "small scale" map even though the area shown is large. Conversely, the second map, a city map, may be drawn at a scale of 1:250,000. That is still a very small number but it is a great deal larger than 1:150,000,000! And so we'd refer to the city map as a "large scale" map, even though it shows only a small area. On our world map, geographical features are generalized greatly and many features can't even be shown at all. On the city map, much less generalization occurs–we can show specific features that we couldn't on the world map–but generalization still takes place. The general rule is that the smaller the map scale, the greater the degree of generalization; the larger the map scale, the less the degree of generalization. The only map that would not generalize would be a map at a scale of 1:1. and that map wouldn't be very handy to use. Examine the relationship between scale and generalization in the four maps below.

Map 1: Small Scale Map of the United States

Map 2: Map of the Northeast

Map 3: Map of Southeastern New England

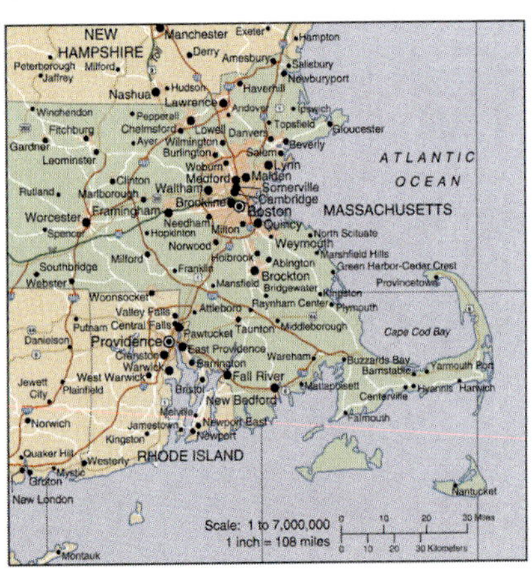

Map 4: Large Scale Map of Boston, MA

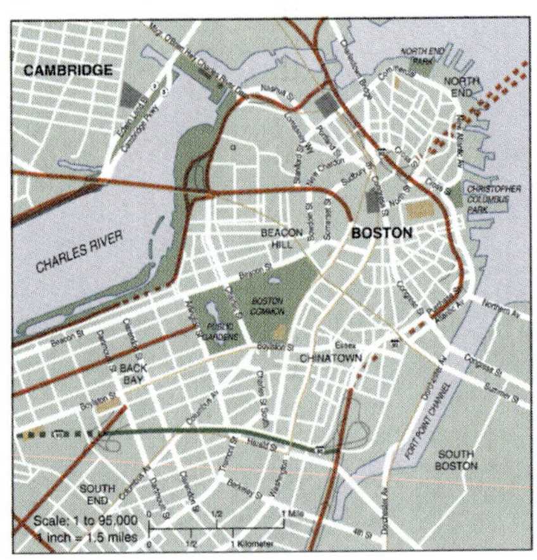

GENERALIZATION ON MAPS

A review of the four maps on the previous page should give you some indication of how cartographers generalize on maps. One thing that you should have noticed is that the first map, that of the United States, is much simpler than the other three and that the level of *simplification* decreases with each map. When a cartographer simplifies map data, information that is not important for the purposes of the map is just left off. For example, on the first map the objective may have been to show cities over 1 million in population. To do that clearly and effectively, it is not necessary to show and label rivers and lakes. The map has been simplified by leaving those items out. The final map, on the other hand, is more complex and shows and labels geographic features that are important to the character of the city of Boston; therefore, the Charles River is clearly indicated on the map.

Another type of generalization is *classification*. Map 1 on the previous page shows cities over 1 million in population. Map 2 shows cities of several different sizes and a different symbol is used for each size classification or category. Many of the thematic maps used in this atlas rely on classification to show data. A thematic map showing population growth rates (see Map 21 on page 36) will use different colors to show growth rates in different classification levels or what are sometimes called "class intervals." Thus, there will be one color applied to all countries with population growth rates between 1.0% and 1.4%, another color applied to all countries with population growth rates between 1.5% and 2.1%, and so on. Classification is necessary because it is impossible to find enough symbols or colors to represent precise values. Classification may also be used for qualitative data, such as the national or regional origin of migrating populations. Cartographers show both quantitative and qualitative classification levels or class intervals in important sections of maps called "legends." These legends, as in the samples shown below, make it possible for the reader of the map to interpret the patterns shown.

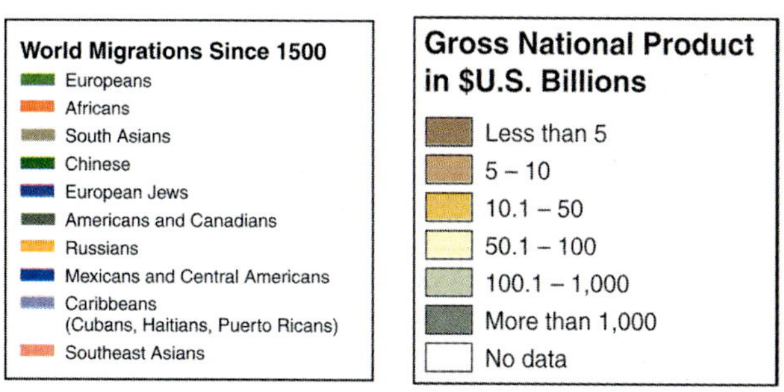

Map Legends from Maps 20 and 31

A third technique of generalization is *symbolization* and we've already noted several different kinds of symbols: those used to represent cities on the preceding maps, or the colors used to indicate population growth levels on Map 21. One general category of map symbols is quantitative in nature and this category can further be divided into a number of different types. For example, the symbols showing city size on Maps 1 and 2 on the preceding page can be categorized as *ordinal* in that they show relative differences in quantities (the size of cities). A cartographer might also use lines of different widths to express the quantities of movement of people or goods between two or more points as on Map 20 (see page 34).

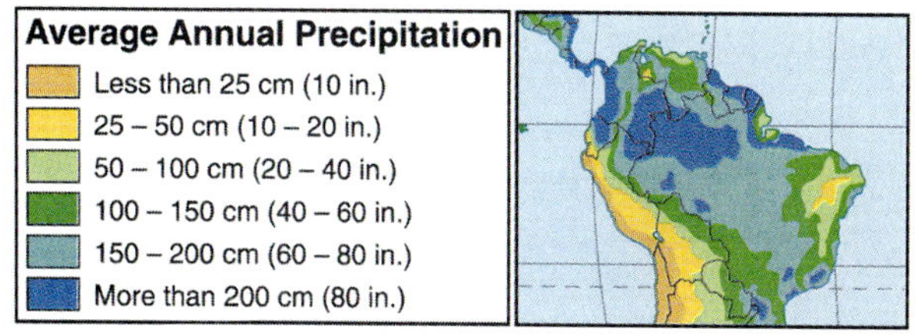

Interval Symbols

The color symbols used to show rates of population growth can be categorized as *interval* in that they express certain levels of a mathematical quantity (the percent of population growth). Interval symbols are often used to show physical geographic characteristics such as inches of precipitation, degrees of temperature, or elevation above sea level. The sample above, for example, shows precipitation (from Map 3a, page 10).

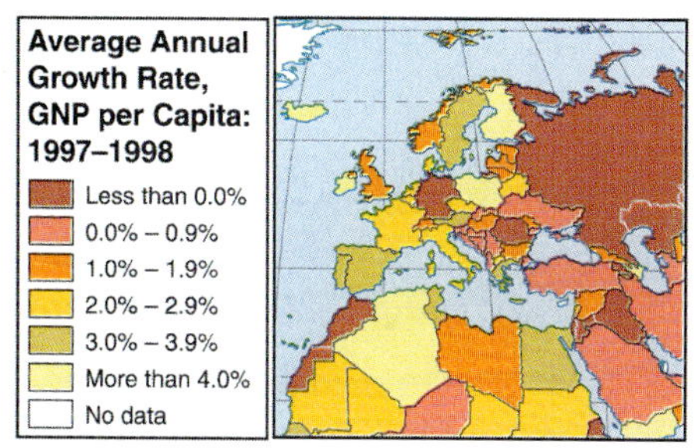

Ratio Symbols

Still another type of mathematical symbolization is the *ratio* in which sets of mathematical quantities are compared: the number of persons per square mile (population density) or the growth in gross national product per capita (per person). The map above shows GNP change per capita (from Map 33, page 50).

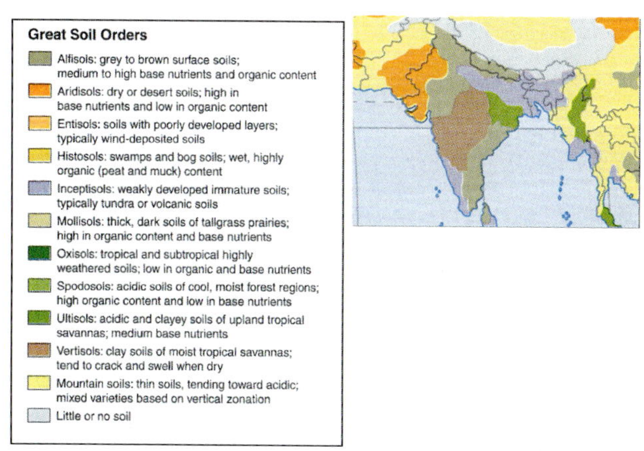

Nominal Symbols

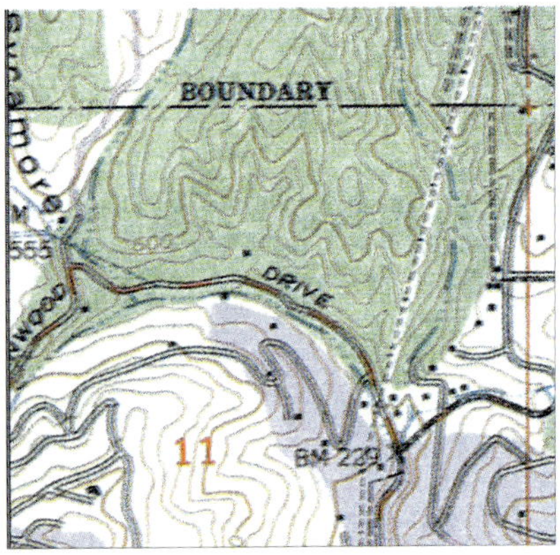

Interpolation

Finally, there are a vast number of cartographic symbols that are not mathematical but show differences in the kind of information being portrayed. These symbols are called *nominal* and they range from the simplest differences such as land and water to more complex differences such as those between different types of vegetation. Shapes or patterns or colors or iconographic drawings may all be used as nominal symbols on maps. The sample map at the bottom of page 3 uses color to show the distribution of soil types.

The final technique of generalization is what cartographers refer to as *interpolation.* Here, the maker of a map may actually show more information on the map than is actually supplied by the original data. In understanding the process of interpolation is it necessary for you to visualize the quantitative data shown on maps as being three dimensional: *x* values provide geographic location along a north-south axis of the map; *y* values provide geographic location along the east-west axis of the map; and *z* values are those values of whatever data (for example, temperature) are being shown on the map at specific points. We all can imagine a real three-dimensional surface in which the *x* and *y* values are directions and the *z* values are the heights of mountains and the depths of valleys. On a topographic map showing a real three-dimensional surface, contour lines are used to connect points of equal elevation above sea level. These contour lines are not measured directly; they are estimated by interpolation on the basis of the elevation points that are provided.

It is harder to imagine the statistical surface of a temperature map in which the *x* and *y* values are directions and the *z* values represent degrees of temperature at precise points. But that is just what cartographers do. And to obtain the values between two or more specific points where *z* values exist, they interpolate based on a class interval they have decided is appropriate and use *isolines* (which are statistical equivalents of a contour line) to show increases or decreases in value. The diagram below shows an example of an interpolation process. Occasionally interpolation is referred to as *induction.* By whatever name, it is one of the most difficult parts of the cartographic process.

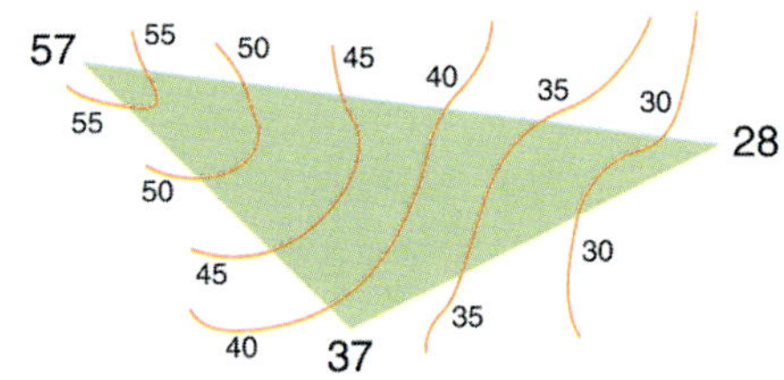

Degrees of Temperature (Celsius)
Interval = 5 degrees

And you thought all you had to do to read an atlas was look at the maps! You've now learned that it is a bit more involved than that. As you read and study this atlas, keep in mind the principles of projection and scale and generalization (including simplification, classification, symbolization, and interpolation) and you'll do just fine. Good luck and enjoy your study of the world of maps as well as maps of the world!

Part I

Global Physical Patterns

Map 1 World Countries
Map 2 World Physical Map
Map 3a Average Annual Precipitation
Map 3b Seasonal Average Precipitation—November through April
Map 3c Seasonal Average Precipitation—May through October
Map 3d Variation in Annual Precipitation
Map 4a Temperature Regions and Ocean Currents
Map 4b Average July Temperature
Map 4c Average January Temperature
Map 5a Atmospheric Pressure and Predominant Surface Winds—January
Map 5b Atmospheric Pressure and Predominant Surface Winds—July
Map 6 World Climate Regions
Map 7 Vegetation Types
Map 8 World Soil Orders
Map 9 World Ecological Regions
Map 10 Plate Tectonics
Map 11 World Topography
Map 12a World Resources: Mineral Fuels
Map 12b World Resources: Critical Metals
Map 13 World Natural Hazards

Map [1] World Countries

The international system includes the political units called "states" or countries as the most important component. The boundaries of countries are the primary source of political division in the world and for most people nationalism is the strongest source of political identity. State boundaries are an important indicator of cultural, linguistic, economic, and other geographic divisions as well, and the states themselves normally serve as the base level for which most global statistics are available. The subfield of geography known as "Political Geography" has as its primary concern the geographic or spatial character of this international system and its components.

Scale: 1 to 125,000,000 — 0, 1000, 2000 Miles; 0, 1000, 2000, 3000 Kilometers

Note: All world maps are Robinson projection.

NORTH SEA
NORWAY
SWEDEN
BALTIC SEA
ESTONIA
0 100 Miles
0 100 Kilometers
DENMARK
LATVIA
RUSSIA
LITHUANIA
NETHERLANDS
BELARUS
GERMANY
POLAND
BELGIUM
UKRAINE
CZECH REPUBLIC
LUXEMBOURG
FRANCE
LIECHTENSTEIN
SLOVAKIA
MOLDOVA
SWITZERLAND
AUSTRIA
HUNGARY
ROMANIA
SLOVENIA
CROATIA
YUGOSLAVIA (SERBIA-MONTENEGRO)
BLACK SEA
SAN MARINO
BOSNIA-HERZEGOVINA
MONACO
BULGARIA
ITALY
ALBANIA
MACEDONIA
GREECE
TURKEY
MEDITERRANEAN SEA
MALTA
ARCTIC OCEAN
Arctic Circle
ICELAND
FINLAND
R U S S I A
UNITED KINGDOM
IRELAND
ANDORRA
SPAIN
PORTUGAL
KAZAKSTAN
MONGOLIA
NORTH PACIFIC OCEAN
UZBEKISTAN
KYRGYZSTAN
TURKMENISTAN
TAJIKISTAN
NORTH KOREA
SOUTH KOREA
JAPAN
C H I N A
TUNISIA
CYPRUS
LEBANON
SYRIA
IRAQ
IRAN
AFGHANISTAN
MOROCCO
ISRAEL
JORDAN
KUWAIT
NEPAL
BHUTAN
ALGERIA
LIBYA
EGYPT
BAHRAIN
QATAR
PAKISTAN
SAUDI ARABIA
MYANMAR (BURMA)
Tropic of Cancer
TAIWAN
MALI
NIGER
ERITREA
UNITED ARAB EMIRATES
OMAN
INDIA
BANGLADESH
LAOS
CHAD
SUDAN
YEMEN
THAILAND
VIETNAM
PHILIPPINES
MARSHALL ISLANDS
NIGERIA
DJIBOUTI
ETHIOPIA
SRI LANKA
CAMBODIA (KAMPUCHEA)
UGANDA
SOMALIA
BRUNEI
PALAU
MICRONESIA
CAMEROON
MALDIVES
MALAYSIA
KIRIBATI
RWANDA
Equator
SINGAPORE
NAURU
KENYA
I N D O N E S I A
DEM. REP. OF THE CONGO
BURUNDI
SEYCHELLES
PAPUA NEW GUINEA
SOLOMON ISLANDS
TUVALU
EQUATORIAL GUINEA
GABON
TANZANIA
MALAWI
CONGO REPUBLIC
COMOROS
INDIAN OCEAN
ANGOLA
MOZAMBIQUE
EAST TIMOR
ZAMBIA
VANUATU
FIJI
MADAGASCAR
MAURITIUS
NAMIBIA
Tropic of Capricorn
BOTSWANA
AUSTRALIA
ZIMBABWE
SWAZILAND
SOUTH AFRICA
LESOTHO
NEW ZEALAND
MAURITANIA
MALI
SENEGAL
NIGER
GAMBIA
GUINEA-BISSAU
BURKINA FASO
GUINEA
BENIN
ATLANTIC OCEAN
SIERRA LEONE
NIGERIA
IVORY COAST
GHANA
LIBERIA
0 150 300 Miles
0 150 300 Kilometers
TOGO
0 100 Miles
0 100 Kilometers
CASPIAN SEA
RUSSIA
BLACK SEA
GEORGIA
AZERBAIJAN
ARMENIA
TURKEY
AZERBAIJAN
IRAN

Map 2 World Physical Map

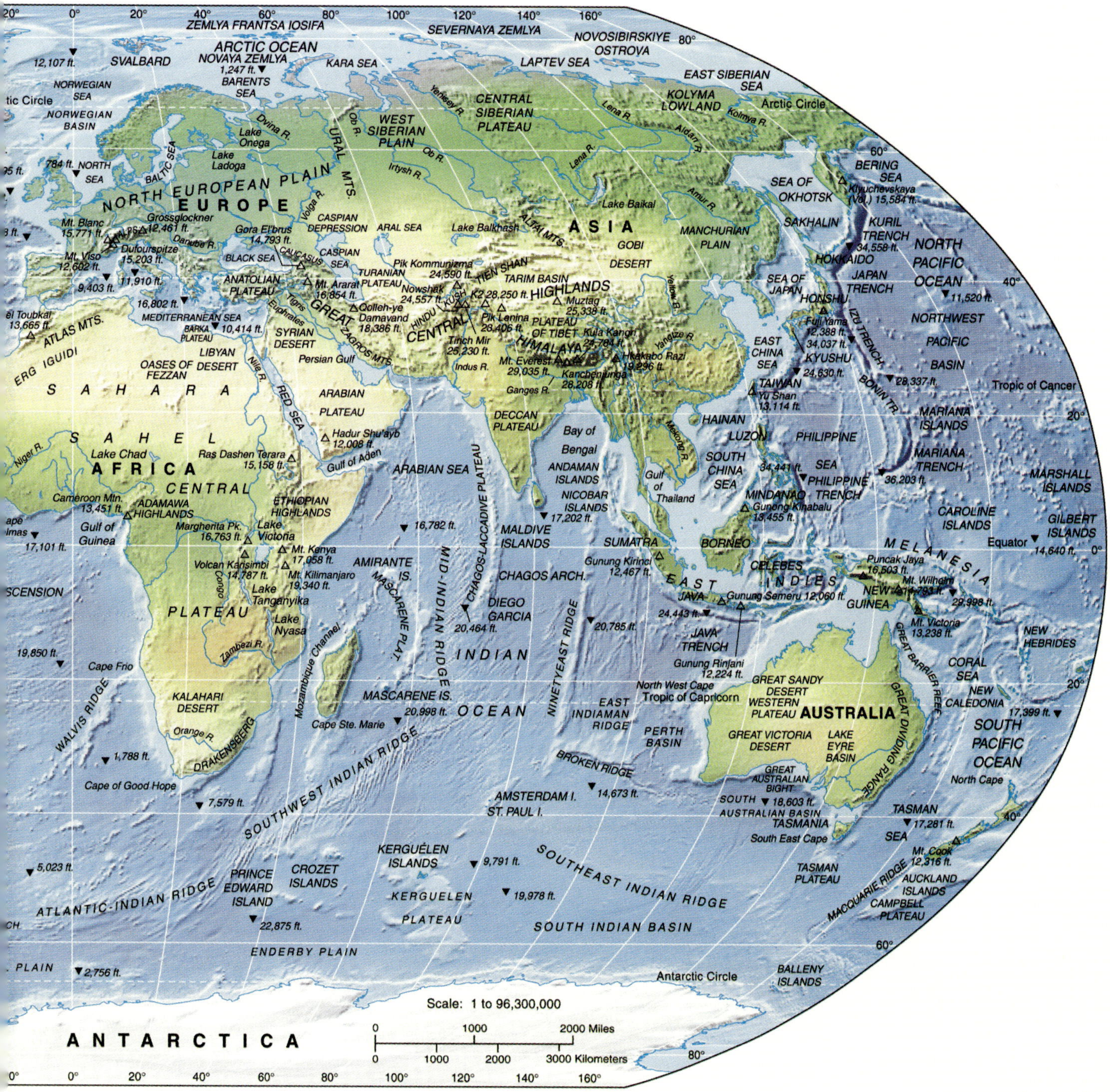
ZEMLYA FRANTSA IOSIFA
SEVERNAYA ZEMLYA
NOVOSIBIRSKIYE OSTROVA
ARCTIC OCEAN
NOVAYA ZEMLYA
1,247 ft.
12,107 ft.
SVALBARD
KARA SEA
LAPTEV SEA
BARENTS SEA
EAST SIBERIAN SEA
NORWEGIAN SEA
Arctic Circle
NORWEGIAN BASIN
KOLYMA LOWLAND
CENTRAL SIBERIAN PLATEAU
WEST SIBERIAN PLAIN
URAL MTS.
Lake Onega
Lake Ladoga
Dvina R.
Ob R.
Yenisey R.
Lena R.
Kolyma R.
Aldan R.
Irtysh R.
BALTIC SEA
784 ft.
NORTH SEA
NORTH EUROPEAN PLAIN
EUROPE
Volga R.
BERING SEA
SEA OF OKHOTSK
Kluchevskaya (Vol.) 15,584 ft.
Lake Baikal
Amur R.
Grossglockner 12,461 ft.
Mt. Blanc 15,771 ft.
CASPIAN DEPRESSION
ARAL SEA
Lake Balkhash
ALTAI MTS.
ASIA
SAKHALIN
KURIL TRENCH
34,558 ft.
NORTH PACIFIC OCEAN
Gora El'brus 18,481 ft.
Danube R.
Dufourspitze 15,203 ft.
Mt. Viso 12,602 ft.
BLACK SEA
CAUCASUS
CASPIAN SEA
GOBI DESERT
MANCHURIAN PLAIN
HOKKAIDO
JAPAN TRENCH
11,910 ft.
9,403 ft.
ANATOLIAN PLATEAU
Mt. Ararat 16,854 ft.
TURANIAN PLATEAU
Pik Kommunizma 24,590 ft.
TIEN SHAN
TARIM BASIN
HIGHLANDS
SEA OF JAPAN
HONSHU
11,520 ft.
16,802 ft.
MEDITERRANEAN SEA
Tigris
Euphrates
Qolleh-ye Damavand 18,386 ft.
GREAT
ZAGROS MTS.
HINDU KUSH
Nowshak 24,557 ft.
K2 28,250 ft.
Pik Lenina 23,406 ft.
Muztag 25,338 ft.
PLATEAU OF TIBET
Kula Kangri 24,784 ft.
Yellow R.
Fuji Yama 12,388 ft.
34,037 ft.
IZU TRENCH
NORTHWEST PACIFIC BASIN
Toubkal 13,665 ft.
ATLAS MTS.
BARKA PLATEAU
10,414 ft.
SYRIAN DESERT
CENTRAL
Tirich Mir 25,230 ft.
HIMALAYA
Yangtze R.
EAST CHINA SEA
KYUSHU
24,630 ft.
BONIN TR.
ERG IGUIDI
OASES OF FEZZAN
LIBYAN DESERT
Nile R.
Persian Gulf
Indus R.
Mt. Everest 29,035 ft.
Kanchenjunga 28,208 ft.
Hkakabo Razi 19,296 ft.
28,337 ft.
Tropic of Cancer
SAHARA
RED SEA
ARABIAN PLATEAU
Ganges R.
TAIWAN
Yu Shan 13,114 ft.
MARIANA ISLANDS
DECCAN PLATEAU
HAINAN
Mekong R.
LUZON
PHILIPPINE SEA
SAHEL
Hadur Shu'ayb 12,008 ft.
Bay of Bengal
MARIANA TRENCH
Niger R.
Lake Chad
AFRICA
Ras Dashen Terara 15,158 ft.
Gulf of Aden
ARABIAN SEA
CHAGOS-LACCADIVE PLATEAU
ANDAMAN ISLANDS
Gulf of Thailand
SOUTH CHINA SEA
34,441 ft.
PHILIPPINE TRENCH
36,203 ft.
MARSHALL ISLANDS
CENTRAL
Cameroon Mtn. 13,451 ft.
ADAMAWA HIGHLANDS
ETHIOPIAN HIGHLANDS
NICOBAR ISLANDS
17,202 ft.
MINDANAO
Gunung Kinabalu 13,455 ft.
CAROLINE ISLANDS
GILBERT ISLANDS
17,101 ft.
Gulf of Guinea
Margherita Pk. 16,763 ft.
Lake Victoria
16,782 ft.
MALDIVE ISLANDS
SUMATRA
BORNEO
MELANESIA
Equator
14,640 ft.
Mt. Kenya 17,058 ft.
AMIRANTE IS.
MID-INDIAN RIDGE
Gunung Kirinci 12,467 ft.
CELEBES
Puncak Jaya 16,503 ft.
Volcan Kansimbi 14,787 ft.
Congo
Mt. Kilimanjaro 19,340 ft.
MASCARENE PLAT.
CHAGOS ARCH.
EAST INDIES
Mt. Wilhelm 14,793 ft.
ASCENSION
Lake Tanganyika
DIEGO GARCIA
JAVA
Gunung Semeru 12,060 ft.
NEW GUINEA
29,988 ft.
PLATEAU
Lake Nyasa
Mozambique Channel
20,464 ft.
NINETYEAST RIDGE
20,785 ft.
24,443 ft.
JAVA TRENCH
Mt. Victoria 13,238 ft.
NEW HEBRIDES
19,850 ft.
Zambezi R.
INDIAN
Gunung Rinjani 12,224 ft.
GREAT BARRIER REEF
Cape Frio
WALVIS RIDGE
KALAHARI DESERT
MASCARENE IS.
20,998 ft.
OCEAN
EAST INDIAMAN RIDGE
North West Cape
Tropic of Capricorn
GREAT SANDY DESERT
WESTERN PLATEAU
AUSTRALIA
CORAL SEA
NEW CALEDONIA
17,399 ft.
Orange R.
DRAKENSBERG
Cape Ste. Marie
PERTH BASIN
GREAT VICTORIA DESERT
LAKE EYRE BASIN
GREAT DIVIDING RANGE
SOUTH PACIFIC OCEAN
1,788 ft.
SOUTHWEST INDIAN RIDGE
BROKEN RIDGE
GREAT AUSTRALIAN BIGHT
North Cape
Cape of Good Hope
7,579 ft.
AMSTERDAM I.
ST. PAUL I.
14,673 ft.
SOUTH AUSTRALIAN BASIN
18,603 ft.
TASMAN SEA
17,281 ft.
TASMANIA
South East Cape
5,023 ft.
PRINCE EDWARD ISLAND
CROZET ISLANDS
KERGUÉLEN ISLANDS
9,791 ft.
SOUTHEAST INDIAN RIDGE
TASMAN PLATEAU
Mt. Cook 12,316 ft.
AUCKLAND ISLANDS
ATLANTIC-INDIAN RIDGE
KERGUELEN PLATEAU
19,978 ft.
MACQUARIE RIDGE
CAMPBELL PLATEAU
22,875 ft.
SOUTH INDIAN BASIN
ENDERBY PLAIN
PLAIN
2,756 ft.
Antarctic Circle
BALLENY ISLANDS
Scale: 1 to 96,300,000
0
1000
2000 Miles
1000
2000
3000 Kilometers
ANTARCTICA
0°
20°
40°
60°
80°
100°
120°
140°
160°

Map 3a Average Annual Precipitation

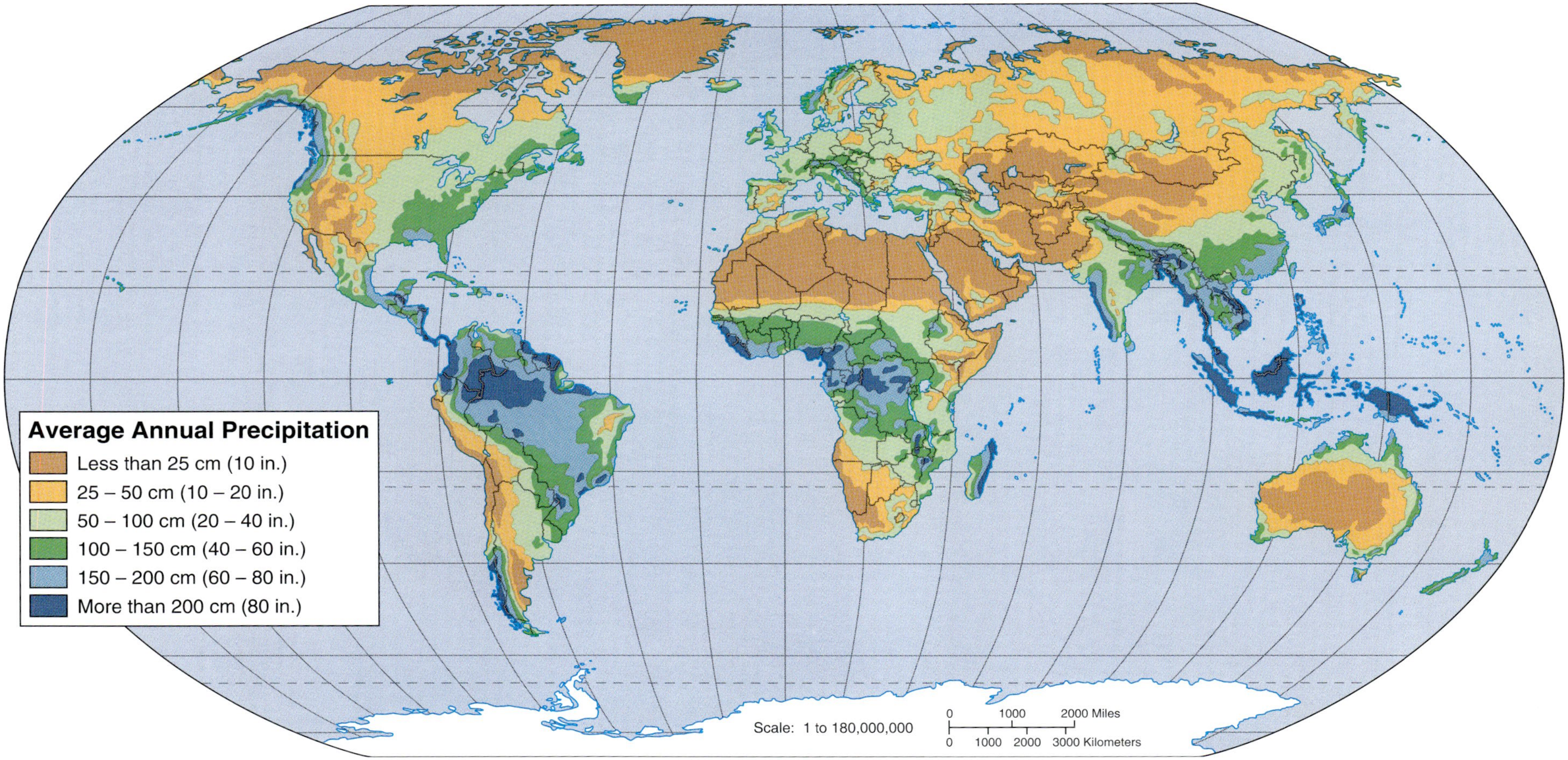

The two most important physical geographic variables are precipitation and temperature, the essential elements of weather and climate. Precipitation is a conditioner of both soil type and vegetation. More than any other single environmental element, it influences where people do or do not live. Water is the most precious resource available to humans, and water availability is largely a function of precipitation. Water availability is also a function of several precipitation variables that do not appear on this map: the seasonal distribution of precipitation (is precipitation or drought concentrated in a particular season?), the ratio between precipitation and temperature (how much of the water that comes to the earth in the form of precipitation is lost through mechanisms such as evaporation and transpiration that are a function of temperature?), and the annual variability of precipitation (how much do annual precipitation totals for a place or region tend to vary from the "normal" or average precipitation?). In order to obtain a complete understanding of precipitation, these variables should be examined along with the more general data presented on this map. The study of precipitation and other climatic elements is the concern of the branch of physical geography called "climatology."

Map 3b Seasonal Average Precipitation–November through April

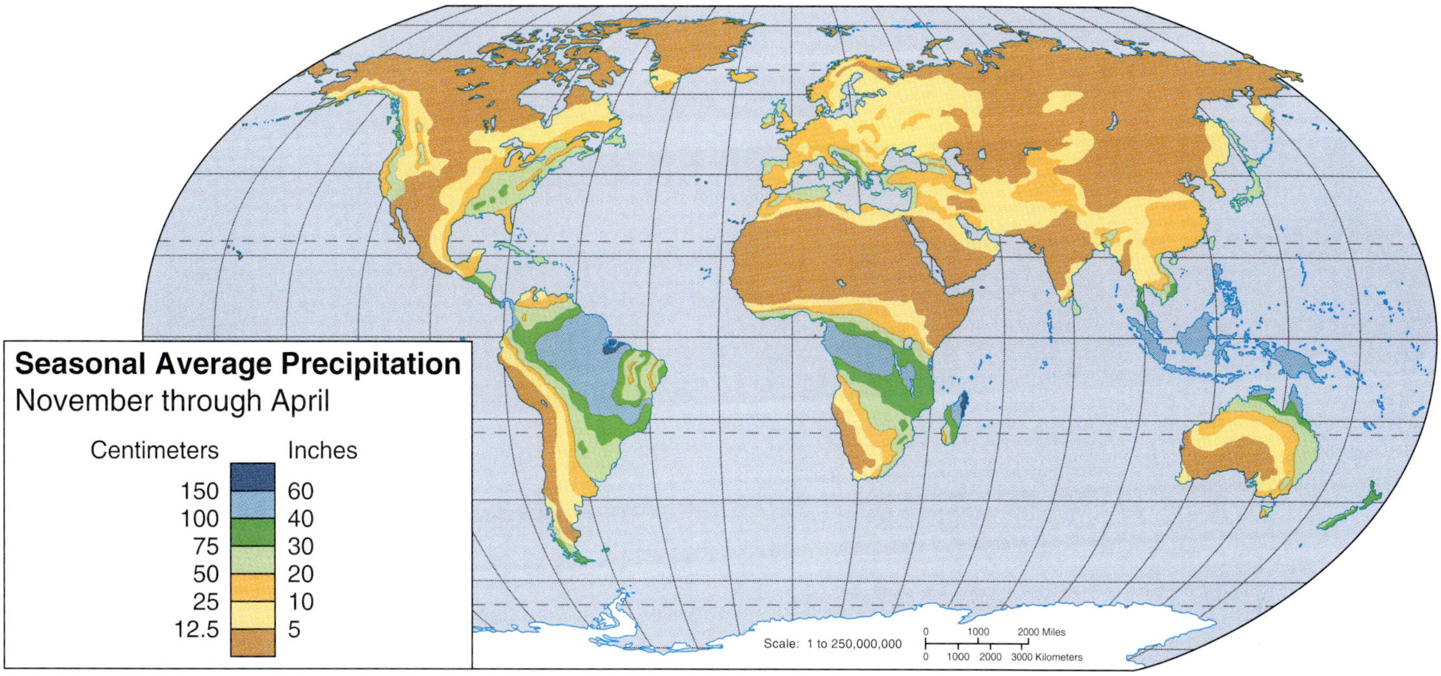

Map 3c Seasonal Average Precipitation–May through October

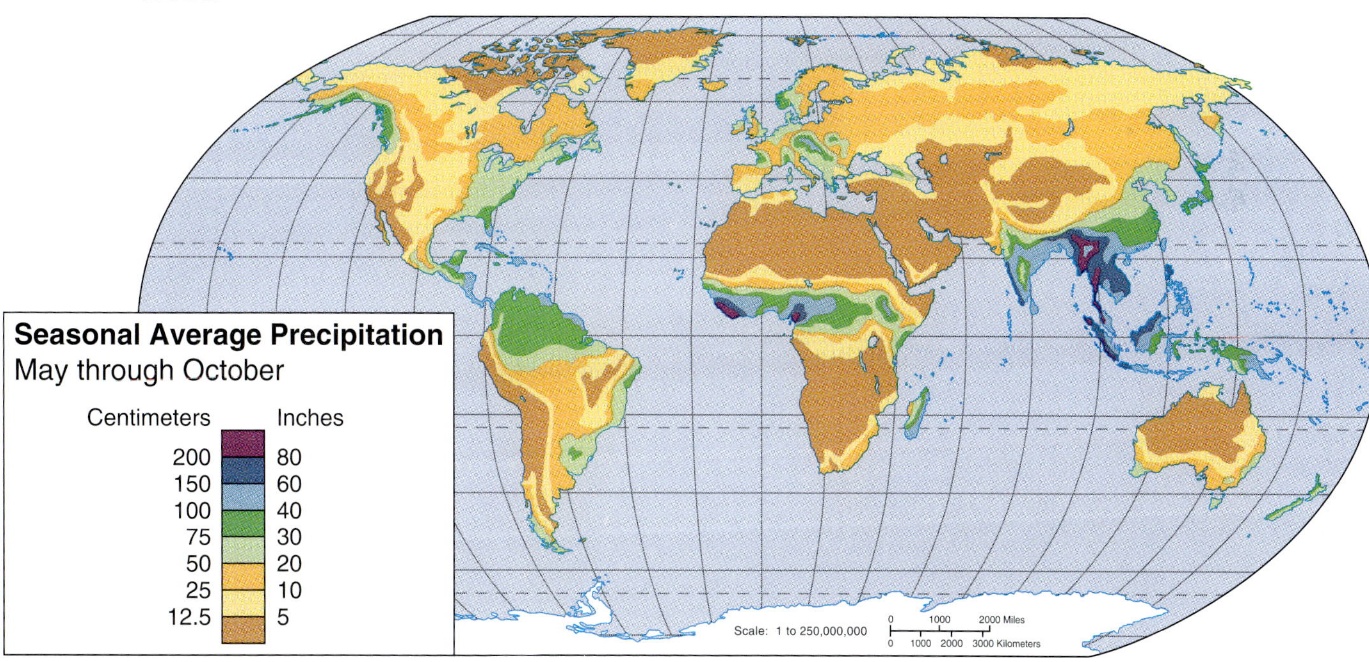

Seasonal average precipitation is nearly as important as annual precipitation totals in determining the habitability of an area. Critical factors are such things as whether precipitation coincides with the growing season and thus facilitates agriculture or during the winter when it is less effective in aiding plant growth, and whether precipitation occurs during summer with its higher water loss through evaporation and transpiration or during the winter when more of it can go into storage. Several of the world's great climate zones have pronounced seasonal precipitation rhythms. The tropical and subtropical savanna grasslands have a long winter dry season and abundant precipitation in the summer. The Mediterranean climate is the only major climate with a marked dry season during the summer, making agriculture possible only through irrigation or other adjustments to cope with drought during the period of plant growth. And the great monsoon climates of south and southeast Asia have their winter dry season and summer rain that has conditioned the development of Asian agriculture and the rhythms of Asian life.

Map 3d Variation in Annual Precipitation

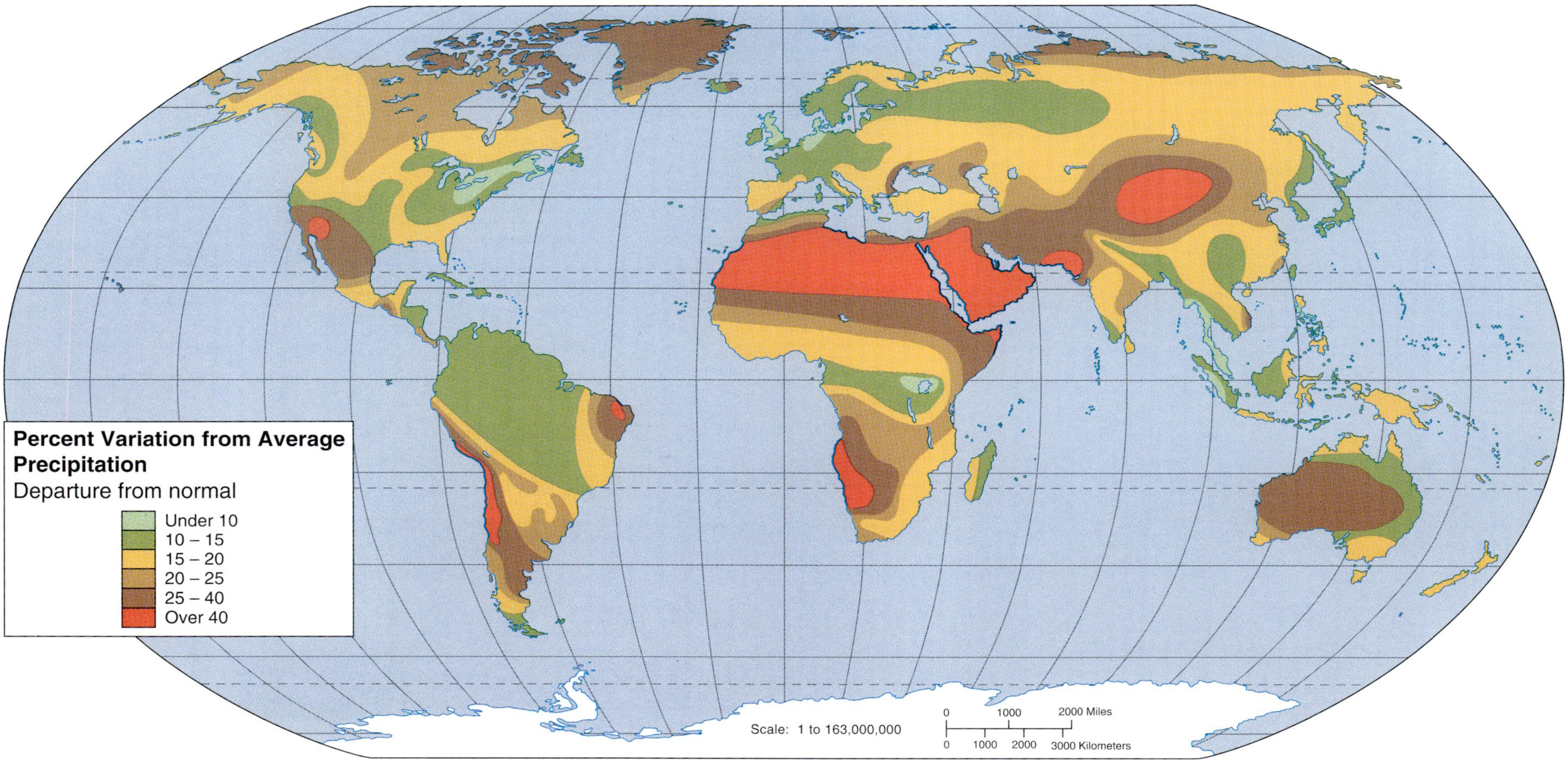

While annual precipitation totals and seasonal distribution of precipitation are important variables, the variability of precipitation from one year to the next may be even more critical. You will note from the map that there is a general spatial correlation between the world's drylands and the amount of annual variation in precipitation. Generally, the drier the climate, the more likely it is that there will be considerable differences in rainfall and/or snowfall from one year to the next. We might determine that the average precipitation of the mid-Sahara is 2 inches per year. What this really means is that a particular location in the Sahara during one year might receive .5", during the next year 3.5", and during a third year 2". If you add these together and divide by the number of years, the "average" precipitation is 2" per year. The significance of this is that much of the world's crucial agricultural output of cereals (grains) comes from dryland climates (the Great Plains of the United States, the Pampas of Argentina, the steppes of Ukraine and Russia, for example) and variations in annual rainfall totals can have significant impacts on levels of grain production and, therefore, important consequences for both economic and political processes.

Map 4a Temperature Regions and Ocean Currents

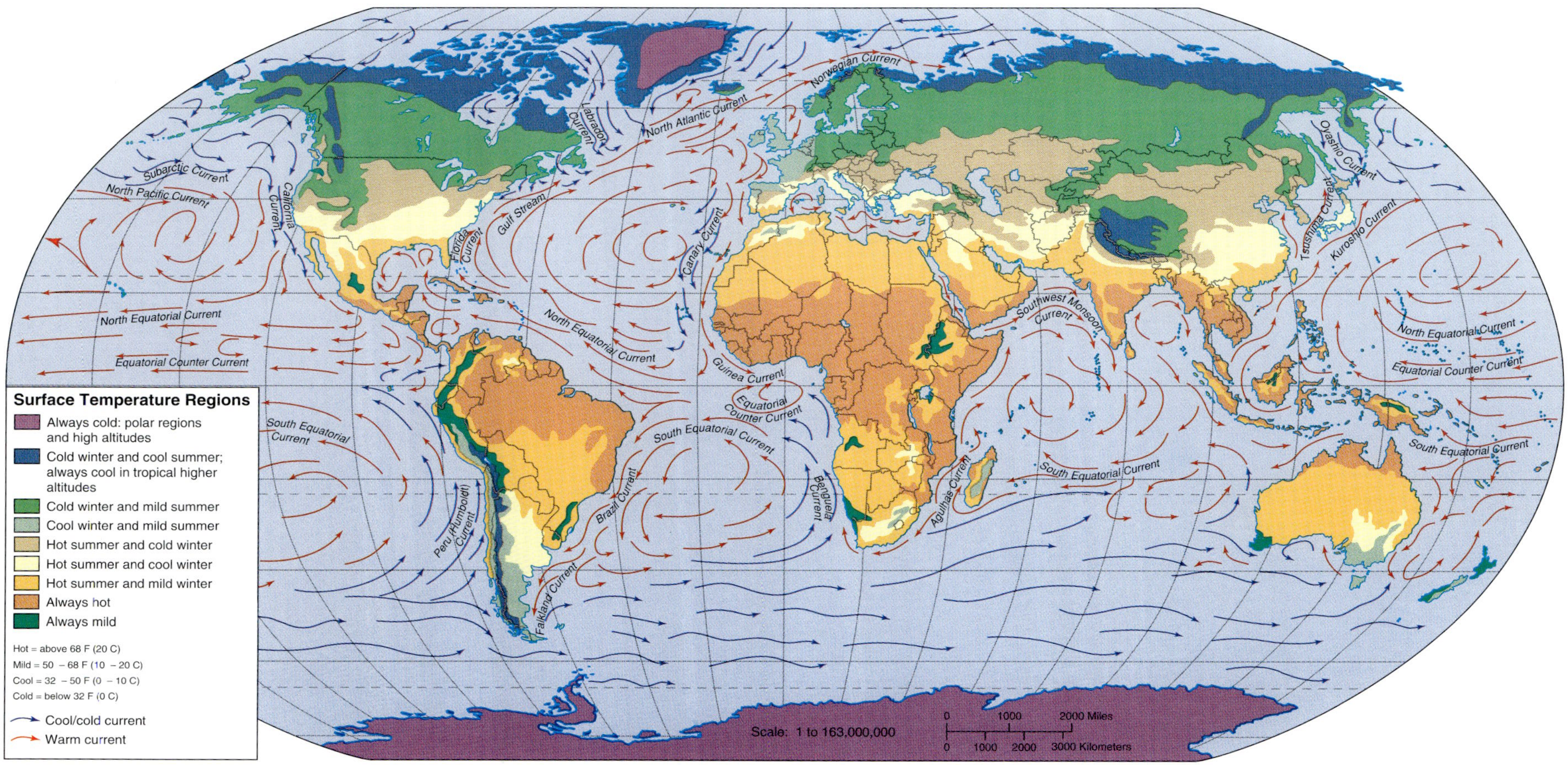

Along with precipitation, temperature is one of the two most important environmental variables, defining the climate conditions so essential for the distribution of such human activities as agriculture and the distribution of the human population. The seasonal rhythm of temperature, including such measures as the average annual temperature range (difference between the average temperature of the warmest month and that of the coldest month), is an additional variable not shown on the map but, like the seasonality of precipitation, should be a part of any comprehensive study of climate. The ocean currents illustrated exert a significant influence over the climate of adjacent regions and are the most important mechanism for redistributing surplus heat from the equatorial region into middle and high latitudes. Physical geographers known as "climatologists" study the phenomenon of temperature and related climatic characteristics.

Map 4b Average July Temperature

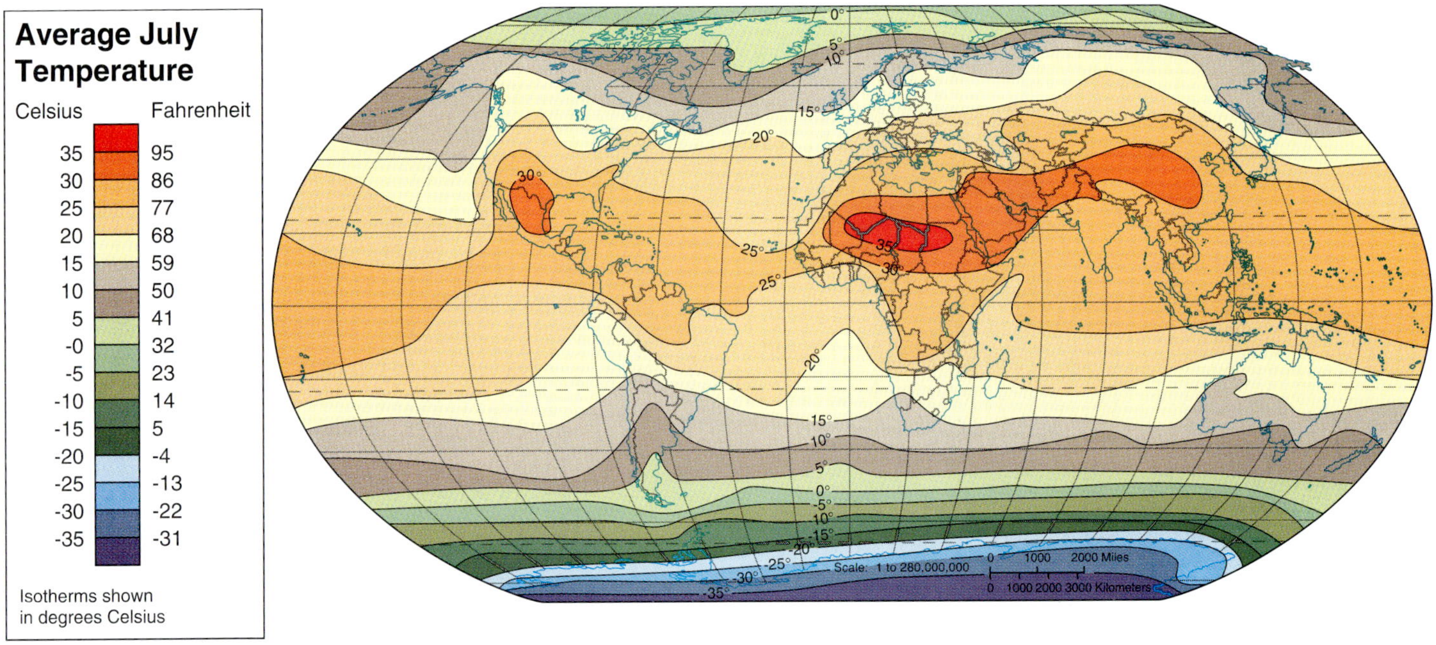

Map 4c Average January Temperature

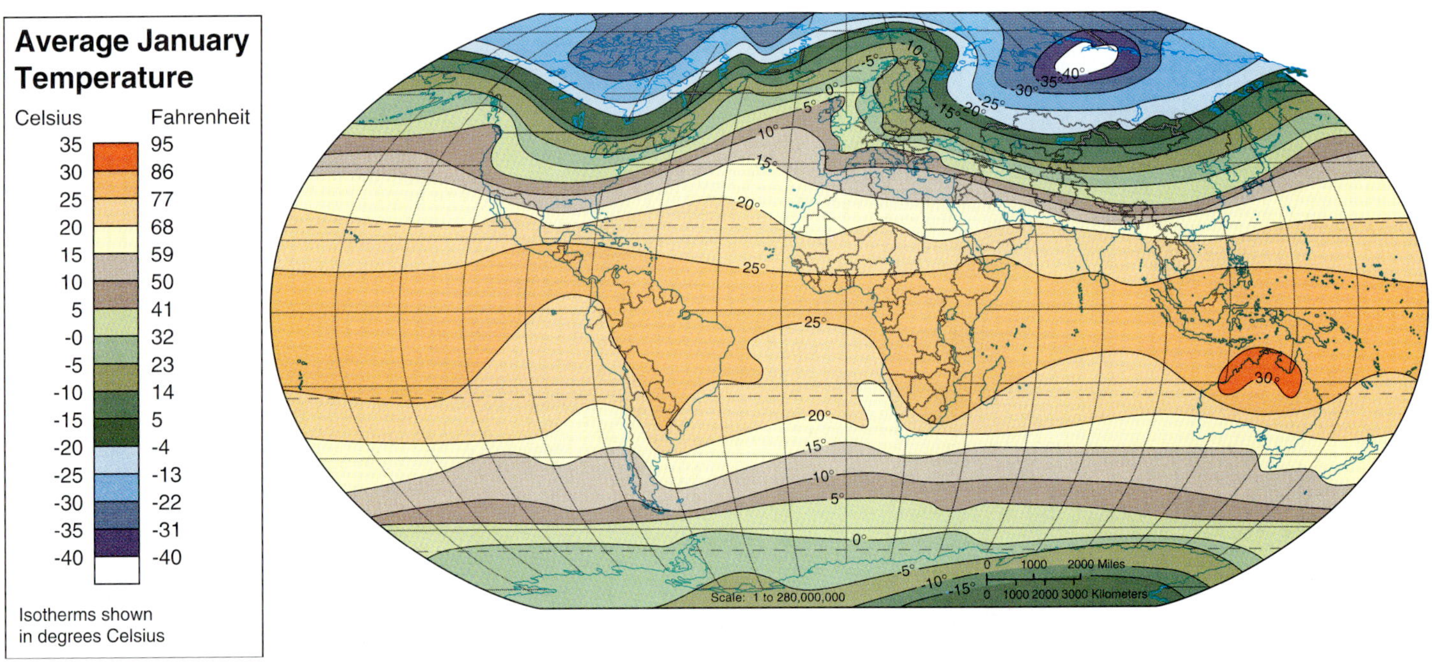

Where moisture availability tends to mark the seasons in the tropics and subtropics, in the mid-latitudes, seasons are defined by temperature. Temperature is determined by latitudinal position, by altitude or elevation above sea level, and by the location of a place relative to the world's land masses and oceans. The most important of these controls is latitude, and temperatures generally become lower with increasing latitude. However, proximity to water tends to moderate temperature extremes, and "maritime" climates influenced by the oceans will be warmer in the winter and cooler in the summer than continental climates in the same general latitude. Maritime climates will also show smaller temperature ranges, the difference between January and July temperatures, while climates of continental interiors, far from the moderating influences of the oceans, will tend to have great temperature ranges. In the Northern Hemisphere, where there are both large land masses and oceans, the range is great. But in the Southern Hemisphere, dominated by water and, hence, by the more moderate maritime air masses, the temperature range is comparatively small. Significant temperature departures from the "normal" produced by latitude may also be the result of elevation. With exceptions, lower temperatures produced by topography are difficult to see on maps of this scale.

Map 5a Atmospheric Pressure and Predominant Surface Winds–January

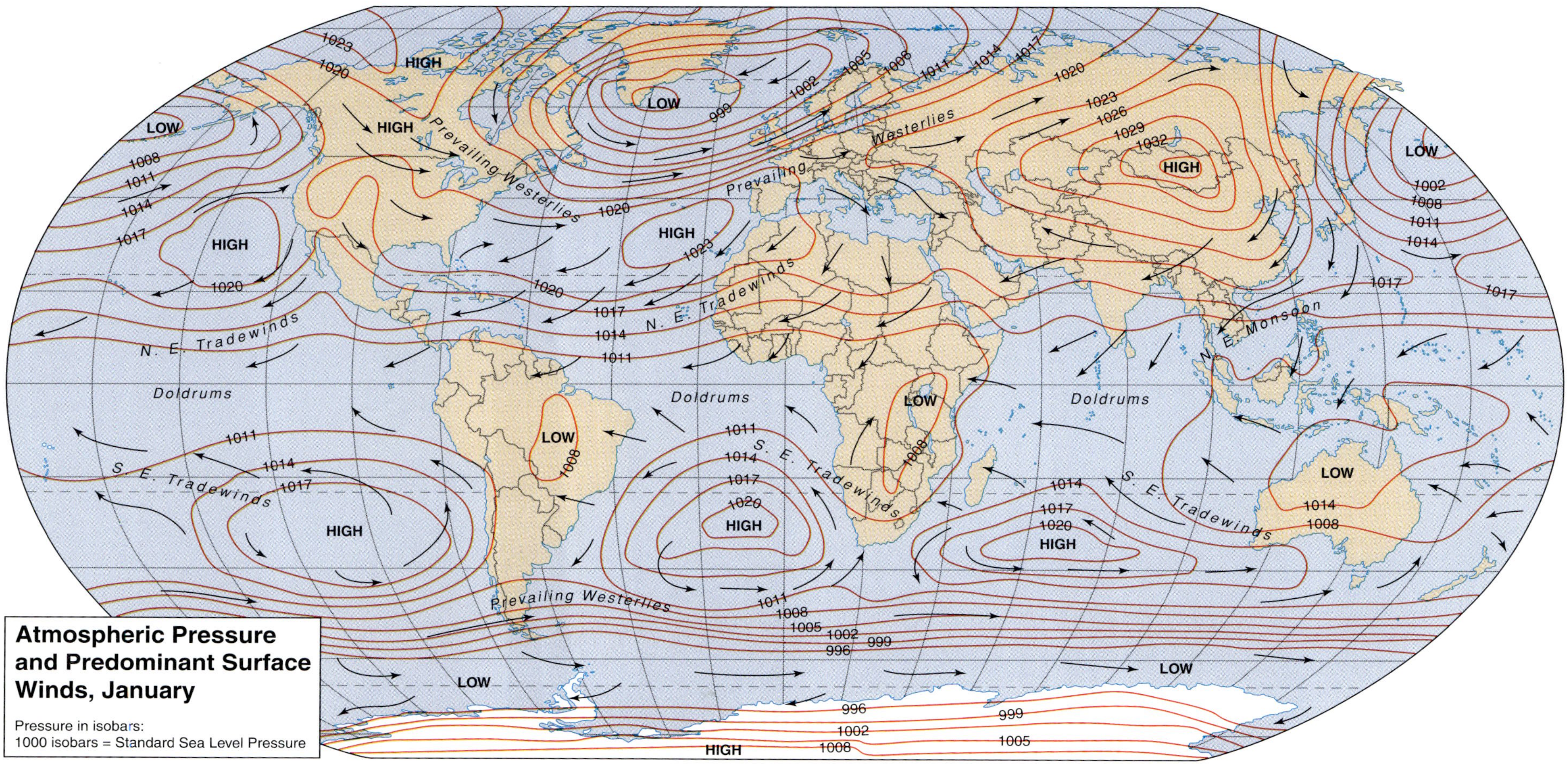

Map 5b Atmospheric Pressure and Predominant Surface Winds–July

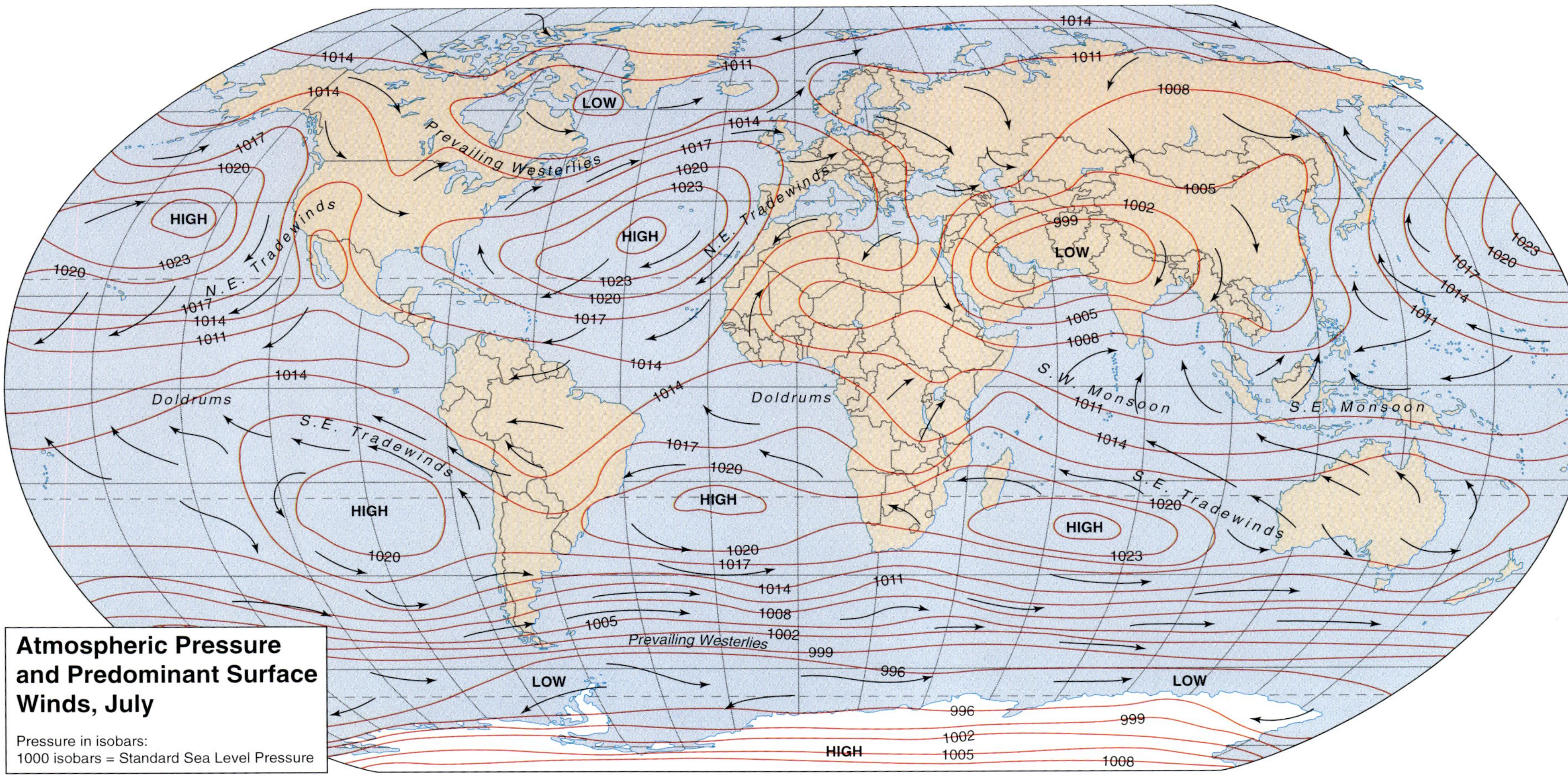

Atmospheric pressure, or the density of air, is a function largely of air temperature: the colder the air, the denser and heavier it is, hence the higher its pressure; the warmer the air, the lighter and less stable it is, hence the lower its pressure. Global pressure systems are the alternating low and high pressure systems that, from the equator north and south, include: the equatorial low (sometimes called the intertropical convergence) centered on the equator for much of the year; the subtropical highs with their centers near the 30th degrees of north and south latitude; the subpolar lows or polar front centered near the 60th parallel of north and south latitude, and the polar highs near the north and south poles. Air flows from high pressure to low pressure regions and this air flow constitutes the earth's major surface winds such as the tropical tradewinds and the prevailing westerlies. This flow of air is one of the chief mechanisms by which surplus heat energy from the equatorial region is redistributed to higher latitudes. It is also the primary conditioner of the world's major precipitation belts, with rainfall and snowfall associated primarily with lower atmospheric pressure conditions.

Map 6 World Climate Regions

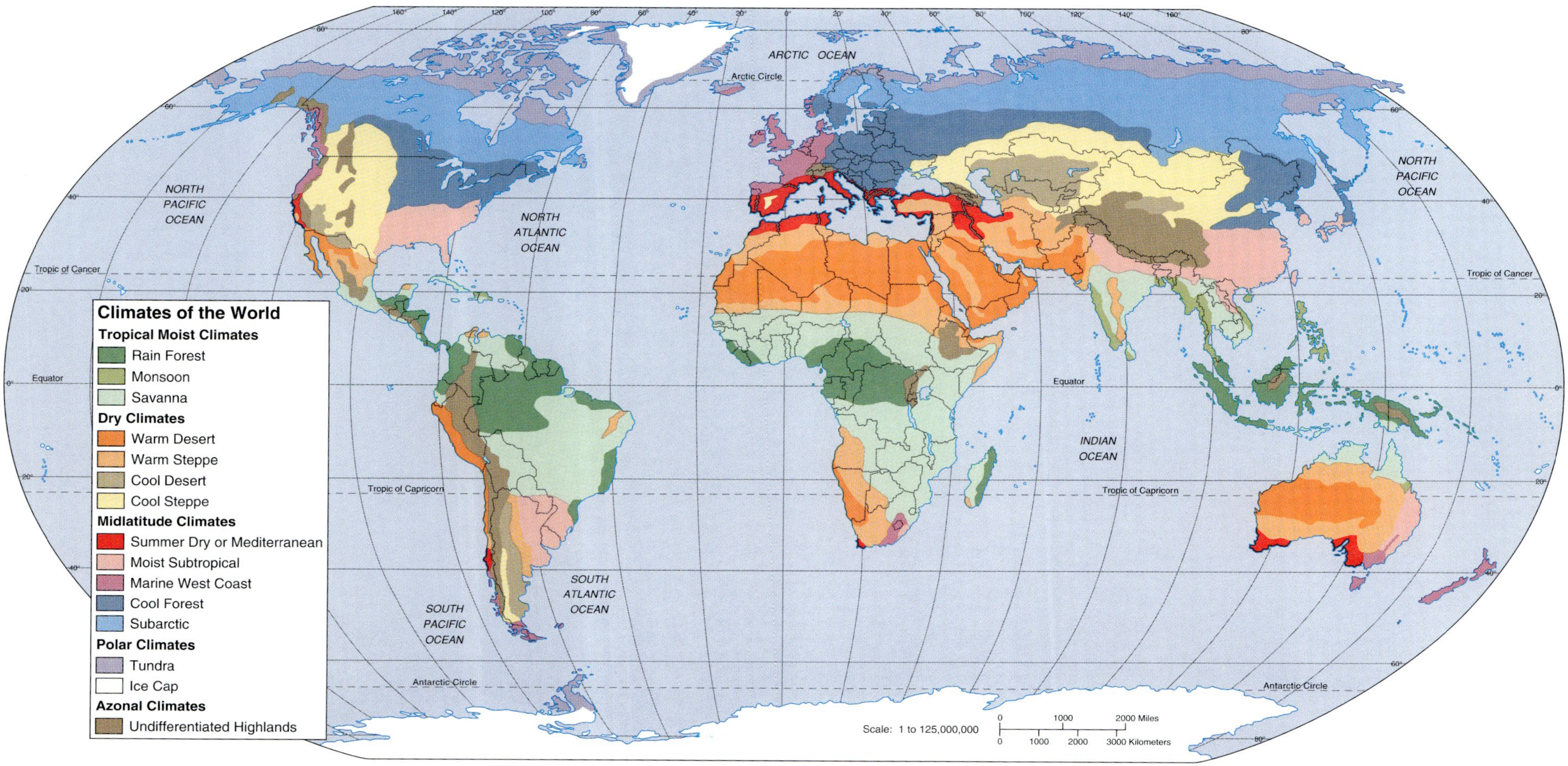

Of the world's many patterns of physical geography, climate or the long-term average of weather conditions such as temperature and precipitation is the most important. It is climate that conditions the distribution of natural vegetation and the types of soils that will exist in an area. Climate also influences the availability of our most crucial resource: water. From an economic standpoint, the world's most important activity is agriculture; no other element of physical geography is more important for agriculture than climate. Ultimately, it is agricultural production that determines where the bulk of human beings live and, therefore, climate is a basic determinant of the distribution of human populations as well. The study of climates or "climatology" is one of the most important branches of physical geography.

Map 7 Vegetation Types

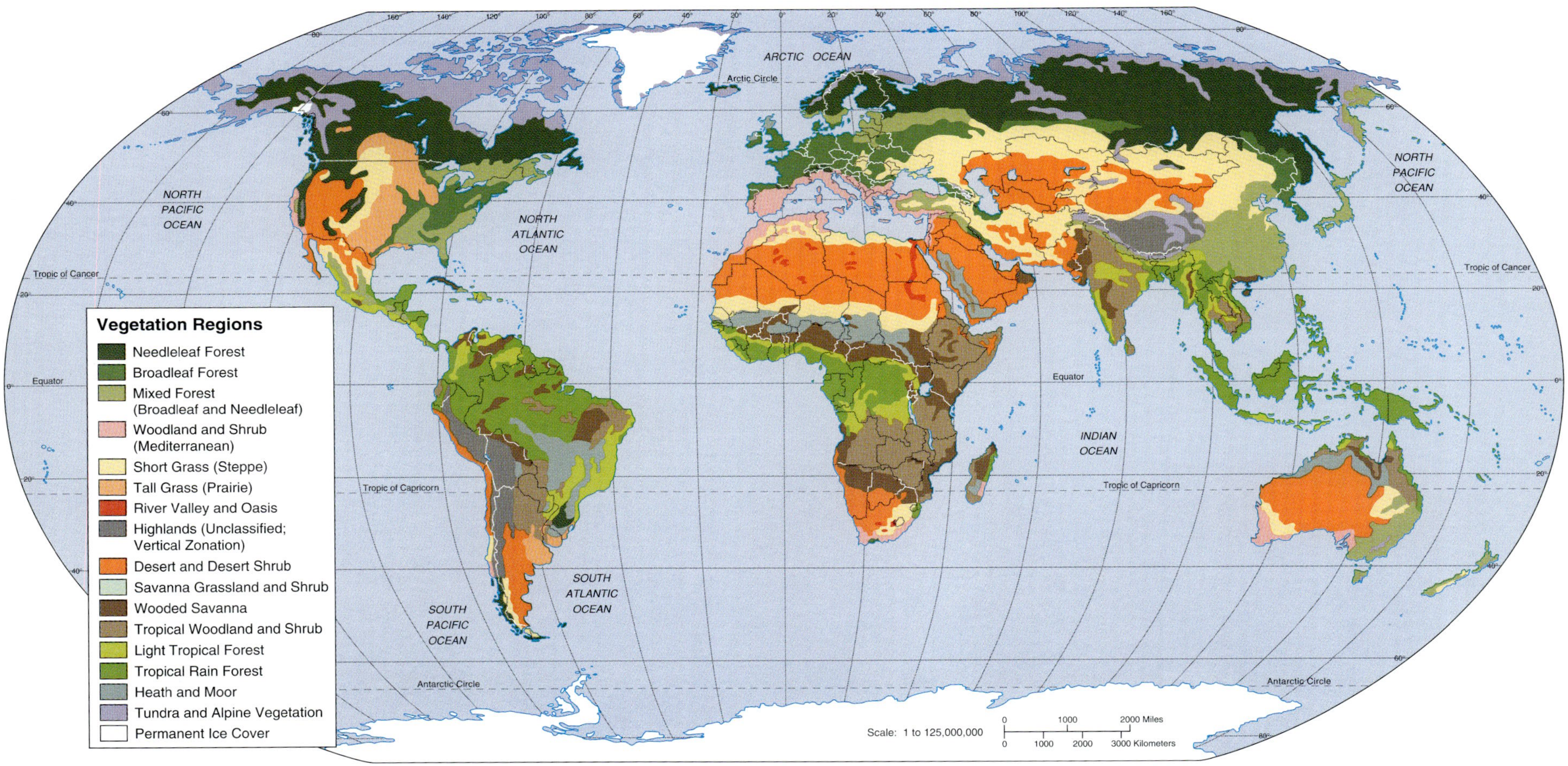

Vegetation is the most visible consequence of the distribution of temperature and precipitation. The global pattern of vegetative types or "habitat classes" and the global pattern of climate are closely related and make up one of the great global spatial correlations. But not all vegetation types are the consequence of temperature and precipitation or other climatic variables. Many types of vegetation in many areas of the world are the consequence of human activities, particularly the grazing of domesticated livestock, burning, and forest clearance. This map shows the pattern of natural or "potential" vegetation, or vegetation as it might be expected to exist without significant human influences, rather than the actual vegetation that results from a combination of environmental and human factors. Physical geographers who are interested in the distribution and geographic patterns of vegetation are "biogeographers."

Map 8 World Soil Orders

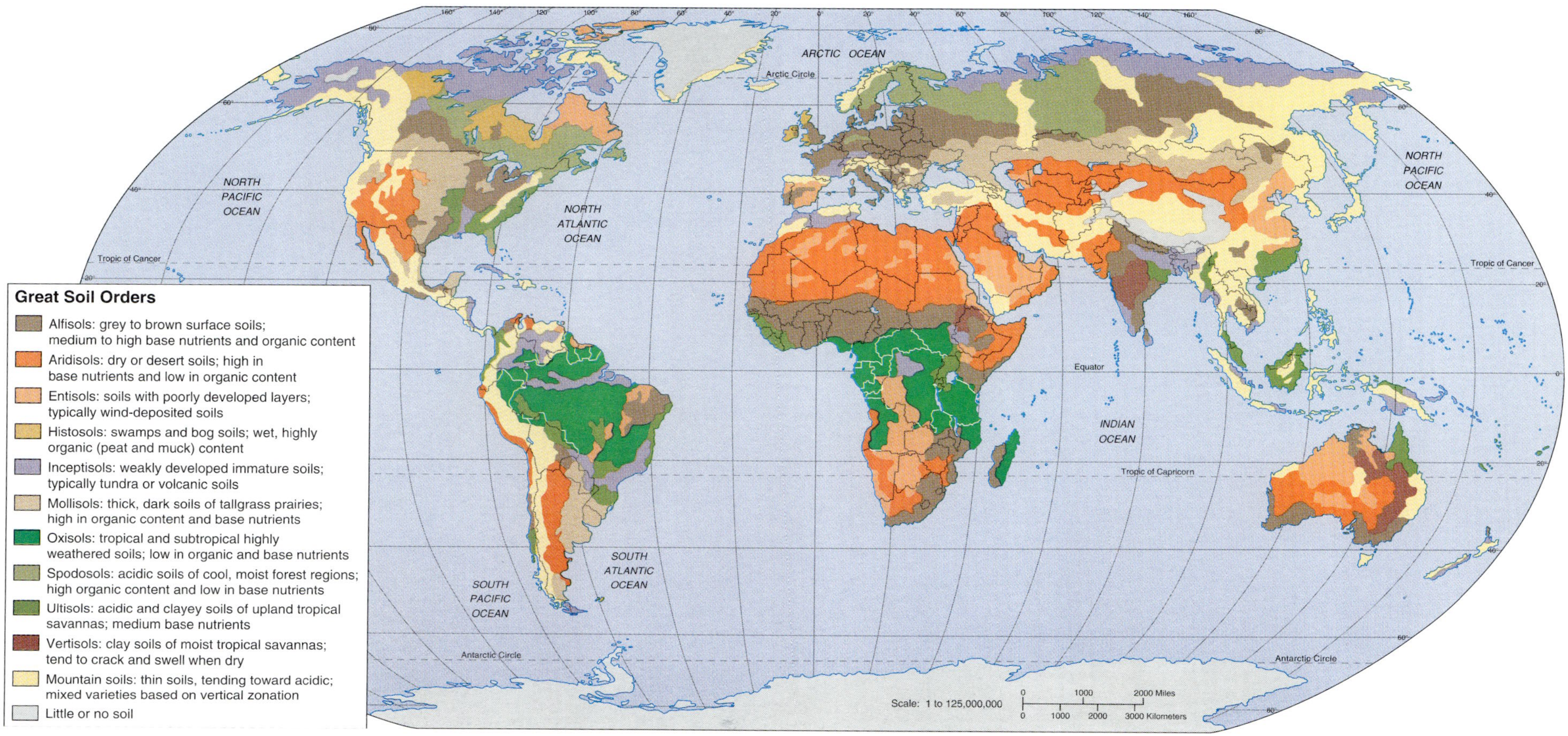

The characteristics of soil are one of the three primary physical geographic factors, along with climate and vegetation, that determine the habitability of regions for humans. In particular, soils influence the kinds of agricultural uses to which land is put. Since soils support the plants that are the primary producers of all food in the terrestrial food chain, their characteristics are crucial to the health and stability of ecosystems. Two types of soil are shown on this map: zonal soils, the characteristics of which are based on climatic patterns; and azonal soils, such as alluvial (water-deposited) or aeolian (wind-deposited) soils, the characteristics of which are derived from forces other than climate. However, many of the azonal soils, particularly those dependent upon drainage conditions, appear over areas too small to be readily shown on a map of this scale. Thus, almost none of the world's swamp or bog soils appear on this map. People who study the geographic characteristics of soils are most often "soil scientists," a discipline closely related to that branch of physical geography called "geomorphology."

Map 9 World Ecological Regions

World Ecological Regions

Arctic and Subarctic Zone

- Ice Cap
- Tundra Province: moss-grass and moss-lichen tundra
- Tundra Altitudinal Zone: polar desert (no vegetation)
- Subarctic Province: evergreen forest, needleleaf taiga; mixed coniferous and small-leafed forest
- Subarctic Altitudinal Zone: open woodland; wooded tundra

Humid Temperate Zone

- Moderate Continental Province: mixed coniferous and broadleaf forest
- Moderate Continental Altitudinal Zone: coastal and alpine forest; open woodland
- Warm Continental Province: broadleaf deciduous forest
- Warm Continental Altitudinal Zone: upland broadleaf and alpine needleleaf forest
- Marine Province: lowland, west-coastal humid forest
- Marine Altitudinal Zone: humid coastal and alpine coniferous forest
- Humid Subtropical Province: broadleaf evergreen and broadleaf deciduous forest
- Humid Subtropical Altitudinal Zone: upland, subtropical broadleaf forest
- Prairie Province: tallgrass and mixed prairie
- Prairie Altitudinal Zone: upland mixed prairie and woodland
- Mediterranean Province: sclerophyll woodland, shrub, and steppe grass
- Mediterranean Altitudinal Zone: upland shrub and steppe

Humid Tropical Zone

- Savanna Province: seasonally dry forest; open woodland; tallgrass savanna
- Savanna Altitudinal Zone: open woodland steppe
- Rain Forest Province: constantly humid, broadleaf evergreen forest
- Rain Forest Altitudinal Zone: broadleaf evergreen and subtropical deciduous forest

Arid and Semiarid Zone

- Tropical/Subtropical Steppe Province: dry steppe (short grass), desert shrub, semidesert savanna
- Tropical/Subtropical Steppe Altitudinal Zone: upland steppe (short grass) and desert shrub
- Tropical/Subtropical Desert Province: hot, lowland desert in subtropical and coastal locations; xerophytic vegetation
- Tropical/Subtropical Desert Altitudinal Zone: desert shrub
- Temperate Steppe Province: medium to shortgrass prairie
- Temperate Steppe Altitudinal Zone: alpine meadow and coniferous woodland
- Temperate Desert Province: midlatitude rainshadow desert; desert shrub
- Temperate Desert Altitudinal Zone: extreme continental desert steppe; desert shrub, xerophytic vegetation, shortgrass steppe

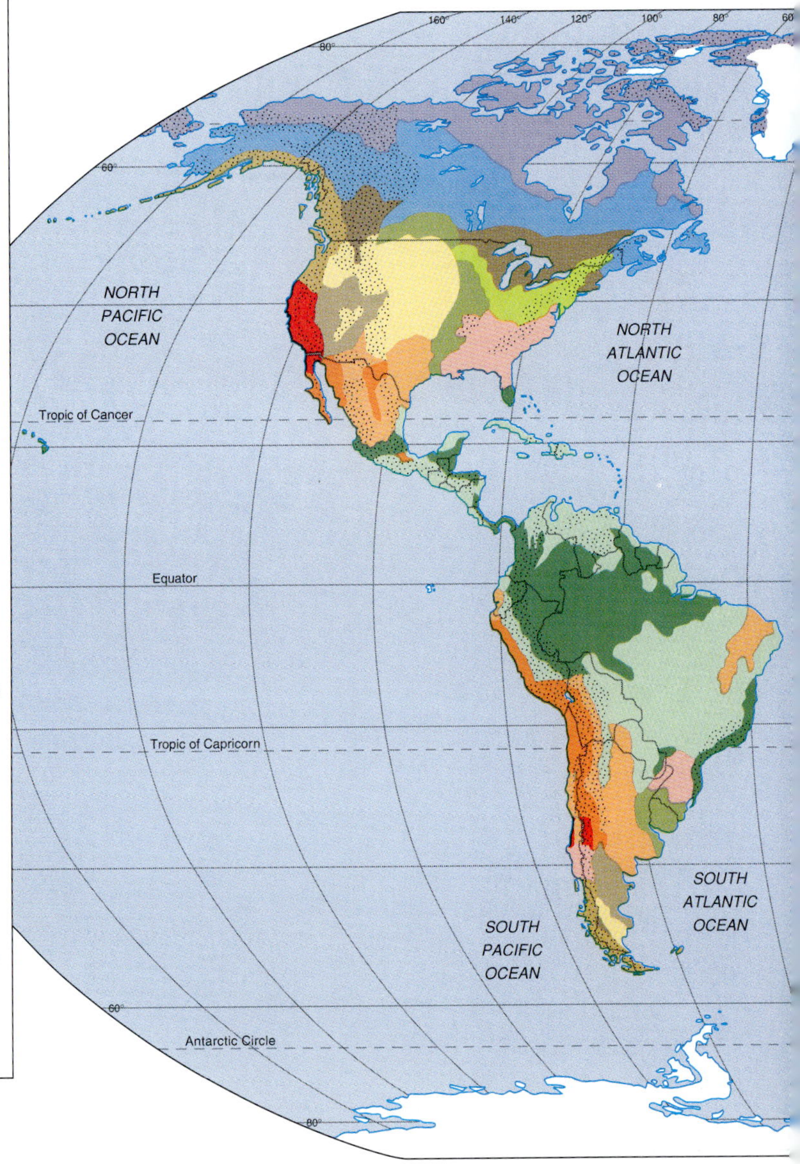

Ecological regions are distinctive areas within which unique sets of organisms and environments are found. We call the study of the relationships between organisms and their environmental surroundings "ecology." Within each of the ecological regions portrayed on the map, a particular combination of vegetation, wildlife, soil, water, climate, and terrain defines that region's habitability, or ability to support life, including human life. Like climate and landforms, ecological relationships are crucial to the existence of agriculture, the most basic of our economic activities, and important for many other kinds of economic activity as well. Biogeographers are especially concerned with the concept of ecological regions since such regions so clearly depend upon the geographic distribution of plants and animals in their environmental settings.

Map 10 Plate Tectonics

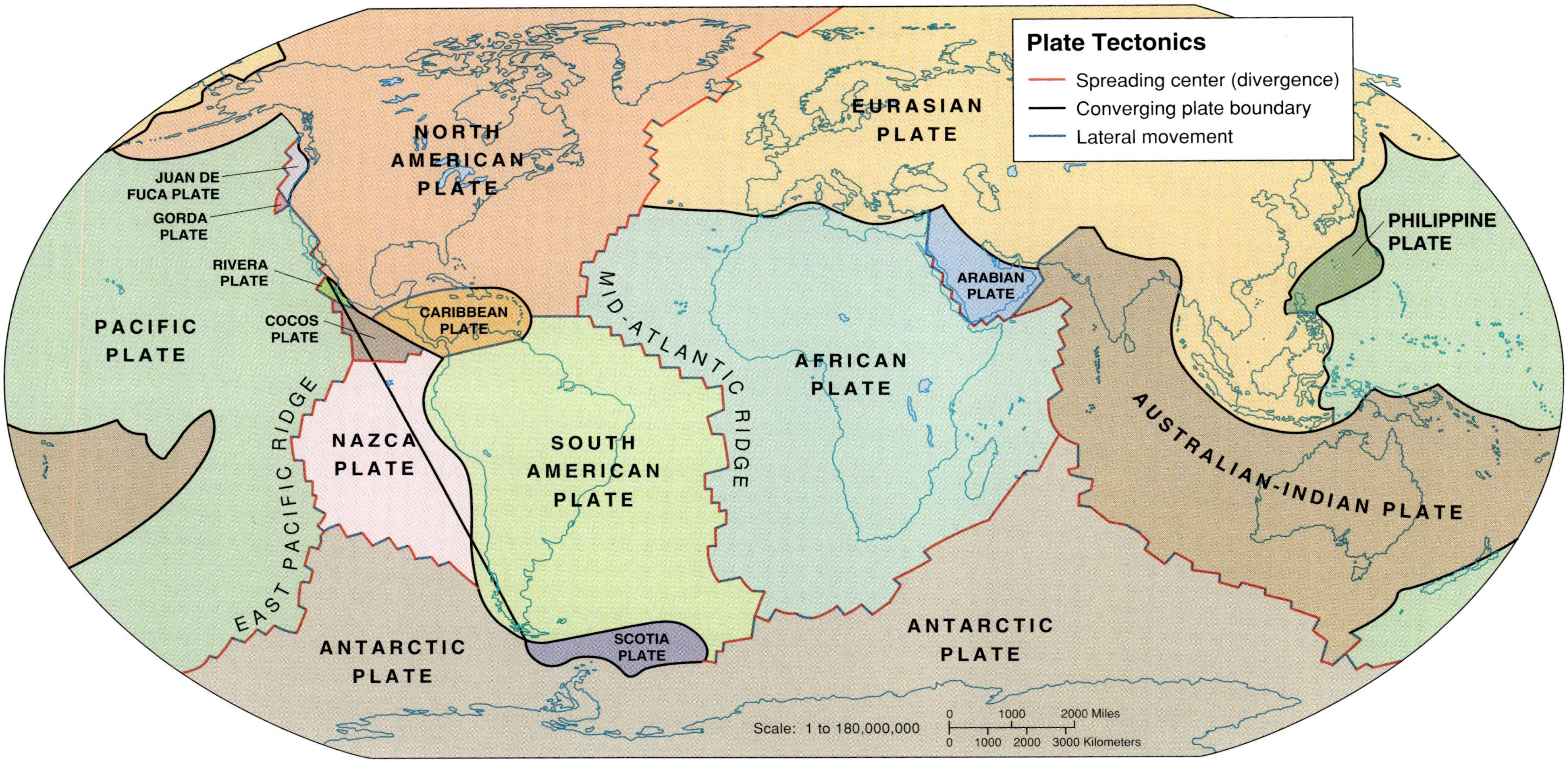

An understanding of the forces that shape the primary features of the earth's surface—the continents and ocean basins—requires a view of the earth's crust as fragments or "lithospheric plates" that shift position relative to one another. There are three dominant types of plate movement: *convergence,* in which plates move together, compressing former ocean floor or continental rocks together to produce mountain ranges, or producing mountain ranges through volcanic activity if one plate slides beneath another; *divergence,* in which the plates move away from one another, producing rifts in the earth's crust through which molten material wells up to produce new sea floors and mid-oceanic ridges; and *lateral shift,* in which plates move horizontally relative to one another, causing significant earthquake activity. All the major forms of these types of shifts are extremely slow and take place over long periods of geologic time. The movement of crustal plates, or what is known as "plate tectonics," is responsible for the present shape and location of the continents but is also the driving force behind some much shorter-term earth phenomena like earthquakes and volcanoes. A comparison of the map of plates with maps of hazards and terrain will reveal some interesting relationships.

Map 11 World Topography

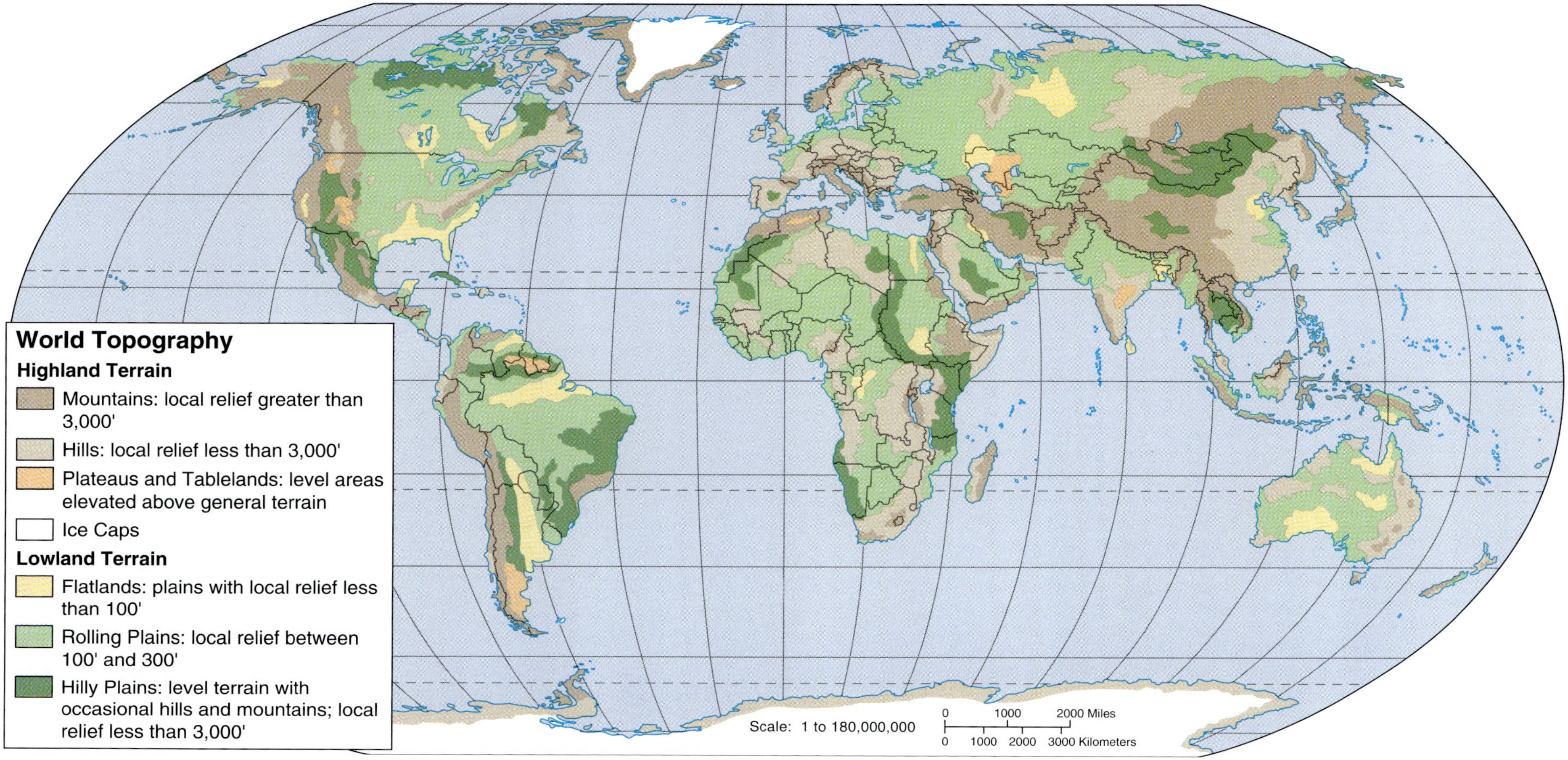

Topography or terrain, also called "landforms," is second only to climate as a conditioner of human activity, particularly agriculture but also the location of cities and industry. A comparison of this map of mountains, valleys, plains, plateaus, and other features of the earth's surface with a map of land use (Map 15) shows that most of the world's productive agricultural zones are located in lowland and relatively level regions. Where large regions of agricultural productivity are found, we also tend to find urban concentrations and, with cities, we find industry. There is also a good spatial correlation between the map of topography and the map showing the distribution and density of the human population (Map 14). Normally the world's major landforms are the result of extremely gradual primary geologic activity such as the long-term movement of crustal plates. This activity occurs over hundreds of millions of years. Also important is the more rapid (but still slow by human standards) geomorphological or erosional activity of water, wind, glacial ice, and waves, tides, and currents. Some landforms may be produced by abrupt or "cataclysmic" events such as a major volcanic eruption or a meteor strike, but such events are relatively rare and their effects are usually too minor to show up on a map of this scale. The study of the processes that shape topography is known as "geomorphology" and is an important branch of physical geography.

Map 12a World Resources: Mineral Fuels

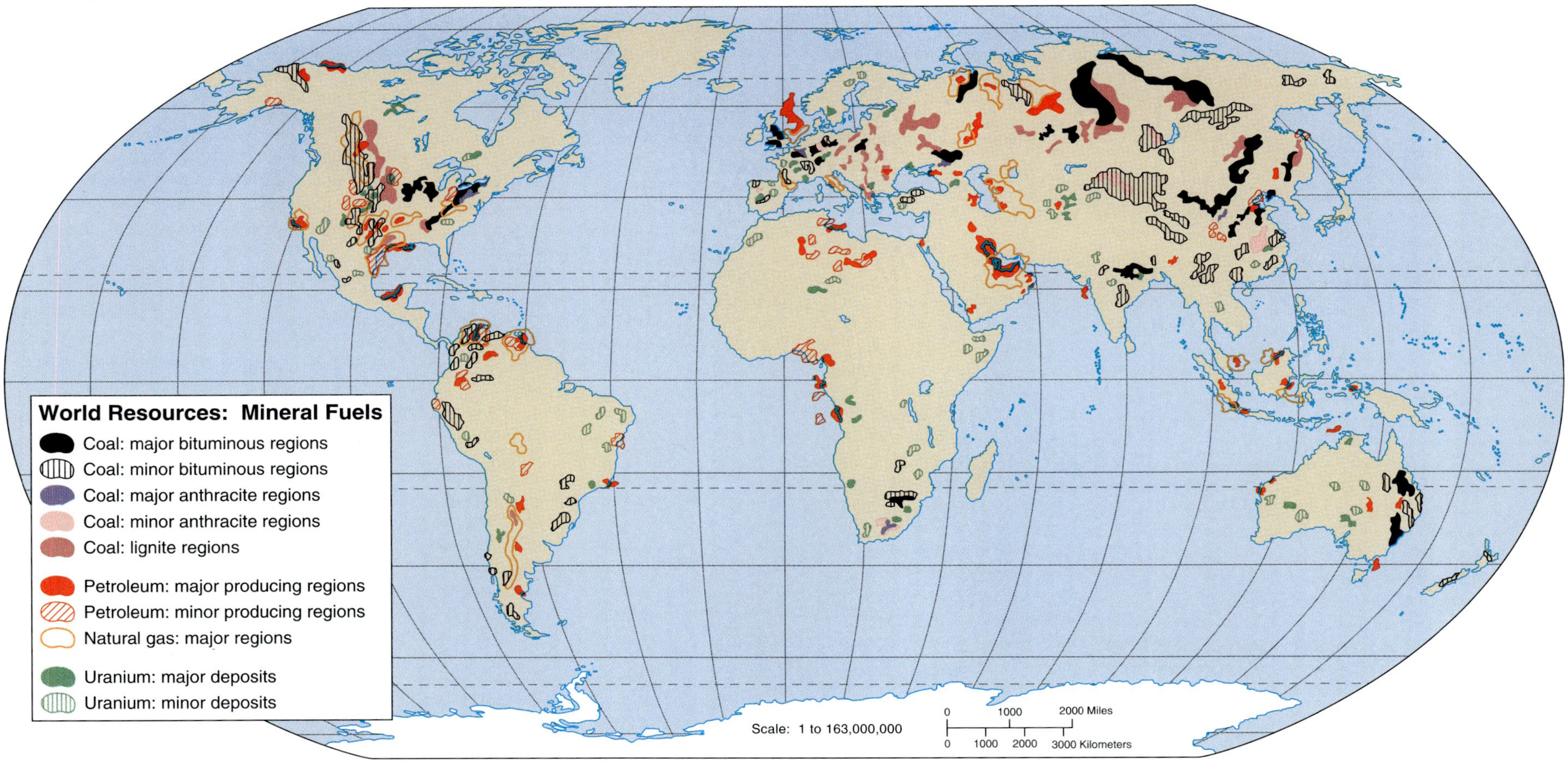

The extraction and transportation of mineral fuels ranks with agriculture and forestry as "primary" human activities that impact on the environment at a global scale. Nearly all of the most highly publicized environmental disasters of recent decades—the Prince William Sound oil spill or the Chernobyl nuclear accident, for example—have involved mineral fuels that were being stored, transported, or used. And the continuing extraction of mineral fuels like oil, natural gas, coal, and uranium produces high levels of atmospheric, soil, and water pollution. The location of mineral fuels tells us a great deal about where environmental degradation is likely to be occurring or to occur in the future. One need only look at the levels of atmospheric pollution and vegetative disruption in central and eastern Europe to recognize the damaging consequences of heavy reliance on coal as a domestic and industrial fuel. The location of mineral fuels also tells us something about existing or potential levels of economic development with those countries possessing abundant reserves of mineral fuels having more of a chance to maintain or attain higher levels of prosperity.

Map 12b World Resources: Critical Metals

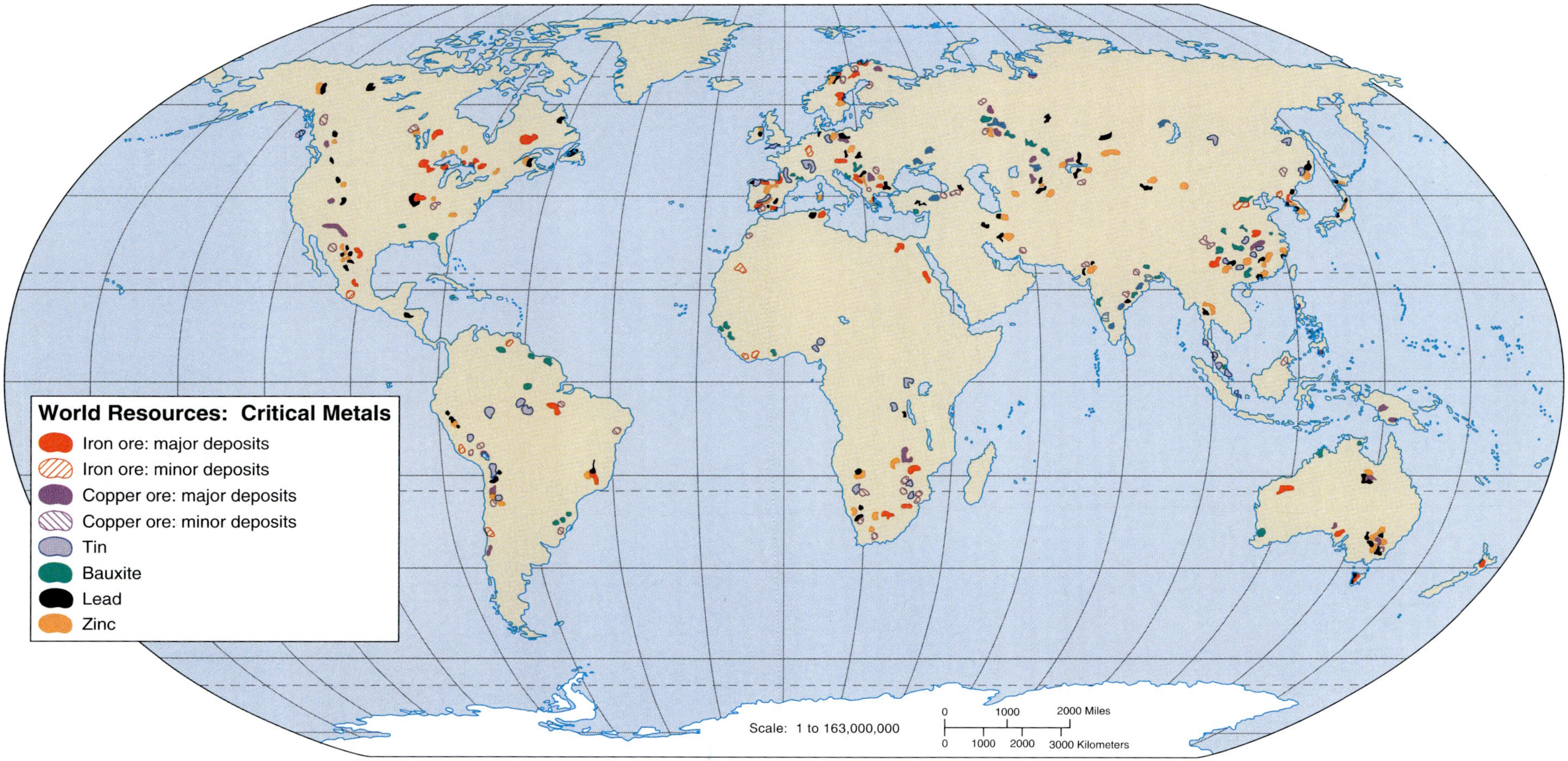

The location of deposits of critical metals such as iron, copper, tin, and others is an important determinant of the location of mining activities, like mineral fuel extraction, a "primary" economic activity. Also like mineral fuel extraction, mining for critical metallic ores makes significant environmental impact, particularly on vegetation, soils, and water resources. Some of the world's most dramatic examples of human modification of environments are located in areas of metallic ore extraction: the open pit copper mining areas of Arizona and Utah, for example. Environmental impact aside, those countries with significant critical metal deposits tend to stand a better chance of reaching higher levels of economic development, as long as they can extract and market the ores themselves rather than having the extraction process controlled by outside concerns. The average Bolivian, for example, does not benefit greatly from the fact that his/her country is an important producer of tin and other metals. Bolivia is a "colonial dependency" country and the wealth generated by metallic ore production there tends to flow out of the country to Europe and North America. On the other hand, another South American country, Brazil, is paying for much of its own current economic development by utilizing its reserves of iron and other metals and more of the wealth from the extraction of those resources stays within the country.

Map 13 World Natural Hazards

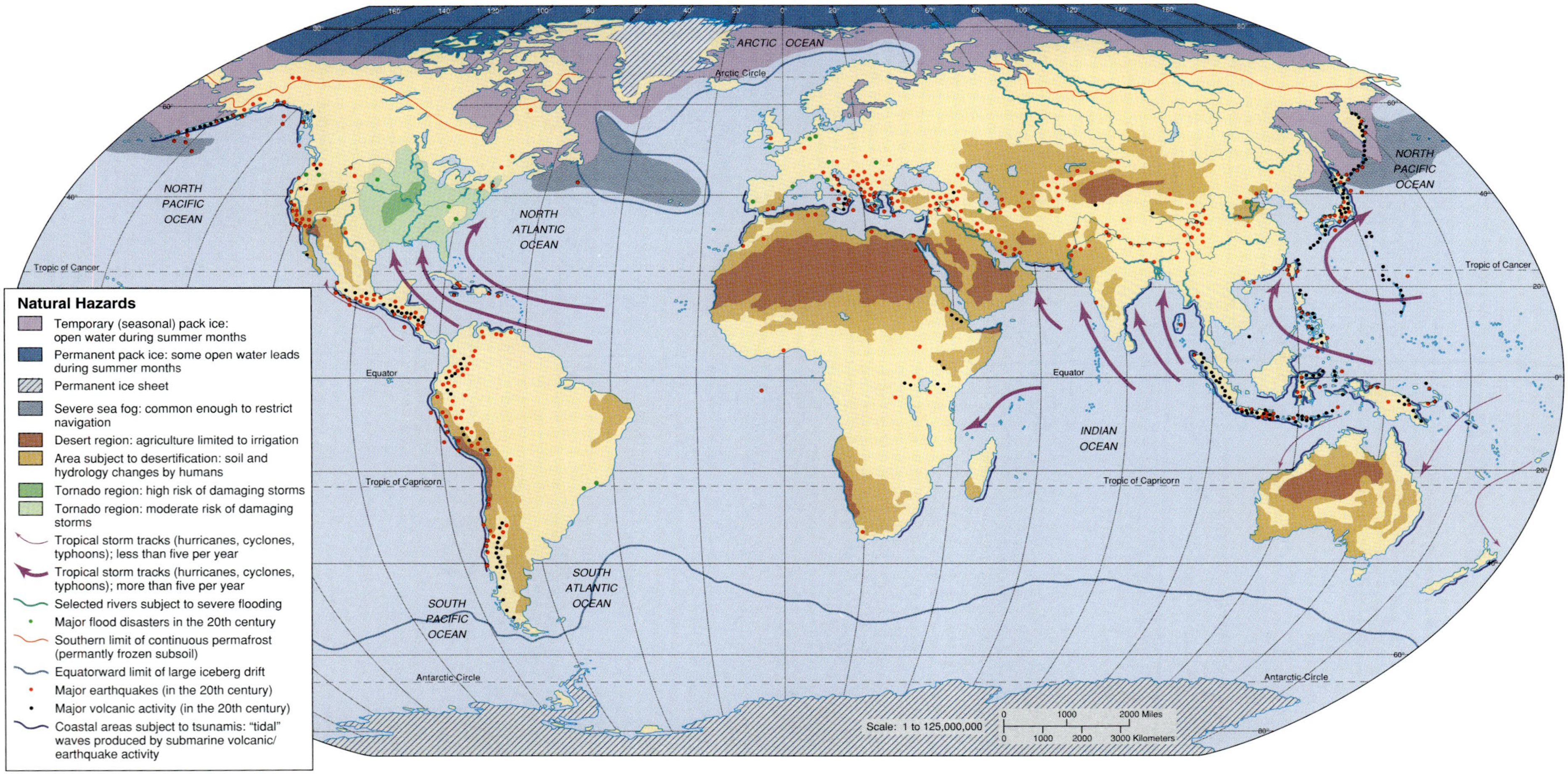

Unlike other elements of physical geography, most natural hazards are unpredictable. However, there are certain regions where the *probability* of the occurrence of a particular natural hazard is high. This map shows regions affected by major natural hazards at rates that are higher than the global norm. The presence of persistent natural hazards may influence the types of modifications that people make in the environment and certainly influence the styles of housing and other elements of cultural geography. Natural hazards may also undermine the utility of an area for economic purposes and some scholars suggest that regions of environmental instability may be regions of political instability as well. The study of natural hazards has become an important activity for "resource geographers" whose areas of interest overlap both human and physical fields of geography.

Part II

The Human Environment: Global Patterns

Map 14 World Population Density

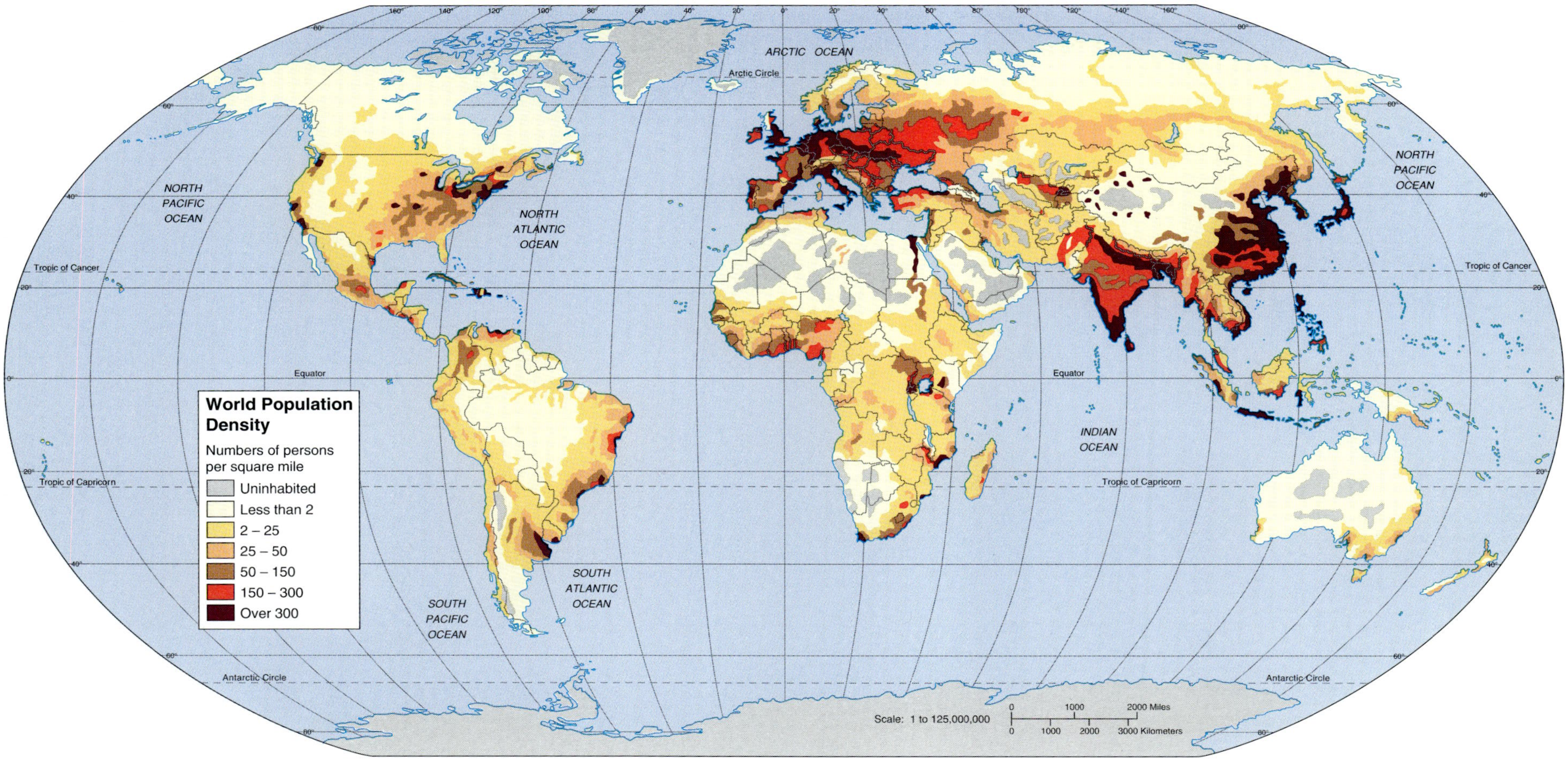

No feature of human activity is more reflective of geographic relationships than where people live. In the areas of densest populations, a mixture of natural and human factors has combined to allow maximum food production, maximum urbanization, and maximum centralization of economic activities. Three great concentrations of human population appear on the map—East Asia, South Asia, and Europe—with a fourth, lesser concentration in eastern North America. While population growth is relatively slow in three of these population clusters, in the fourth—South Asia—growth is still rapid and South Asia is expected to become even more densely populated in the early years of the twenty-first century while density of the other regions is expected to remain about as it now appears. In Europe and North America, the relatively stable population growth rates are the result of economic development that has caused population growth to level off within the last century. In East Asia, the growth rates have also begun to decline. In the case of Japan, Taiwan, the Koreas, and other more highly developed nations of the Pacific Rim, the reduced growth is the result of economic development. In China, at least until recently, lowered population growth rates have resulted from strict family planning. The areas of future high density of population, in addition to those already existing, are likely to be in Middle and South America and in Central Africa, where population growth rates are well above the world average.

Map 15 World Economic Activity

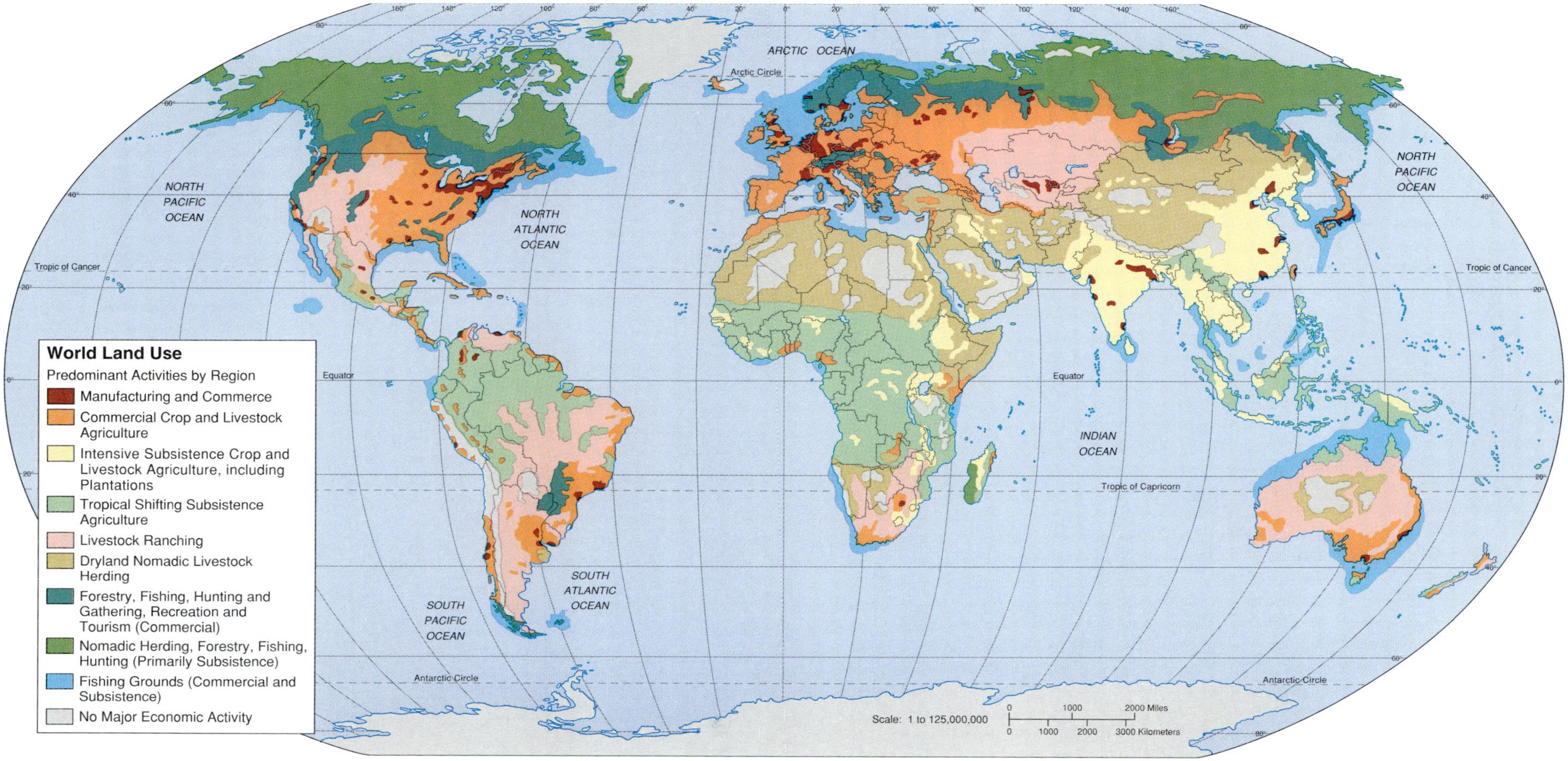

Land uses can be categorized as lying somewhere on a scale between *extensive* uses in which human activities are dispersed over relatively large areas and *intensive* uses in which human activities are concentrated in relatively small areas. Many of the most important land use patterns of the world (such as urbanization, industry, mining, or transportation) are intensive and therefore relatively small in area and not easily seen on maps of this scale. Hence, even in the areas identified as "Manufacturing and Commerce" on the map there are many land uses that are not strictly industrial or commercial in nature and, in fact, more extensive land uses (farming, residential, open space) may actually cover more ground than the intensive industrial or commercial activities. On the other hand, the more extensive land uses, like agriculture and forestry, tend to dominate the areas in which they are found. Thus, primary economic activities such as agriculture and forestry tend to dominate the world map of land use because of their extensive character. Much of this map is, therefore, a map that shows the global variations in agricultural patterns. Note, among other things, the differences between land use patterns in the more developed countries of the temperate zones and the less developed countries of the tropics.

Map 16 World Urbanization

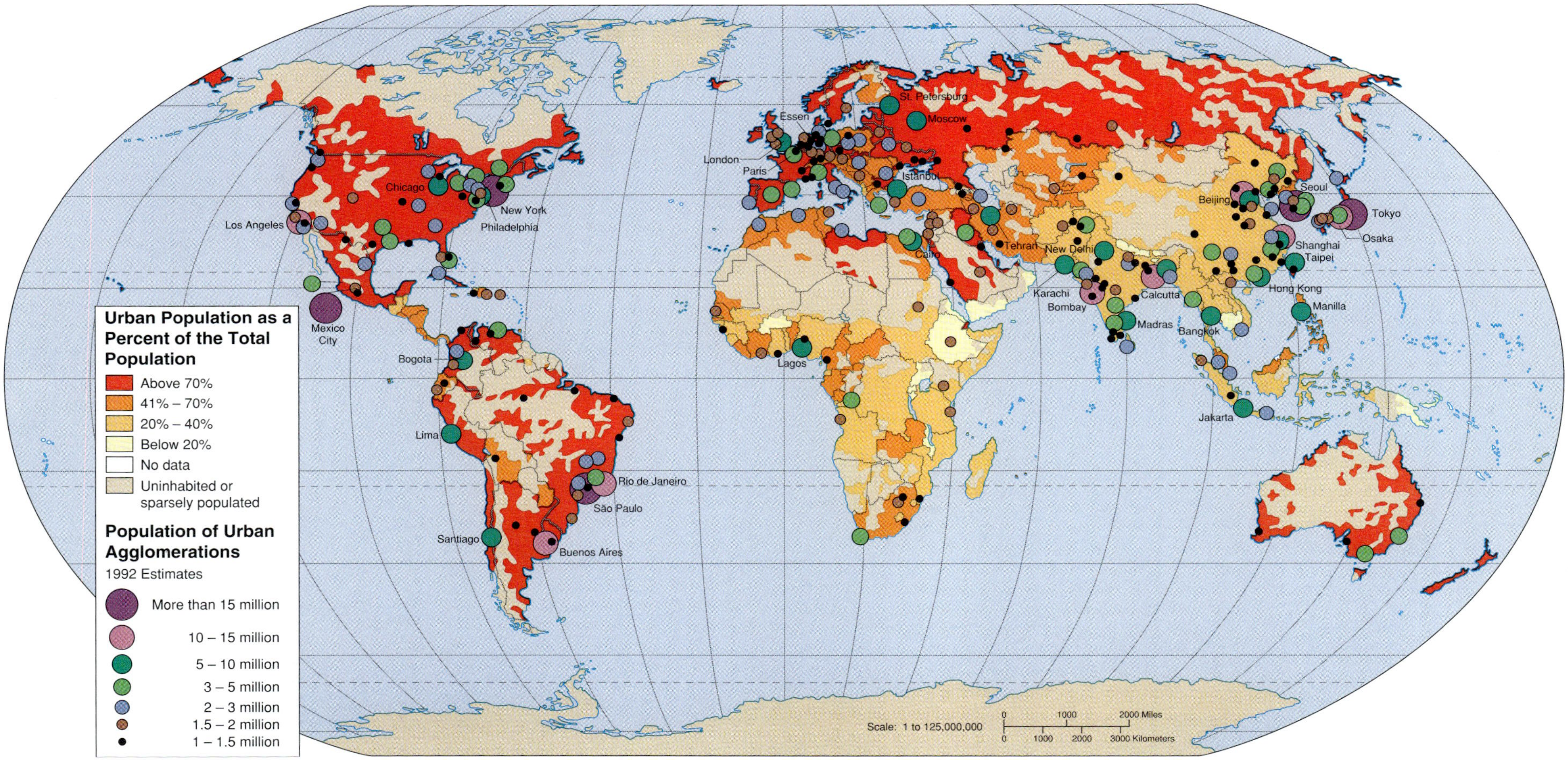

The degree to which a region's population is concentrated in urban areas is a major indicator of a number of things: the potential for environmental impact, the level of economic development, and the problems associated with human concentrations. Urban dwellers are rapidly becoming the norm among the world's people and rates of urbanization are increasing worldwide, with the greatest increases in urbanization taking place in developing regions. Whether in developed or developing countries, those who live in cities exert an influence on the environment, politics, economics, and social systems that go far beyond the confines of the city itself.

Acting as the focal points for the flow of goods and ideas, cities draw resources and people not just from their immediate hinterland but from the entire world. This process creates far-reaching impacts as resources are extracted, converted through industrial processes, and transported over great distances to metropolitan regions, and as ideas spread or *diffuse* along with the movements of people to cities and the flow of communication from them. The significance of urbanization can be most clearly seen, perhaps, in North America where, in spite of vast areas of relatively unpopulated land, well over 90% of the population lives in urban areas.

Map 17 World Transportation Patterns

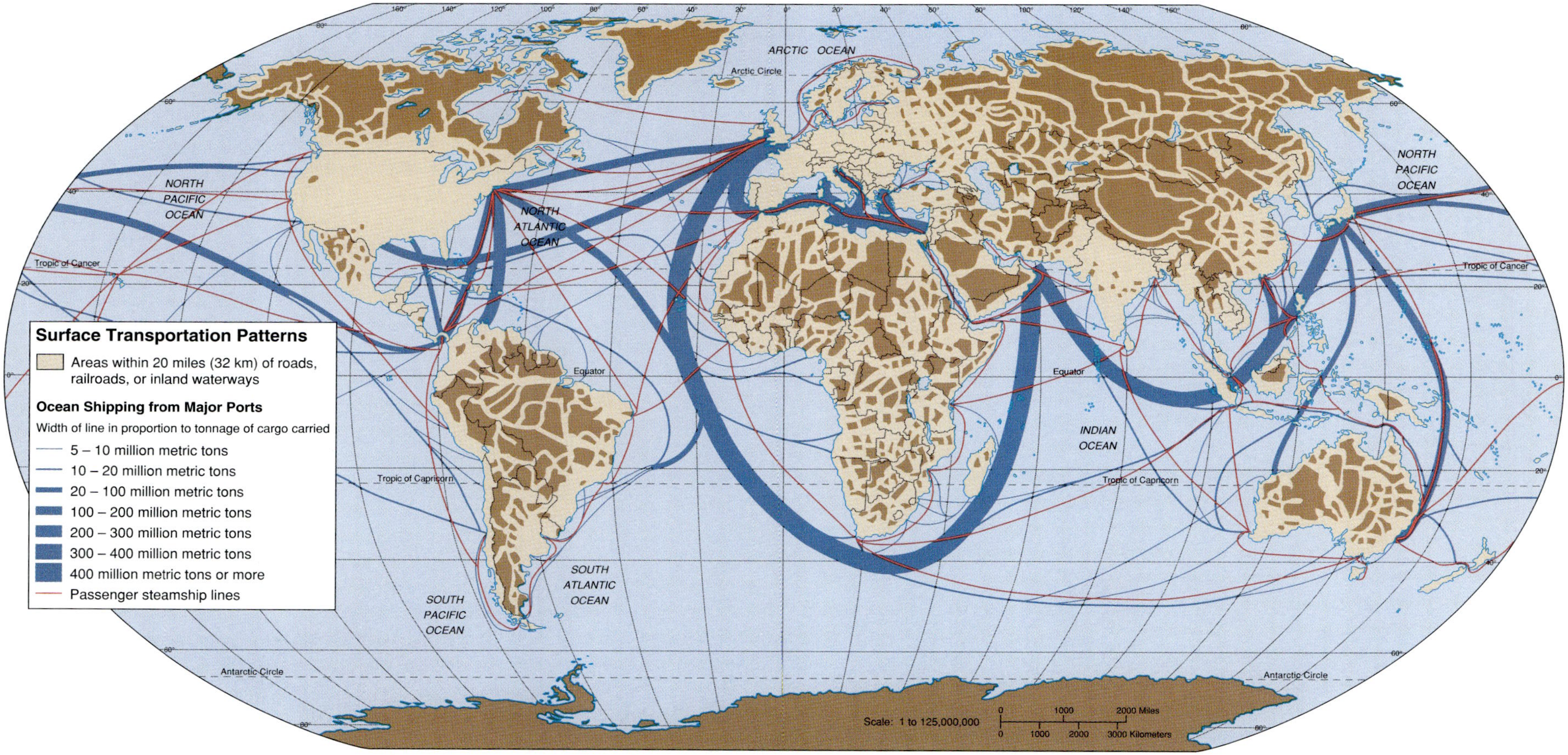

As a form of land use, transportation is second only to agriculture in its coverage of the earth's surface and is one of the clearest examples in the human world of a *network,* a linked system of lines allowing flows from one place to another. The global transportation network and its related communication web is responsible for most of the *spatial interaction* or movement of goods, people, and ideas between places. As the chief mechanism of spatial interaction, transportation is linked firmly with the concept of a shrinking world and the development of a global community and economy. Because transportation systems require significant modification of the earth's surface, transportation is also responsible for massive alterations in the quantity and quality of water, for major soil degradations and erosion, and (indirectly) for the air pollution that emanates from vehicles utilizing the transportation system. In addition, as improved transportation technology draws together places on the earth that were formerly remote, it allows people to impact environments a great distance away from where they live.

Map 18 World Religions

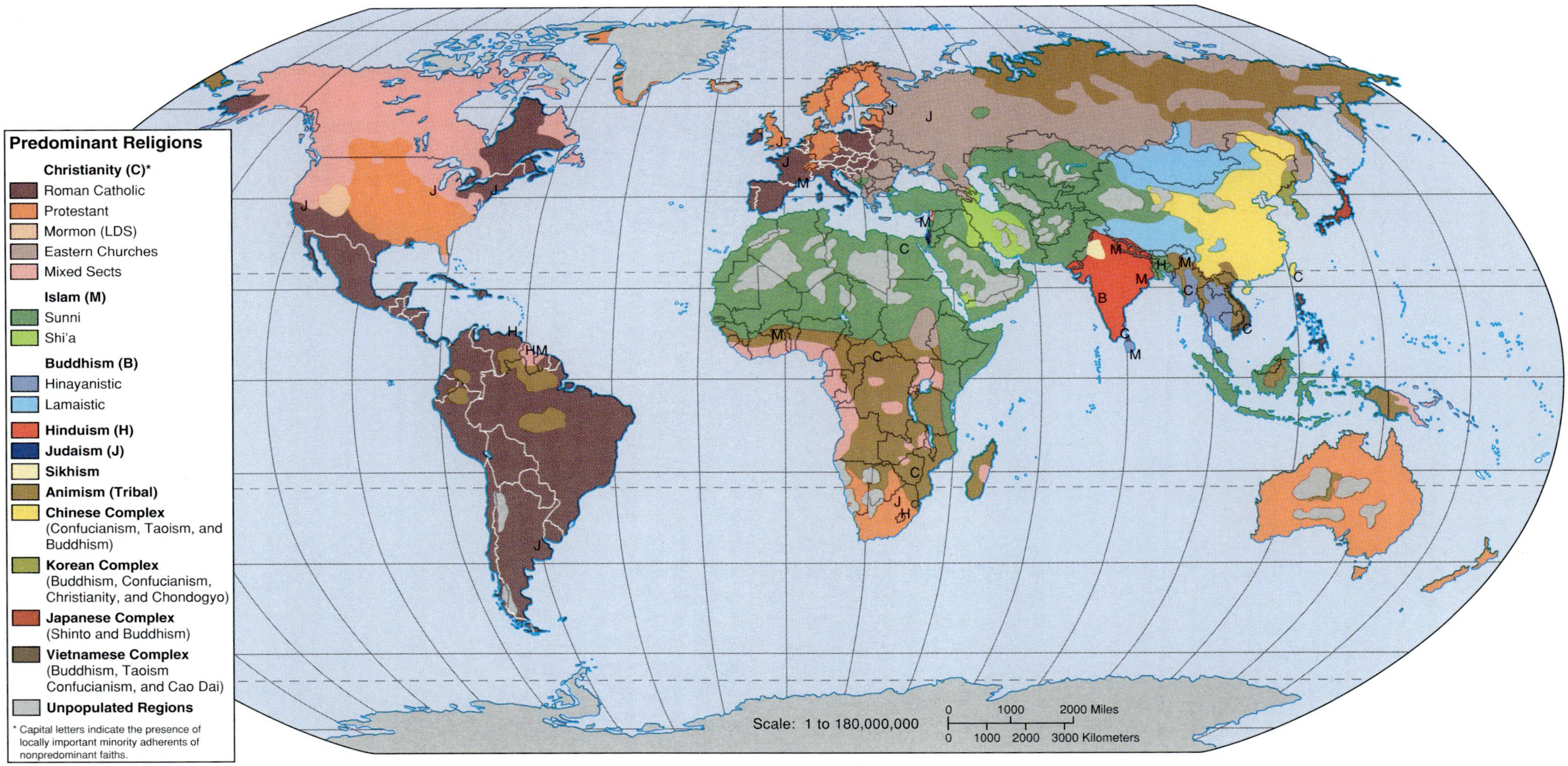

Religious adherence is one of the fundamental defining characteristics of human *culture,* the style of life adopted by a people and passed from one generation to the next. Because of the importance of religion for culture, a depiction of the spatial distribution of religions is as close as we can come to a map of cultural patterns. More than just a set of behavioral patterns having to do with worship and ceremony, religion is a vital conditioner of the ways that people deal with one another, with their institutions, and with the environments they occupy. In many areas of the world, the ways in which people make a living, the patterns of occupation that they create on the land, and the impacts that they make on ecosystems are the direct consequences of their adherence to a religious faith. An examination of the map in the context of international and intranational conflict will also show that tension between countries and the internal stability of states is also a function of the spatial distribution of religion.

Map 19 World Languages

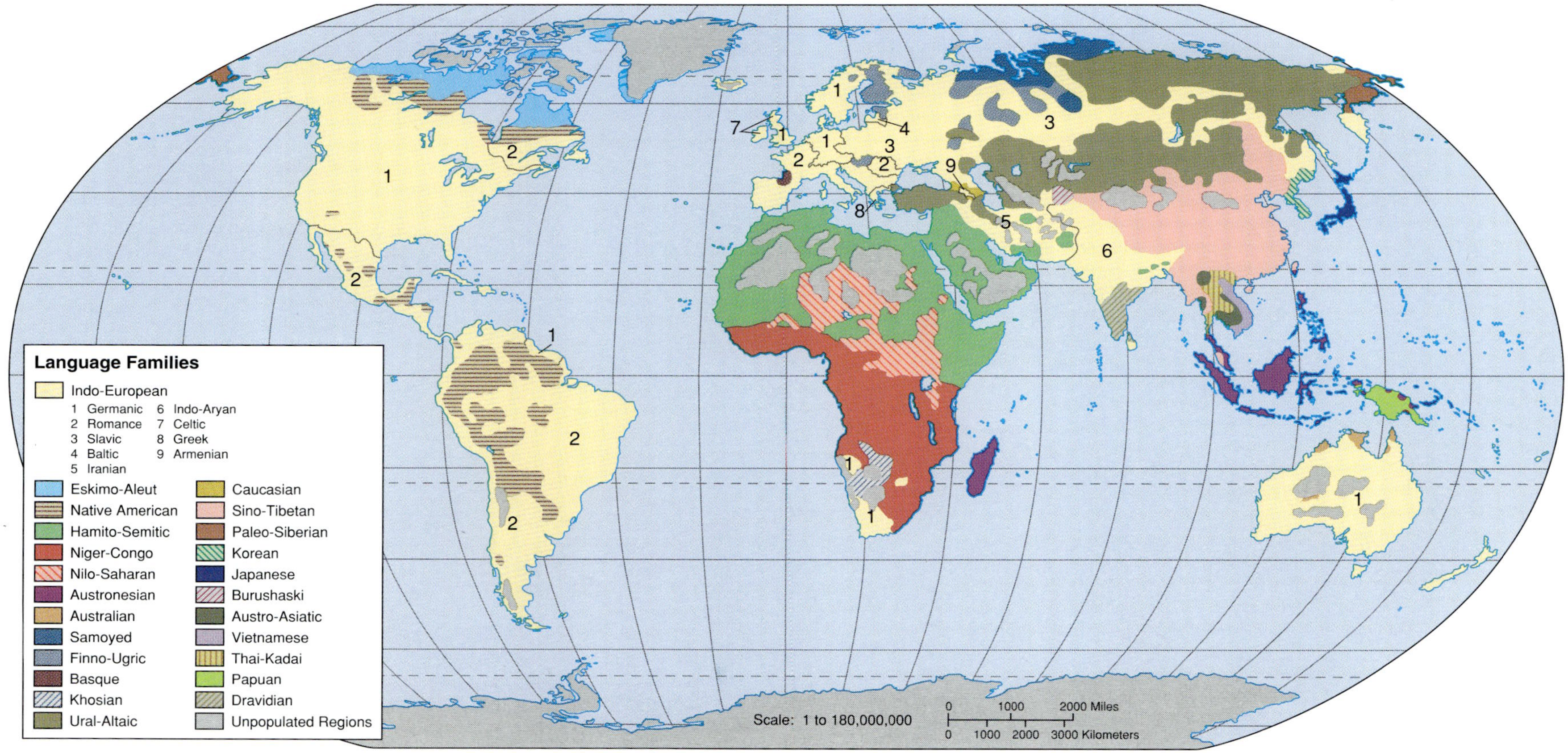

Language, like religion, is an important identifying characteristic of culture. Indeed, it is perhaps the most durable of all those identifying characteristics or *cultural traits:* language, religion, institutions, material technologies, and ways of making a living. After centuries of exposure to other languages or even conquest by speakers of other languages, the speakers of a specific tongue will often retain their own linguistic identity. As a geographic element, language helps us to locate areas of potential conflict, particularly in regions where two or more languages overlap. Many, if not most, of the world's conflict zones are also areas of linguistic diversity and knowing the distribution of languages helps us to understand some of the reasons behind important current events: for example, linguistic identity differences played an important part in the disintegration of the Soviet Union in the early 1990s; and in areas emerging from recent colonial rule, such as Africa, the participants in conflicts over territory and power are often defined in terms of linguistic groups. Language distributions also help us to comprehend the nature of the human past by providing clues that enable us to chart the course of human migrations, as shown in the distribution of Indo-European, Austronesian, or Hamito-Semitic languages. Finally, because languages have a great deal to do with the way people perceive and understand the world around them, linguistic patterns help to explain the global variations in the ways that people interact with their environments.

Map 20 World External Migrations in Modern Times

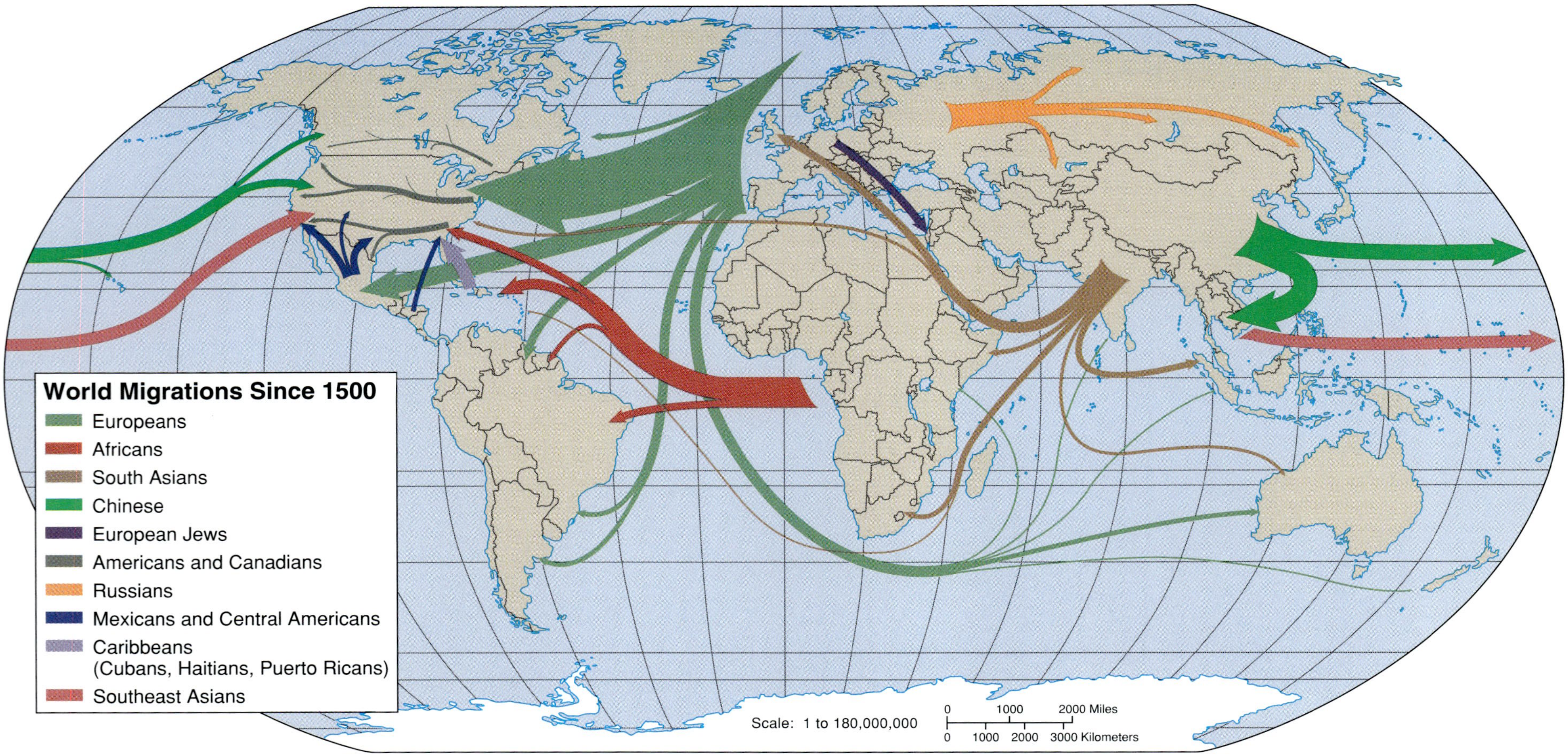

Migration has had a significant effect on world geography, contributing to cultural change and development, to the diffusion of ideas and innovations, and to the complex mixture of people and cultures found in the world today. *Internal migration* occurs within the boundaries of a country; *external migration* is movement from one country or region to another. Over the last 50 years, the most important migrations in the world have been internal, largely the rural-to-urban migration that has been responsible for the recent rise of global urbanization. Prior to the mid-twentieth century, three types of external migrations were most important: *voluntary,* most often in search of better conditions and opportunities; *involuntary* or *forced,* involving people who have been driven from their homelands by war, political unrest, or environmental disasters, or who have been transported as slaves or prisoners; and *imposed,* not entirely forced but which conditions make highly advisable. Human migrations in recorded history have been responsible for major changes in the patterns of languages, religions, ethnic composition, and economies. Particularly during the last 500 years, migrations of both the voluntary and involuntary or forced type have literally reshaped the human face of the earth.

Part III

Global Demographic Patterns

Map 21 Population Growth Rates

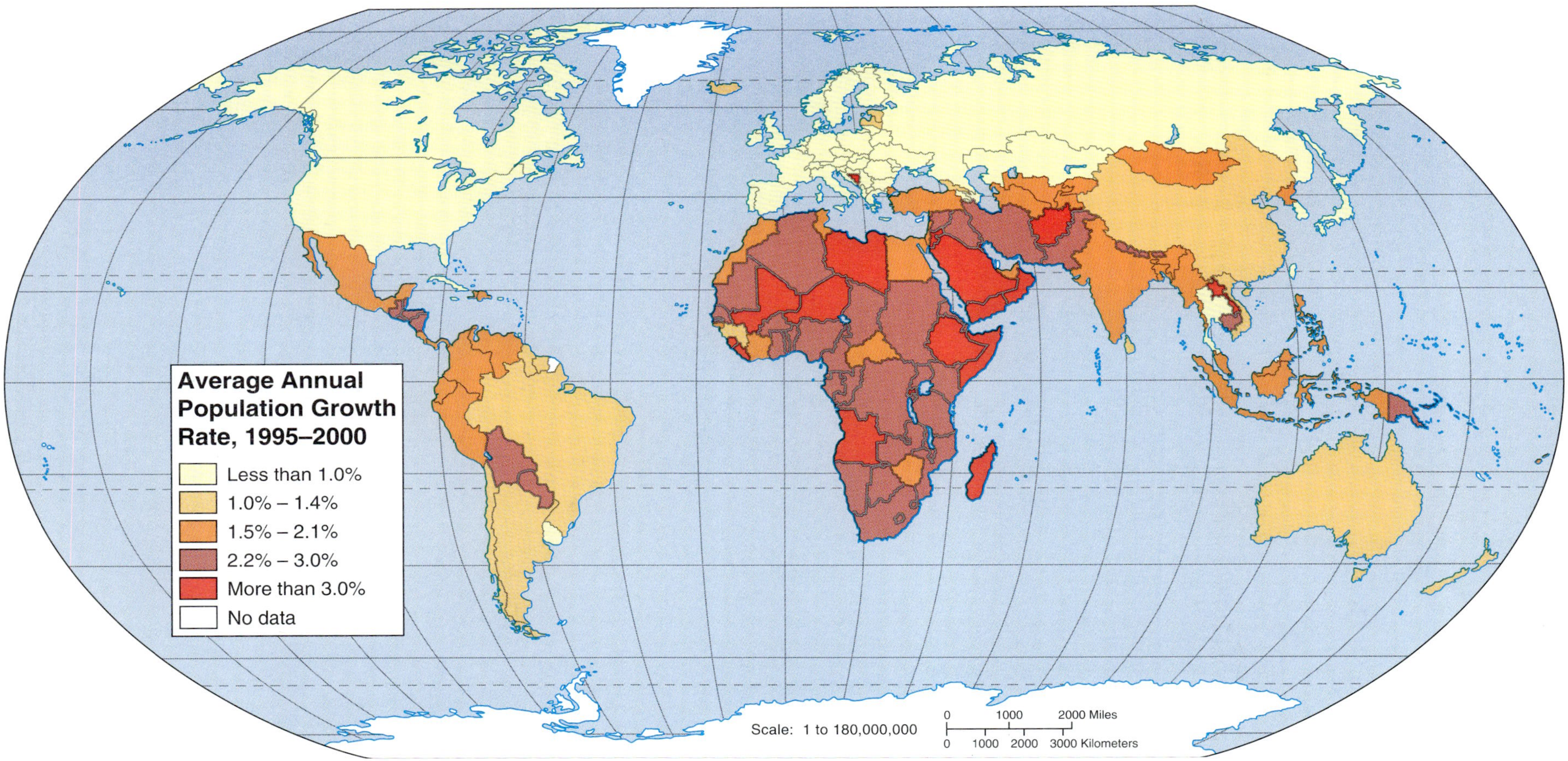

Of all the statistical measurements of human population, that of the rate of population growth is the most important. The growth rate of a population is a combination of natural change (births and deaths), in-migration, and out-migration; it is obtained by adding the number of births to the number of immigrants during a year and subtracting from that total the sum of deaths and emigrants for the same year. For a specific country, this figure will determine many things about the country's future ability to feed, house, educate, and provide medical services to its citizens.

Some of the countries with the largest populations (such as India) also have high growth rates. Since these countries tend to be in developing regions, the combination of high population and high growth rates poses special problems for continuing economic development and carries heightened risks of environmental degradation. Many people believe that the rapidly expanding world population is a potential crisis that may cause environmental and human disaster by the middle of the twenty-first century.

Map 22 Total Fertility Rate

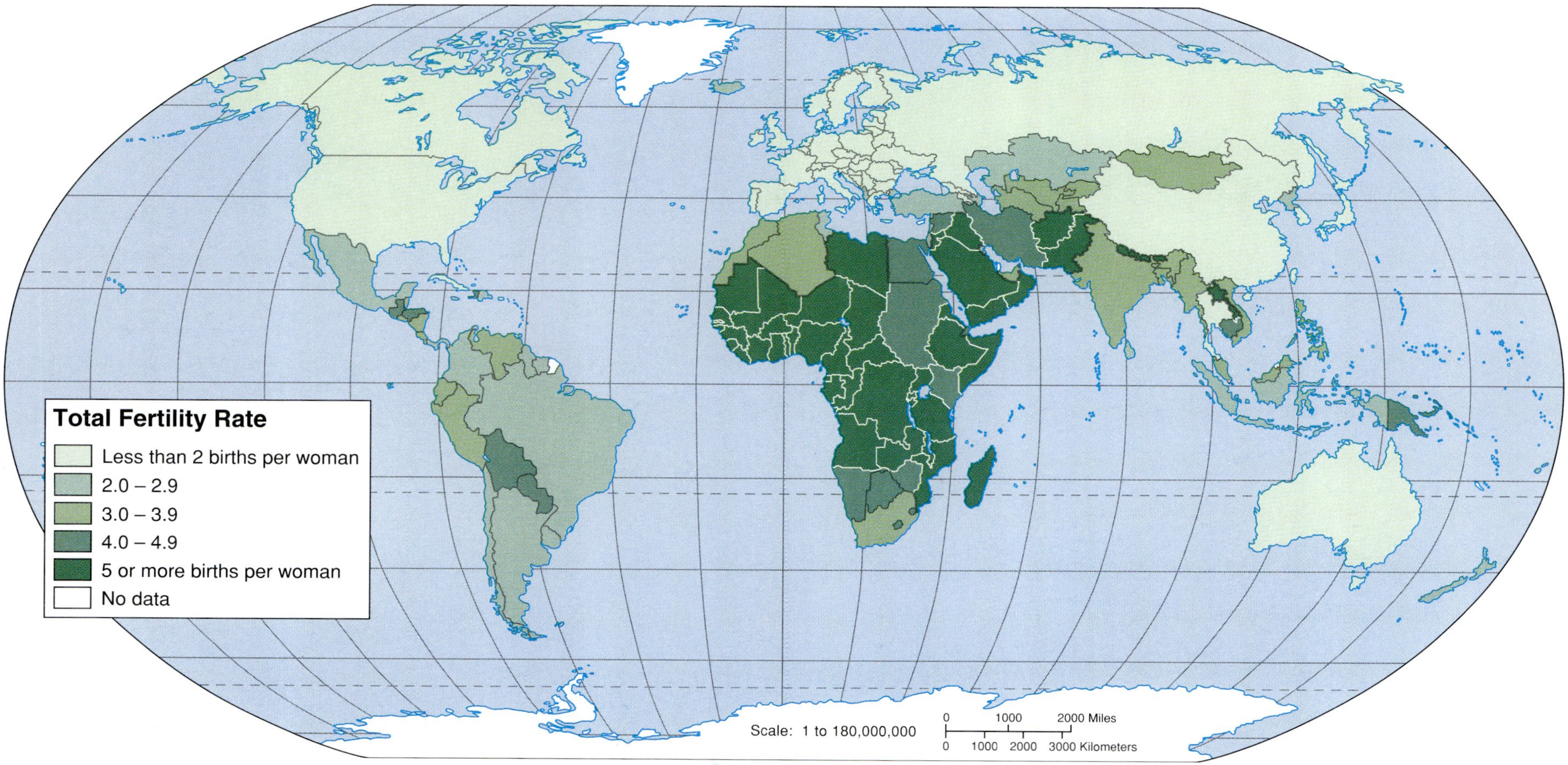

The fertility rate measures the number of children that a woman is expected to bear during her lifetime, based on the age-specific fertility figures of women between 15 and 40 (the normal childbearing years). While fertility rates tell us a great deal about present population growth, with high fertility rates indicating high population growth rates, they are also indicative of potential or projected growth. A country whose women can be expected to bear many children is a country with enormous potential for population growth in the future. Given present fertility rates, for example, the number of offspring from the average German woman over the next three generations (the total number of children, grandchildren, and great-grandchildren) will be 7. During the same three generations, the average American woman will have a total of 17 children, grandchildren, and great-grandchildren. But during this time, assuming that present fertility rates are maintained, the average woman in sub-Saharan Africa will have *258* children, grandchildren, and great-grandchildren. You might be interested in working out some potential population growth rates over two or three generations, using the data as presented on the map.

Note: Total fertility rate figures are based on yearly age-specific fertility rate estimates from 1990–2000.

Map 23 Infant Mortality Rate

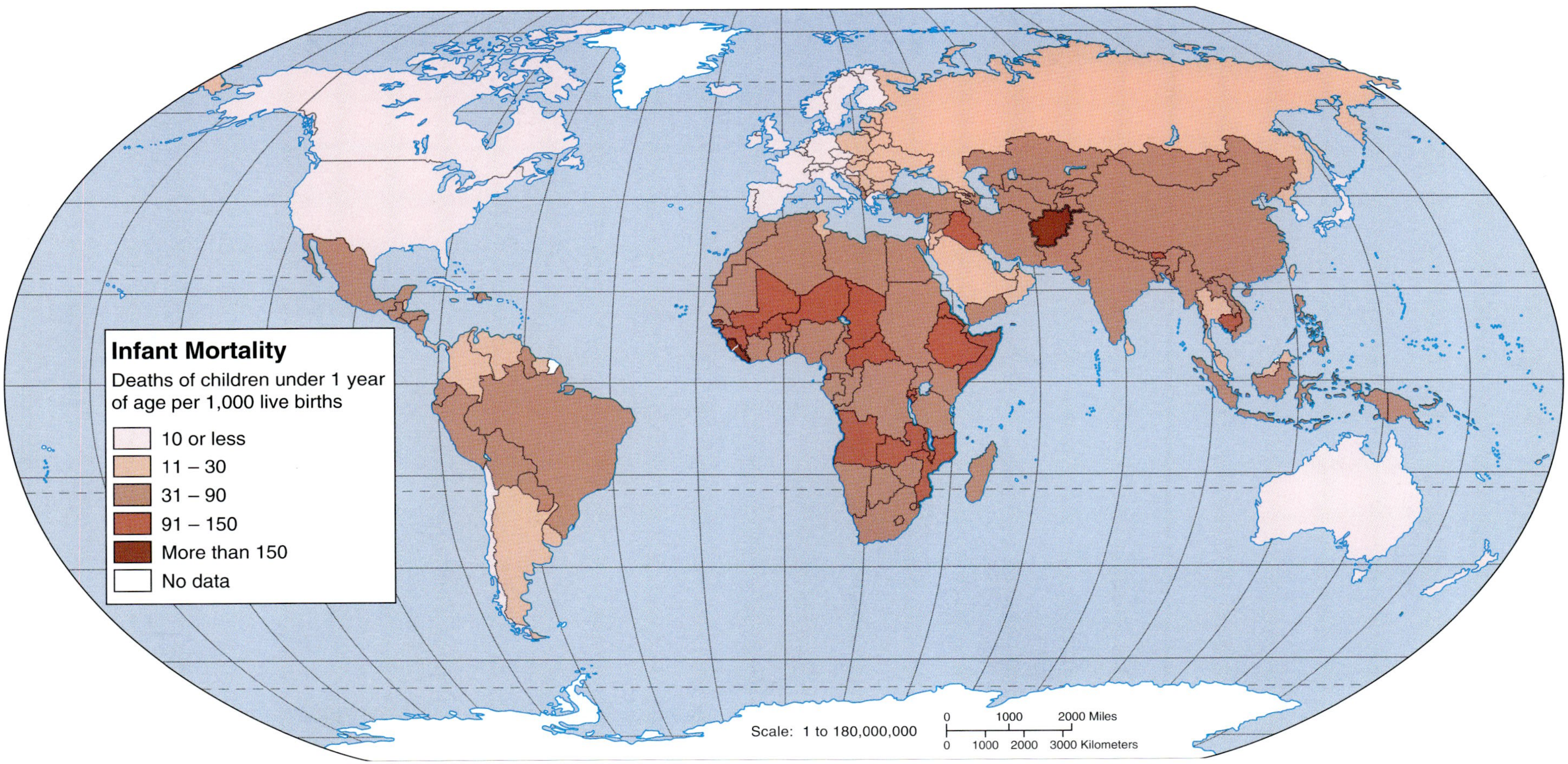

Infant mortality rates are calculated by dividing the number of children born in a given year who die before their first birthday by the total number of children born that year and then multiplying by 1,000; this shows how many infants have died for every 1,000 births. Infant mortality rates are prime indicators of economic development. In highly developed economies, with advanced medical technologies, sufficient diets, and adequate public sanitation, infant mortality rates tend to be quite low. By contrast, in less developed countries, with the disadvantages of poor diet, limited access to medical technology, and the other problems of poverty, infant mortality rates tend to be high. Although worldwide infant mortality has decreased significantly during the last 2 decades, many regions of the world still experience infant mortality above the 10 percent level (100 deaths per 1,000 live births). Such infant mortality rates represent not only human tragedy at its most basic level, but also are powerful inhibiting factors for the future of human development. Comparing infant mortality rates in the midlatitudes and the tropics shows that children in most African countries are more than 10 times as likely to die within a year of birth as children in European countries.

Map 24 Average Life Expectancy at Birth

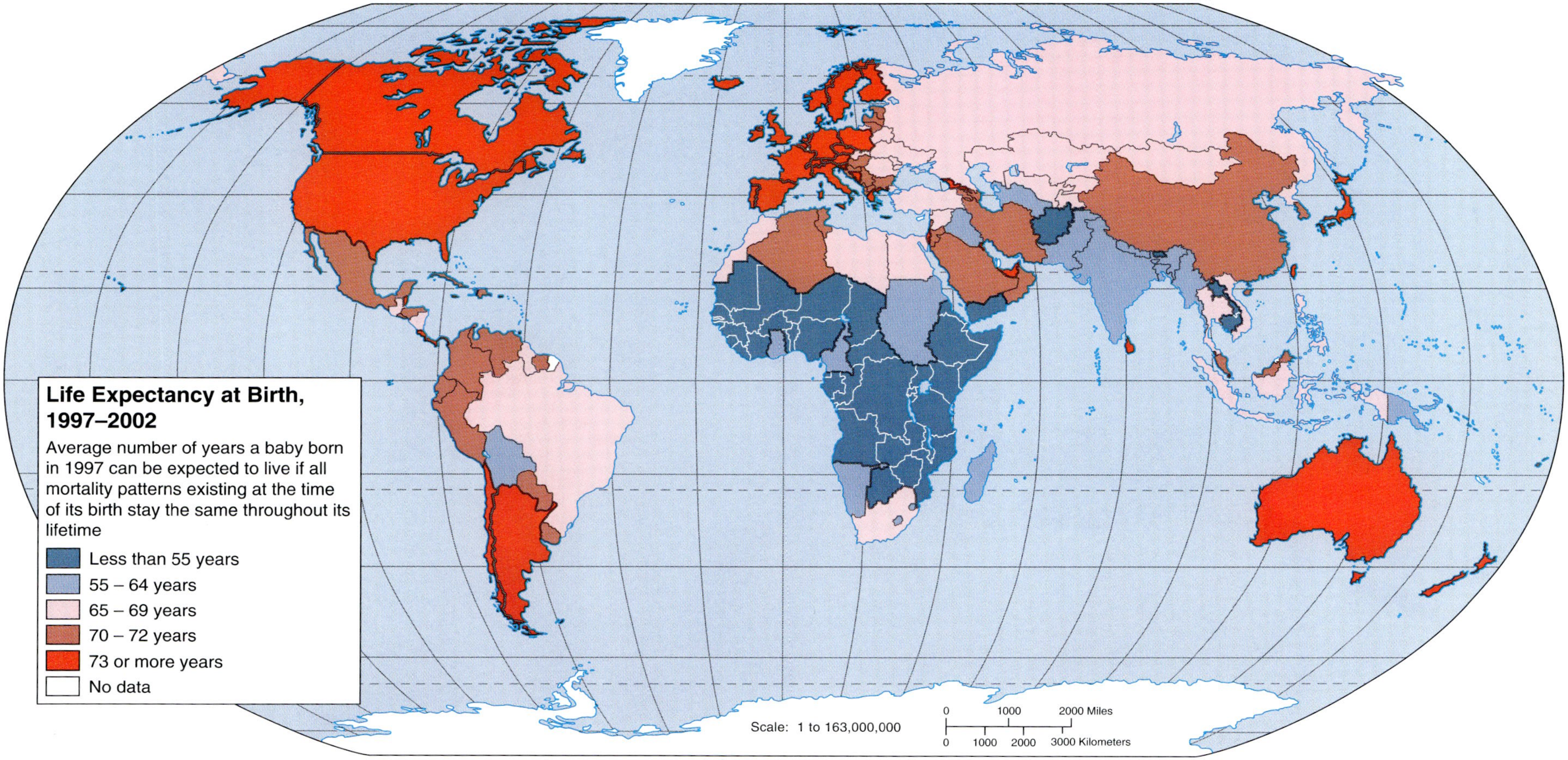

Average life expectancy at birth is a measure of the average longevity of the population of a country. Like all average measures, it is distorted by extremes. For example, a country with a high mortality rate among children will have a low average life expectancy. Thus, an average life expectancy of 45 years does not mean that everyone can be expected to die at the age of 45. More normally, what the figure means is that a substantial number of children die between birth and 5 years of age, thus reducing the average life expectancy for the entire population. In spite of the dangers inherent in misinterpreting the data, average life expectancy (along with infant mortality and several other measures) is a valid way of judging the relative health of a population. It reflects the nature of the health care system, public sanitation and disease control, nutrition, and a number of other key human need indicators. As such, it is a measure of well-being that is significant in indicating economic development.

Map 25 Population by Age Group

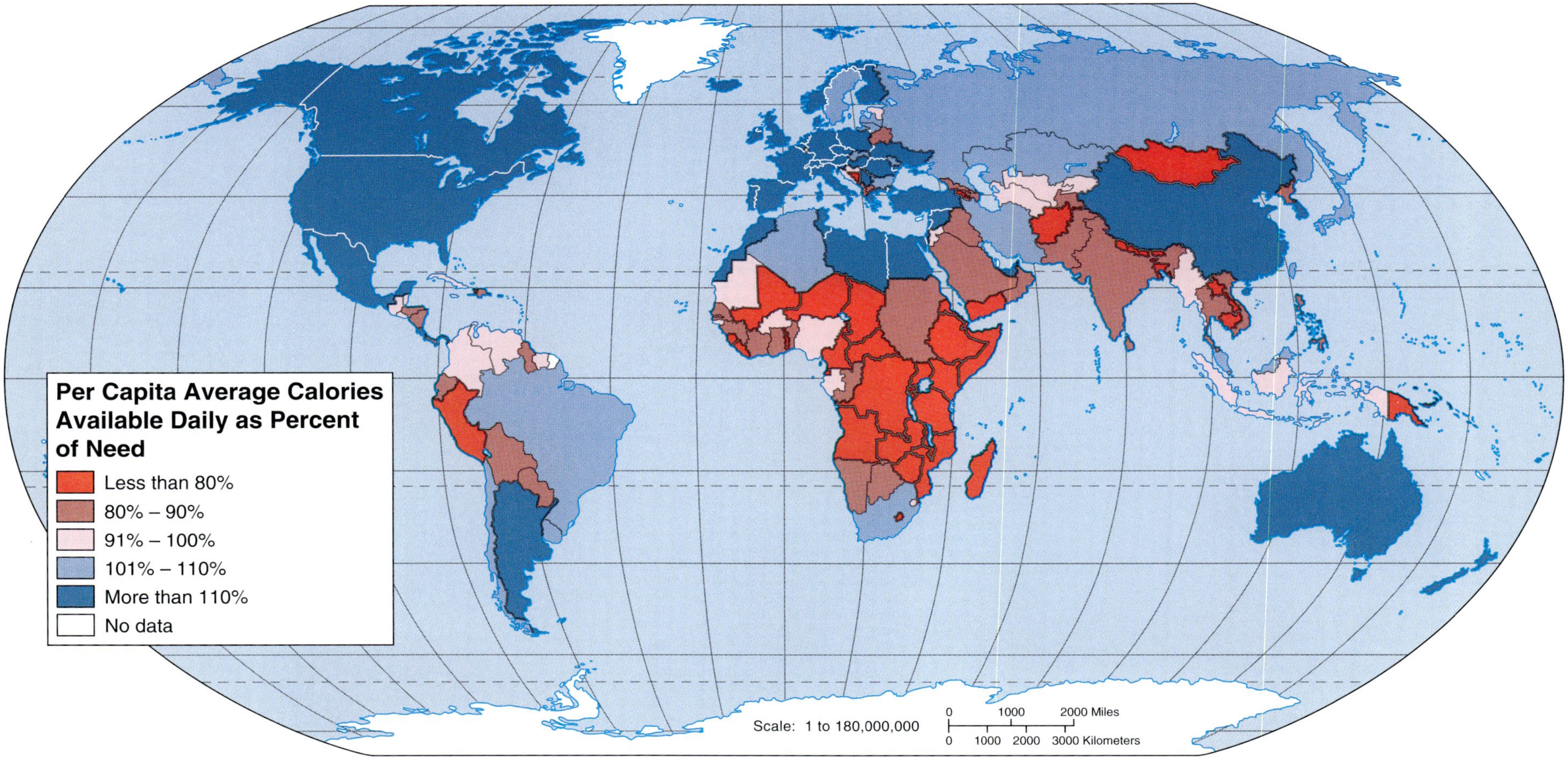

Of all the measurements that illustrate the dynamics of a population, age distribution may be the most significant, particularly when viewed in combination with average growth rates. The particular relevance of age distribution is that it tells us what to expect from a population in terms of growth over the next generation. If, for example, approximately 40–50 percent of a population is below the age of 15, that suggests that in the next generation about one-quarter of the total population will be women of childbearing age. When age distribution is combined with fertility rates (the average number of children born per woman in a population), an especially valid measurement of future growth potential may be derived. A simple example: Nigeria, with a 1995 population of 127 million, has 47 percent of its population below the age of 15 and a fertility rate of 6.4; the United States, with a 1995 population of 263 million, has 22 percent of its population below the age of 15 and a fertility rate of 2.1. During the period in which those women presently under the age of 15 are in their childbearing years, Nigeria can be expected to add a total of approximately 197 million persons to its total population. Over the same period, the United States can be expected to add only 61 million.

Map 26 World Daily Per Capita Food Supply

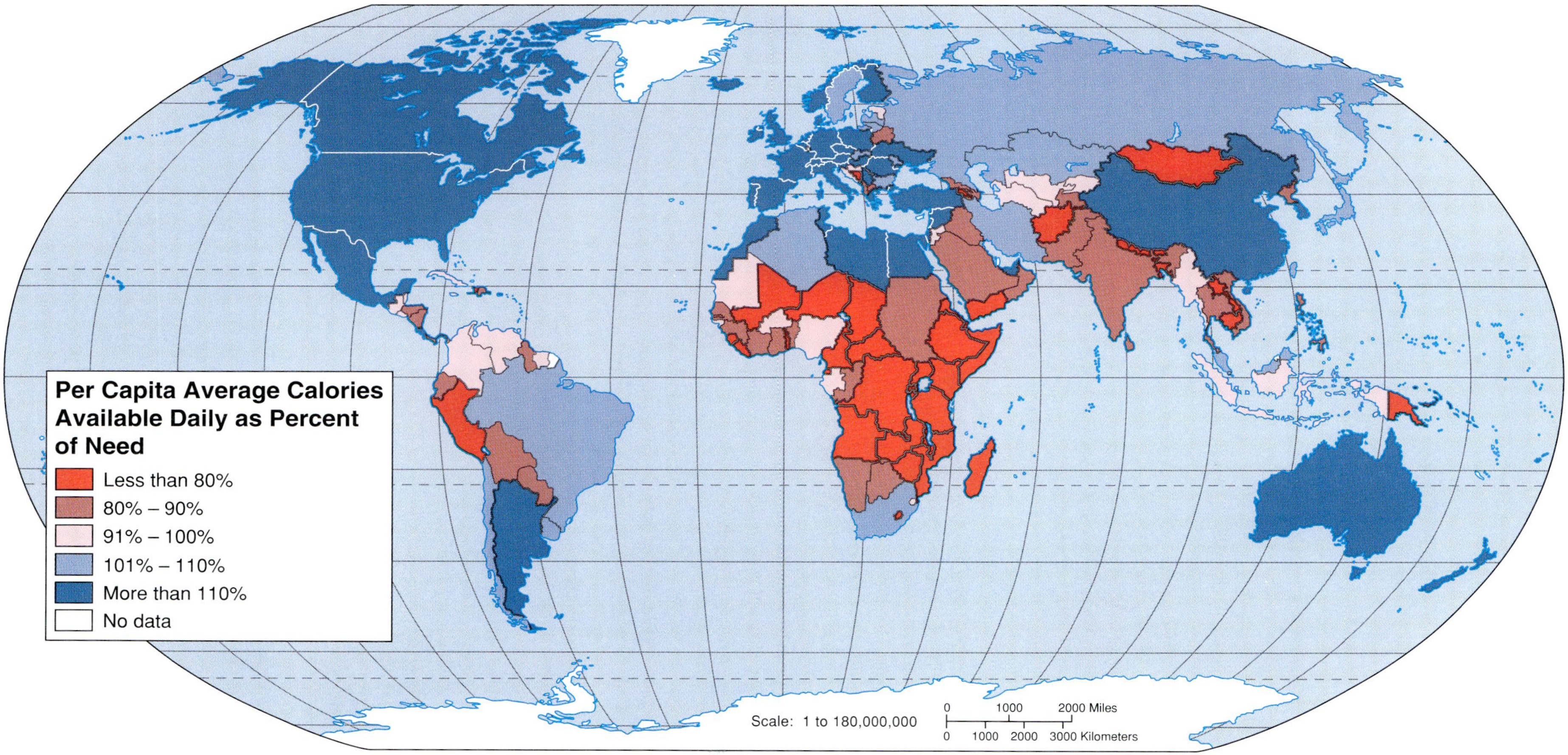

The data shown on this map indicate the presence or absence of critical food shortages. While they do not necessarily indicate the presence of starvation or famine, they certainly do indicate potential problem areas for the next decade. The measurements are in calories from *all* food sources: domestic production, international trade, drawdown on stocks or food reserves, and direct foreign contributions or aid. The quantity of calories available is that amount, estimated by the UN's Food and Agriculture Organization (FAO), that actually reaches consumers. The calories actually consumed may be lower than the figures shown, depending on how much is lost in a variety of ways: in home storage (to pests such as rats and mice), in preparation and cooking, through consumption by pets and domestic animals, and as discarded foods, for example. The former practice in such maps was to evaluate available calories as a percent of "need" or minimum daily requirements to maintain health. Such a statistical measure was virtually impossible to standardize for the variety of human types in the world and for such variables as age and sex distribution. A newer form of measure—available calories as a percent of the world average available—eliminates many of the problems of the former set of numbers while still maintaining a good relative picture of global hunger.

Map 27 Illiteracy Rate

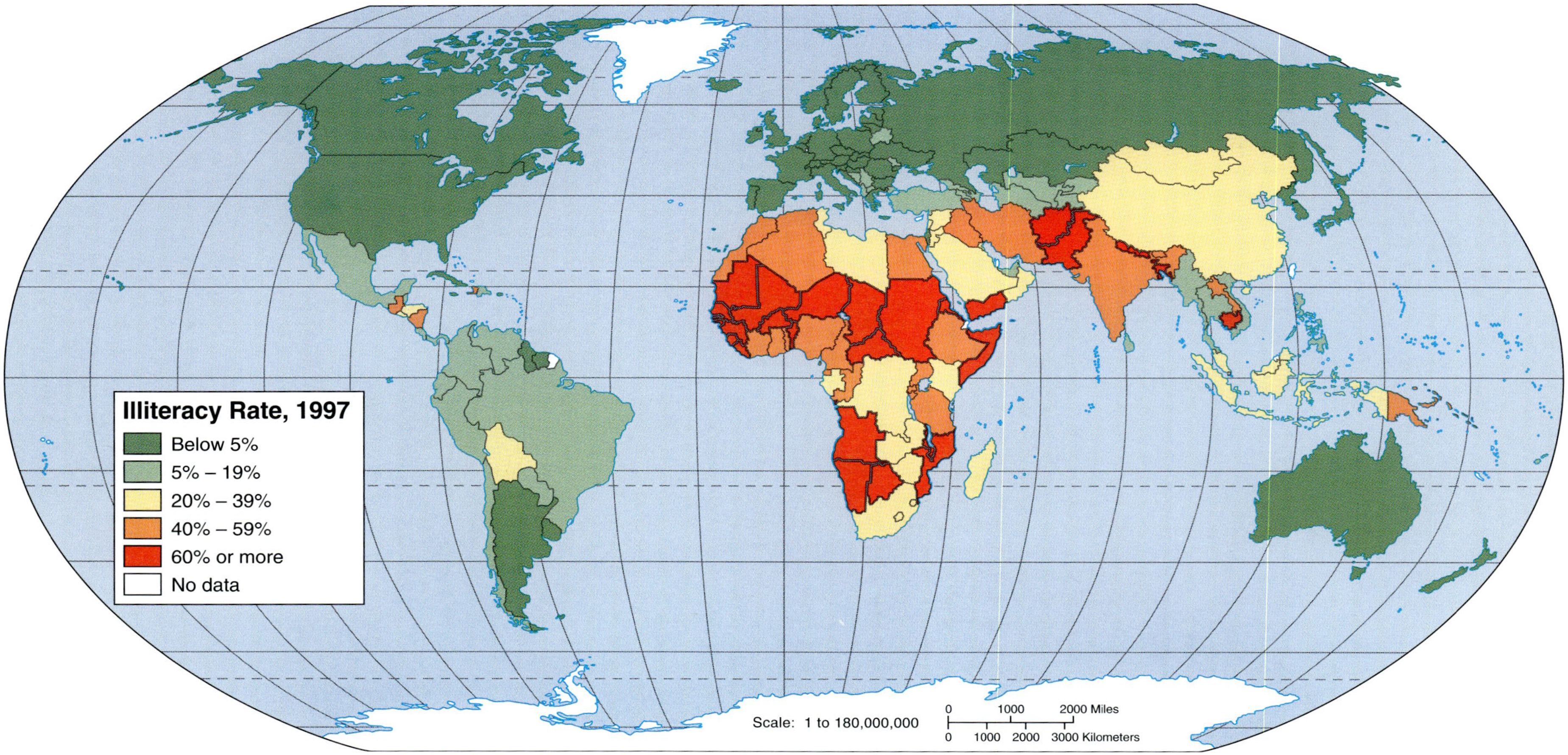

The gains in living standards that developing countries have experienced during the last two decades are manifested in two major areas: life expectancy and literacy. The increase in global literacy is largely the consequence of an increase in primary school enrollment, particularly throughout Middle and South America, Africa, and Asia. Worldwide, education is perceived as a way to advance economic status. Unfortunately, although gains have been made, there are still countries where illiteracy rates—particularly among the females of the population—are well above global norms. The long-term potential of these countries is severely compromised as a result. **A word of caution:** Most countries view their literacy or illiteracy rates as hallmarks of their status in the world community and there is, therefore, a tendency to overstate or overestimate literacy (or, conversely, to underestimate illiteracy). In the United States for example, the stated illiteracy rate is less than 2%. Yet many experts indicate that somewhere between 10% and 15% of the U.S. population may, in fact, be functionally illiterate—that is, unable to read street signs, advertisements, or newspapers.

Map 28 Female/Male Inequality in Education and Employment

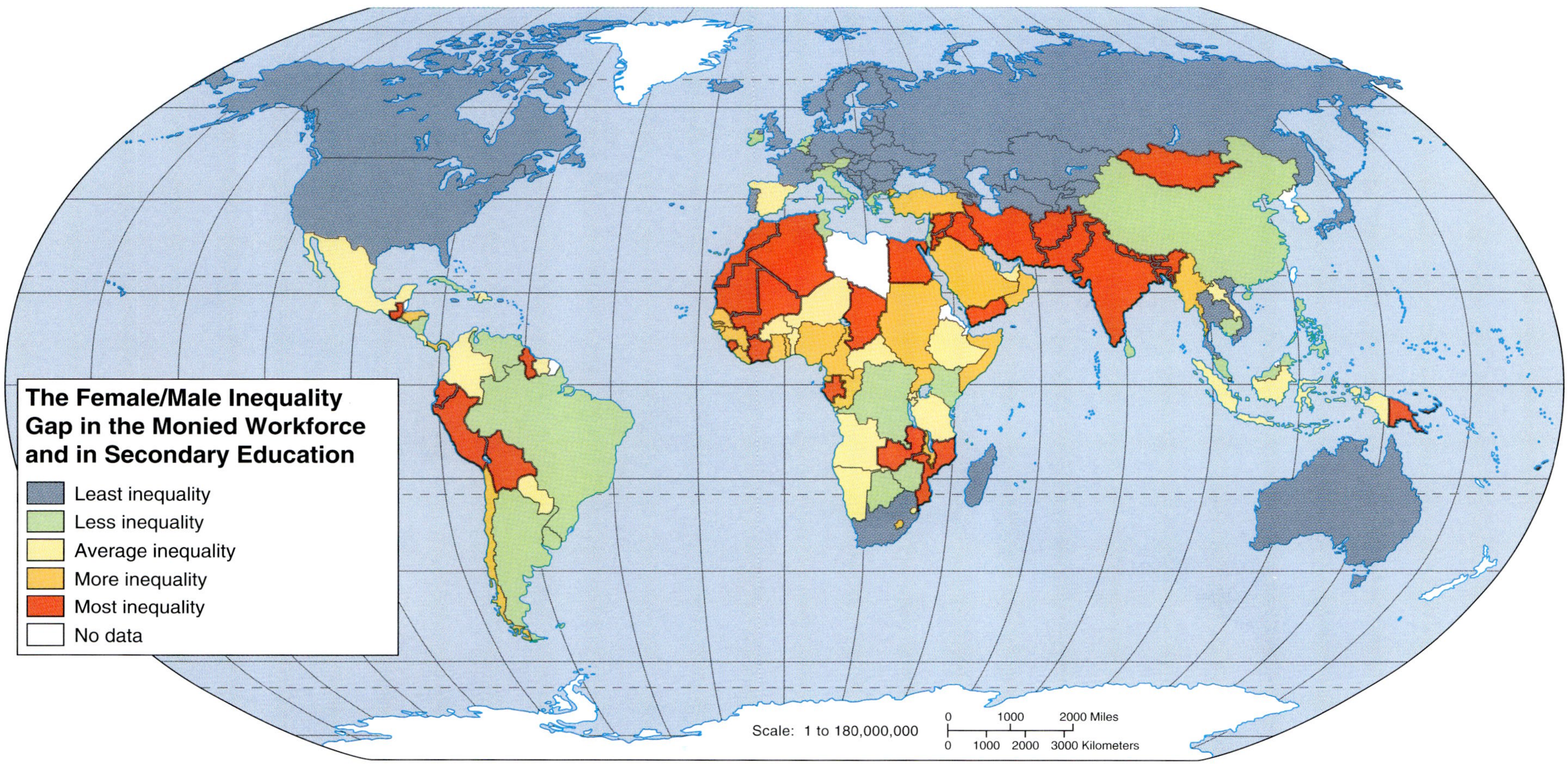

While women in developed countries, particularly in North America and Europe, have made significant advances in socioeconomic status in recent years, in most of the world females suffer from significant inequality when compared with their male counterparts. Although women have received the right to vote in most of the world's countries, in over 90 percent of these countries that right has only been granted in the last 50 years. In most regions, literacy rates for women still fall far short of those for men; In Africa and Asia, for example, only about half as many women are as literate as men. Women marry considerably younger than men and attend school for shorter periods of time. Inequalities in education and employment are perhaps the most telling indicators of the unequal status of women in most of the world. Lack of secondary education in comparison with men prevents women from entering the workforce with equally high-paying jobs. Even where women are employed in positions similar to those held by men, they still tend to receive less compensation. The gap between rich and poor involves not only a clear geographic differentiation, but a clear gender differentiation as well.

Map 29 Global Scourges: Major Infectious Diseases

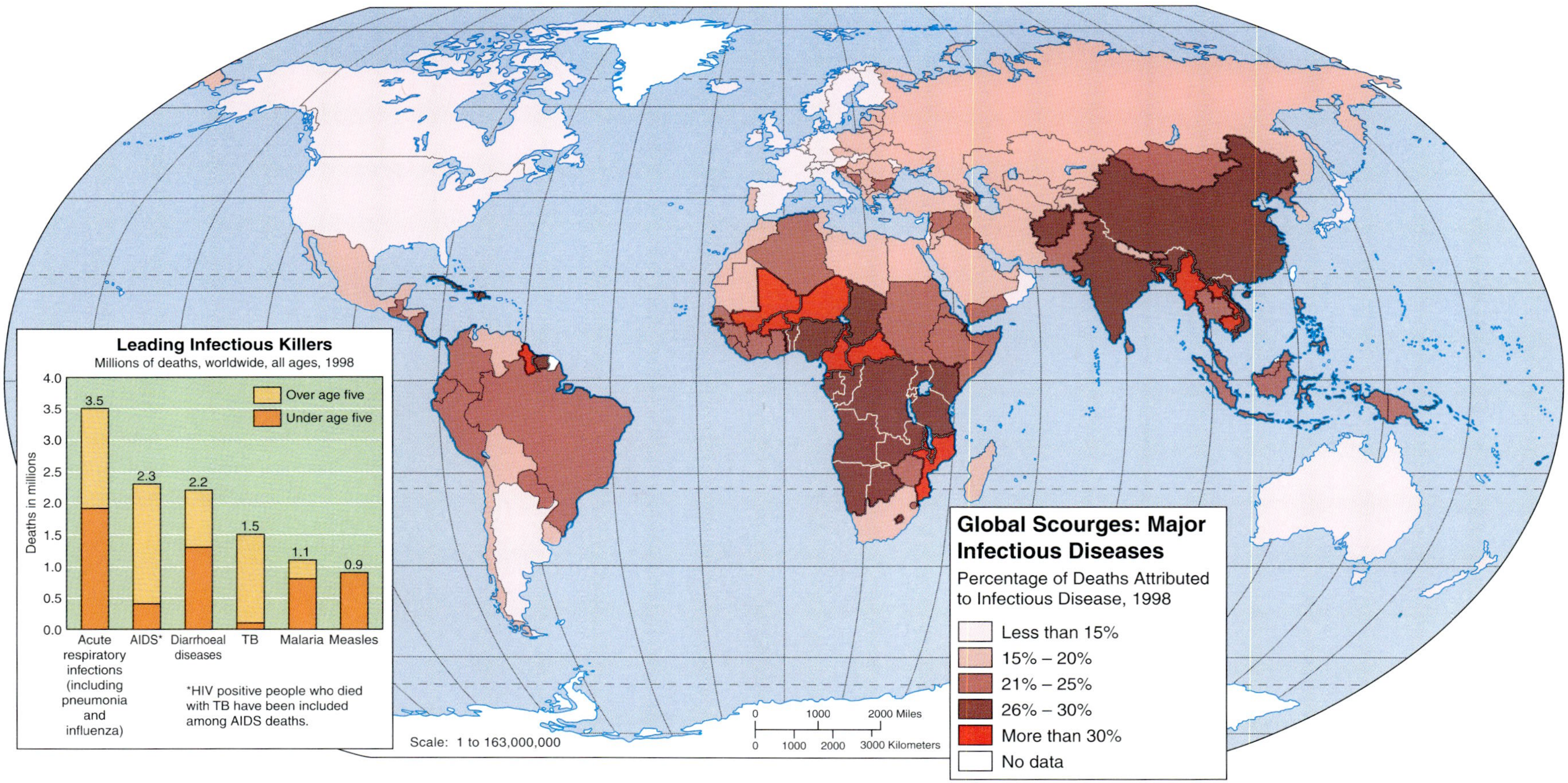

Infectious diseases are the world's leading cause of premature death and at least half of the world's population is, at any time, at risk of contracting an infectious disease. While we often think of infectious diseases as being restricted to the tropical world (malaria, dengue fever, etc.), many if not most of them have attained global proportions. A major case in point is HIV/AIDS, which quite probably originated in Africa but has, over the last two decades, spread throughout the entire world. Major diseases of the nineteenth century, such as cholera and tuberculosis, are making a major comeback in many parts of the world, in spite of being preventable or treatable. Part of the problem with infectious diseases is that they tend to be associated with poverty (poor nutrition, poor sanitation, substandard housing, and so on) and, therefore, are seen as a problem of undeveloped countries, with the consequent lack of funding for prevention and treatment. Infectious diseases are also tending to increase because lifesaving drugs, such as antibiotics and others used in the fight against diseases, are losing their effectiveness as bacteria develop genetic resistance to them. The problem of global warming is also associated with a spread of infectious diseases as many disease vectors (certain species of mosquito, for example) are spreading into higher latitudes with increasingly warm temperatures and are spreading diseases into areas where populations have no resistance to them. Infectious diseases have become something greater than simply a health issue of poor countries. They are now major social problems with potentially enormous consequences for the entire world.

Map [30] Quality of Life–Human Development Index

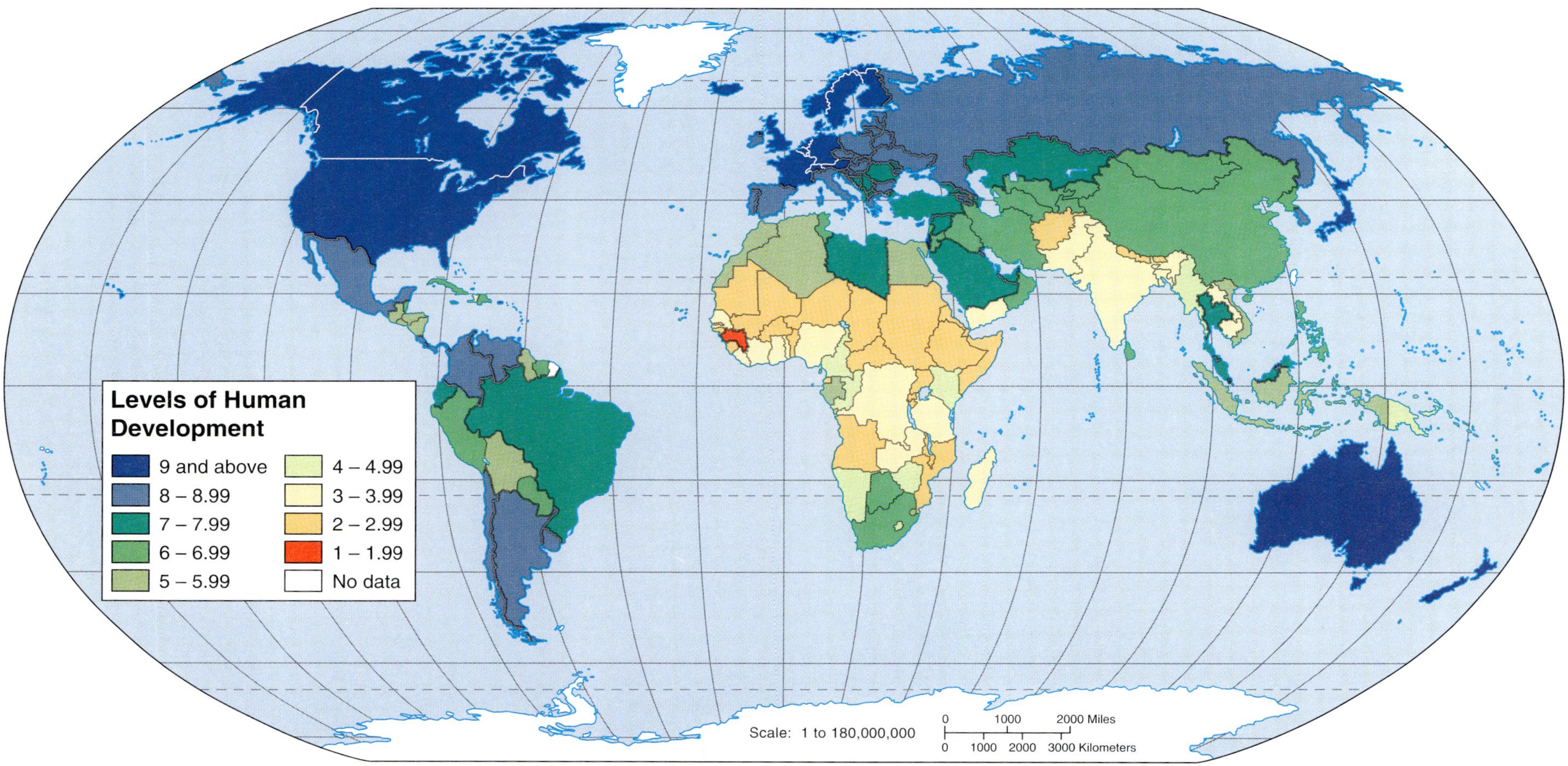

The development index upon which this map is based takes into account a wide variety of demographic, health, and educational data, including population growth, per capita gross domestic product, longevity, literacy, and years of schooling. The map reveals significant improvement in the quality of life in Middle and South America, although it is questionable whether the gains made in those regions can be maintained in the face of the dramatic population increases expected over the next 30 years. More clearly than anything else, the map illustrates the near-desperate situation in Africa and South Asia. In those regions, the unparalleled growth in population threatens to overwhelm all efforts to improve the quality of life. In Africa, for example, the population is increasing by 20 million persons per year. With nearly 45 percent of the continent's population aged 15 years or younger, this growth rate will accelerate as the women reach childbearing age. Africa, along with South Asia, faces the very difficult challenge of providing basic access to health care, education, and jobs for a rapidly increasing population. The map also illustrates the striking difference in quality of life between those who inhabit the world's equatorial and tropical regions and those fortunate enough to live in the temperate zones, where the qualify of life is significantly higher.

Part IV

Global Economic Patterns

Map 31 Rich and Poor Countries–Gross National Product

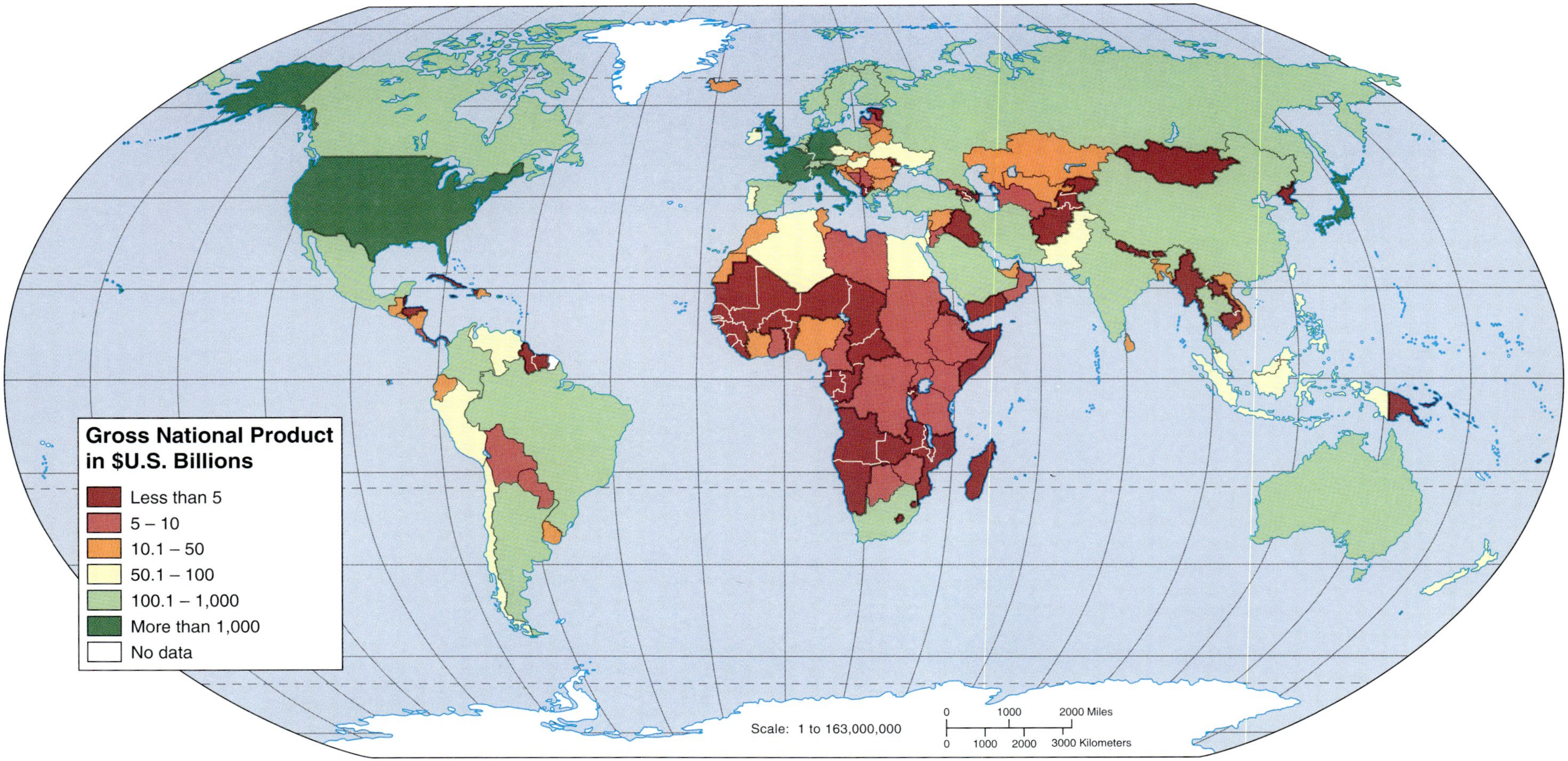

Gross National Product (GNP) is the value of all the goods and services produced by a country, including its net income from abroad, during a year. Although GNP is often misleading and commonly incomplete, it is commonly used by economists, geographers, political scientists, policy makers, development experts, and others not only as a measure of relative well-being but also as an instrument of assessing the effectiveness of economic and political policies. What is wrong with GNP? First of all, it does not take into account a number of real economic factors such as environmental deterioration, the accumulation or degradation of human and social capital, or the value of household work. Yet in spite of these deficiencies, GNP is still a reasonable way to assess the relative wealth of nations: the vast differences in wealth that separate the poorest countries from the richest. One of the more striking features of the map is the evidence it presents that such a small number of countries possess so many of the world's riches (keeping in mind that GNP provides no measure of the distribution of wealth within a country).

Map 32 Gross National Product Per Capita

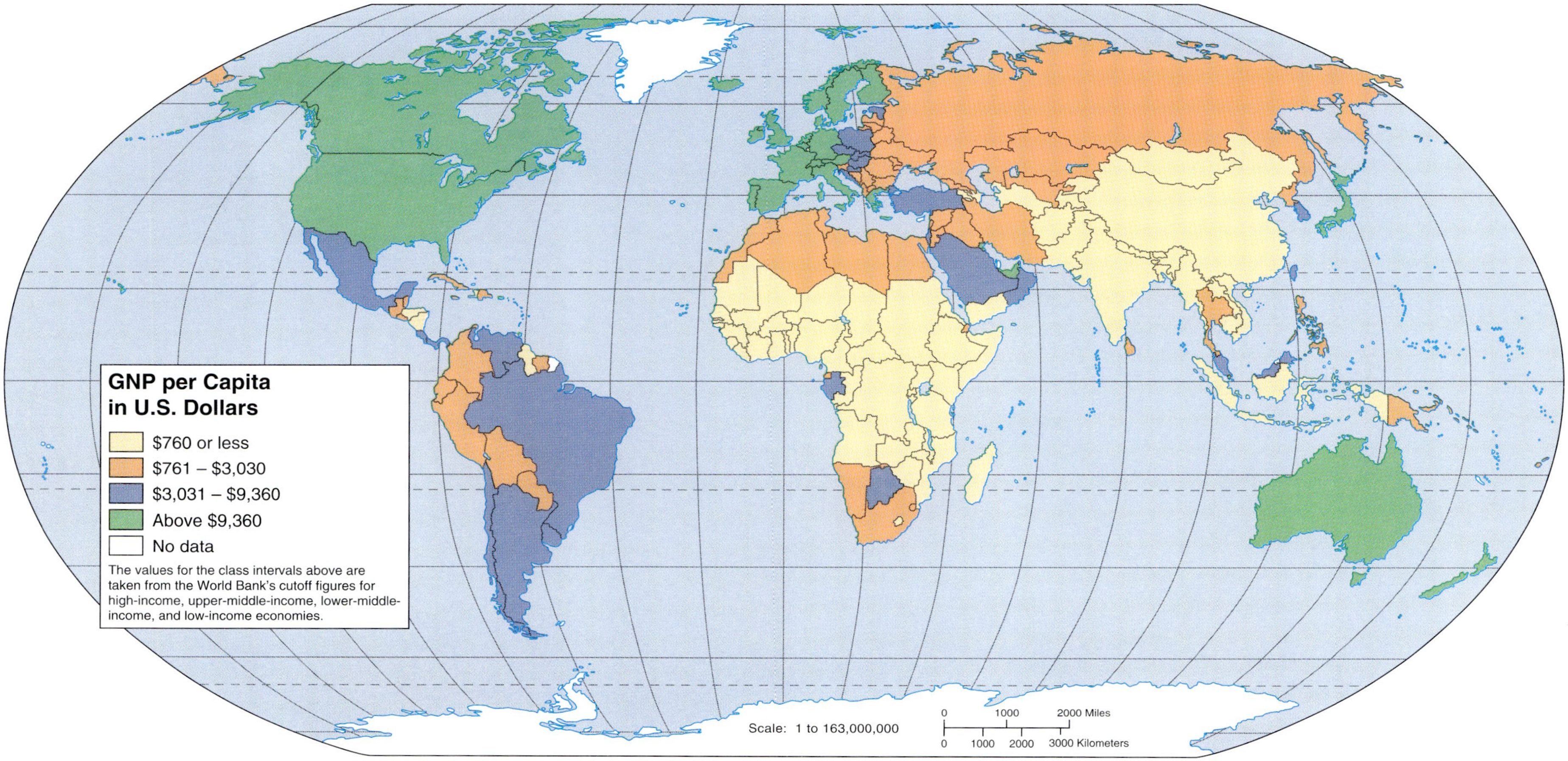

Gross National Product in either absolute or per capita form should be used cautiously as a yardstick of economic strength, because it does not measure the distribution of wealth among a population. There are countries (most notably, the oil-rich countries of the Middle East) where per capita GNP is high but where the bulk of the wealth is concentrated in the hands of a few individuals, leaving the remainder in poverty. Even within countries in which wealth is more evenly distributed (such as those in North America or western Europe), there is a tendency for dollars or pounds sterling or francs or marks to concentrate in the bank accounts of a relatively small percentage of the population. Yet the maldistribution of wealth tends to be greatest in the less developed countries, where the per capita GNP is far lower than in North America and western Europe, and poverty is widespread. In fact, a map of GNP per capita offers a reasonably good picture of comparative economic well-being. It should be noted that a low per capita GNP does not automatically condemn a country to low levels of basic human needs and services. There are a few countries, such as Costa Rica and Sri Lanka, that have relatively low per capita GNP figures but rank comparatively high in other measures of human well-being, such as average life expectancy, access to medical care, and literacy.

Map 33 Economic Growth–GNP Change Per Capita

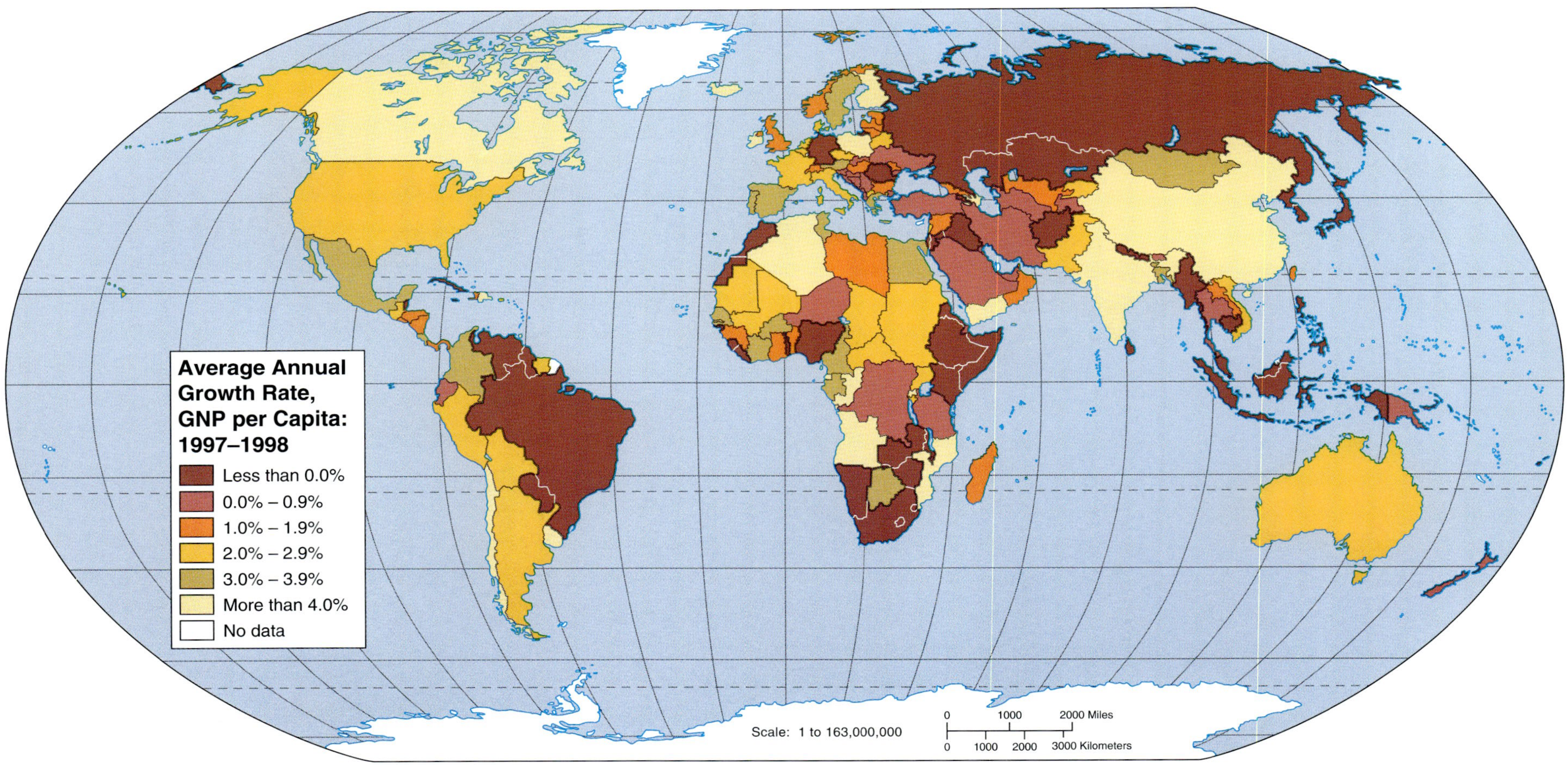

As more and more of the world's countries move into the international trade mainstream, the share of the total global production under the control of developing countries increases. During the decade for which these data are available, developing economies in South, Southeast, and East Asia grew at rates far greater than the growth rates of the middle-income and high-income economies of Europe and North and South America. This should not necessarily be viewed as a case of the poor catching up with the rich; in fact, it shows the huge impact even relatively small production increases will have in countries with small GNPs. Nevertheless, the growth rate in the Gross National Products of some of the world's poorer countries is an encouraging trend.

Map 34 Total Labor Force

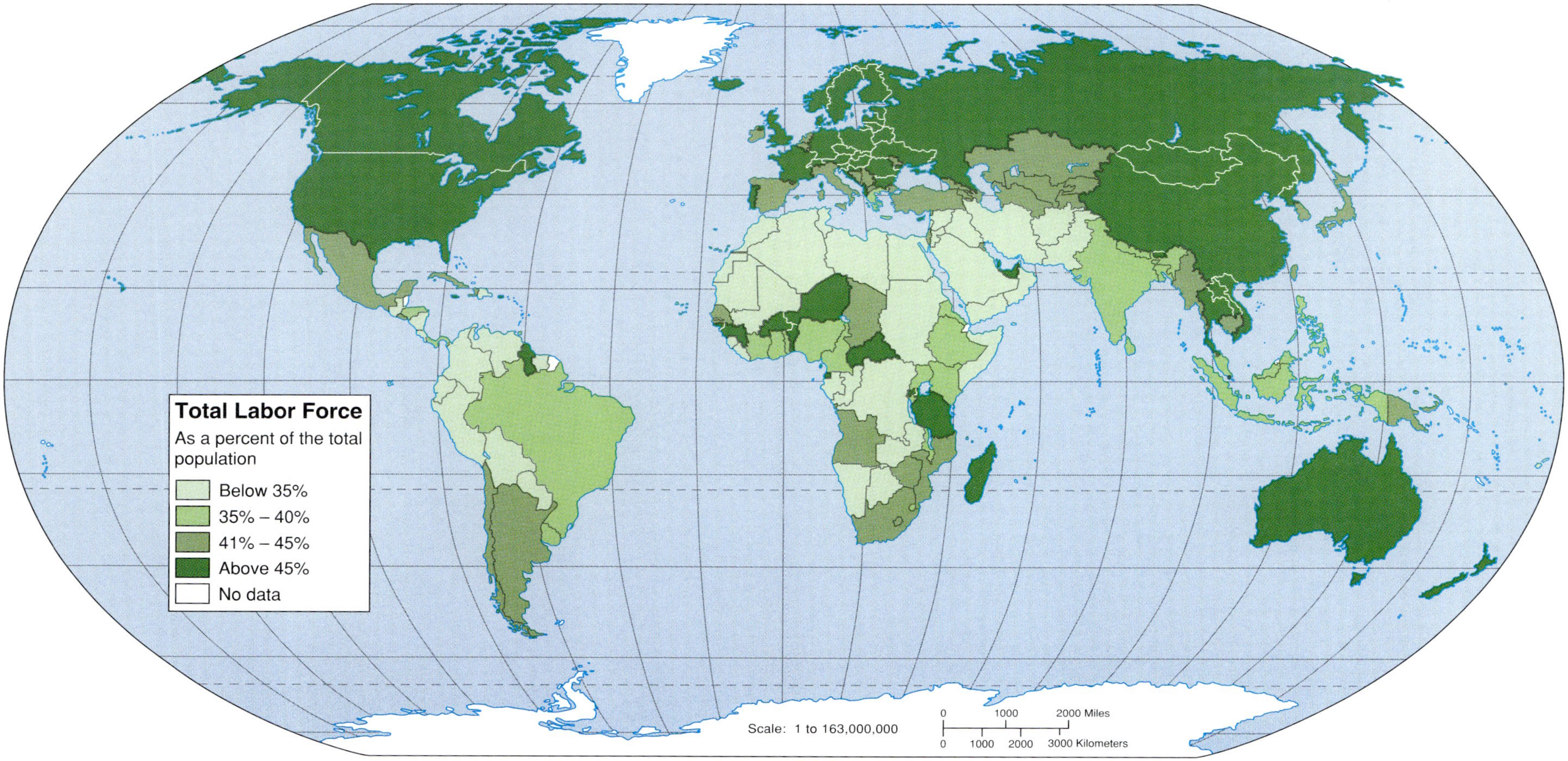

The term *labor force* refers to the economically active portion of a population, that is, all people who work or are without work but are available for and are seeking work to produce economic goods and services. The total labor force thus includes both the employed and the unemployed (as long as they are actively seeking employment). Labor force is considered a better indicator of economic potential than employment/unemployment figures, since unemployment figures will include experienced workers with considerable potential who are temporarily out of work. Unemployment figures will also incorporate persons seeking employment for the first time (many recent college graduates, for example). Generally, countries with higher percentages of total population within the labor force will be countries with higher levels of economic development. This is partly a function of levels of education and training and partly a function of the age distribution of populations. In developing countries, substantial percentages of the total population are too young to be part of the labor force. Also in developing countries a significant percentage of the population is women engaged in household activities or subsistence cultivation. These people seldom appear on lists of either employed or unemployed seeking employment and are the world's forgotten workers.

Map 35 Employment by Sector

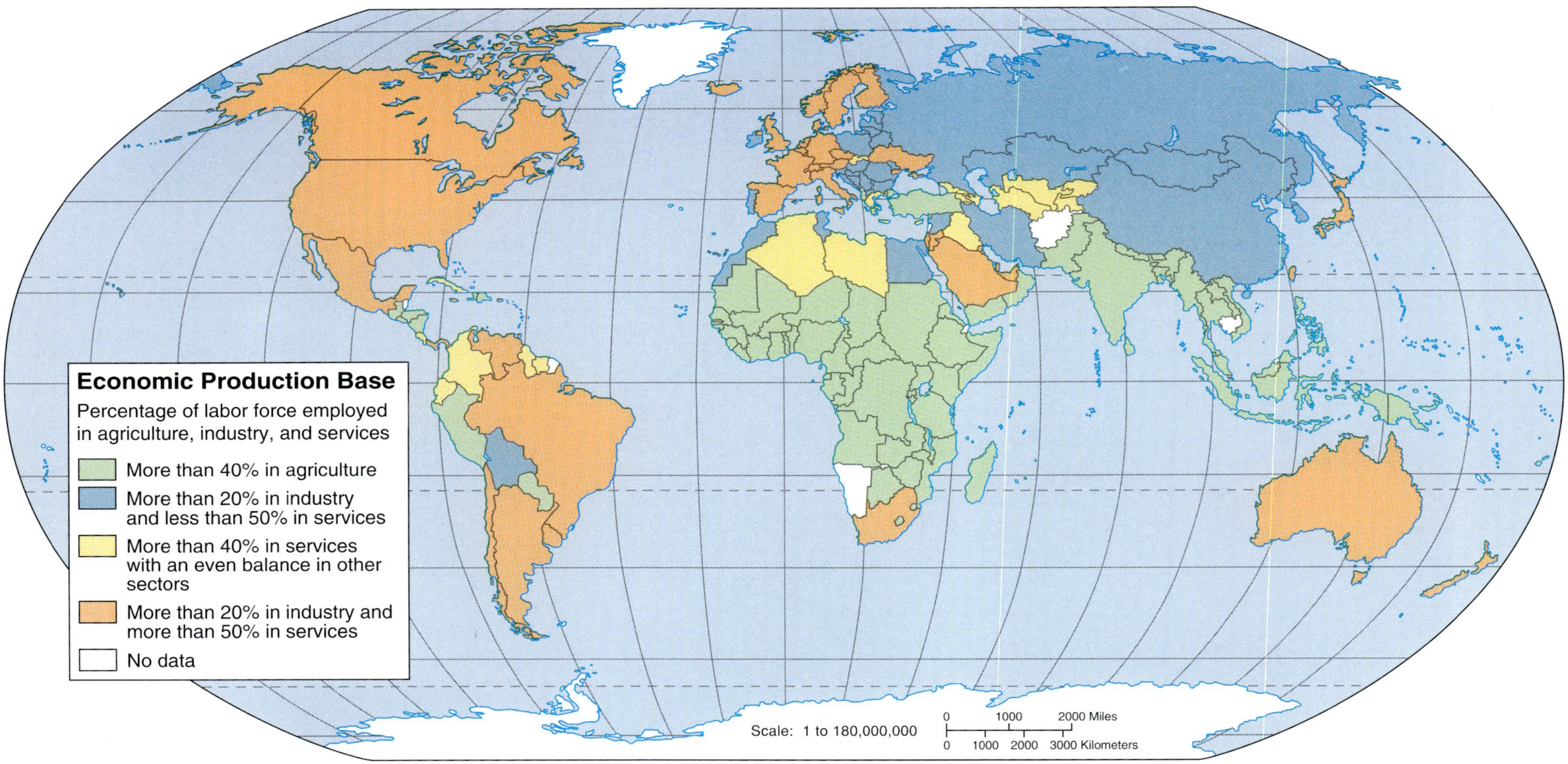

The employment structure of a country's population is one of the best indicators of the country's position on the scale of economic development. At one end of the scale are those countries with more than 40 percent of their labor force employed in agriculture. These are almost invariably the least developed, with high population growth rates, poor human services, significant environmental problems, and so on. In the middle of the scale are two types of countries: those with more than 20 percent of their labor force employed in industry and those with a fairly even balance among agricultural, industrial, and service employment but with at least 40 percent of their labor force employed in service activities. Generally, these countries have undergone the industrial revolution fairly recently and are still developing an industrial base while building up their service activities. This category also includes countries with a disproportionate share of their economies in service activities primarily related to resource extraction. On the other end of the scale from the agricultural economies are countries with more than 20 percent of their labor force employed in industry and more than 50 percent in service activities. These countries are, for the most part, those with a highly automated industrial base and a highly mechanized agricultural system (the "postindustrial," developed countries). They also include, particularly in Middle and South America and Africa, industrializing countries that are also heavily engaged in resource extraction as a service activity.

Map 36 Agricultural Production Per Capita

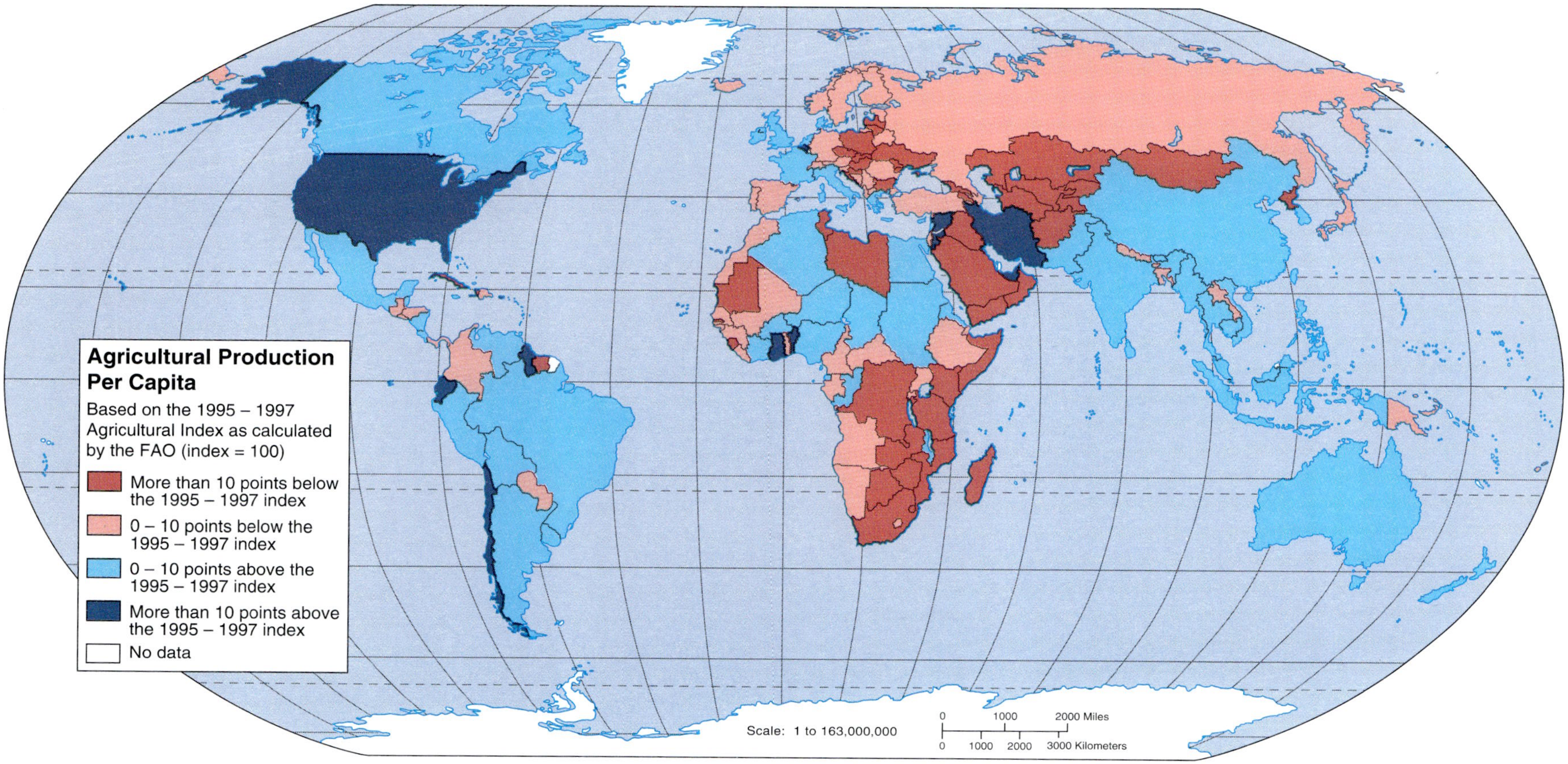

Agricultural production includes the value of all crop and livestock products originating within a country for the base period of 1995–1997. The index value portrays the disposable output (after deductions for livestock feed and seed for planting) of a country's agriculture in comparison with the base period 1989–1991. Thus, the production values show not only the relative ability of countries to produce food but also show whether or not that ability has increased or decreased over a 10-year period. In general, global food production has kept up with or very slightly exceeded population growth. However, there are significant regional variations in the trend of food production keeping up with or surpassing population growth. For example, agricultural production in Africa and in Middle America has fallen, while production in South America, Asia, and Europe has risen. In the case of Africa, the drop in production reflects a population growing more rapidly than agricultural productivity. Where rapid increases in food production per capita exist (as in certain countries in South America, Asia, and Europe), most often the reason is the development of new agricultural technologies that have allowed food production to grow faster than population. In much of Asia, for example, the so-called Green Revolution of new, highly productive strains of wheat and rice made positive index values possible. Also in Asia, the cessation of major warfare allowed some countries (Cambodia, Laos, and Vietnam) to show substantial increases over the 1982–1984 index. In some cases, a drop in production per capita reflects government decisions to limit production in order to maintain higher prices for agricultural products. The United States and Japan fall into this category.

Map 37 Exports of Primary Products

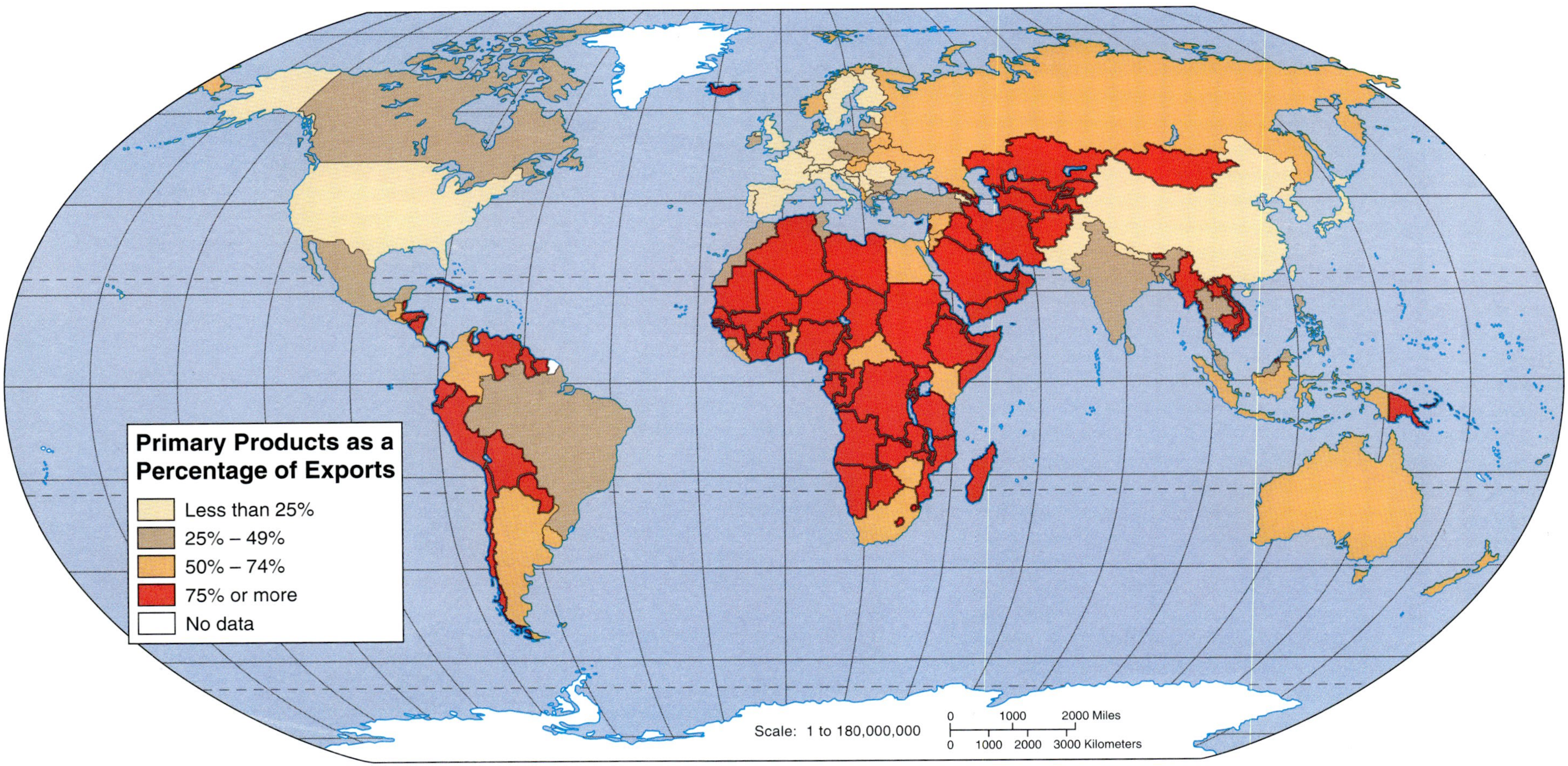

Primary products are those that require additional processing before they enter the consumer market: metallic ores that must be converted into metals and then into metal products such as automobiles or refrigerators; forest products such as timber that must be converted to lumber before they become suitable for construction purposes; and agricultural products that require further processing before being ready for human consumption. It is an axiom in international economics that the more a country relies on primary products for its export commodities, the more vulnerable its economy is to market fluctuations. Those countries with only primary products to export are hampered in their economic growth. A country dependent on only one or two products for export revenues is unprotected from economic shifts, particularly a changing market demand for its products. Imagine what would happen to the thriving economic status of the oil-exporting states of the Persian Gulf, for example, if an alternate source of cheap energy were found. A glance at this map shows that those countries with the lowest levels of economic development tend to be concentrated on primary products and, therefore, have economies that are especially vulnerable to economic instability.

Map 38 Dependence on Trade

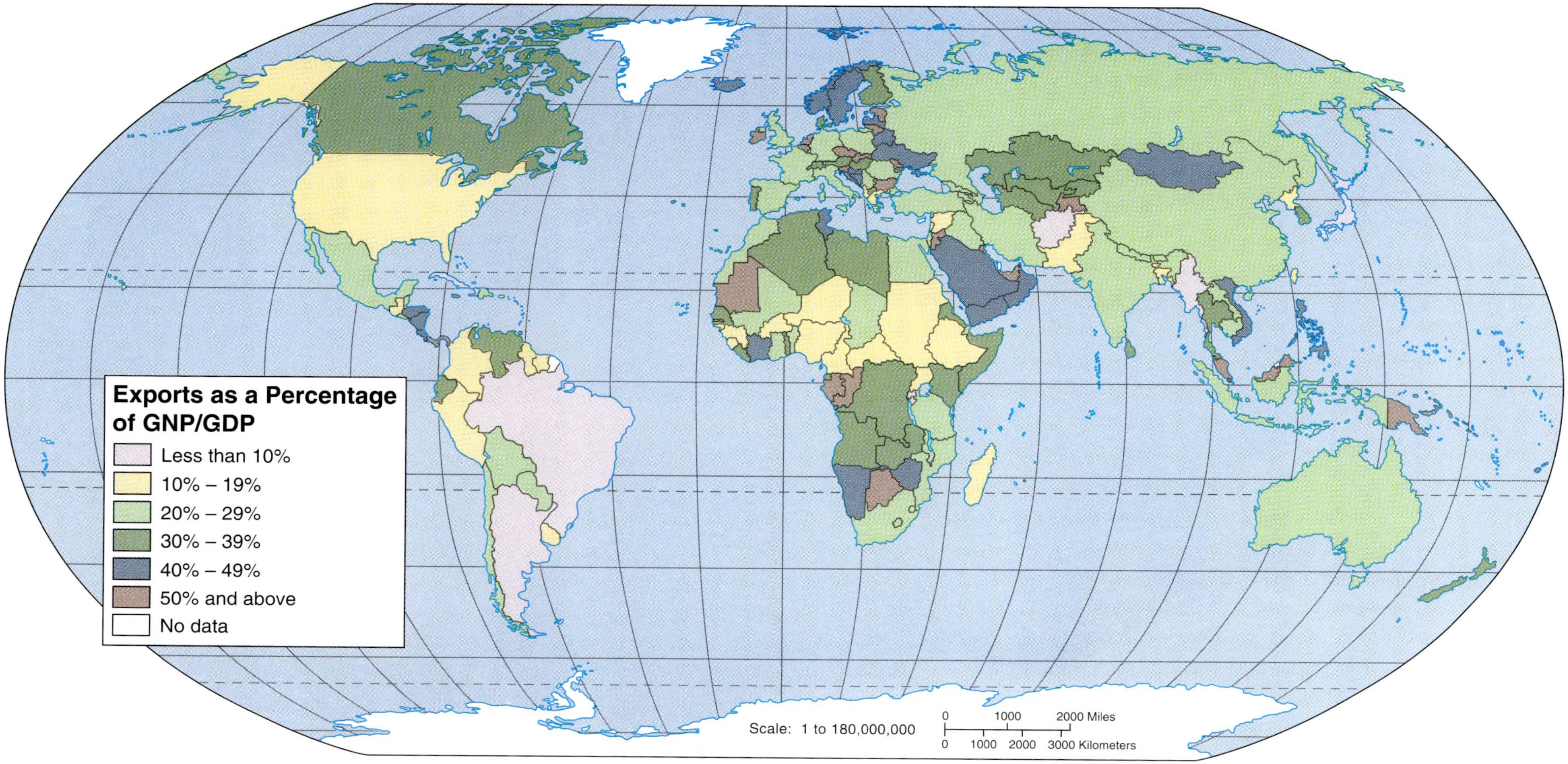

As the global economy becomes more and more a reality, the economic strength of virtually all countries is increasingly dependent upon trade. For many developing nations, with relatively abundant resources and limited industrial capacity, exports provide the primary base upon which their economies rest. Even countries like the United States, Japan, and Germany, with huge and diverse economies, depend on exports to generate a significant percentage of their employment and wealth. Without imports, many products that consumers want would be unavailable or more expensive; without exports, many jobs would be eliminated. But exports alone do not provide the full story on trade dependence; part of what a map such as this masks is "what kind of exports?" For the more developed parts of the world, exports tend to be industrial products, perhaps along with some few raw materials (the United States and Russia are exceptions here in that they export a significant quantity of raw materials). But for the lesser developed countries, the exports are largely in the raw materials category. While this, as noted, provides jobs, it also means that countries may not have the necessary quantity of raw materials with which to develop their own industries and further their economic development.

Map 39 International Flows of Capital

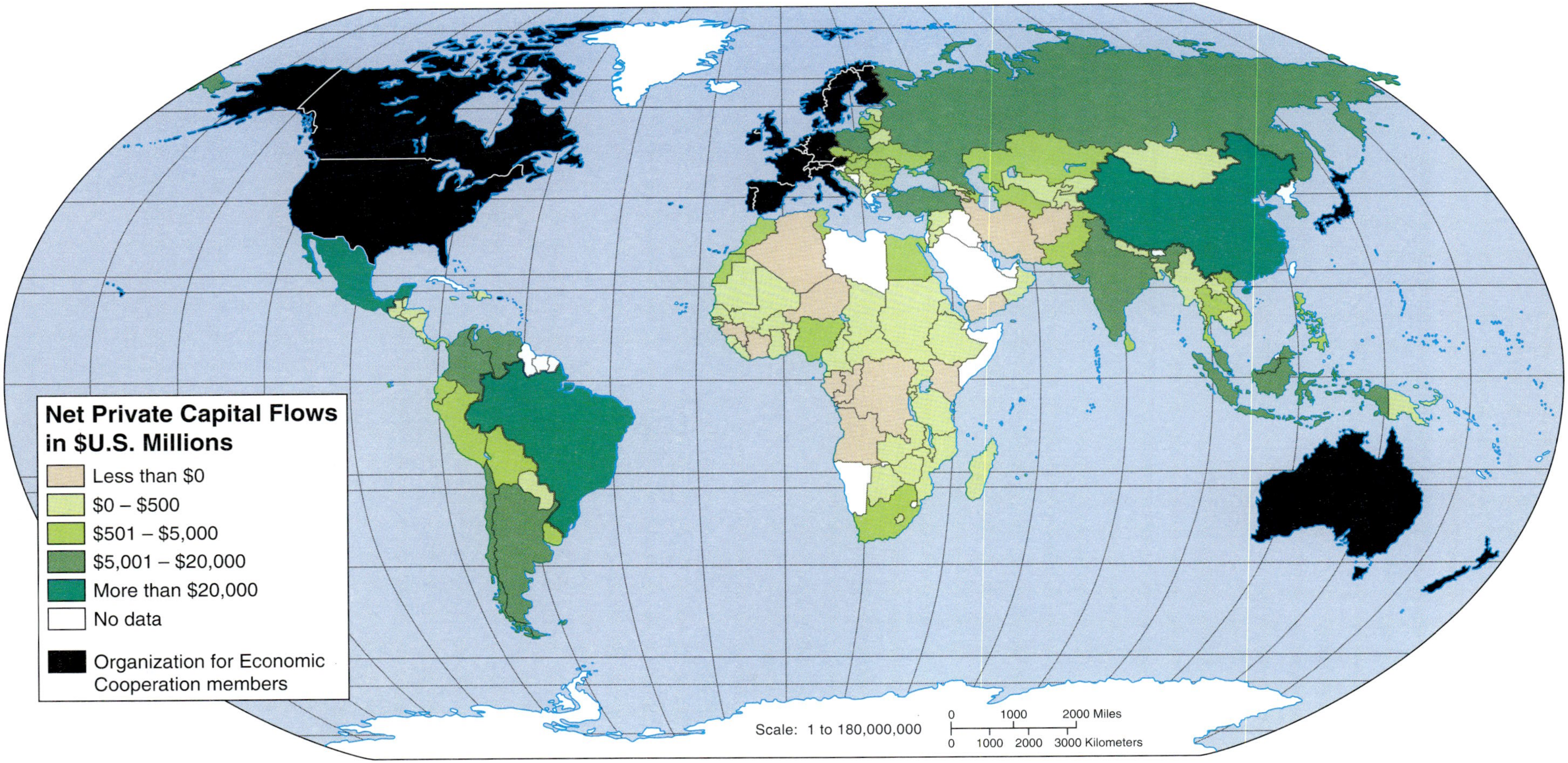

International capital flows include private debt and nondebt flows from one country to another, shown on the map as flows into a country. Nearly all of the capital comes from those countries that are members of the Organization for Economic Cooperation and Development (OECD), shown in black on the map. Capital flows include commercial bank lending, bonds, other private credits, foreign direct investment, and portfolio investment. Most of these flows are indicators of the increasing influence developed countries exert over the developing economies. Foreign direct investment or FDI, for example, is a measure of the net inflow of investment monies used to acquire long-term management interest in businesses located somewhere other than in the economy of the investor. Usually this means the acquisition of at least 10% of the stock of a company by a foreign investor and is, then, a measure of what might be termed "economic colonialism": control of a region's economy by foreign investors that could, in the world of the future, be as significant as colonial political control was in the past. International capital flows have increased greatly in the last decade as the result of the increasing liberalization of developing countries, the strong economic growth exhibited by many developing countries, and the falling costs and increased efficiency of communication and transportation services.

Map 40 Central Government Expenditures Per Capita

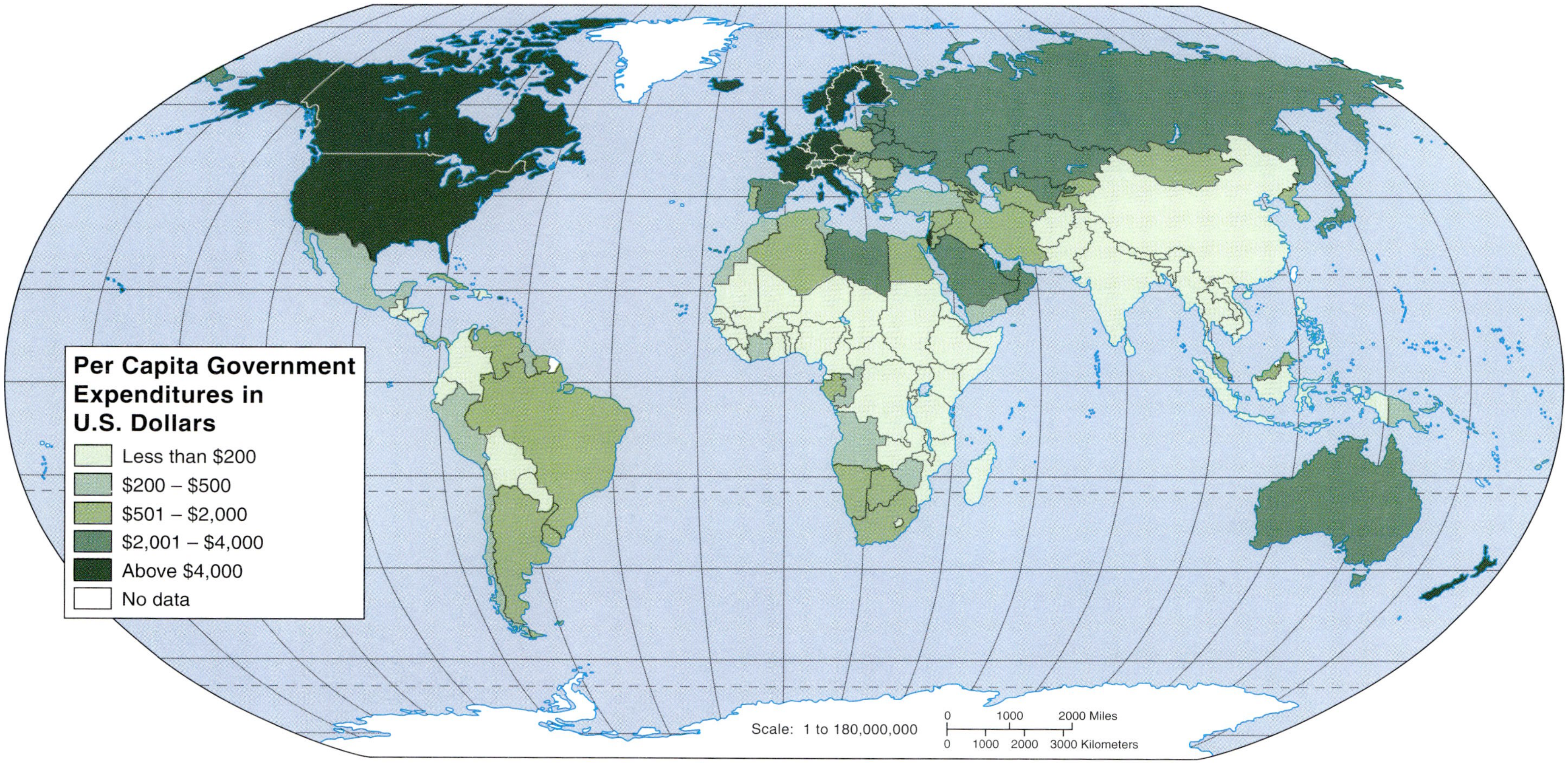

The amount of money that the central government of a country spends upon a variety of essential governmental functions is a measure of relative economic development, particularly when it is viewed on a per-person basis. These functions include such governmental responsibilities as agriculture, communications, culture, defense, education, fishing and hunting, health, housing, recreation, religion, social security, transportation, and welfare. Generally, the higher the level of economic development, the greater the per capita expenditures on these services. However, the data do mask some internal variations. For example, countries that spend 20 percent or more of their central government expenditures on defense will often show up in the more developed category when, in fact, all that the figures really show is that a disproportionate amount of the money available to the government is devoted to purchasing armaments and maintaining a large standing military force. Thus, the fact that Libya spends $2,937 per capita—more than 10 times the average for Africa—does not suggest that the average Libyan is 10 times better off than the average Tanzanian. Nevertheless, this map—particularly when compared with Map 43, Energy Consumption Per Capita—does provide a reasonable approximation of economic development levels.

Map 41 Purchasing Power Parity

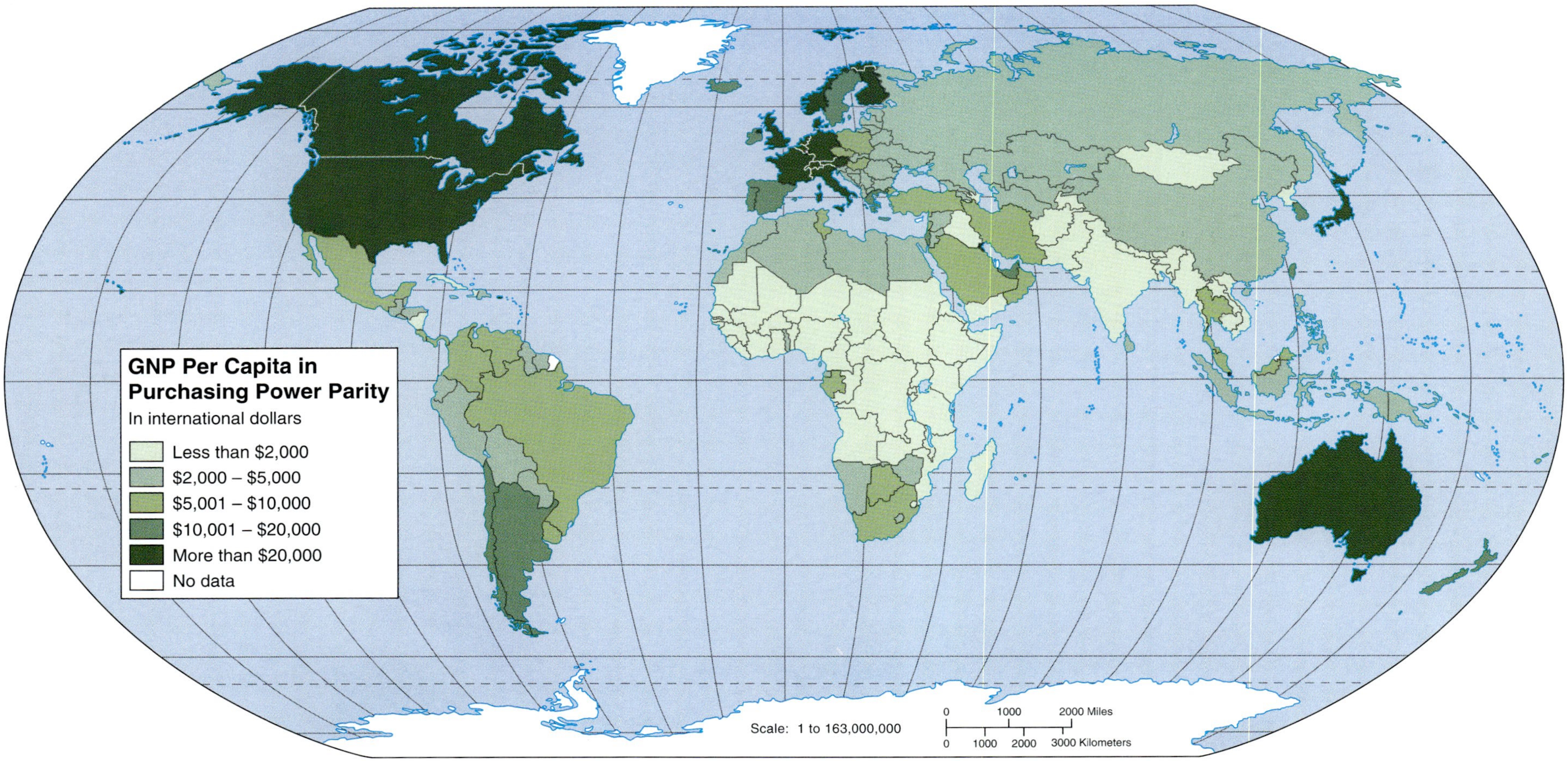

Among all the economic measures that separate the "haves" from the "have-nots," per capita Purchasing Power Parity (PPP) may be the most meaningful. Per capita GNP and GDP (Gross Domestic Product) figures, and even per capita income, have the limitation of seldom reflecting the true purchasing power of a country's currency at home. In order to get around this limitation, international economists seeking to compare national currencies developed the PPP measure, which shows the level of goods and services that holders of a country's money can acquire locally. By converting all currencies to the "international dollar," the World Bank and other organizations using PPP can now show more truly comparative values, since the new currency value shows the number of units of a country's currency required to buy the same quantity of goods and services in the local market as one U.S. dollar would buy in an average country. The use of PPP currency values can alter the perceptions about a country's true comparative position in the world economy. PPP provides a valid measurement of the ability of a country's population to provide for itself the things that people in the developed world take for granted: adequate food, shelter, clothing, education, and access to medical care. A glance at the map shows a clear-cut demarcation between temperate and tropical zones, with most of the countries with a PPP above $5,000 in the midlatitude zones and most of those with lower PPPs in the tropical and equatorial regions.

Map 42 Energy Production

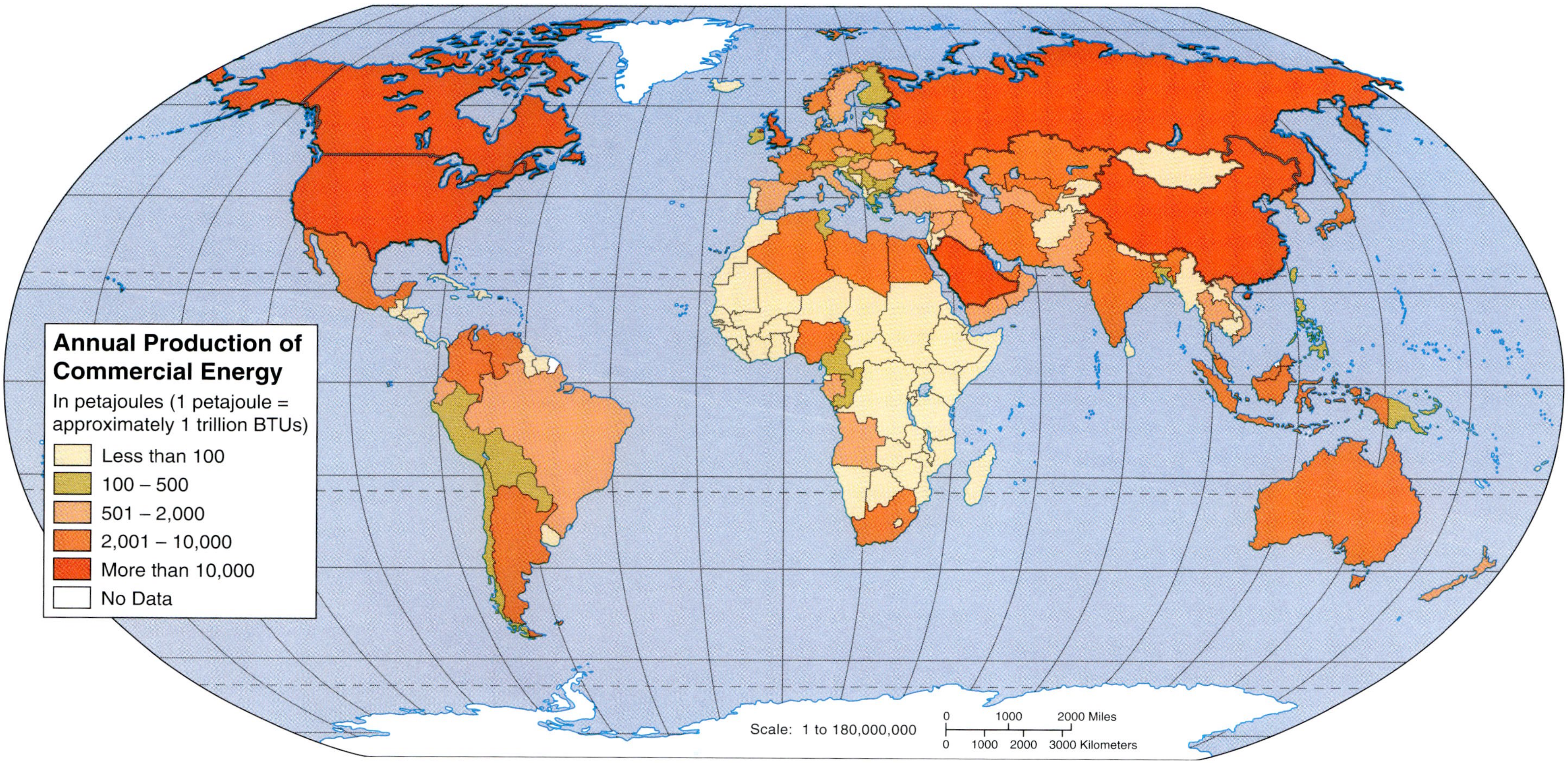

The production of commercial energy in all its forms—solid fuels (primarily coal), liquid fuels (primarily petroleum), natural gas, geothermal, wind, solar, hydroelectric, and nuclear—is a good measure of a country's ability to produce sufficient quantities of energy to meet domestic demands or to provide a healthy export commodity—or, in some instances, both. Commercial energy production is also a measure of the level of economic development, although a fairly subjective one. With exceptions, wealthier countries produce more energy from all sources than do poorer countries. Countries such as Japan and many European states rank among the world's wealthiest, but are energy-poor and produce relatively little of their own energy. They have the ability, however, to pay for it. On the other hand, countries such as those of the Persian Gulf or the oil-producing states of Middle and South America may rank relatively low on the scale of economic development but rank high as producers of energy. The map does not show the enormous amounts of energy from noncommercial sources (traditional fuels like firewood and animal dung) used by the world's poor, particularly in Middle and South America, Africa, South Asia, and East Asia. In these regions, firewood and animal dung may account for more actual energy production than coal or oil. Indeed, for many in the developing world, the real energy crisis is a shortage of wood for cooking and heating.

Map 43 Energy Consumption Per Capita

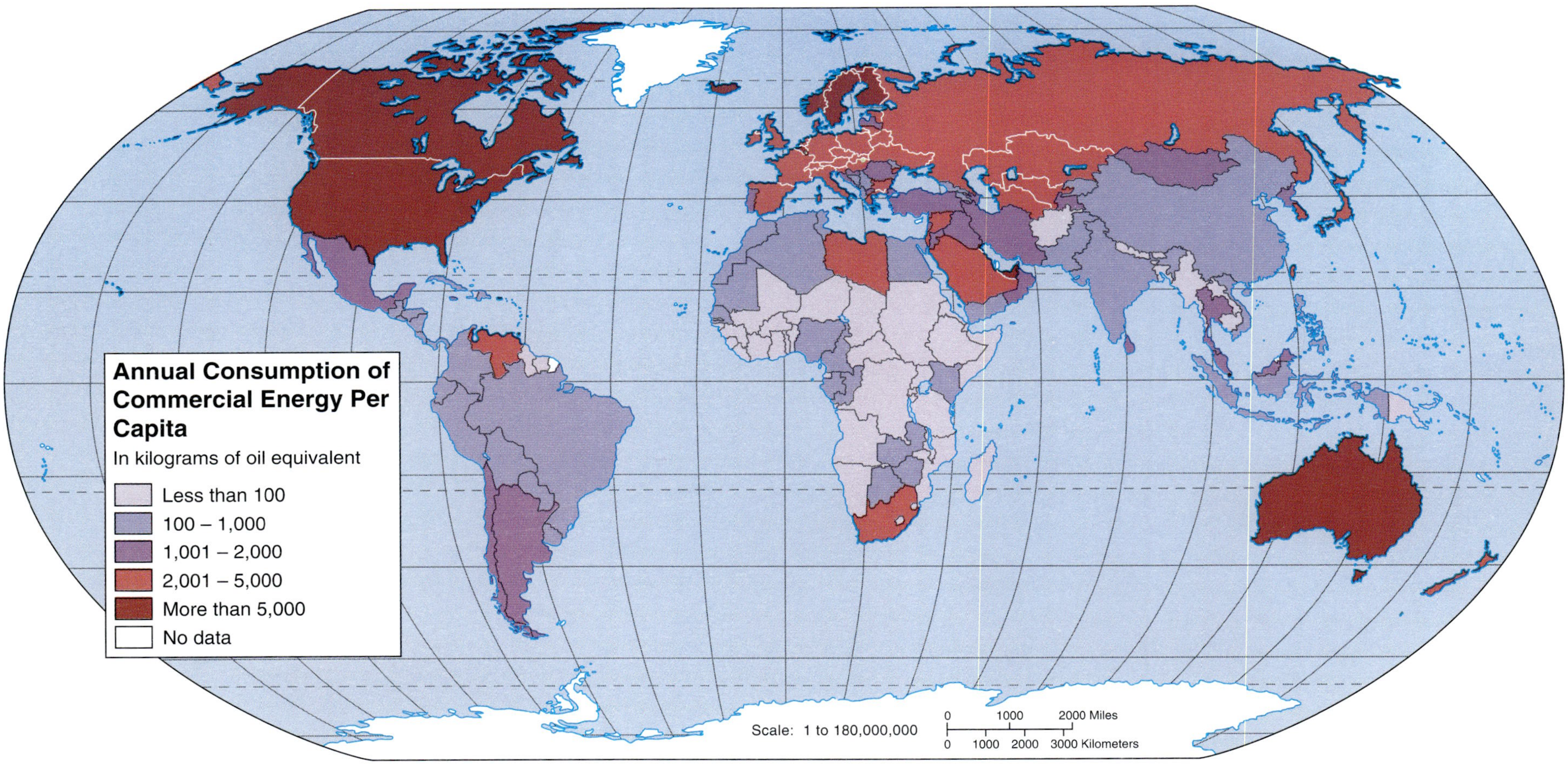

Of all the quantitative measures of economic well-being, energy consumption per capita may be the most expressive. All of the countries defined by the World Bank as having high incomes consume at least 100 gigajoules of commercial energy (the equivalent of about 3.5 metric tons of coal) per person per year, with some, such as the United States and Canada, having consumption rates in the 300 gigajoule range (the equivalent of more than 10 metric tons of coal per person per year). With the exception of the oil-rich Persian Gulf states, where consumption figures include the costly "burning off" of excess energy in the form of natural gas flares at wellheads, most of the highest-consuming countries are in the Northern Hemisphere, concentrated in North America and Western Europe. At the other end of the scale are low-income countries, whose consumption rates are often less than 1 percent of those of the United States and other high consumers. These figures do not, of course, include the consumption of noncommercial energy—the traditional fuels of firewood, animal dung, and other organic matter—widely used in the less developed parts of the world.

Part V

Global Patterns of Environmental Disturbance

Map 44 Global Air Pollution: Sources and Wind Currents

Almost all processes of physical geography begin and end with the flows of energy and matter among land, sea, and air. Because of the primacy of the atmosphere in this exchange system, air pollution is potentially one of the most dangerous human modifications in environmental systems. Pollutants such as various oxides of nitrogen or sulfur cause the development of acid precipitation, which damages soil, vegetation, and wildlife and fish. Air pollution in the form of smog is often dangerous for human health. And most atmospheric scientists believe that the efficiency of the atmosphere in retaining heat—the so-called "greenhouse effect"—is being enhanced by increased carbon dioxide, methane, and other gases produced by agricultural and industrial activities. The result, they fear, will be a period of global warming that will dramatically alter climates in all parts of the world.

Map 45 The Acid Deposition Problem: Air, Water, Soil

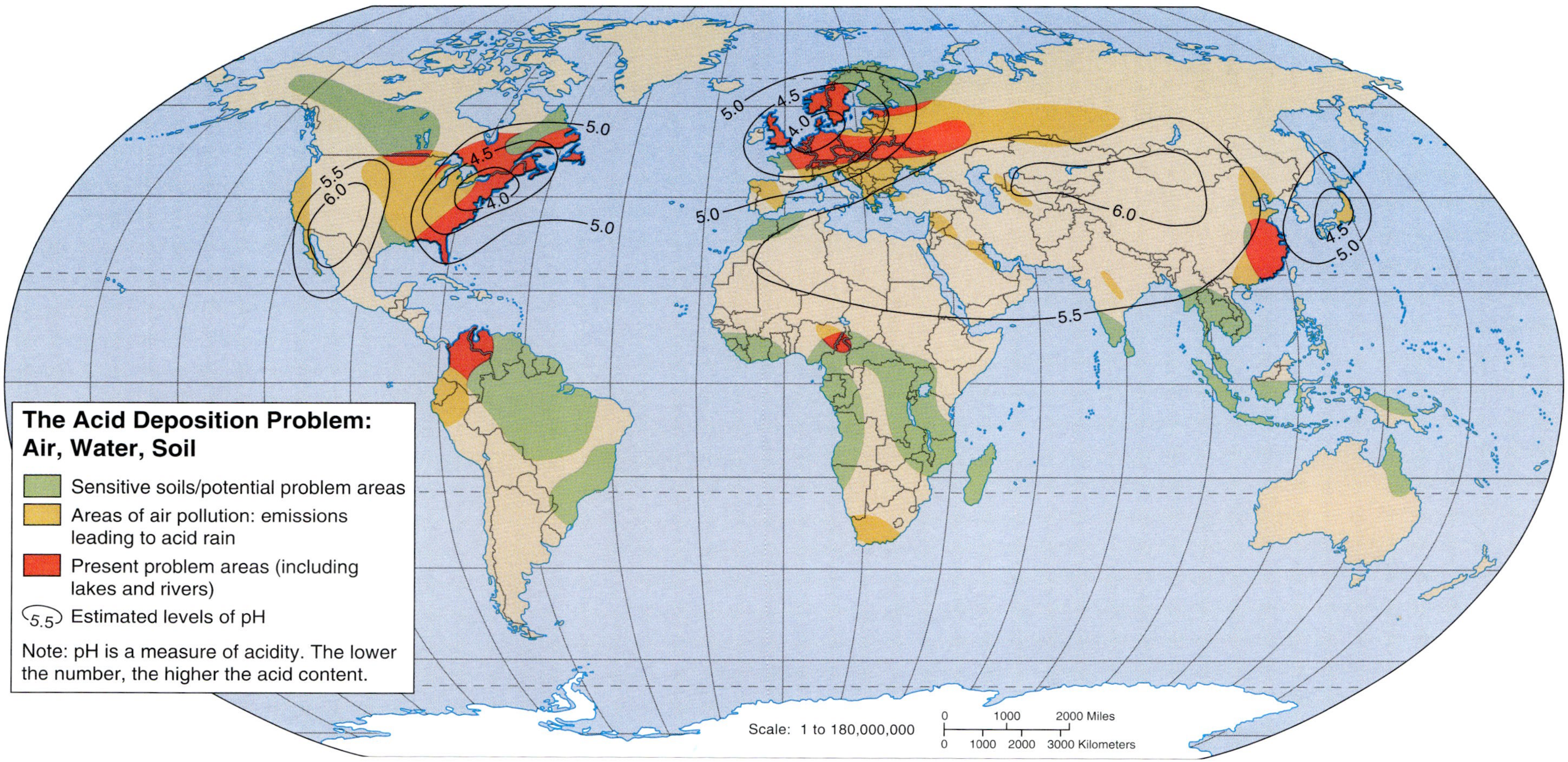

The term "acid precipitation" refers to increasing levels of acidity in snowfall and rainfall caused by atmospheric pollution. Oxides of nitrogen and sulfur resulting from incomplete combustion of fossil fuels (coal, oil, and natural gas) combine with water vapor in the atmosphere to produce weak acids that then "precipitate" or fall along with water or ice crystals. Some atmospheric acids formed by this process are known as "dry-acid" precipitates and they too will fall to earth, although not necessarily along with rain or snow. In some areas of the world, the increased acidity of streams and lakes stemming from high levels of acid precipitation or dry acid fallout has damaged or destroyed aquatic life. Acid precipitation and dry acid fallout also harms soil systems and vegetation, producing a characteristic burned appearance in forests that lends the same quality to landscapes that forest fires would. The region most dramatically impacted by acid precipitation is Central Europe where decades of destructive environmental practices, including the burning of high sulfur coal for commercial, industrial, and residential purposes, has produced the destruction of hundreds of thousands of acres of woodlands—a phenomenon described by the German foresters who began their study of the area following the lifting of the Iron Curtain as "Waldsterben": Forest Death.

Map 46 Major Polluters and Common Pollutants

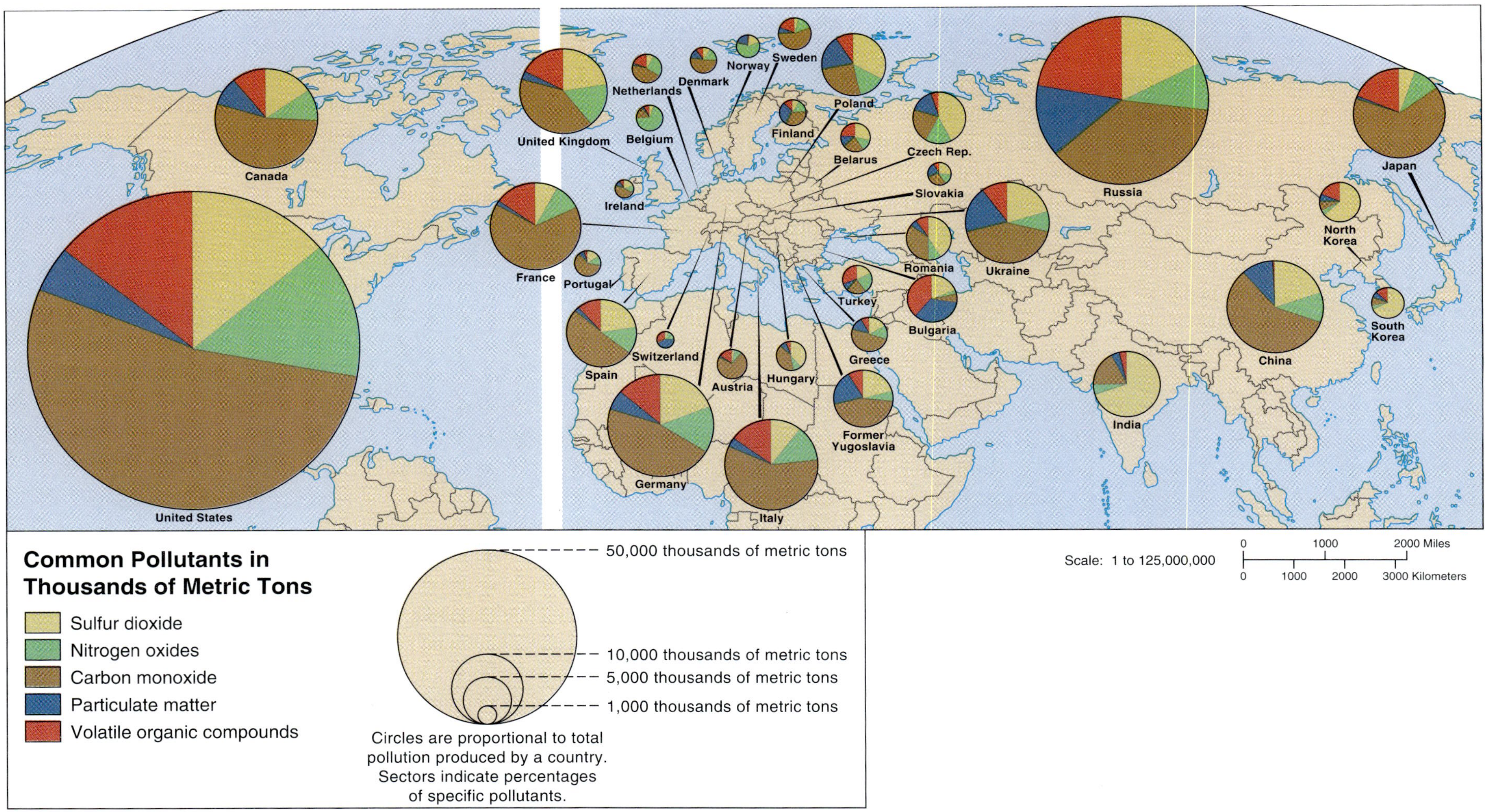

More than 90 percent of the world's total of anthropogenic (human-generated) air pollutants come from the heavily populated industrial regions of North America, Europe, South Asia (primarily in India), and East Asia (mainly in China, Japan, and the two Koreas). This map shows the origins of the five most common pollutants: sulfur dioxide, nitrogen oxide, carbon monoxide, particulate matter, and volatile organic compounds. These substances are produced both by industry and by the combustion of fossil fuels that generate electricity and power trains, planes, automobiles, buses, and trucks. In addition to combining with other components of the atmosphere and with one another to produce smog, they are the chief ingredients in acid accumulations in the atmosphere, which ultimately result in acid deposition, either as acid precipitation or dry acid fallout. Like other forms of pollutants, these air pollutants do not recognize political boundaries, and regions downwind of major polluters receive large quantities of pollutants from areas over which they often have no control.

Map 47 Global Carbon Dioxide Emissions

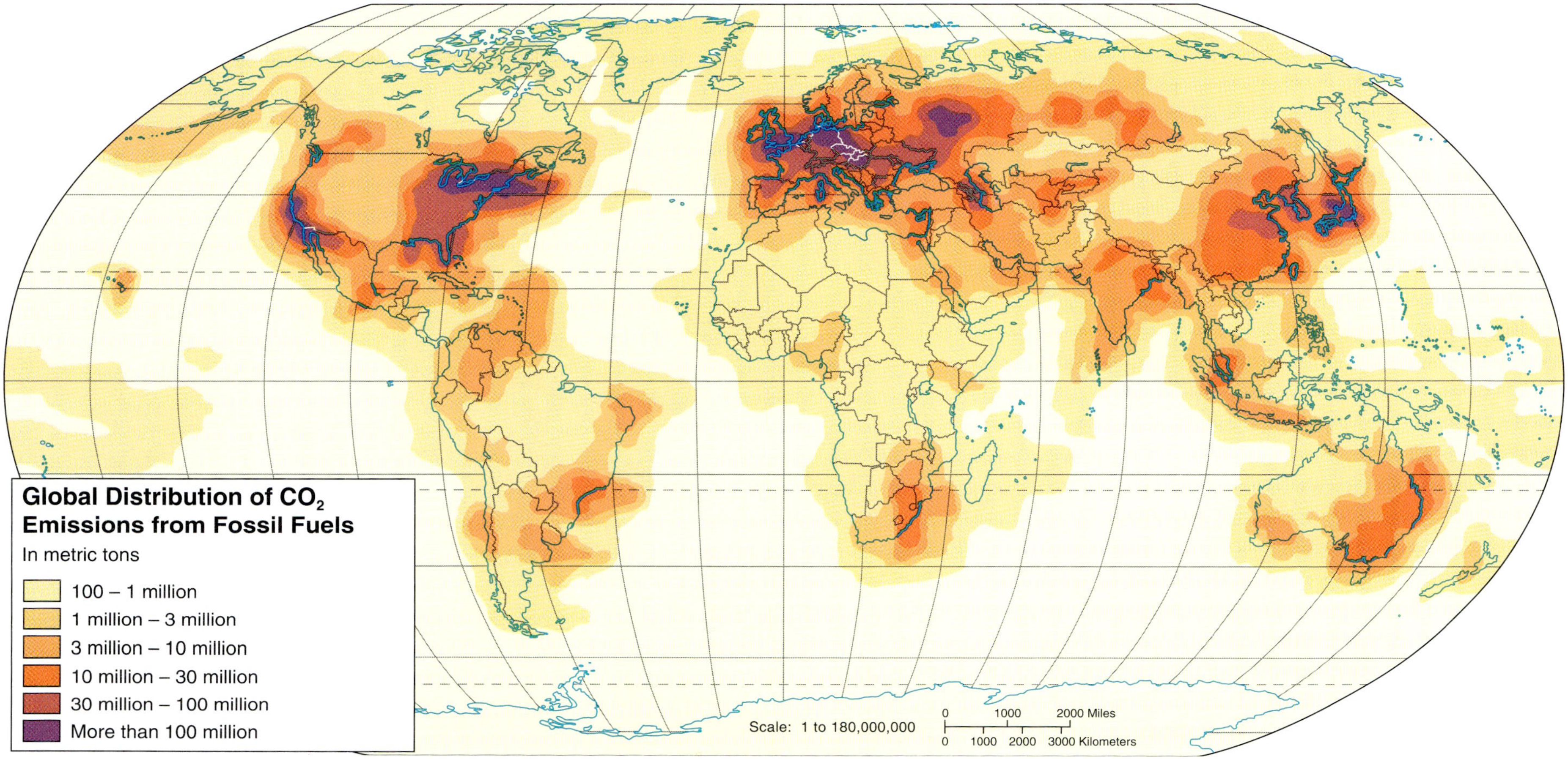

One of the most important components of the atmosphere is the gas carbon dioxide, the byproduct of animal respiration, of decomposition, and of combustion. During the past 200 years, atmospheric CO_2 has risen dramatically, largely as the result of the tremendous increase in fossil fuel combustion brought on by the industrialization of the world's economy and the burning and clearing of forests by the expansion of farming. While carbon dioxide by itself is relatively harmless, it is an important "greenhouse gas." The gases in the atmosphere act like the panes of glass in a greenhouse roof, allowing light in but preventing heat from escaping. The greenhouse capacity of the atmosphere is crucial for organic life and is a purely natural component of the global energy cycle. But too much carbon dioxide and other greenhouse gases such as methane could cause the earth's atmosphere to warm up too much, producing the global warming that atmospheric scientists are concerned about. Researchers estimate that if greenhouse gases such as carbon dioxide continue to increase at their present rates, the earth's mean temperature could rise between 1.5 and 4.5 degrees Celsius by the middle of the next century. Such a rise in global temperatures would produce massive alterations in the world's climate patterns.

Map 48 Potential Global Temperature Change

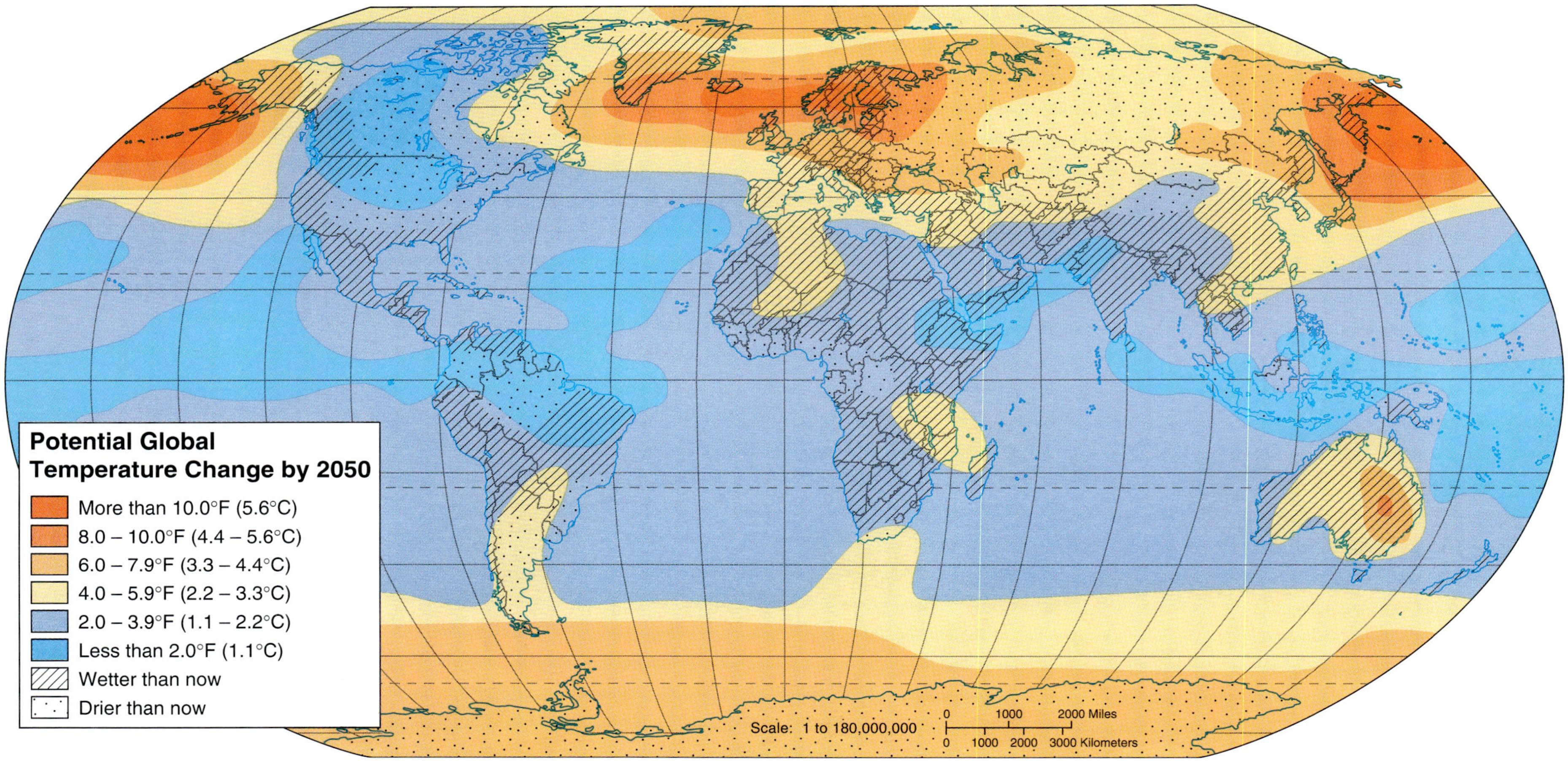

According to atmospheric scientists, one of the major problems of the twenty-first century will be "global warming," produced as the atmosphere's natural ability to trap and retain heat is enhanced by increased percentages of carbon dioxide, methane, chlorinated fluorocarbons or "CFCs," and other "greenhouse gases" in the earth's atmosphere. Computer models based on atmospheric percentages of carbon dioxide resulting from present use of fossil fuels show that warming is not just a possibility but a probability. Increased temperatures would cause precipitation patterns to alter significantly as well and would produce a number of other harmful effects, including a rise in the level of the world's oceans that could flood most coastal cities. International conferences on the topic of the enhanced greenhouse effect have resulted in several international agreements to reduce the emission of carbon dioxide or to maintain it at present levels. Unfortunately, the solution is not that simple since reduction of carbon dioxide emissions is, in the short run, expensive—particularly as long as the world's energy systems continue to be based on fossil fuels. Chief among the countries that could be hit by serious international mandates to reduce emissions are those highest on the development scale who use the highest levels of fossil fuels and, therefore, produce the highest emissions, and those on the lowest end of the development scale whose efforts to industrialize could be severely impeded by the more expensive energy systems that would replace fossil fuels.

Map 49a World Water Resources: Availability of Renewable Water Per Capita

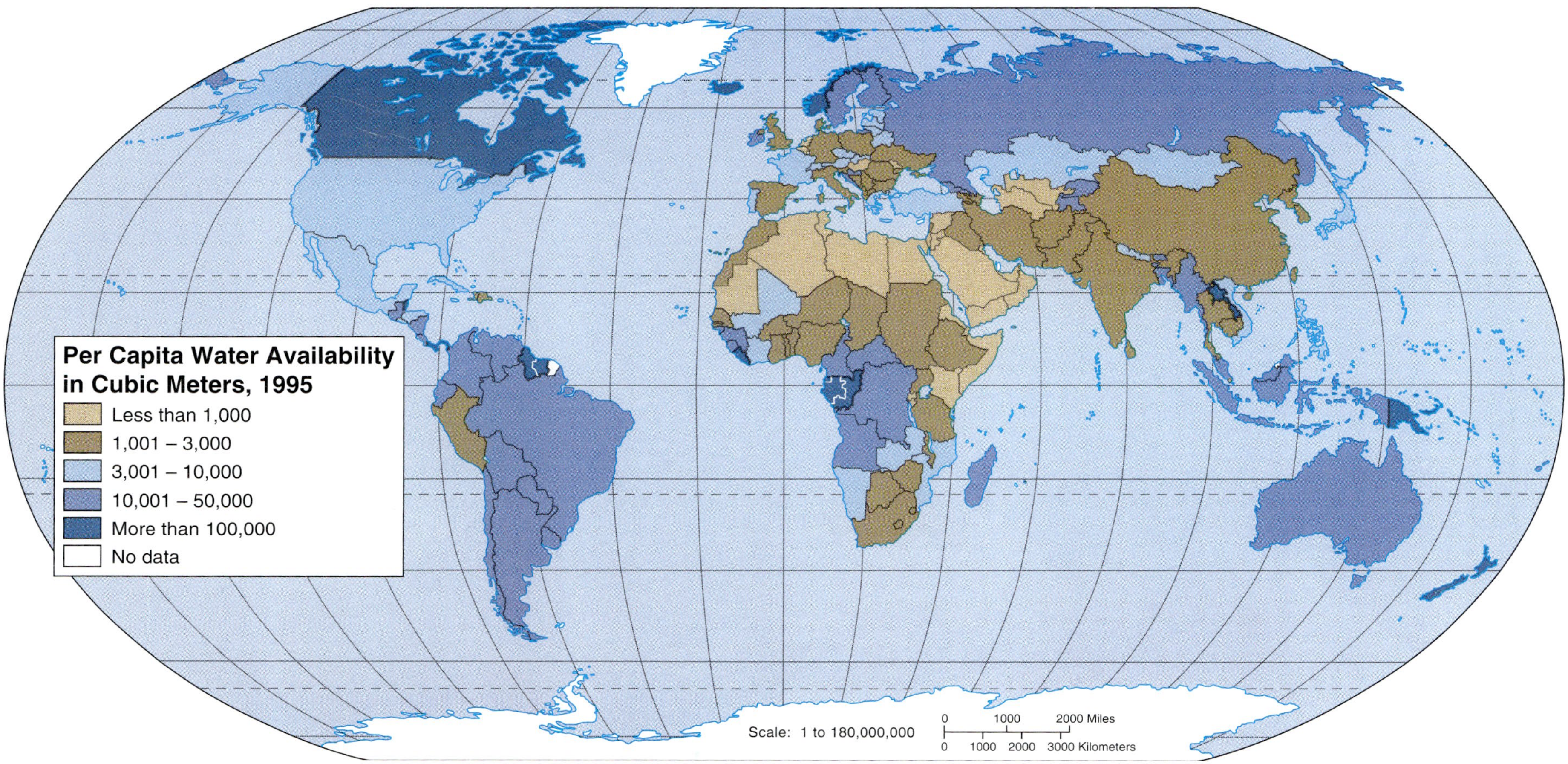

Renewable water resources are usually defined as the total water available from streams and rivers (including flows from other countries), ponds and lakes, and groundwater storage or aquifers. Not included in the total of renewable water would be water that comes from such nonrenewable sources as desalinization plants or melted icebergs. While the concept of renewable or flow resources is a traditional one in resource management, in fact, few resources, including water, are truly renewable when their use is excessive. The water resources shown here are indications of that principle. A country like the United States possesses truly enormous quantities of water. But the United States also used enormous quantities of water. The result is availability of renewable water that is—largely because of excess use—much less than in many other parts of the world where the total supply of water is significantly less.

Map 49b World Water Resources: Annual Withdrawal Per Capita

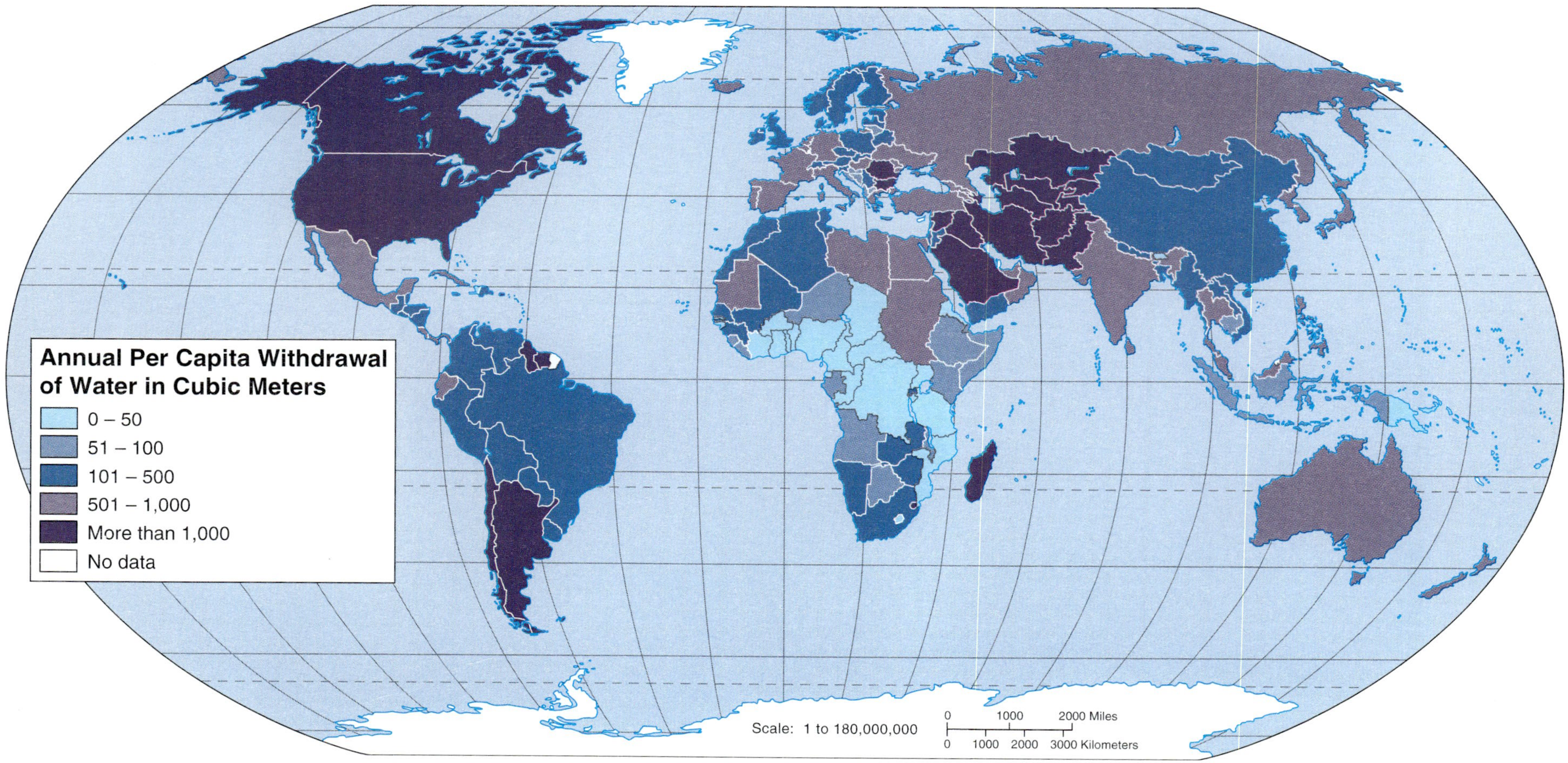

Water resources must be viewed like a bank account in which deposits and withdrawals are made. As long as the deposits are greater than the withdrawals, a positive balance remains. But when the withdrawals begin to exceed the deposits, sooner or later (depending on the relative sizes of the deposits and withdrawals) the account becomes overdrawn. For many of the world's countries, annual availability of water is insufficient to cover the demand. In these countries, reserves stored in groundwater are being tapped, resulting in depletion of the water supply (think of this as shifting money from a savings account to a checking account). The water supply can maintain its status as a renewable resource only if deposits continue to be greater than withdrawals, and that seldom happens. In general, countries with high levels of economic development and countries that rely on irrigation agriculture are the most spendthrift when it comes to their water supplies.

Map 50 Pollution of the Oceans

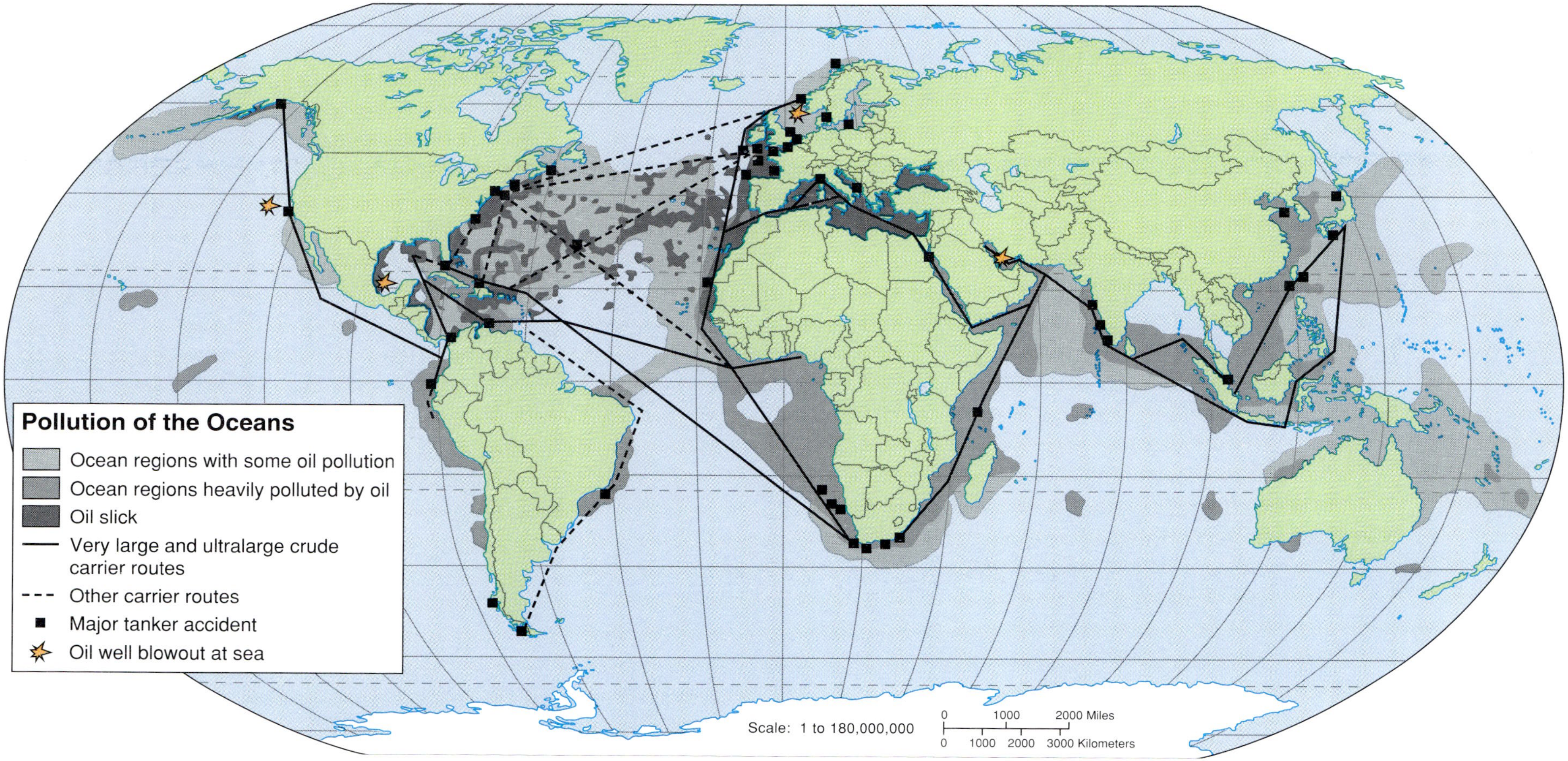

The pollution of the world's oceans has long been a matter of concern to physical geographers, oceanographers, and other environmental scientists. The great circulation systems of the ocean are one of the controlling factors of the earth's natural environment, and modifications to those systems have unknown consequences. This map is based on what we can measure: (1) areas of oceans where oil pollution has been proven to have inflicted significant damage to ocean ecosystems and life-forms (including phytoplankton, the oceans' primary food producers, equivalent to land-based vegetation) and (2) areas of oceans where unusually high concentrations of hydrocarbons from oil spills may have inflicted some damage to the oceans' biota. A glance at the map shows that there are few areas of the world's oceans where some form of pollution is not a part of the environmental system. What the map does not show in detail, because of the scale, are the dramatic consequences of large individual pollution events: the wreck of the *Exxon Valdez* and the polluting of Prince William Sound or the environmental devastation produced by the Gulf War in the Persian Gulf.

Map 51 Food Supply from the World's Marine and Freshwater Systems

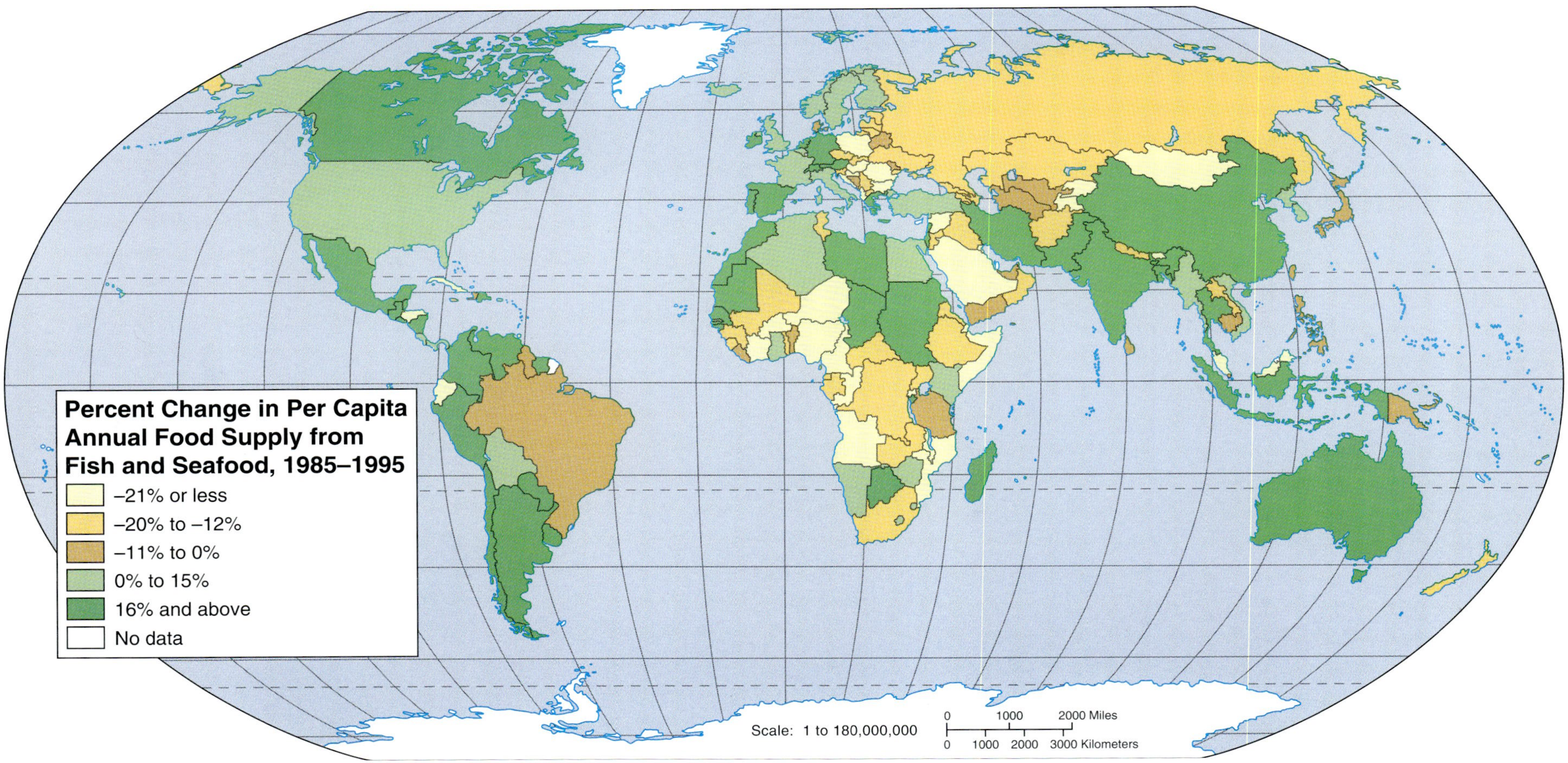

Not that many years ago, food supply experts were confidently predicting that the "starving millions" of the world of the future could be fed from the unending bounty of the world's oceans. While the annual catch from the sea helped to keep hunger at bay for a time, by the late 1980s it had become apparent that without serious human intervention in the form of aquaculture, the supply of fish would not be sufficient to offset the population/food imbalance that was beginning to affect so many of the world's regions. The development of factory-fishing with advanced equipment to locate fish and process them before they went to market increased the supply of food from the ocean, but in that increase was sown the seeds of future problems. The factory-fishing system, efficient in terms of economics, was costly in terms of fish populations. In some well-fished areas, the stock of fish that was viewed as near infinite just a few decades ago has dwindled nearly to the point of disappearance. This map shows both increases and decreases in the amount of individual countries' food supplies from the ocean. The increases are often the result of more technologically advanced fishing operations. The decreases are usually the result of the same thing: increased technology has brought increased harvests, which has reduced the supply of fish and shellfish and that, in turn, has increased prices. Most of the countries that have experienced sharp decreases in their supply of food from the world's oceans are simply no longer able to pay for an increasingly scarce commodity.

Map 52 Cropland Per Capita: Changes, 1985–1995

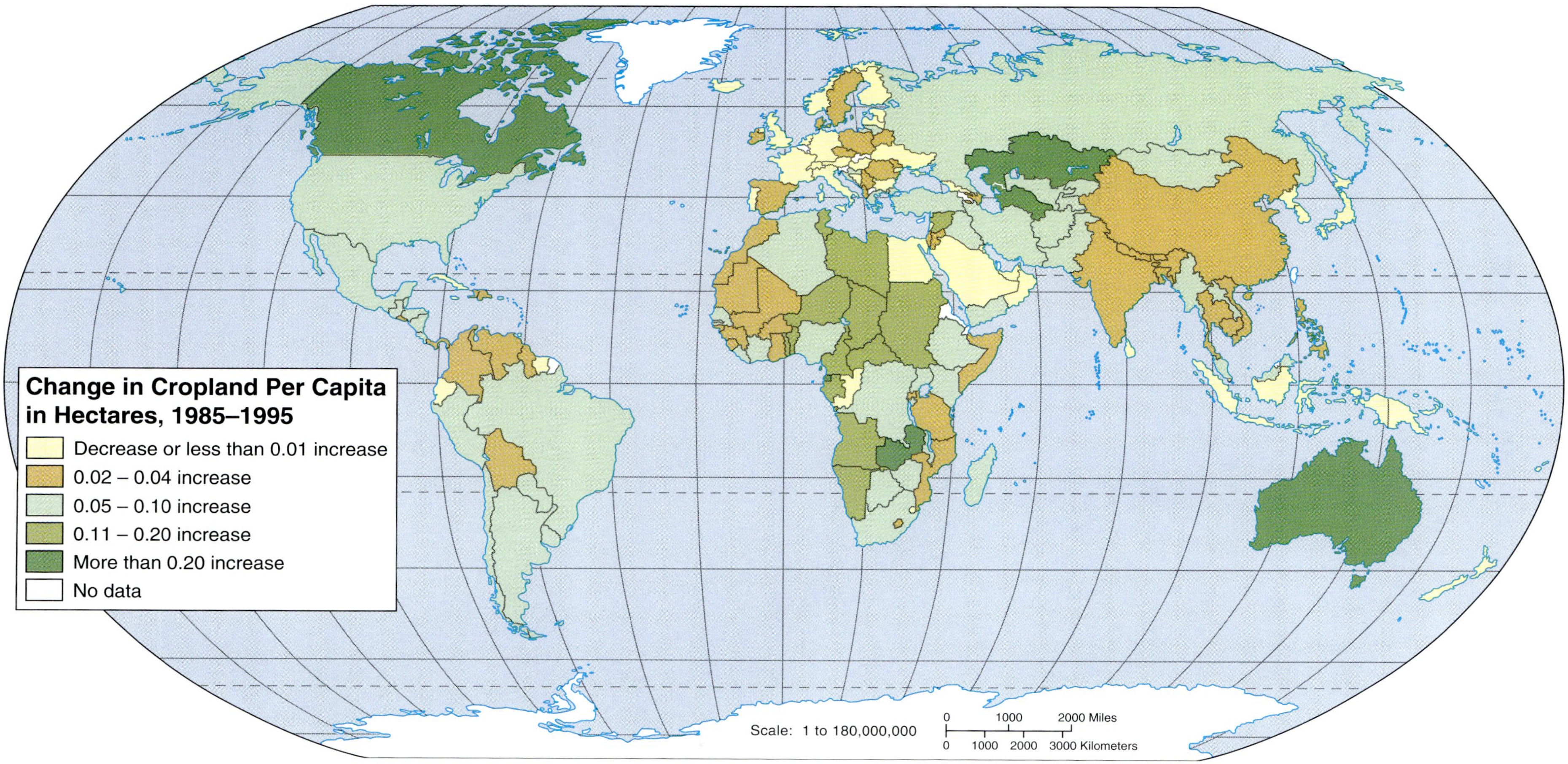

As population has increased rapidly throughout the world, area in cultivated land has increased at the same time; in fact, the amount of farmland per person has gone up slightly. Unfortunately, the figures that show this also tell us that since most of the best (or even good) agricultural land in 1985 was already under cultivation, most of the agricultural area added since the early 1980s involves land that would have been viewed as marginal by the fathers and grandfathers of present farmers—marginal in that it was too dry, too wet, too steep to cultivate, too far from a market, and so on. The continued expansion of agricultural area is one reason that serious famine and starvation have struck only a few regions of the globe. But land, more than any other resource we deal with, is finite, and the expansion cannot continue indefinitely. Future gains in agricultural production are most probably going to come through more intensive use of existing cropland, heavier applications of fertilizers and other agricultural chemicals, and genetically engineered crops requiring heavier applications of energy and water, than from an increase in the amount of the world's cropland.

Map 53 Annual Change in Forest Cover, 1981–1995

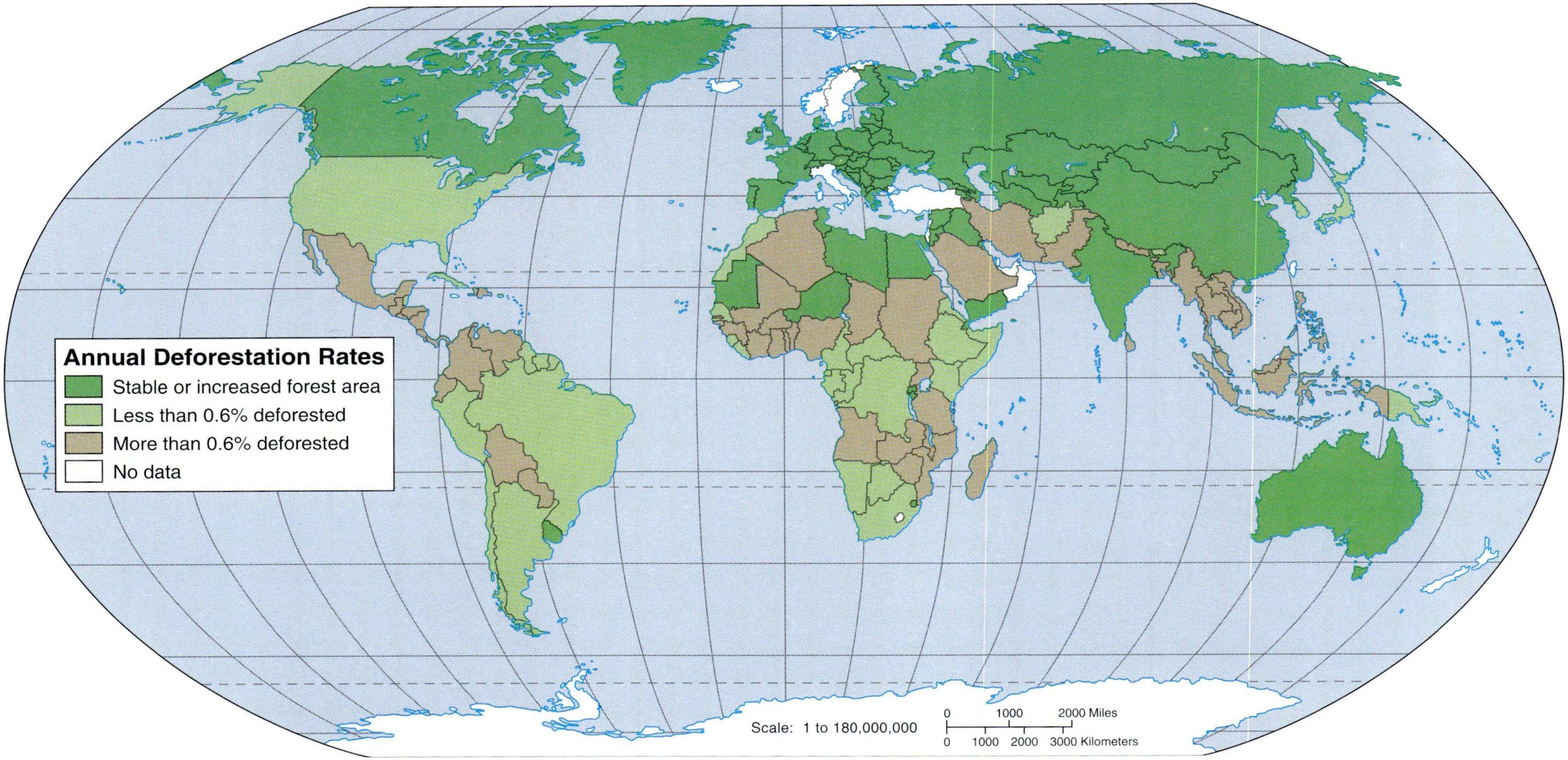

One of the most discussed environmental problems is that of deforestation. For most people, deforestation means clearing of tropical rain forests for agricultural purposes. Yet nearly as much forest land per year—much of it in North America, Europe, and Russia—is impacted by commercial lumbering as is cleared by tropical farmers and ranchers. Even in the tropics, much of the forest clearance is undertaken by large corporations producing high-value tropical hardwoods for the global market in furniture, ornaments, and other fine wood products. Still, it is the agriculturally driven clearing of the great rain forests of the Amazon Basin, west and central Africa, Middle America, and Southeast Asia that draws public attention. Although much concern over forest clearance focuses on the relationship between forest clearance and the reduction in the capacity of the world's vegetation system to absorb carbon dioxide (and thus delay global warming), of just as great concern are issues having to do with the loss of biodiversity (large numbers of plants and animals), the near-total destruction of soil systems, and disruptions in water supply that accompany clearing.

Map 54a The Loss of Biodiversity: Globally Threatened Animal Species

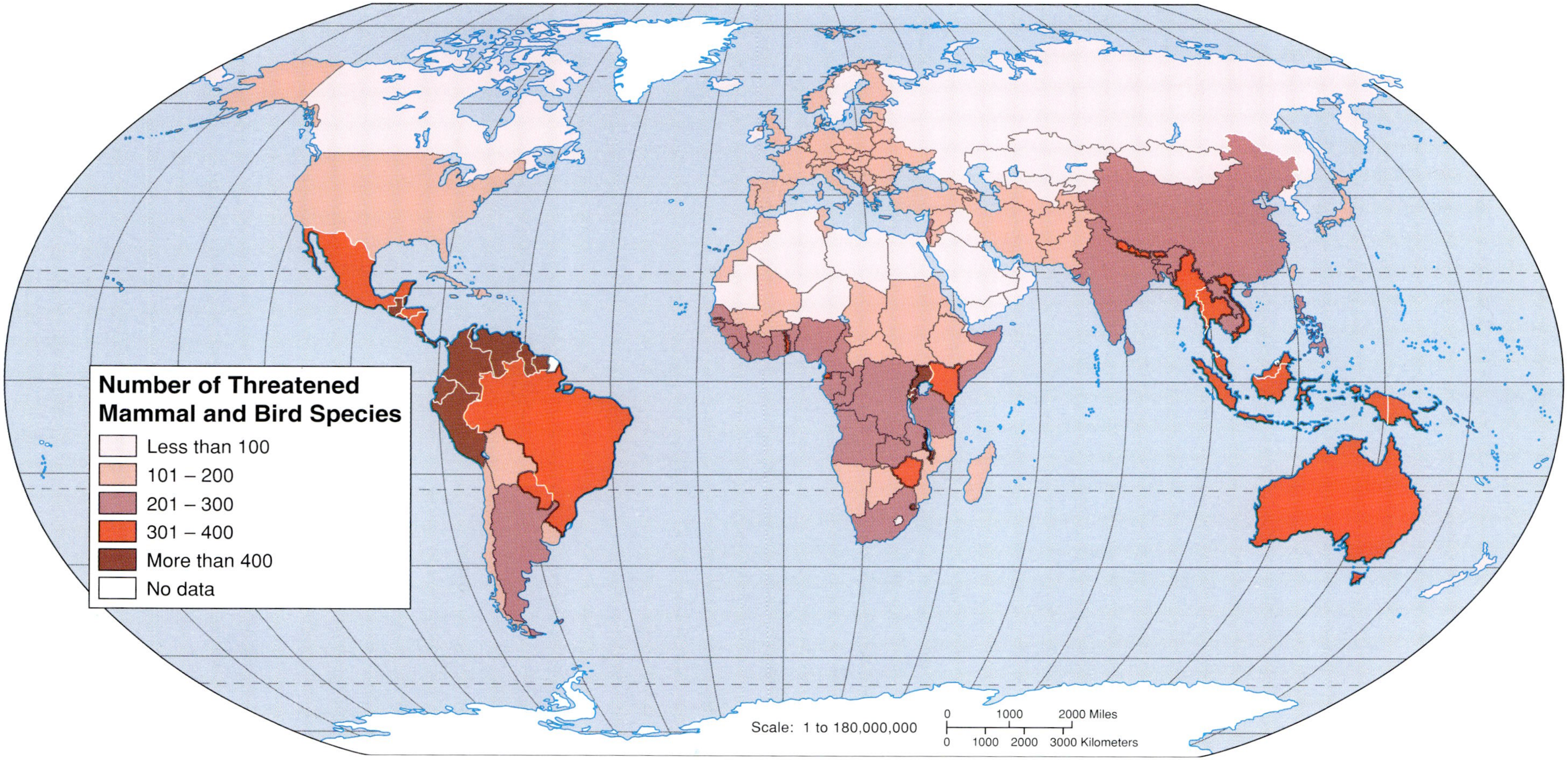

Threatened species are those in grave danger of going extinct. Their populations are becoming restricted in range, and the size of the populations required for sustained breeding is nearing a critical minimum. *Endangered species* are in immediate danger of becoming extinct. Their range is already so reduced that the animals may no longer be able to move freely within an ecozone, and their populations are at the level where the species may no longer be able to sustain breeding. Most species become threatened first and then endangered as their range and numbers continue to decrease. When people think of animal extinction, they think of large herbivorous species like the rhinoceros or fierce carnivores like lions, tigers, or grizzly bears. Certainly these animals make almost any list of endangered or threatened species. But there are literally hundreds of less conspicuous animals that are equally threatened. Extinction is normally nature's way of informing a species that it is inefficient. But conditions in the late twentieth century are controlled more by human activities than by natural evolutionary processes. Species that are endangered or threatened fall into that category because, somehow, they are competing with us or with our domesticated livestock for space and food. And in that competition the animals are always going to lose.

Map 54b The Loss of Biodiversity: Globally Threatened Plant Species

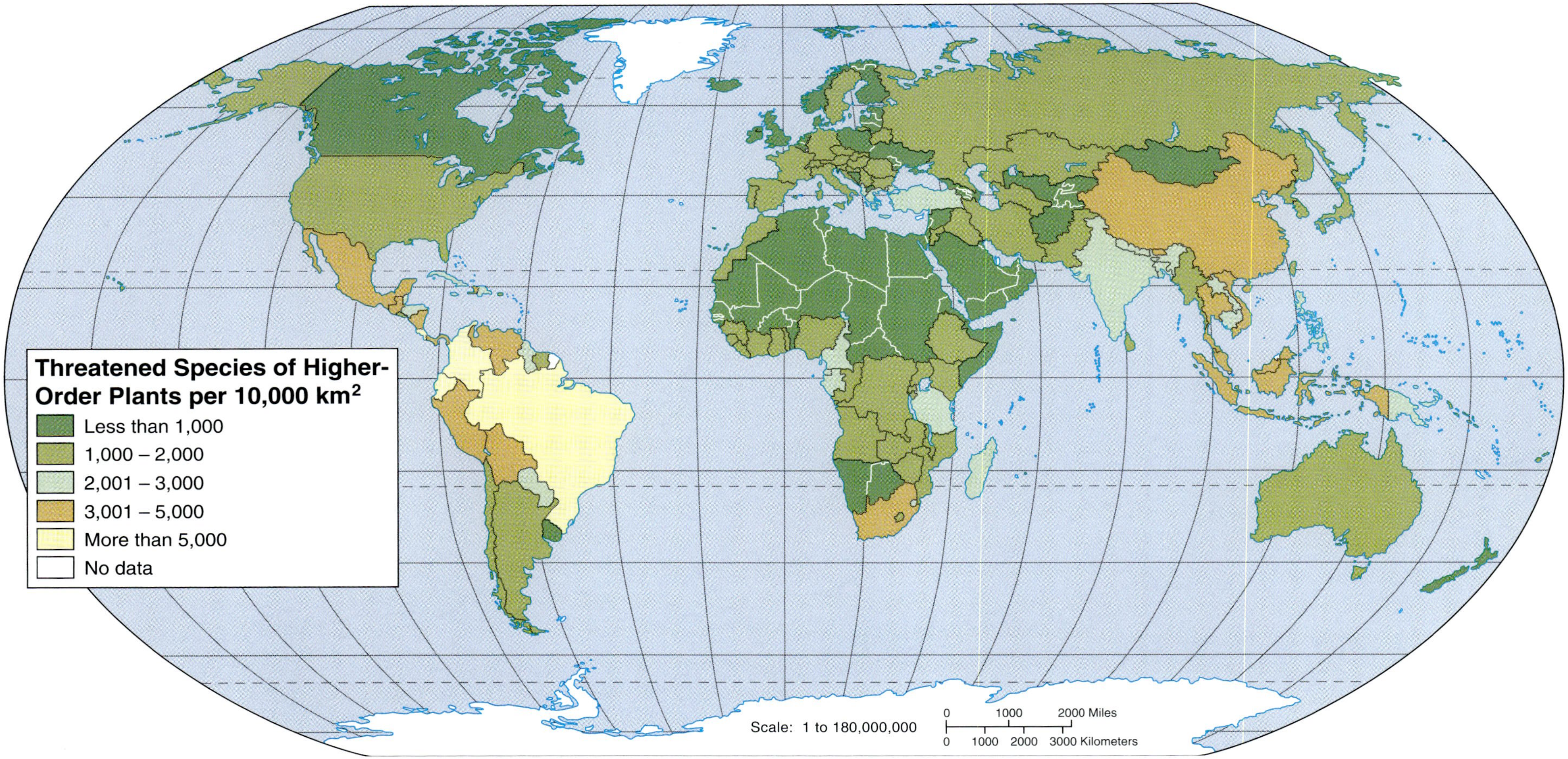

While most people tend to be more concerned about the animals on threatened and endangered species lists, the fact is that many more plants are in jeopardy, and the loss of plant life is, in all ecological regions, a more critical occurrence than the loss of animal populations. Plants are the primary producers in the ecosystem; that is, plants produce the food upon which all other species in the food web, including human beings, depend for sustenance. It is plants from which many of our critical medicines come, and it is plants that maintain the delicate balance between soil and water in most of the world's regions. When biogeographers and other environmental scientists speak of a loss of "biodiversity," what they are most often describing is a loss of the richness and complexity of plant life that lends stability to ecosystems. Systems with more plant life tend to be more stable than those with less. For these and other reasons, the scientific concern over extinction is greater when applied to plants than to animals. It is difficult for people to become as emotional over a teak tree as they would over an elephant. But as great a tragedy as the loss of the elephant would be, the loss of the teak would be greater.

Map 55 The Risks of Desertification

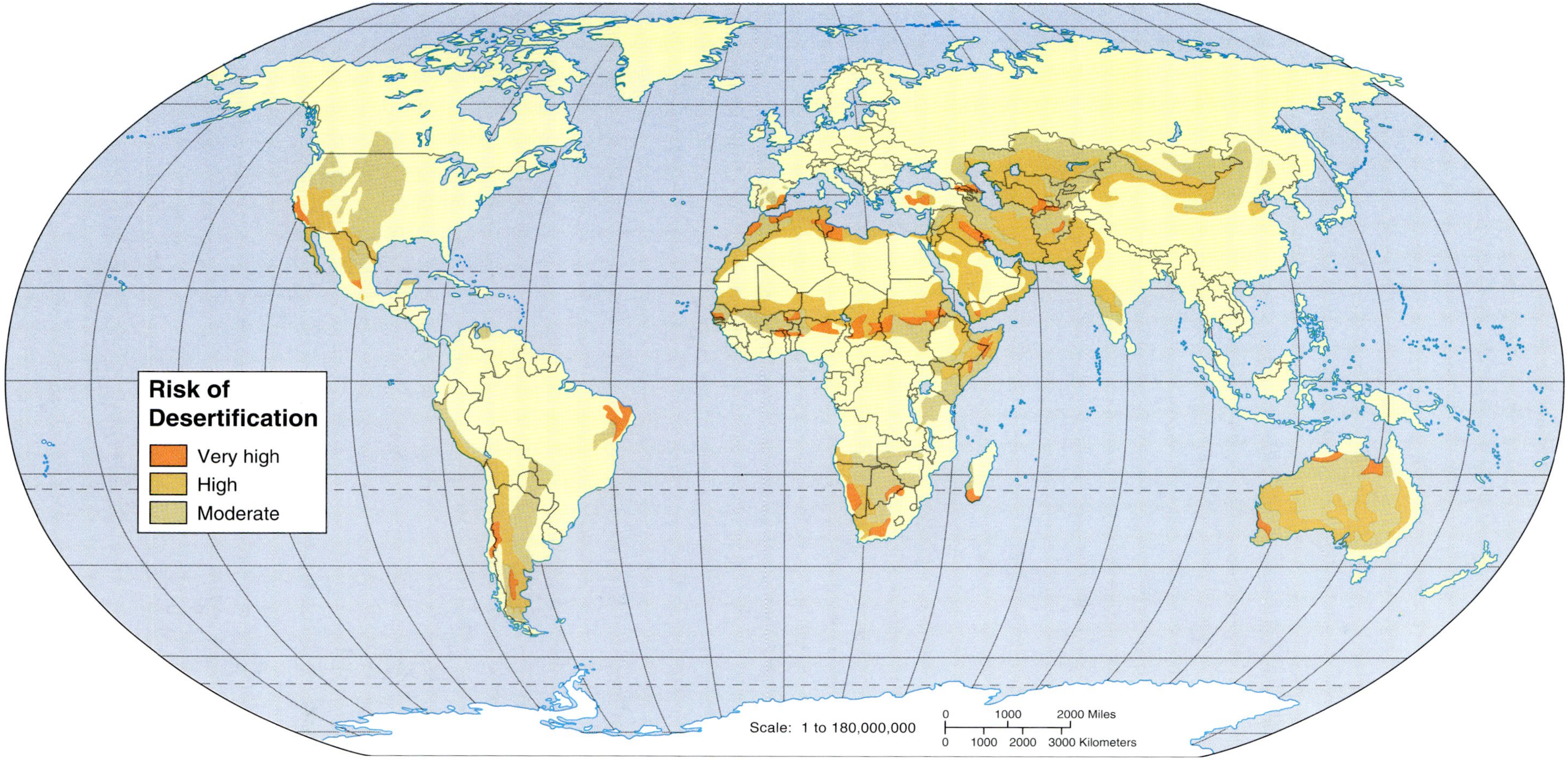

The awkward-sounding term "desertification" refers to a reduction in the food-producing capacity of drylands through vegetation, soil, and water changes that culminate in either a drier climate or in soil and plant systems that are less efficient in their use of water. Most of the world's existing drylands—the shortgrass steppes, the tropical savannas, the bunchgrass regions of the desert fringe—are fairly intensively used for agriculture and are, therefore, subject to the kinds of pressures that culminate in desertification. Most desertification is a natural process that occurs near the margins of desert regions. It is caused by dehydration of the soil's surface layers during periods of drought and by high water loss through evaporation in an environment of high temperature and high winds. This natural process is greatly enhanced by human agricultural activities that expose topsoil to wind and water erosion. Among the most important practices that cause desertification are (1) overgrazing of rangelands, resulting from too many livestock on too small an area of land; (2) improper management of soil and water resources in irrigation agriculture, leading to accelerated erosion and to salt buildup in the soil; (3) cultivation of marginal terrain with soils and slopes that are unsuitable for farming; (4) surface disturbances of vegetation (clearing of thorn scrub, mesquite, chaparral, and similar vegetation) without soil protection efforts being made or replanting being done; and (5) soil compaction by agricultural implements, domesticated livestock, and rain falling on an exposed surface.

Map 56 Global Soil Degradation

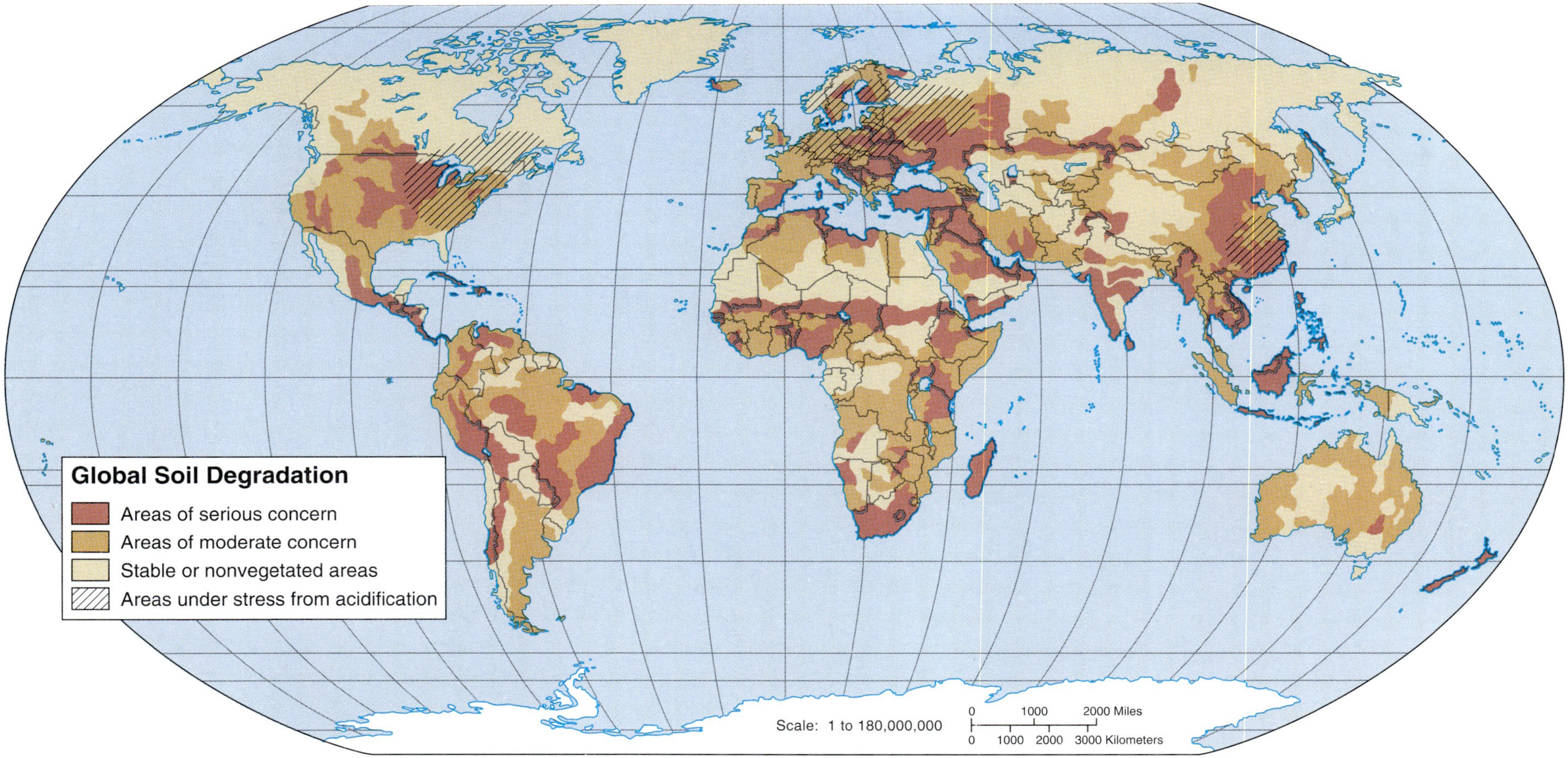

Recent research has shown that more than 3 billion acres of the world's surface suffer from serious soil degradation, with more than 22 million acres so severely eroded or poisoned with chemicals that they can no longer support productive crop agriculture. Most of this soil damage has been caused by poor farming practices, overgrazing of domestic livestock, and deforestation. These activities strip away the protective cover of natural vegetation forests and grasslands, allowing wind and water erosion to remove the topsoil that contains necessary nutrients and soil microbes for plant growth. But millions of acres of topsoil have been degraded by chemicals as well. In some instances these chemicals are the result of overapplication of fertilizers, herbicides, pesticides, and other agricultural chemicals. In other instances, chemical deposition from industrial and urban wastes and from acid precipitation has poisoned millions of acres of soil. As the map shows, soil erosion and pollution are not problems just in developing countries with high population densities and increasing use of marginal lands. They also afflict the more highly developed regions of mechanized, industrial agriculture. While many methods for preventing or reducing soil degradation exist, they are seldom used because of ignorance, cost, or perceived economic inefficiency.

Map 57 Degree of Human Disturbance

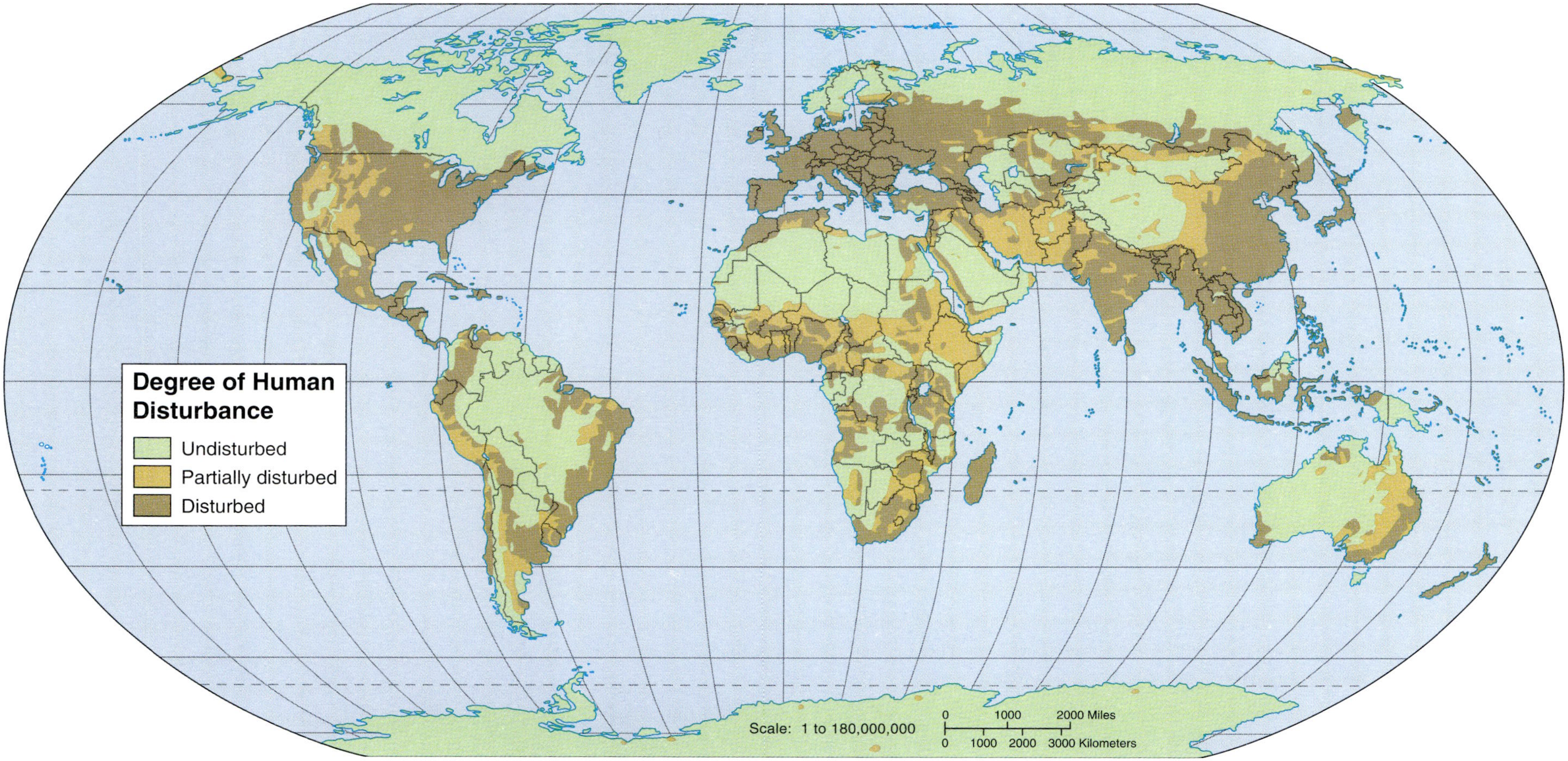

The data on human disturbance have been gathered from a wide variety of sources, some of them conflicting and not all of them reliable. Nevertheless, at a global scale this map fairly depicts the state of the world in terms of the degree to which humans have modified its surface. The undisturbed areas, covered with natural vegetation, generally have population densities under 10 persons per square mile. These areas are, for the most part, in the most inhospitable parts of the world: too high, too dry, too cold for permanent human habitation in large numbers. The partially disturbed areas are normally agricultural areas, either subsistence (such as shifting cultivation) or extensive (such as livestock grazing). They often contain areas of secondary vegetation, regrown after removal of original vegetation by humans. They are also often marked by a density of livestock in excess of carrying capacity, leading to overgrazing, which further alters the condition of the vegetation. The disturbed areas are those of permanent and intensive agriculture and urban settlement. The primary vegetation of these regions has been removed, with no evidence of regrowth or with current vegetation that is quite different from natural (potential) vegetation. Soils are in a state of depletion and degradation, and, in drier lands, desertification is a factor of human occupation. The disturbed areas match closely those areas of the world with the densest human populations.

Part VI

Global Political Patterns

Map 58 Political Systems

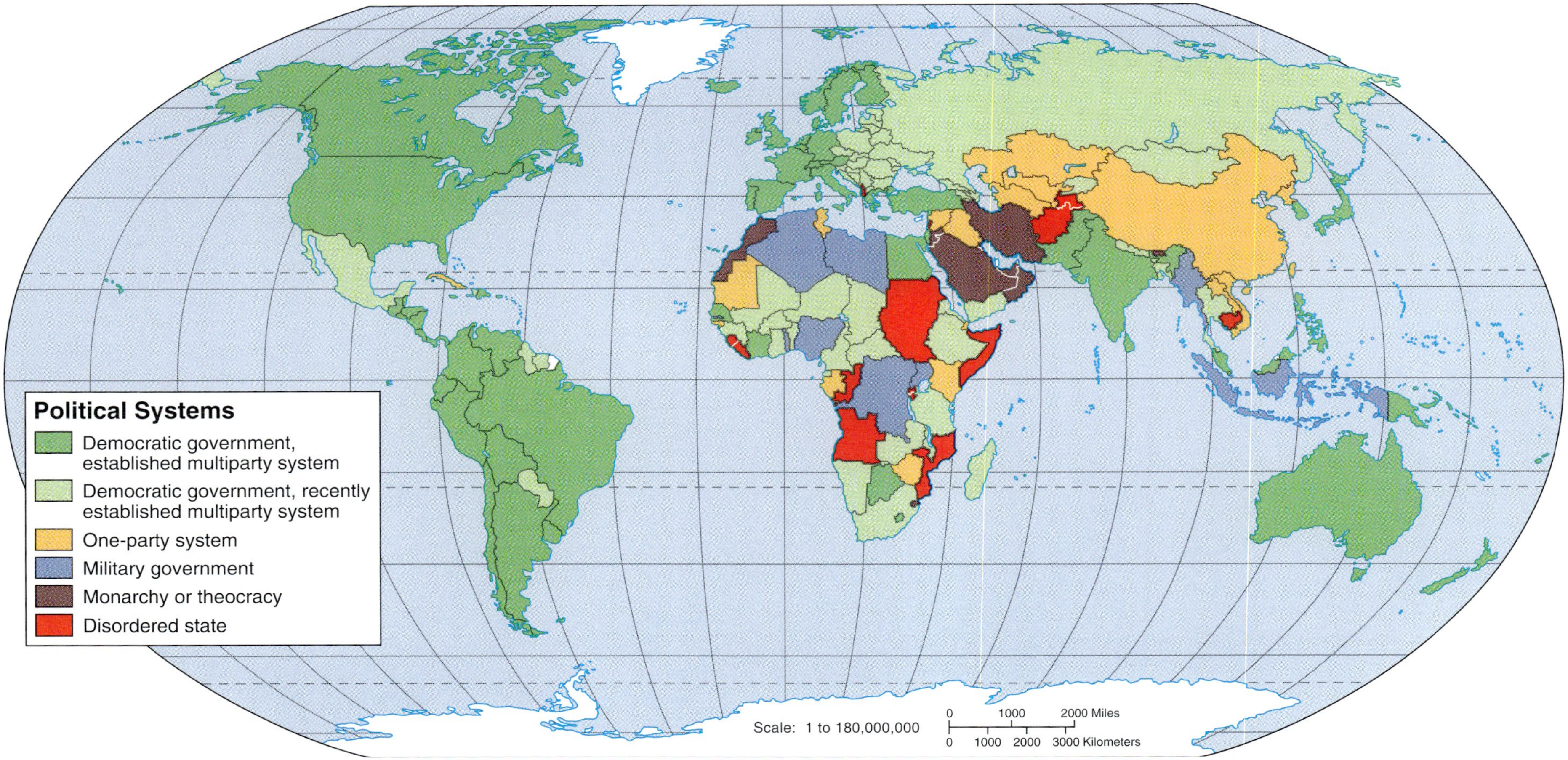

The world map of political systems has changed dramatically during the 1990s. The categories of political systems shown are subject to some interpretation: established multiparty democracies are those in which elections by secret ballot with adult suffrage are long-term features of the political landscape; recently established multiparty democracies are those in which this distinguishing feature has only recently emerged. The former Soviet satellites of eastern Europe and the republics that formerly constituted the USSR are in this category; so are states in emerging regions that are beginning to throw off the single-party rule that often followed the violent upheavals of the immediate postcolonial governmental transitions. The other categories are more-or-less obvious. One-party systems define states where single party rule provided for by constitution is a fact of political life. Monarchies are countries with heads of state who are members of a royal family. Some countries with monarchs do not fall into this category because their monarchs are titular heads of state only. Theocracies are countries in which rule is within the hands of a priestly or clerical class; for example, fundamentalist Islamic countries. Military governments are often organized around a junta that has seized control of the government from civil authority; such states are often technicially transitional—the military claims that it will return the reins of government to civil authority "when order is restored." Finally, "disordered states" are countries so beset by civil war or widespread ethnic conflict that no organized government can be said to exist within them.

Map 59 Sovereign States

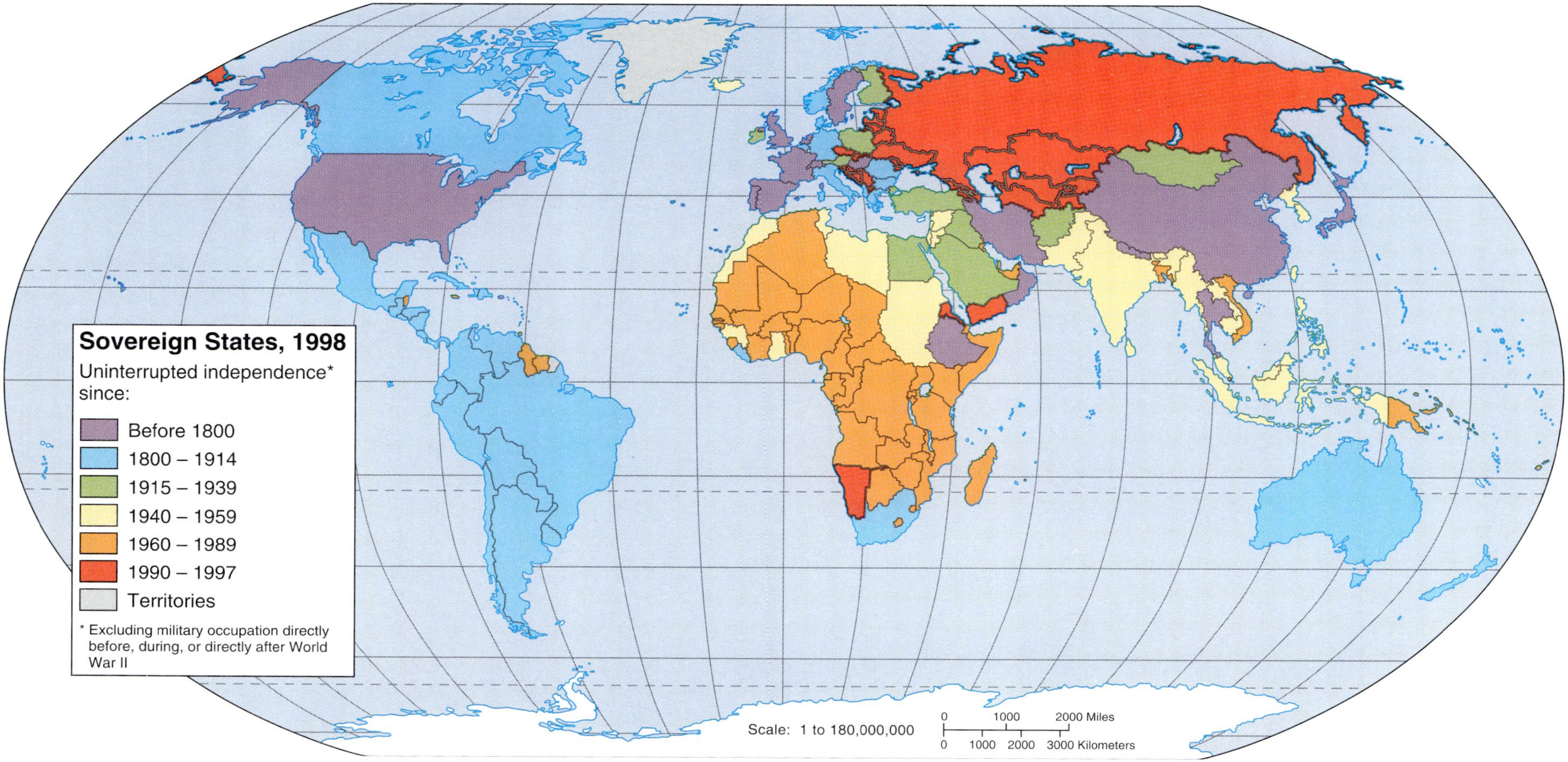

Most countries of the modern world, including such major states as Germany and Italy, became independent after the beginning of the nineteenth century. Of the world's current countries, only 27 were independent in 1800. (Ten of the 27 were in Europe; the others were Afghanistan, China, Colombia, Ethiopia, Haiti, Iran, Japan, Mexico, Nepal, Oman, Paraguay, Russia, Taiwan, Thailand, Turkey, the United States, and Venezuela). Following 1800, there have been five great periods of national independence. During the first of these (1800–1914), most of the mainland countries of the Americas achieved independence.During the second period (1915–1939), the countries of Eastern Europe emerged as independent entities. The third period (1940–1959) includes World War II and the years that followed, when independence for African and Asian nations that had been under control of colonial powers first began to occur. During the fourth period (1960–1989), independence came to the remainder of the colonial African and Asian nations, as well as to former colonies in the Caribbean and the South Pacific. More than half of the world's countries came into being as independent political entities during this period. Finally, in the last few years (1990–1997), the breakup of the existing states of the Soviet Union, Yugoslavia, and Czechoslovakia created 22 countries where only 3 had existed before.

Map 60 Post-Cold War International Alliances

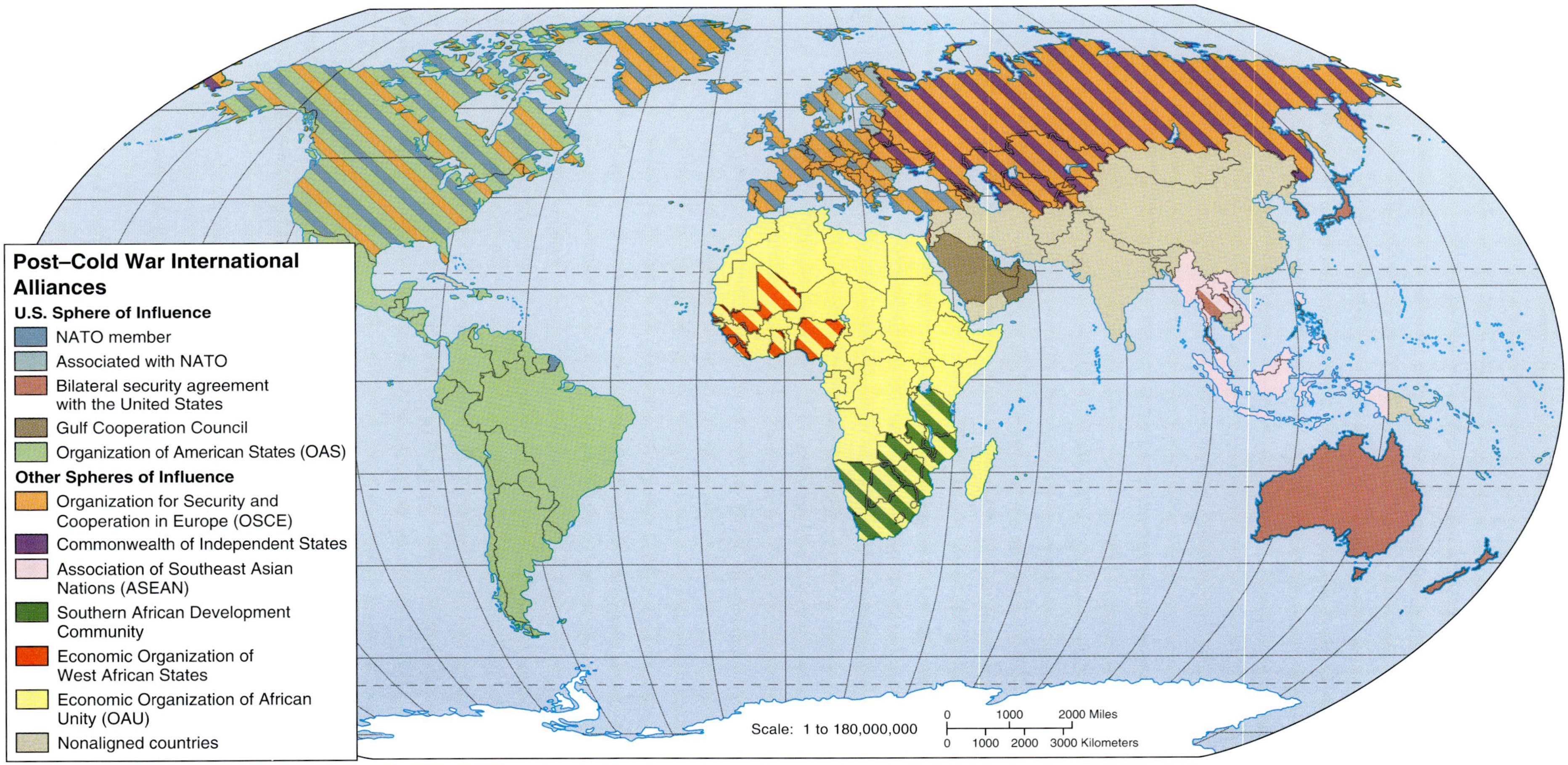

When the Warsaw Pact dissolved in 1992, the North Atlantic Treaty Organization (NATO) was left as the only major military alliance in the world. Some former Warsaw Pact members (Czech Republic, Hungary, and Poland) have joined NATO and others are petitioning for entry. The bipolar division of the world into two major military alliances is over, at least temporarily, leaving the United States alone as the world's dominant political and military power. But other international alliances such as the Commonwealth of Independent States (including most of the former republics of the Soviet Union) will continue to be important. It may well be that, during the first few decades of the twenty-first century, economic alliances will begin to overshadow military ones in their relevance for the world's peoples.

Map 61 International Conflicts in the Post–World War II World

	Conflict[1]	Start Date	Major Belligerent Countries[2] (in alphabetical order)	
1	Palestine	1948	Egypt Iraq Israel	Jordan Lebanon Syria
2	Korean	1950	China North Korea South Korea United Nations: United States and 11 other countries	
3	Soviet-Hungarian	1956	Hungary	Soviet Union
4	Sinai	1956	Egypt France	Israel United Kingdom
5	Sino-Indian	1962	China	India
6	Kashmir	1965	India	Pakistan
7	Vietnam	1965	Australia North Vietnam South Korea	South Vietnam United States
8	Six-Day	1967	Egypt Israel	Jordan Syria
9	Soviet-Czech	1968	Czechoslovakia	Soviet Union
10	Football	1969	El Salvador	Honduras
11	Indo-Pakistani	1971	India	Pakistan
12	Yom Kippur	1973	Egypt Israel	Syria
13	Cyprus	1974	Cyprus	Turkey
14	Ogaden	1977	Ethiopia	Somalia
15	Cambodian-Vietnamese	1978	Cambodia China	Vietnam
16	Ugandan-Tanzanian	1978	Tanzania	Uganda
17	Afghanistan	1979	Afghanistan	Soviet Union
18	Persian Gulf	1980	Iran	Iraq
19	Angola	1981	Angola Cuba	South Africa
20	Falklands	1982	Argentina	United Kingdom
21	Saharan	1983	Chad	Libya
22	Lebanon	1987	France Israel Lebanon	Syria United States
23	Panama	1989	Panama	United States
24	Persian Gulf	1990	Iraq United Nations: United States and 7 other countries	
25	Yugoslavia	1990	Bosnia-Herzegovina	Croatia Serbia
26	Peruvian-Ecuadorian	1995	Ecuador	Peru
27	Albania	1995	Albania	Yugoslavia (Serbia-Montenegro)
28	Rwanda	1995	Burundi	Rwanda
29	East Timor	1995	Indonesia	New Guinea insurgency
30	Cameroon	1996	Cameroon	Nigeria
31	Northern Iraq	1996	Iraq	Kurdish insurgency
32	Eritrea	1997	Eritrea	Yemen
33	Iraq	1998	Great Britain Iraq	United States
34	Kosovo	1999	Albania NATO	Yugoslavia

[1] "Conflict" implies at least 1,000 battle deaths.
[2] "Belligerent" implies country supplied at least 5% of the combat troops in the conflict.

The Korean War and the Vietnam War dominated the post–World War II period in terms of international military conflict. But numerous smaller conflicts have taken place, with fewer numbers of belligerents and with fewer battle and related casualties. These smaller international conflicts have been mostly territorial conflicts, reflecting the continual readjustment of political boundaries and loyalties brought about by the end of colonial empires, and the dissolution of the Soviet Union. Many of these conflicts were not wars in the more traditional sense, in which two or more countries formally declare war on one another, severing diplomatic ties, and devoting their entire national energies to the war effort. Rather, many of these conflicts were and are undeclared wars, sometimes fought between rival groups within the same country with outside support from other countries.

Map 62 Global Distribution of Minority Groups

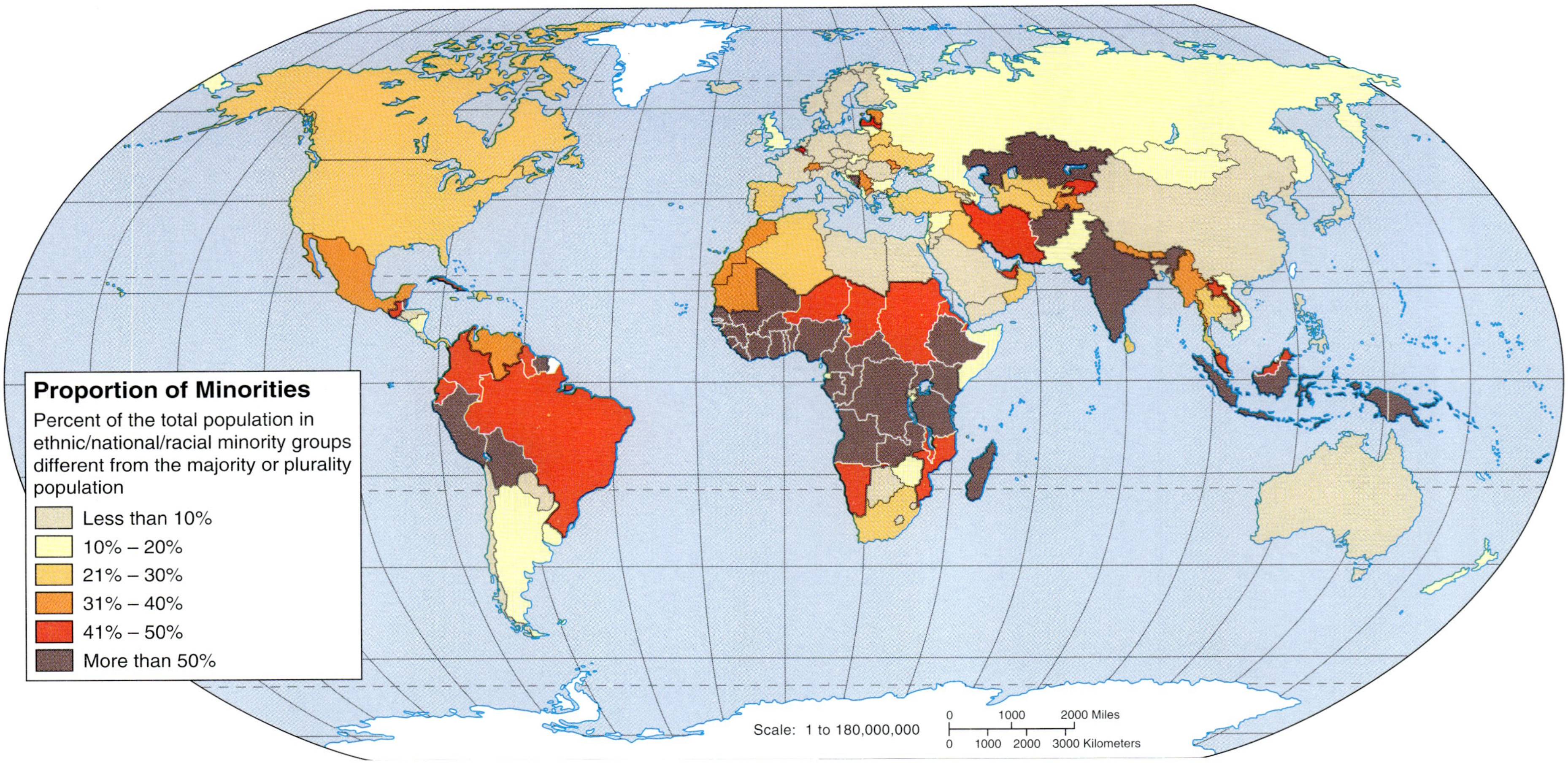

The presence of minority ethnic, national, or racial groups within a country's population can add a vibrant and dynamic mix to the whole. Plural societies with a high degree of cultural and ethnic diversity should, according to some social theorists, be among the world's most healthy. Unfortunately, the reality of the situation is quite different from theory or expectation. The presence of significant minority populations played an important role in the disintegration of the Soviet Union; the continuing existence of minority populations within the new states formed from former Soviet republics threatens the viability and stability of those young political units. In Africa, national boundaries were drawn by colonial powers without regard for the geographical distribution of ethnic groups, and the continuing tribal conflicts that have resulted hamper both economic and political development. Even in the most highly developed regions of the world, the presence of minority ethnic populations poses significant problems: witness the separatist movement in Canada, driven by the desire of some French-Canadians to be independent of the English majority, and the continuing ethnic conflict between Flemish-speaking and Walloon-speaking Belgians. This map, by arraying states on a scale of homogeneity to heterogeneity, indicates areas of existing and potential social and political strife.

Map 63 World Refugee Population

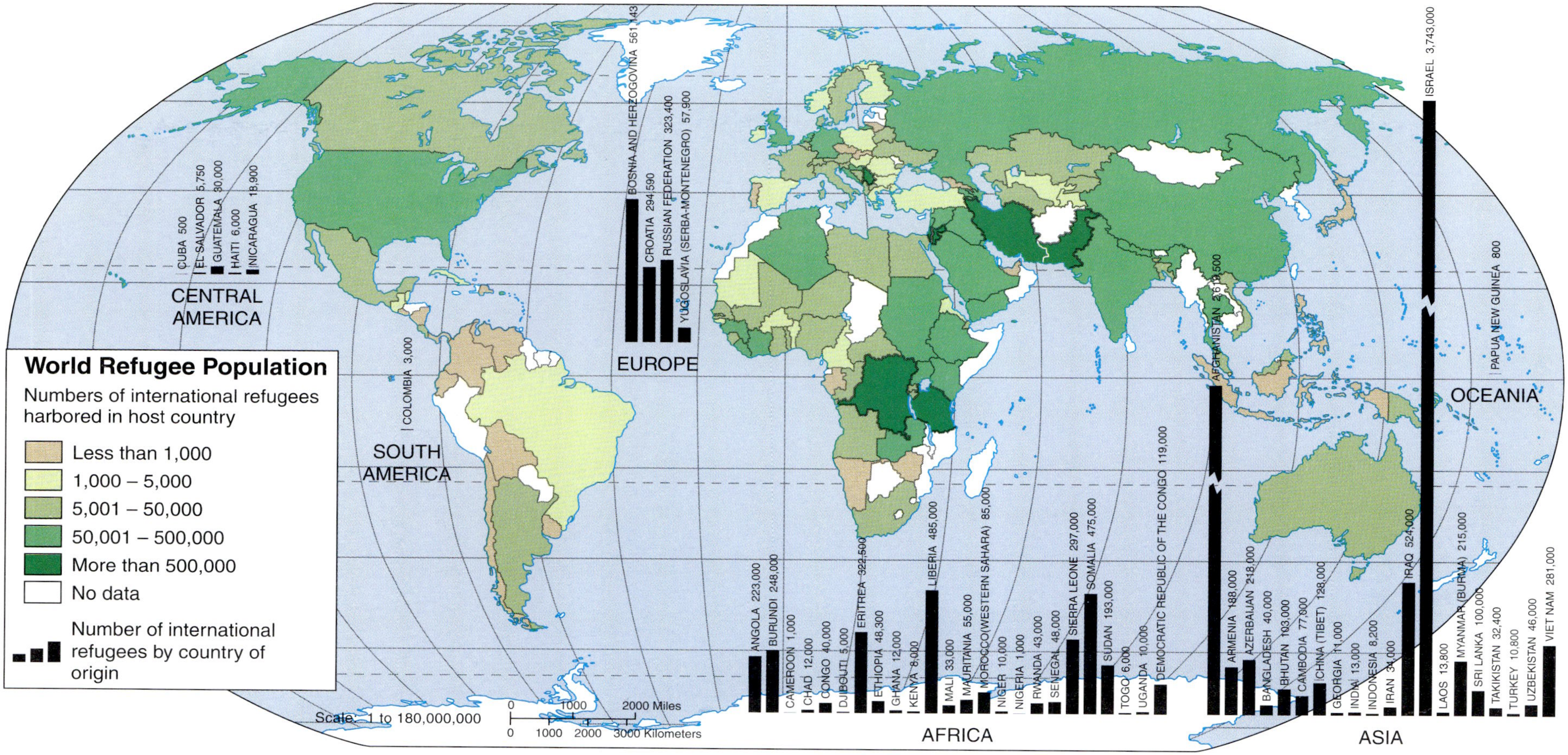

Refugees are persons who have been driven from their homes, normally by armed conflict, and have sought refuge by relocating. The most numerous refugees have traditionally been international refugees, who have crossed the political boundaries of their homelands into other countries. This refugee population is recognized by international agencies, and the countries of refuge are often rewarded financially by those agencies for their willingness to take in externally displaced persons. In recent years, largely because of an increase in civil wars, there have been growing numbers of internally displaced persons—those who leave their homes but stay within their country of origin. There are no rewards for harboring such internal refugee populations.

Part VII

World Regions

Map 64 North America Political Map

Map 65 North America Physical Map

Map 66a Environment and Economy: The Use of Land

The use of land in North America represents a balance between agriculture, resource extraction, and manufacturing that is unmatched. The United States, as the world's leading industrial power, is also the world's leader in commercial agricultural production. Canada, despite its small population, is a ranking producer of both agricultural and industrial products and Mexico has begun to emerge from its developing nation status to become an important industrial and agricultural nation as well. The countries of Middle America and the Caribbean are just beginning the transition from agriculture to modern industrial economies. Part of the basis for the high levels of economic productivity in North America is environmental: a superb blend of soil, climate, and raw materials. But just as important is the cultural and social mix of the plural societies of North America, a mix that historically aided the growth of the economic diversity necessary for developed economies.

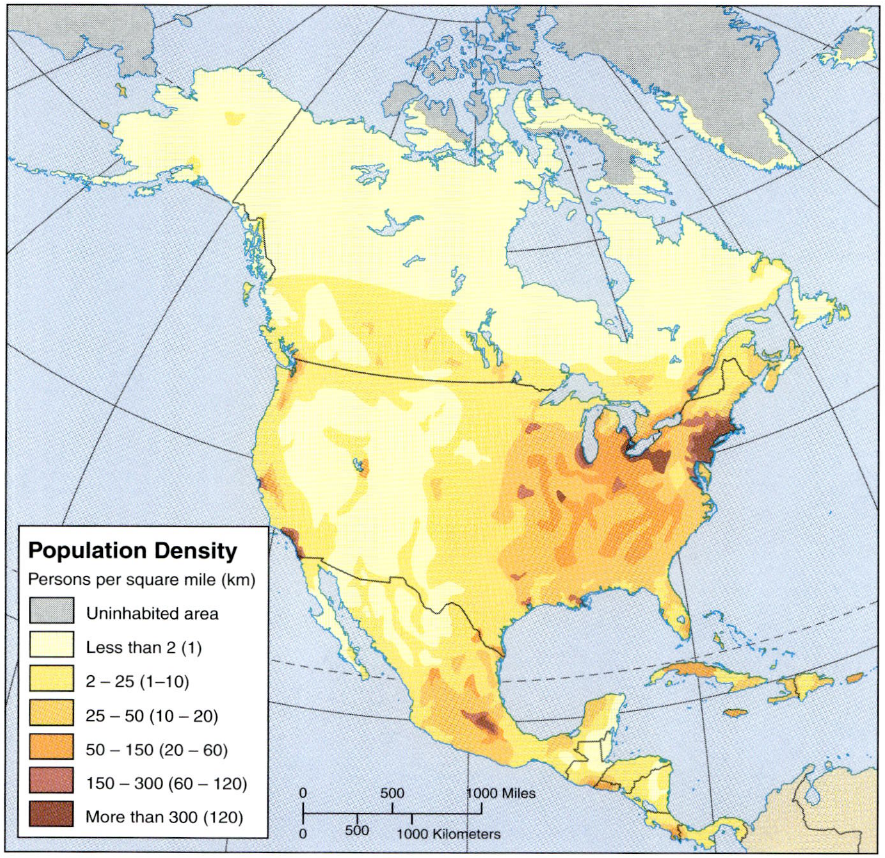

Map 66b Population Density

North America contains nearly 500 million people and the United States, with over 250 million inhabitants, is the third most populous country in the world, after China and India. Most of the present North American population has roots in the Old World. The native populations of the Americas had little or no resistance to Old World diseases in 1500 and within a couple of centuries of first contact with Europeans, most of the native peoples had either died out or preserved their genetic heritage by mixing with disease-resistant Old World populations. This left a North American population that is largely European, but with significant minorities resulting from the slave laborers imported from Africa, and from the mixture of native Americans with Europeans and/or Africans. The density of that population is largely the consequence of environmental factors (good soil, the availability of water, the presence of other resources) and cultural/economic ones (agricultural production, urbanization, industrialization).

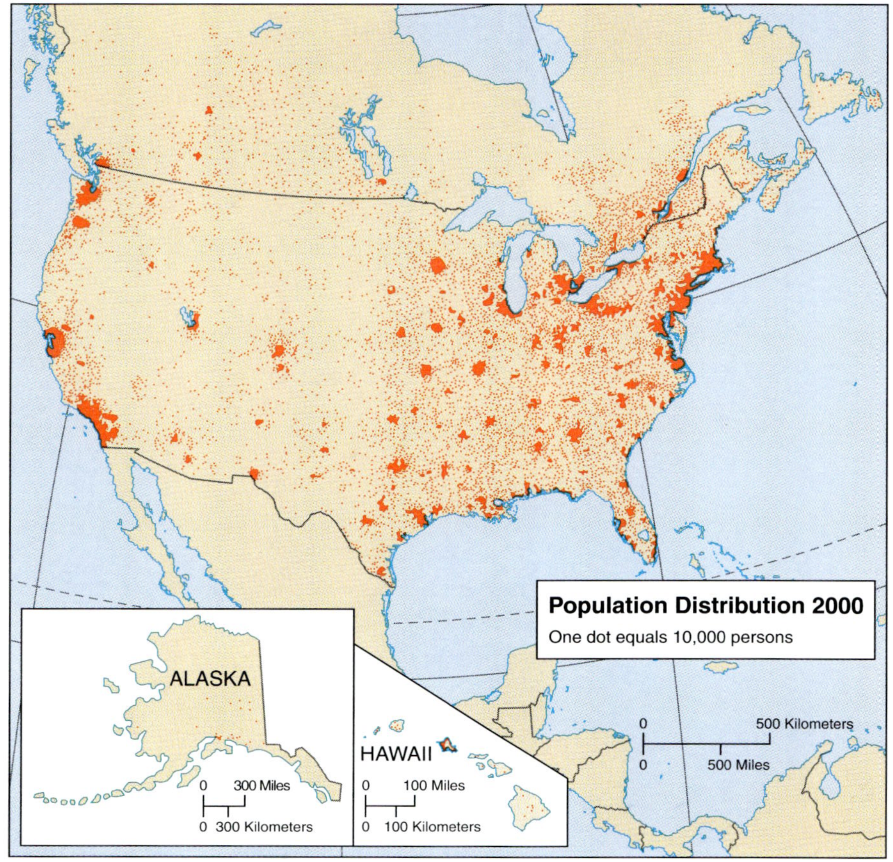

Map 66c Population Distribution

Although population clustering is characteristic of highly economically developed regions, the Anglo-American population exhibits a remarkably clustered pattern. The primary reasons for this remarkable development are agricultural technology and affluence. A highly developed agricultural technology allows a small number of farmers, using sophisticated machinery, to grow and harvest enormous quantities of agricultural produce on large farms. In the United States, the world's leader in commercial agricultural production, only 2% of the population are farmers and that population is thinly distributed over wide areas. The vast majority of Americans live and work in city-suburb systems in which the widespread availability of private automobiles allows people to live considerable distances from where they work, keeping overall urban population densities relatively low but allowing for extensive urbanization—with cities large enough in area to be visible as population clusters on maps at this scale.

Map 67 Canada

Map 68 United States

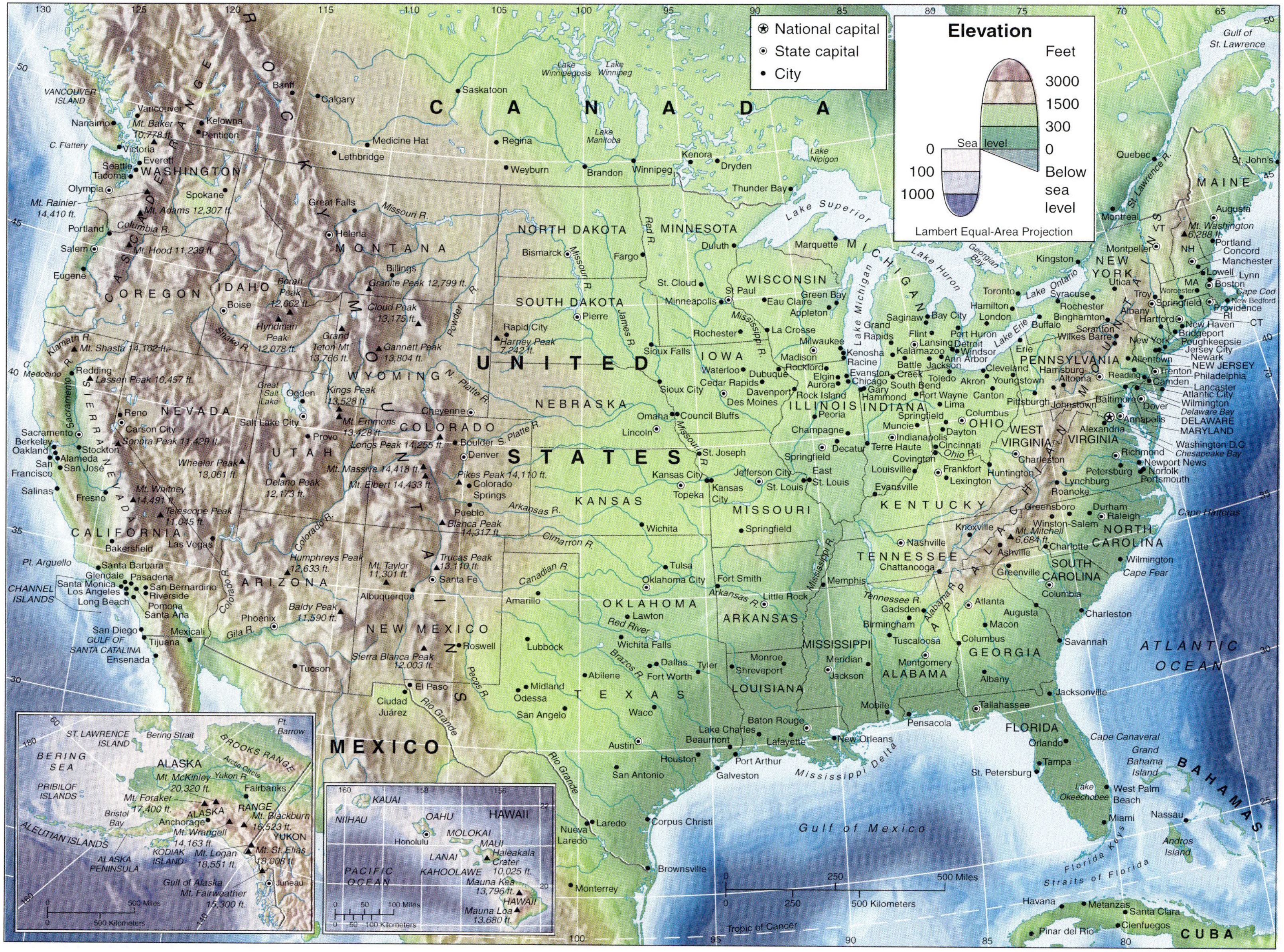

Map 69 Middle America

Map 70 The Caribbean

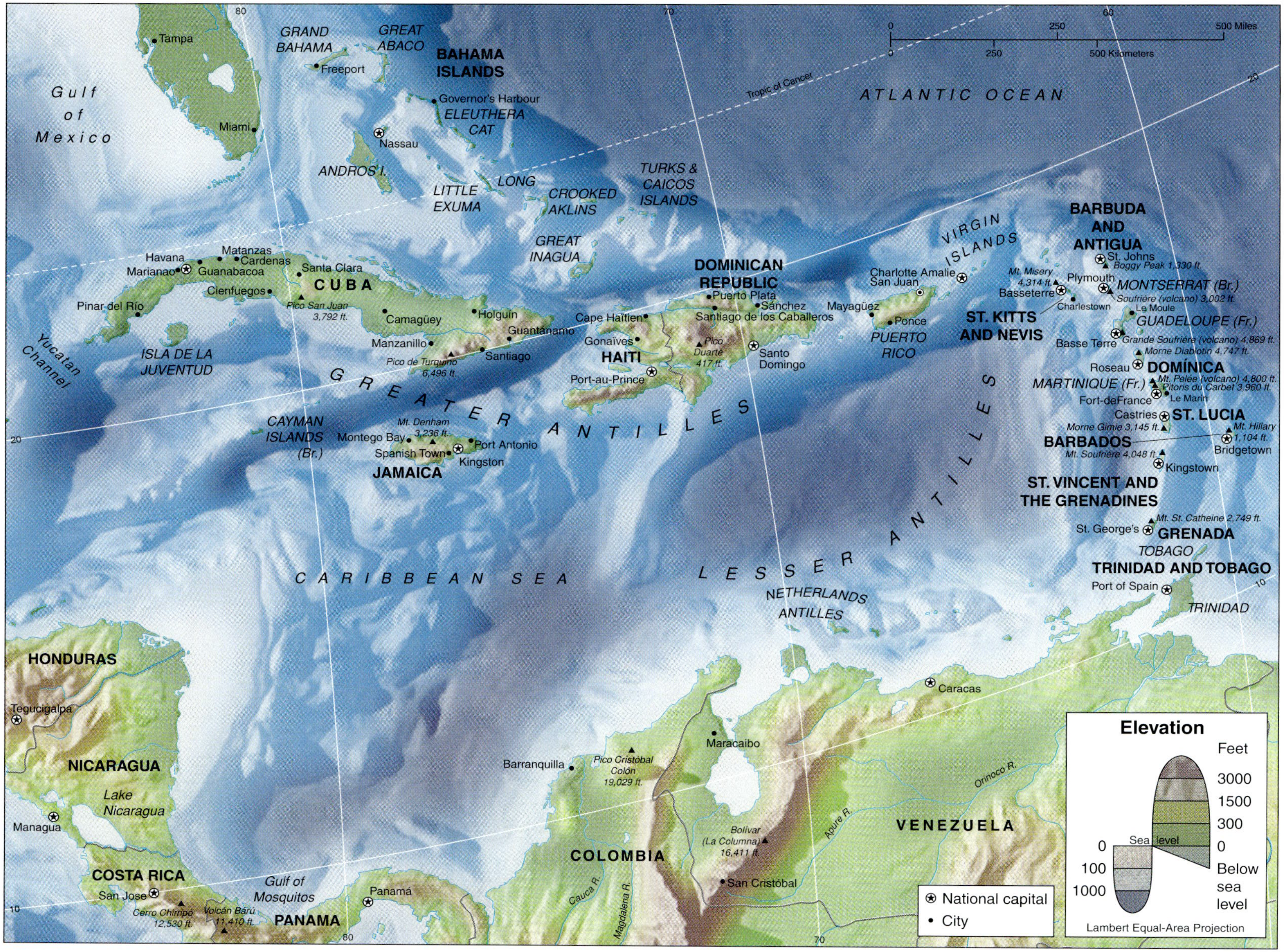

Map [71] South America Political Map

Map 72 South America Physical Map

Map 73a Environment and Economy

South America is a region just beginning to emerge from a colonial-dependency economy in which raw materials flowed from the continent to more highly developed economic regions. With the exception of Brazil, Argentina, Chile, and Uruguay, most of the continent's countries still operate under the traditional mode of exporting raw materials in exchange for capital that tends to accumulate in the pockets of a small percentage of the population. The land use patterns of the continent are, therefore, still dominated by resource extraction and agriculture. A problem posed by these patterns is that little of the continent's land area is actually suitable for either commercial forestry or commercial crop agriculture without extremely high environmental costs. Much of the agriculture, then, is based on high value tropical crops that can be grown in small areas profitably, or on extensive livestock grazing. Even within the forested areas of the Amazon Basin where forest clearance is taking place at unprecedented rates, much of the land use that replaces forest is grazing.

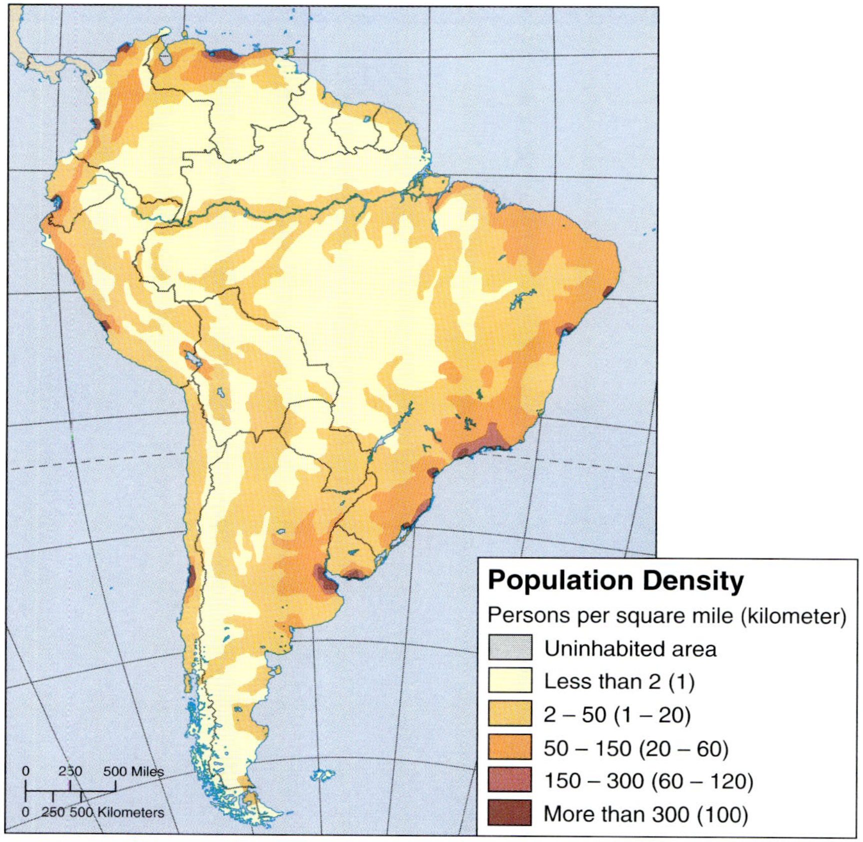

Map 73b Population Density

Since so much of interior South America is uninhabitable (the high Andes) or only sparsely populated (the interior of the Amazon basin), the continent's population tends to be peripheral—approximately 90% of the continent's nearly 375 million people live within 150 miles of the sea. This population also tends to be heavily urbanized. Over 80% of South America's population lives in cities and the continent has three of the world's 15 largest cities—Rio de Janeiro, Saõ Paulo, and Buenos Aires. Saõ Paulo is the world's third largest urban agglomeration after Tokyo and New York. As in North America, most of the population of South America can trace at least part of its ancestry to the Old World. Throughout the Spanish-speaking parts of the continent the population is predominantly *mestizo* or mixed European and native South American. In Portuguese-speaking Brazil, in addition to a *mestizo* population, there is a significant admixture of African blood, the result of a large slave labor force imported from Africa to work the sugar, cotton, and other plantations of the colonial period.

Map 73c Environmental Problems

The drainage basin of the Amazon River and its tributaries, along with adjacent regions, is the world's largest remaining area of tropical forest. Much of the periphery of this vast forested region has already been cleared for farming and grazing and the ax and chainsaw and the flames are working their way steadily toward the interior. Tropical deforestation produces a loss of the biological diversity represented by the world's most biologically productive ecosystem, along with changes in soil and soil-water systems. South America has other environmental problems: *desertification* in which grassland and/or scrub vegetation is converted to desert through overgrazing or other unwise agricultural practices; soil *salinization* in which soils become increasingly salty as the consequence of the over-application of irrigation water; *coastal and estuarine pollution* resulting from unregulated or unchecked use of coastal waters for industrial, commercial, and transportation purposes; and *acid precipitation* resulting from the combination of airborne industrial wastes and automobile-truck exhausts with water vapor to produce dry or wet acidic fallout.

Map 74 Northern South America

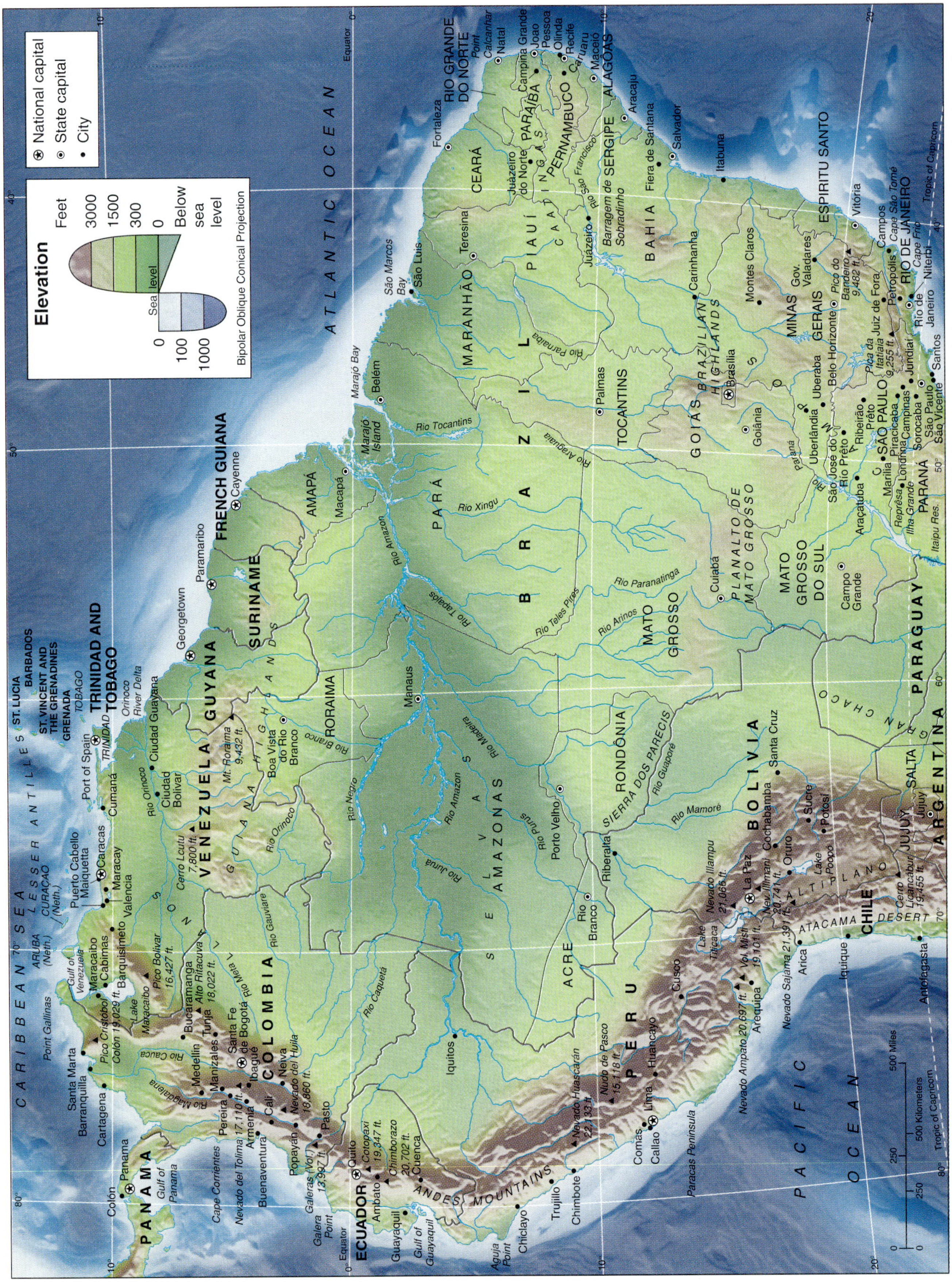

Map 75 Southern South America

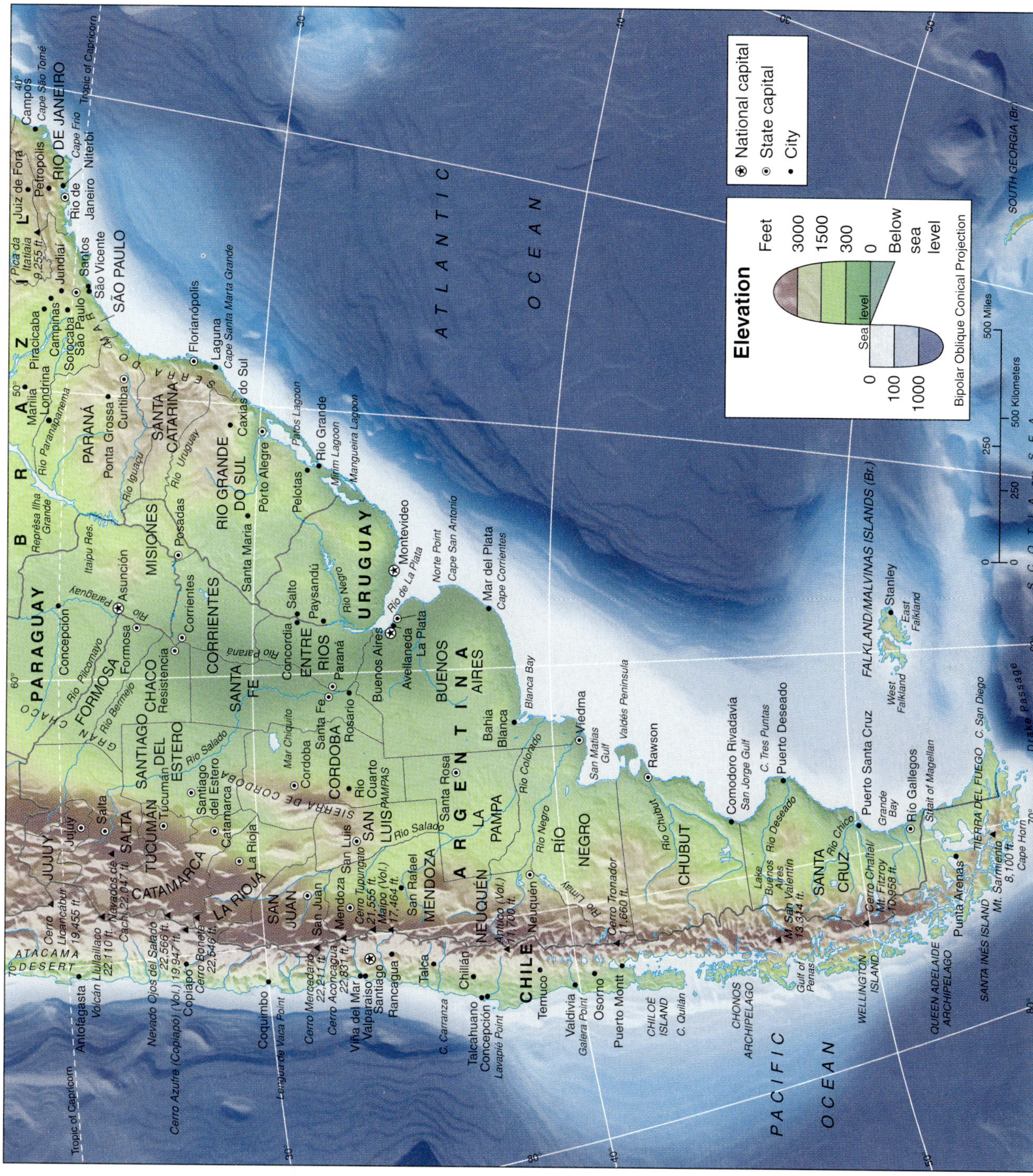

Map 76 Europe Political Map

Map 77 Europe Physical Map

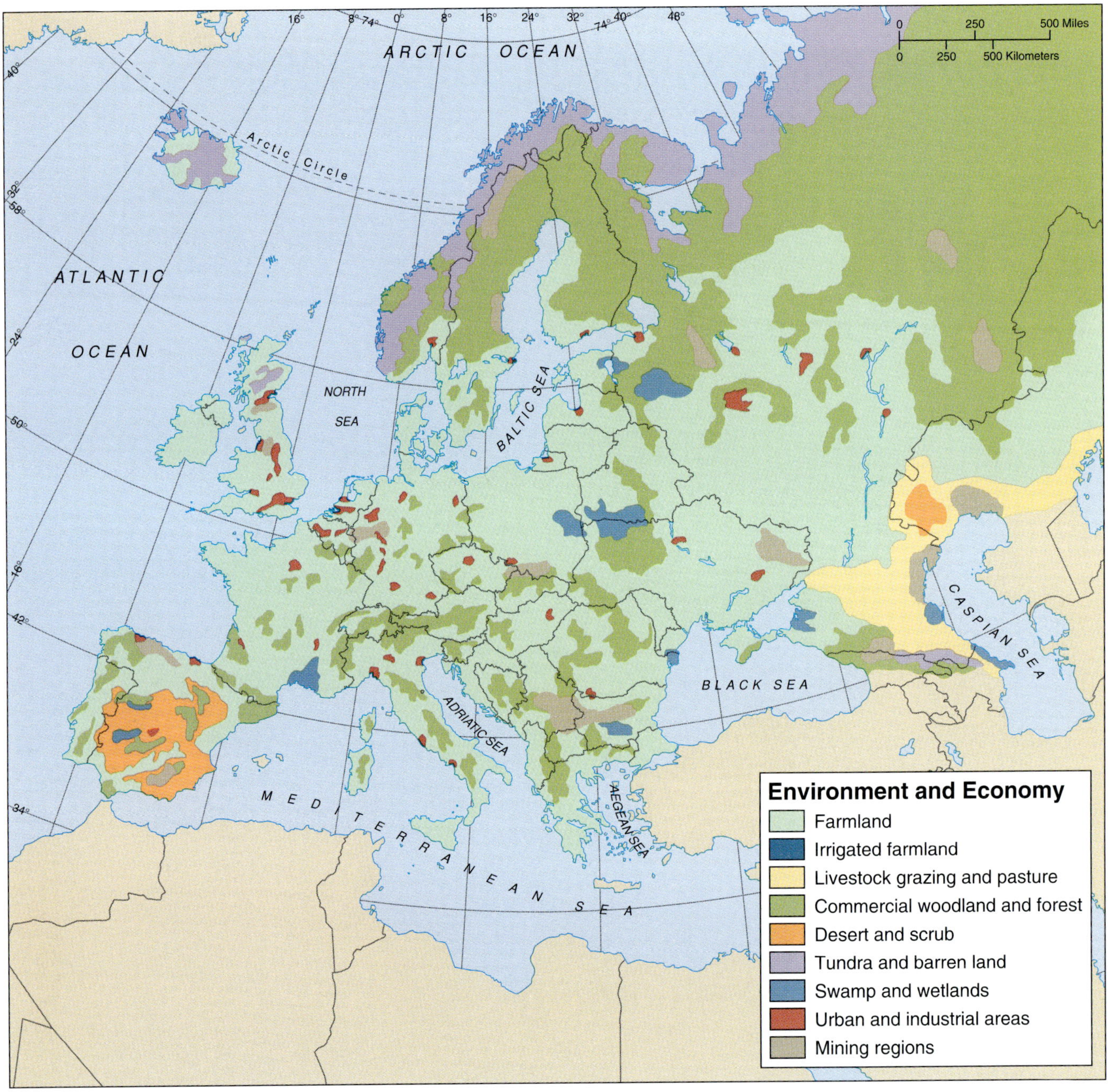

Map 78a Environment and Economy: The Use of Land

More than any other continent, Europe bears the imprint of human activity—mining, forestry, agriculture, industry, and urbanization. Virtually all of western and central Europe's natural forest vegetation is gone, lost to clearing for agriculture beginning in prehistory, to lumbering that began in earnest during the Middle Ages, or more recently, to disease and destruction brought about by acid precipitation. Only in the far north and the east do some natural stands remain. The region is the world's most heavily industrialized and the industrial areas on the map represent only the largest and most significant. Not shown are the industries that are found in virtually every small town and village and smaller city throughout the industrial countries of Europe. Europe also possesses abundant raw materials and a very productive agricultural base. The mineral resources have long been in a state of active exploitation and the mining regions shown on the map are, for the most part, old regions in upland areas that are somewhat less significant now than they may have been in the past. Agriculturally, the northern European plain is one of the world's great agricultural regions but most of Europe contains decent land for agriculture.

Map 78b Population Density

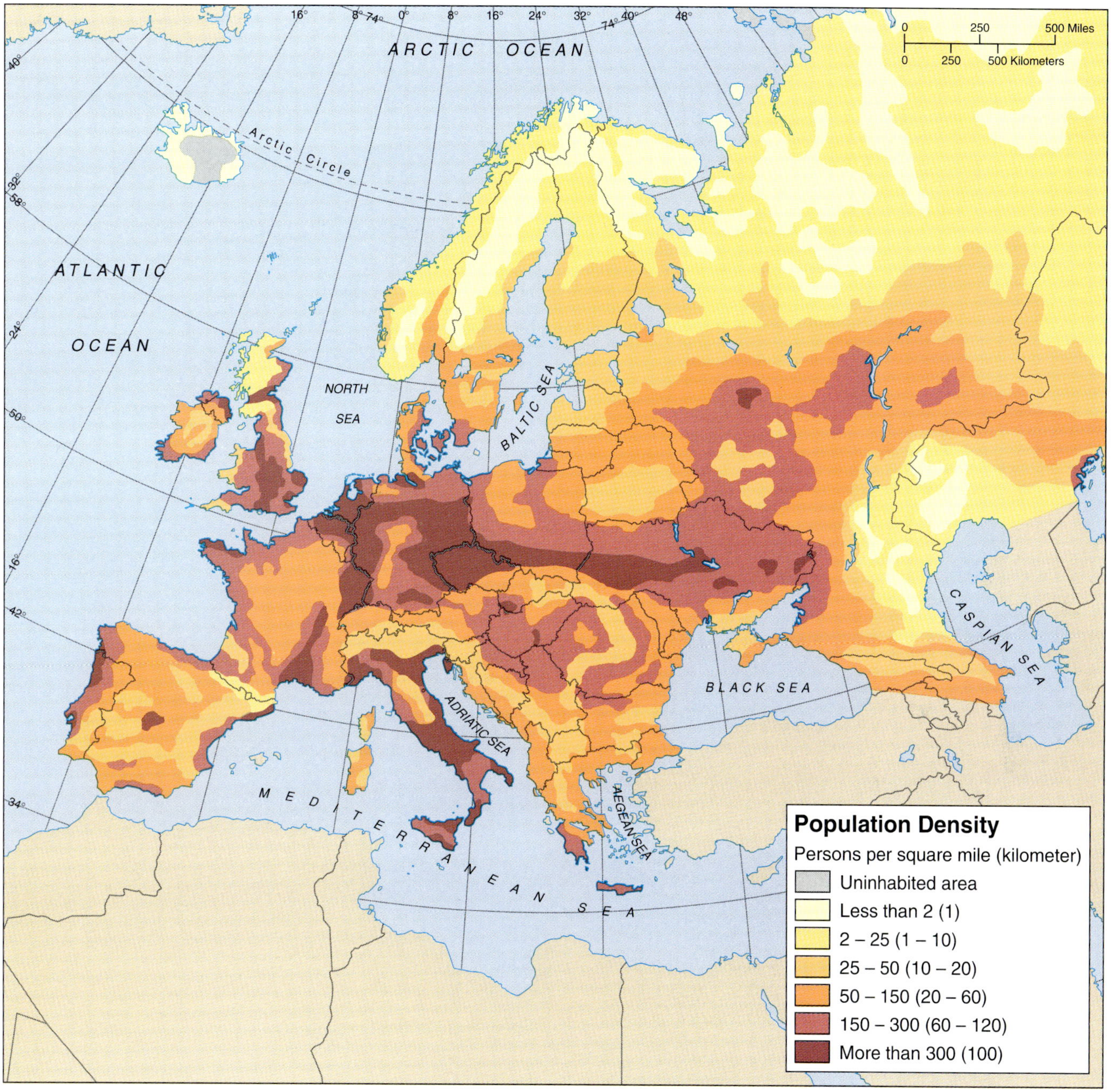

Europe is one of the most densely settled regions of the world with an overall population density nearing 200 persons per square mile (80 per square kilometer), the consequence of a high level of urbanization and an economic system that is heavily industrialized. Even in agricultural regions, the population density is high. Beyond high density, the two chief identifying marks of the European population are remarkable diversity and unusual dynamics. For a small part of the world, Europe has cultural and ethnic diversity that is rarely matched elsewhere; more than 60 languages are spoken in an area not much larger than the United States. The population dynamics of Europe show a mature population that has passed through the "Demographic Transition"—a remarkable increase and then decline in growth rates resulting from the rise of an urban-industrial society. Only in other heavily industrialized regions of the world are found the very small overall growth rates characteristic of Europe.

Map 78c Political Changes in the 1990s

Europe: Political Changes in the 1990s

1989

- Union of Soviet Socialist Republics
- Warsaw Pact Countries (excluding the USSR)
- North Atlantic Treaty Organization Countries
- European Community (formerly the EEC)

1999

- Former Republics of the USSR, now independent countries
- Russian Federation
- New European Countries resulting from reunification
- New European Countries resulting from partition
- NATO Countries, 1999
- Associated with NATO / Petitioned for entry
- European Union (formerly the EC)
- 2000 Year of projected entry into the European Union

During the last decade of the twentieth century, one of the most remarkable series of political geographic changes of the last 500 years took place. The bipolar "East-West" structure that had characterized Europe's political geography since the end of the Second World War altered in the space of a very few years. In the mid-1980s, as Soviet influence over eastern and central Europe weakened, those countries began to turn to the capitalist West. Between 1989, when the country of Hungary was the first Soviet satellite to open its borders to travel, and 1991, when the Soviet Union dissolved into 15 independent countries, abrupt change in political systems occurred. The result is a new map of Europe that includes a number of countries not present on the map of 1989. These countries have emerged as the result of reunification, separation, or independence from the old Soviet Union. The new political structure has been accompanied by growing economic cooperation.

Map 79 Western Europe

Map 80 Eastern Europe

Map 81 Northern Europe

Map 82 Africa Political Map

Map 83 Africa Physical Map

Africa Thematic Maps

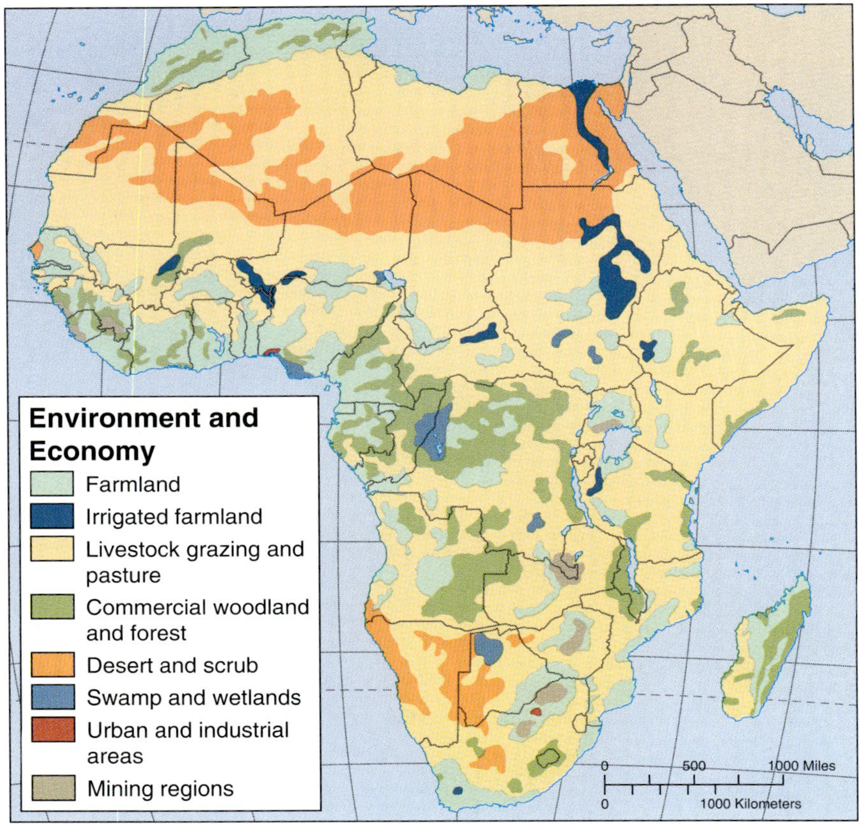

Map 84a Environment and Economy

Africa's economic landscape is dominated by subsistence, or marginally-commercial agricultural activities and raw material extraction, engaging three-fourths of Africa's workers. Much of this grazing land is very poor desert scrub and bunch grass that is easily impacted by cattle, sheep, and goats. Growing human and livestock populations place enormous stress on this fragile support capacity and the result is desertification: the conversion of even the most minimal of grazing environments to desert. Balanced against the enormous reaches of land suitable only for grazing is a small quantity of land suitable for crop farming. Although the continent has approximately 20 percent of the world's total land area, the proportion of Africa's arable land is small. The agricultural environment is also uncertain; unpredictable precipitation and poor soils hamper crop agriculture.

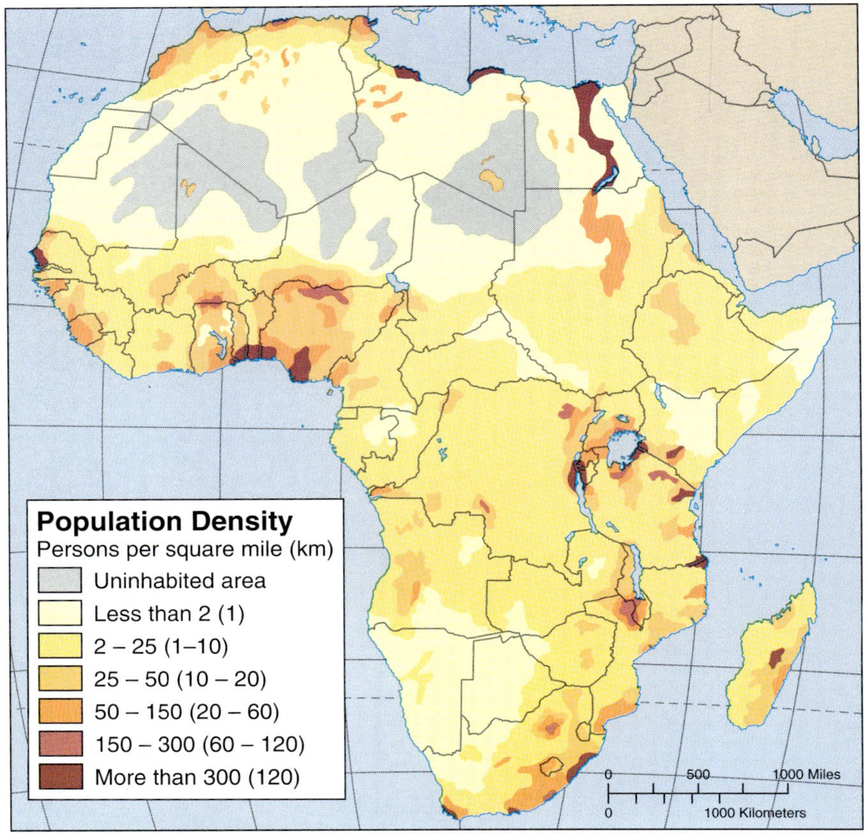

Map 84b Population Density

Nearly 800 million people occupy the African continent, approximately 1/8th of the world's population. In general, this population has two chief characteristics: a low level of quality of life and growth rates that are among the world's highest. On a continent beset by poverty, recurrent internal civil and tribal war, and a host of environmental problems, the populations of many African countries are nevertheless increasing at a rate above 3% per year. The bulk of the population is concentrated in relatively small areas of the Mediterranean coastal regions of the north, the bulge of West Africa, and the eastern coastal and highland zone stretching from South Africa to Kenya. Where populations in other parts of the world tend to avoid highland locations, in Africa highlands often tend to be the most densely settled regions: moister with better soils, freer of insect pests, and somewhat cooler.

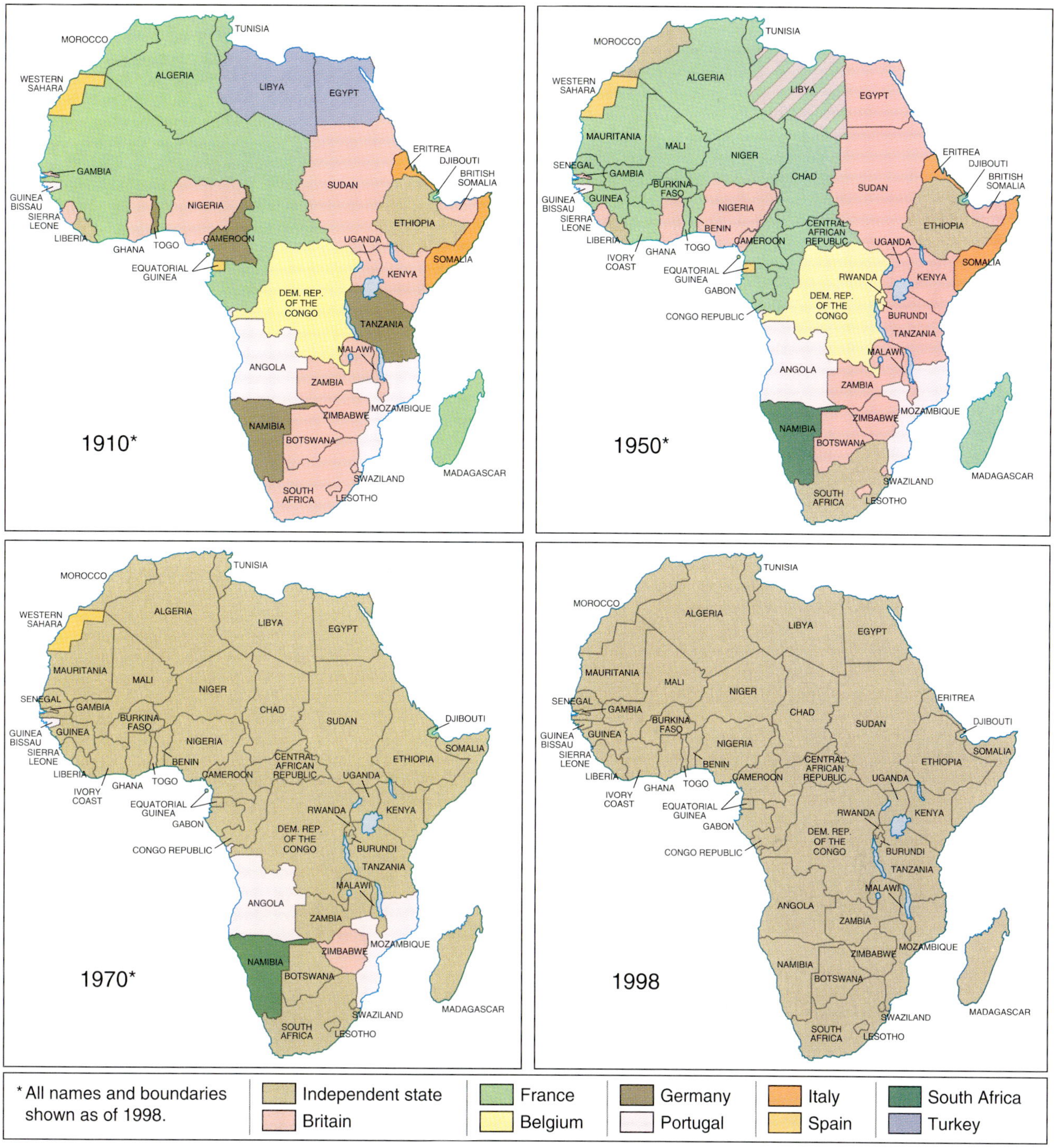

Map 84c Colonialism to Independence: 1910 to 1998

In few parts of the world has the transition from colonialism to independence been as abrupt as on the African continent. Most African states did not become colonies until the nineteenth century and did not become independent until the twentieth, nearly all of them after World War II. Much of the colonial legacy of the European colonial powers in Africa is social and economic. The African colony provided the mother country with raw materials in exchange for marginal economic returns, and many African countries still exist in this colonial dependency relationship. An even more important component of the colonial legacy of Europe in Africa is geopolitical. When the world's colonial powers joined at the Conference of Berlin in 1884, they divided up Africa to fit their own needs, drawing boundary lines on maps without regard for terrain or drainage features, or for tribal/ethnic linguistic, cultural, economic, or political borders. Traditional Africa was enormously disrupted by this process. After independence, African countries retained boundaries that are legacies of the colonial past and African countries today are beset by internal problems related to tribal and ethnic conflicts, the disruption of traditional migration patterns, and inefficient spatial structures of market and supply.

Map 85 Northern Africa

Map 86 Southern Africa

Map 87 Asia Political Map

Map 88 Asia Physical Map

Asia Thematic Maps

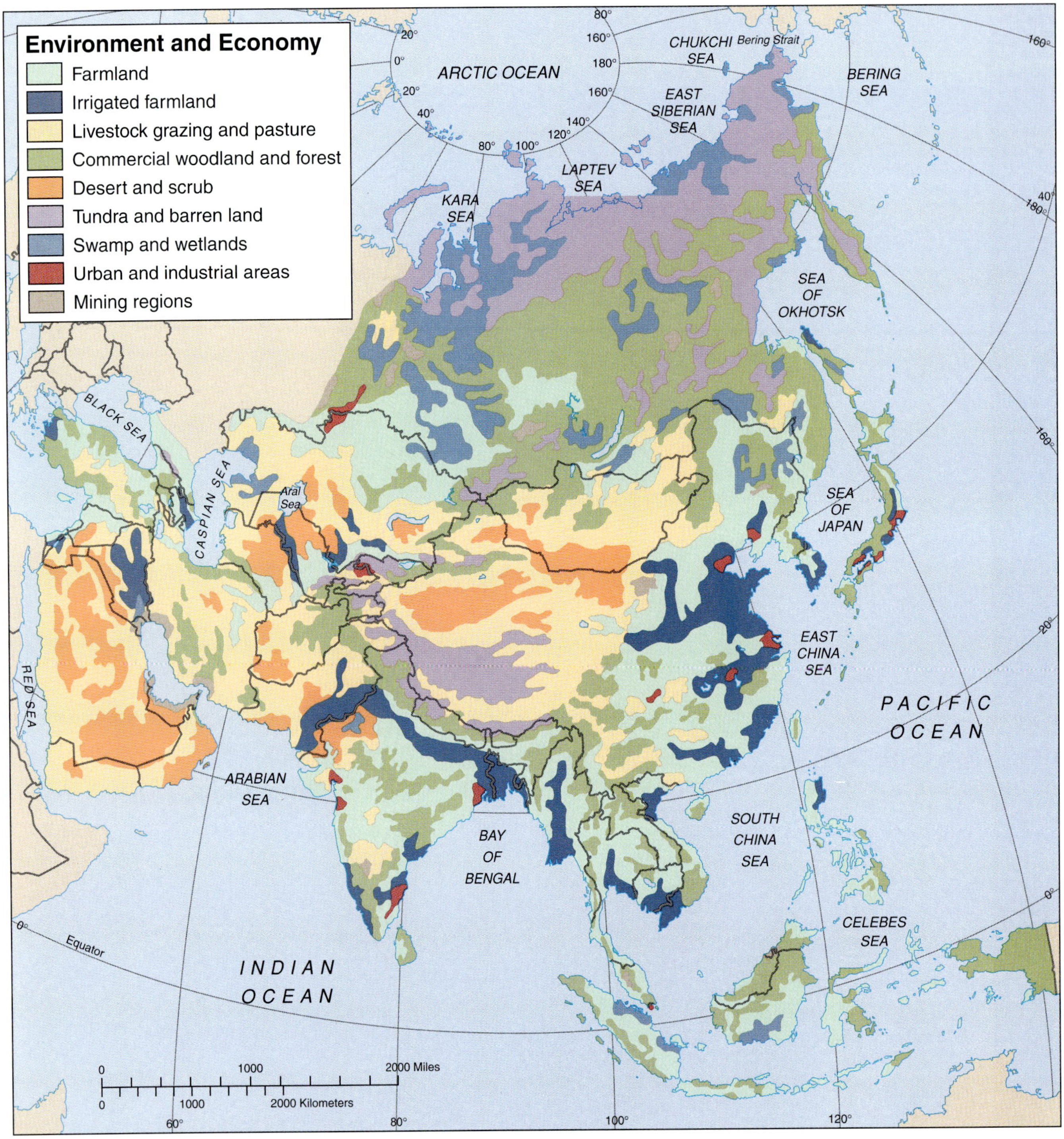

Map 89a Environment and Economy

Asia is a land of extremes of land use with some of the world's most heavily industrialized regions, barren and empty areas, and productive and densely populated farm regions. Asia is a region of rapid industrial growth. Yet Asia remains an agricultural region with three out of every four workers engaged in agriculture. Asian commercial agriculture and intensive subsistence agriculture is characterized by irrigation. Some of Asia's irrigated lands are desert requiring additional water. But most of the Asian irrigated regions have sufficient precipitation for crop agriculture and irrigation is a way of coping with seasonal drought—the wet-and-dry cycle of the monsoon—often gaining more than one crop per year on irrigated farms. Agricultural yields per unit area in many areas of Asia are among the world's highest. Because the Asian population is so large and the demands for agricultural land so great, Asia is undergoing rapid deforestation and some areas of the continent have only small remnants of a once-abundant forest reserve.

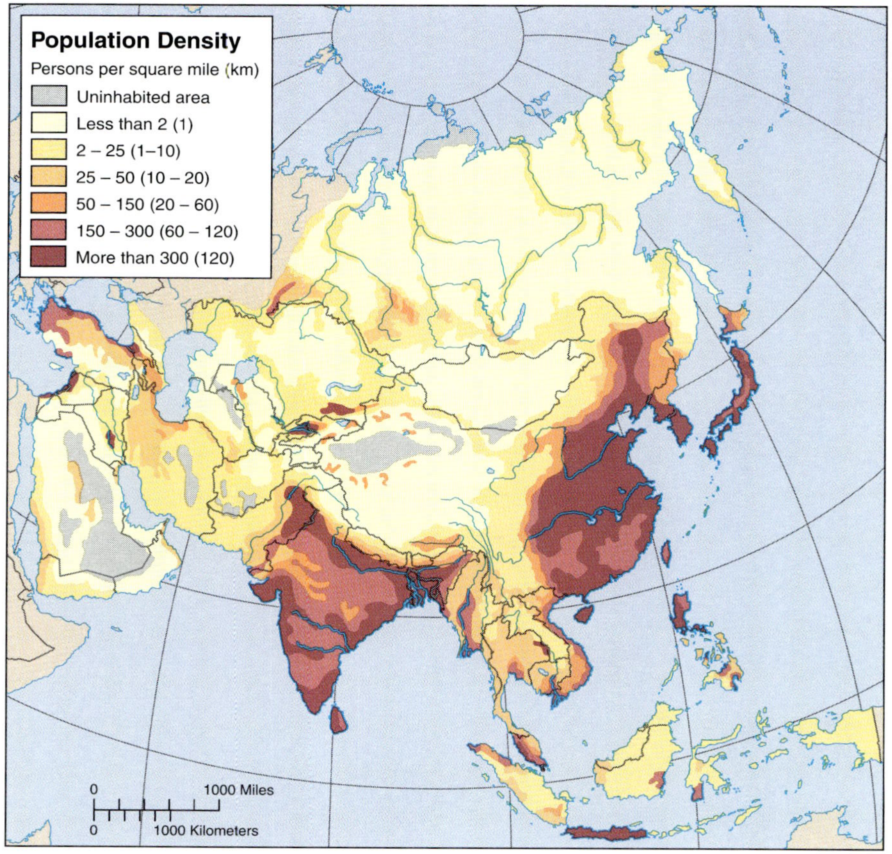

Map 89b Population Density

With one-third of the world's land area and nearly two-thirds of the world's population, Asia is more densely settled than any other region of the world. In some of the continent's farming regions, agricultural population density exceeds 2000 persons per square mile. In some portions of the continent, particularly the Islamic areas of Central and Southwest Asia, this already large population is growing very rapidly with some countries having population growth rates above 3% per year and doubling times between 20 and 25 years. The populations of neither China nor India are growing particularly rapidly but since both countries have population bases that are enormous, the absolute number of Indians and Chinese added to the world's population each year is staggering. In spite of these massive populations, Asia also contains areas that are either completely uninhabited or have population densities that are as low as any on earth.

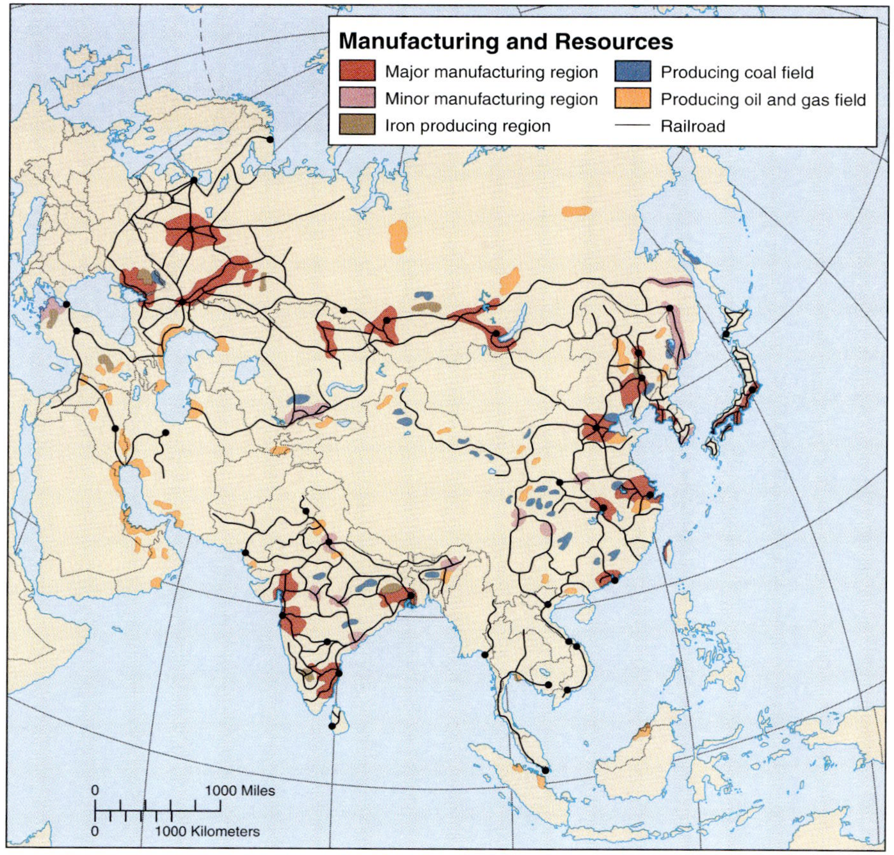

Map 89c Industrialization: Manufacturing and Resources

International economists have predicted that the next century will be one of Asian economic dominance, as other Asian nations approach the economic levels of industrial giant Japan. Asian countries have begun to industrialize rapidly and have increased industrial production more than 100 percent in the last decade. But nothing guarantees that this success will continue. Before Asia can rival Europe and North America in industrial output, it must master the great distances separating critical raw material and production sites from the locations of the markets for them. Such a mastery is achieved only by the development of efficient transportation systems. Usually that means water travel and here Asia is remarkably deficient when compared with Europe and North America. Nevertheless, the mixed prospects for Asian economic growth into the next century are a great deal better than would have been predicted a decade ago.

Map 90 Northern Asia

Map 91 Southwestern Asia

Map 92 Southern Asia

Map 93 East Asia

Map 94 Southeast Asia

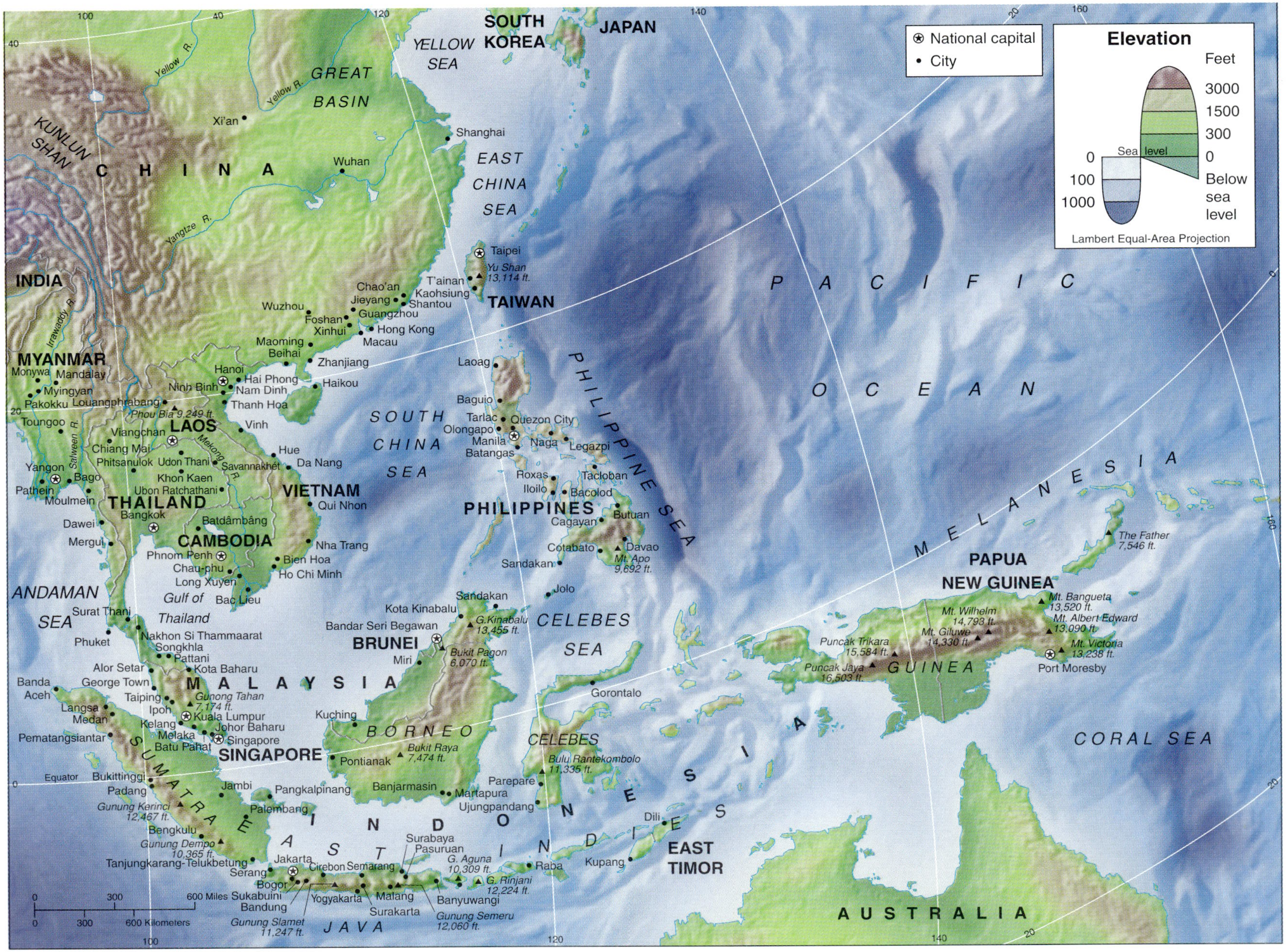

Map 95 Australasia Political Map

Map 96 Australasia Physical Map

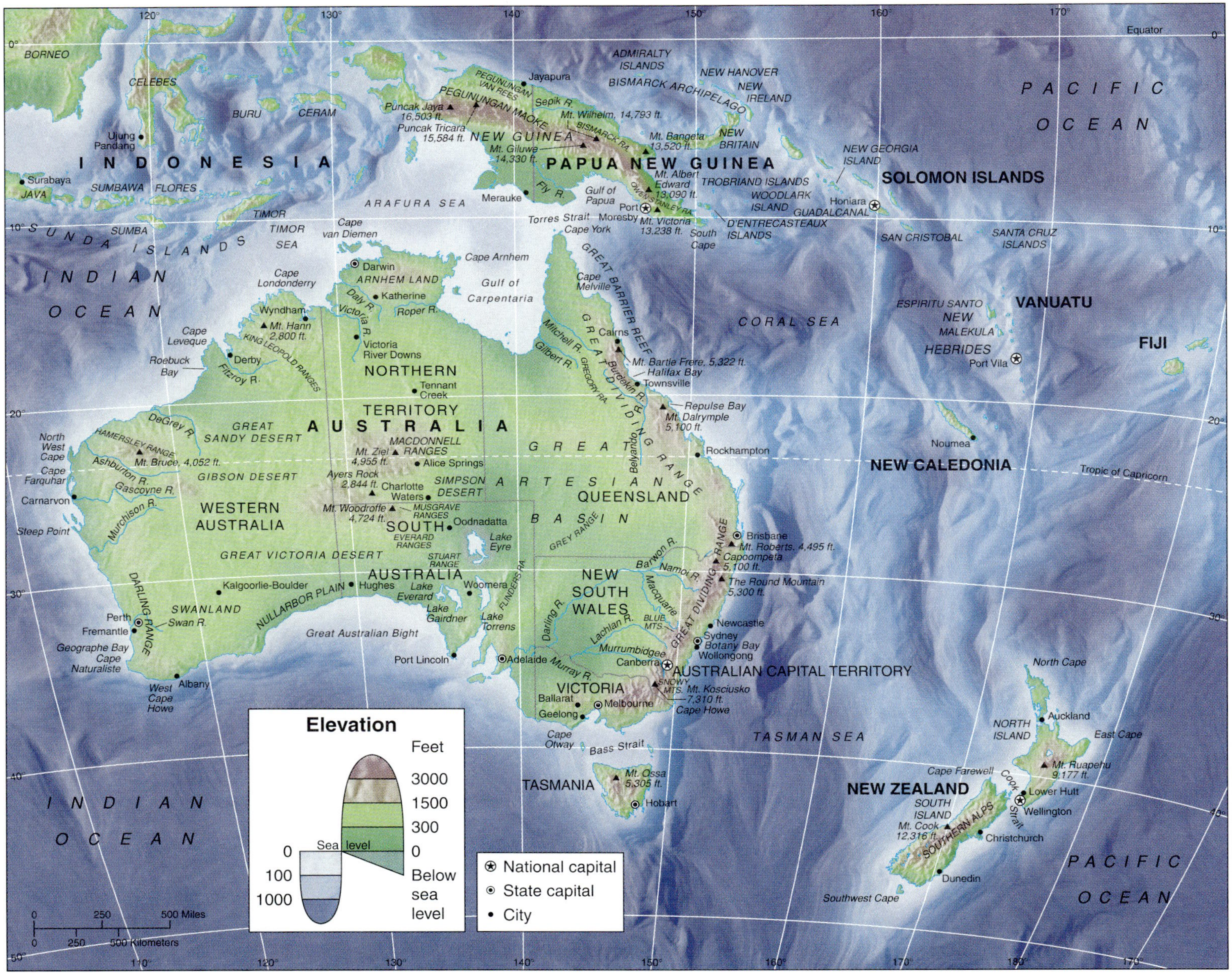

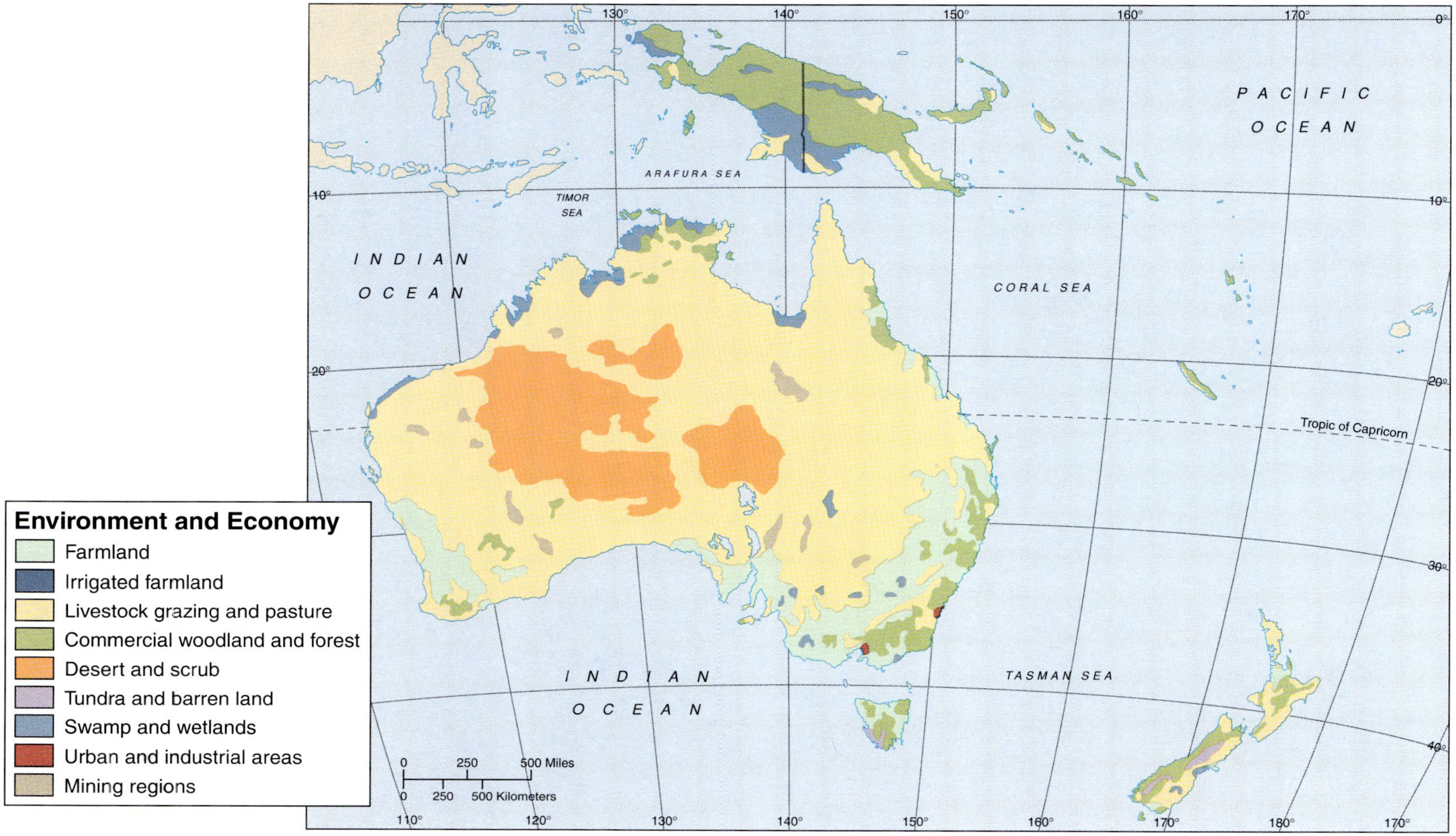

Map 97a Environment and Economy

Australasia is dominated by the world's smallest and most uniform continent. Flat, dry, and mostly hot, Australia has the simplest of land use patterns: where rainfall exists so does agricultural activity. Two agricultural patterns dominate the map: livestock grazing, primarily sheep, and wheat farming, although some sugar cane production exists in the north and some cotton is grown elsewhere. Only about 6 percent of the continent consists of arable land so the areas of wheat farming, dominant as they may be in the context of Australian agriculture, are small. Australia also supports a healthy mineral resource economy, with iron and copper and precious metals making up the bulk of the extraction. Elsewhere in the region, tropical forests dominate Papua New Guinea, with some subsistence agriculture and livestock. New Zealand's temperate climate with abundant precipitation supports a productive livestock industry and little else besides tourism—which is an important economic element throughout the remainder of the region as well.

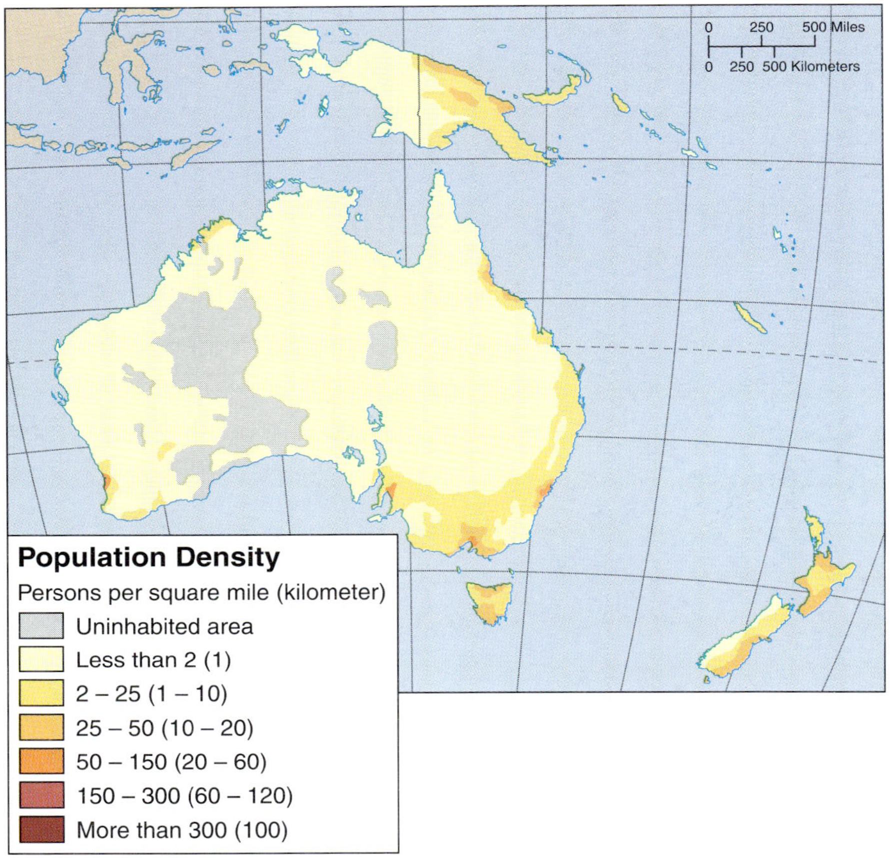

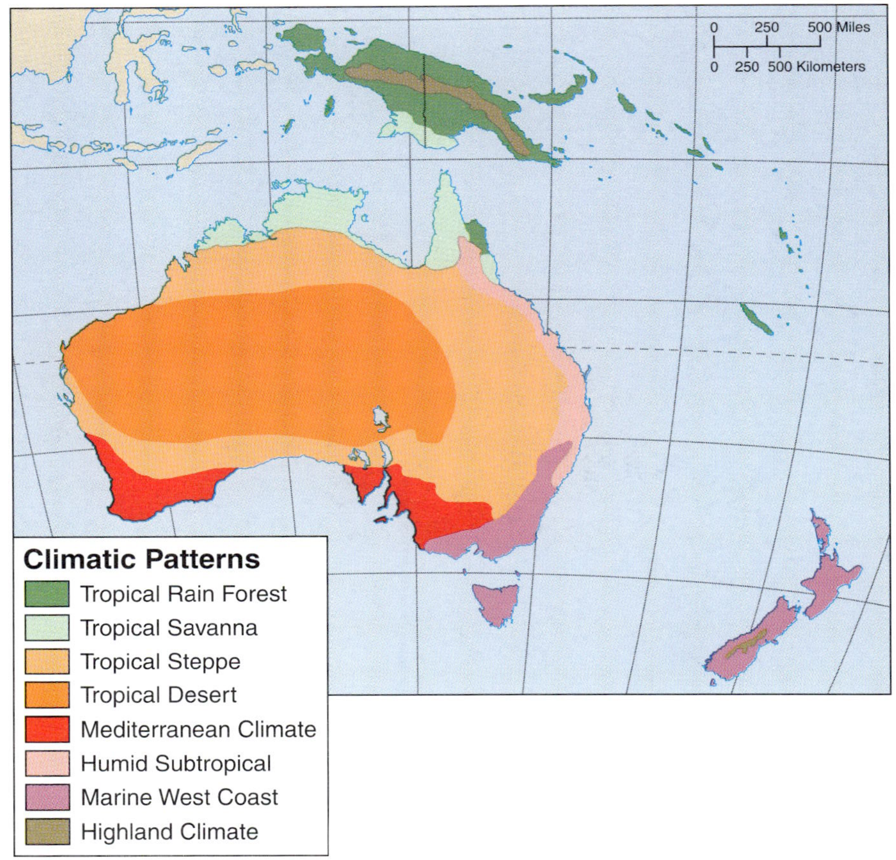

Map 97b Population Density

The region's small population is remarkably diverse. To the north are the Melanesian New Guinea peoples while Europeans dominate the populations of Australia and New Zealand, both of which have significant indigenous populations. Throughout most of the smaller island groups, the bulk of the population is Melanesian but with a scattering of Europeans. The distribution of population is extremely uneven with New Guinea, southeastern Australia, and New Zealand supporting the bulk of the region's people while the remainder of the region—meaning nearly all of Australia—is either sparsely populated or devoid of population altogether. Nowhere do population densities reach the levels they do in other major regions of the world and densities of 50 persons per square mile are the highest to be found. Population location is dependent on precipitation and population growth patterns are culturally variable.

Map 97c Climatic Patterns

Because of its nearly uniform surface, with only a few low and scattered uplands, Australian climate is a consequence only of the two great climate controls—latitudinal position and location relative to continental margin and interior. The continent bestrides the 30th parallel of latitude and its climatic pattern is dominated by the subtropical high pressure system with dry air masses that are responsible for the existence of great deserts. Toward the equator, the desert grades into steppe, savanna, and tropical forest as the subtropical high gives way to equatorial low pressure and abundant precipitation. Toward the pole, arid land fades into more well-watered steppe grasslands, the Mediterranean type climate of the southern margins of the continent, and the marine west coast climate of the Australian southeast and New Zealand. This latter climate is where most of the region's people live.

Map 98 Pacific Ocean

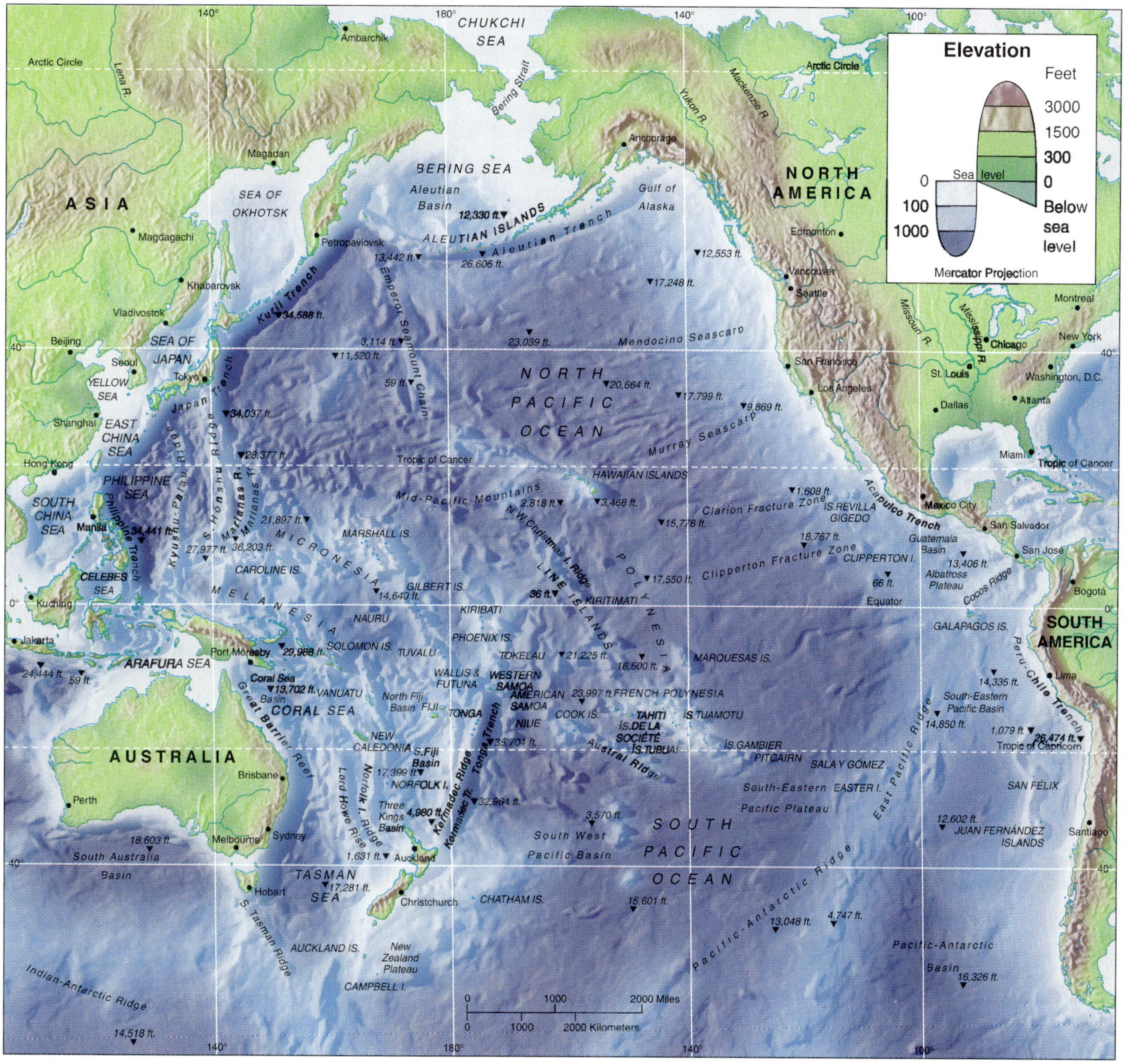

Map 99 Atlantic Ocean

Map 100 The Indian Ocean

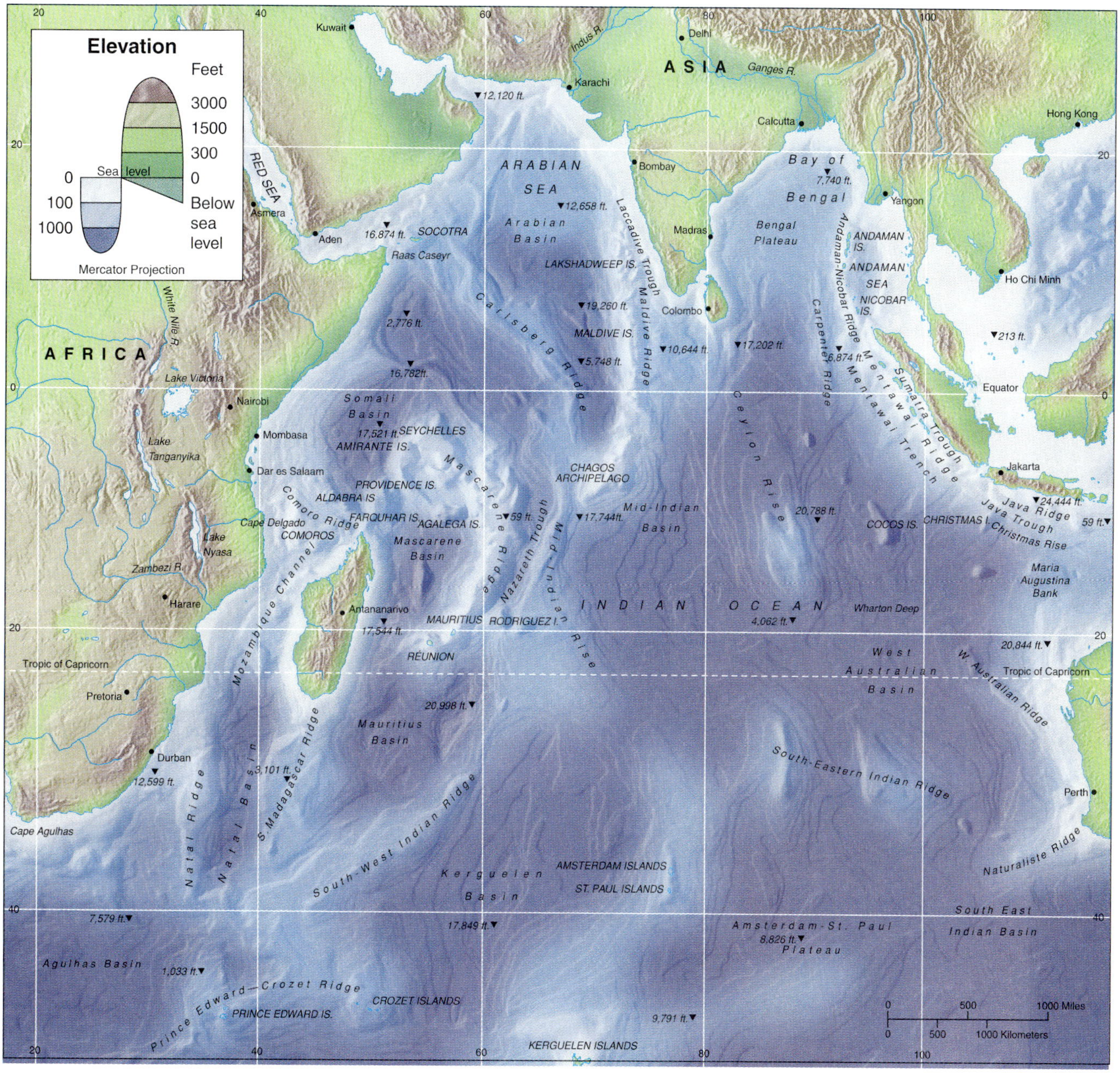

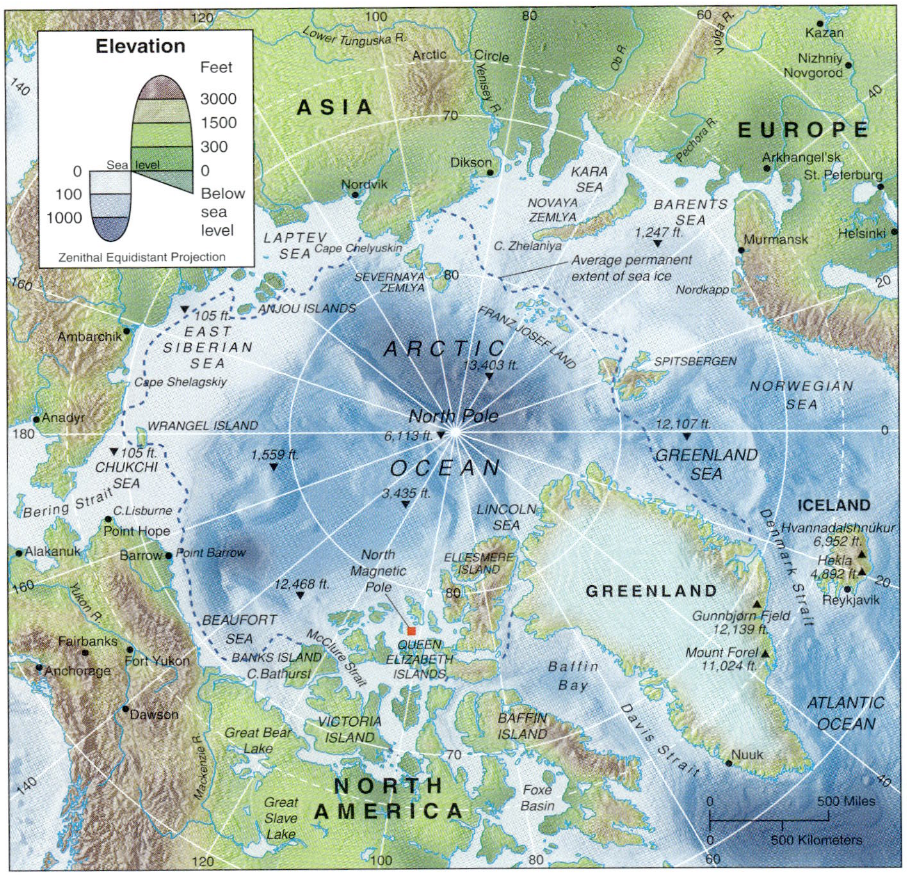

Map 101 The Arctic

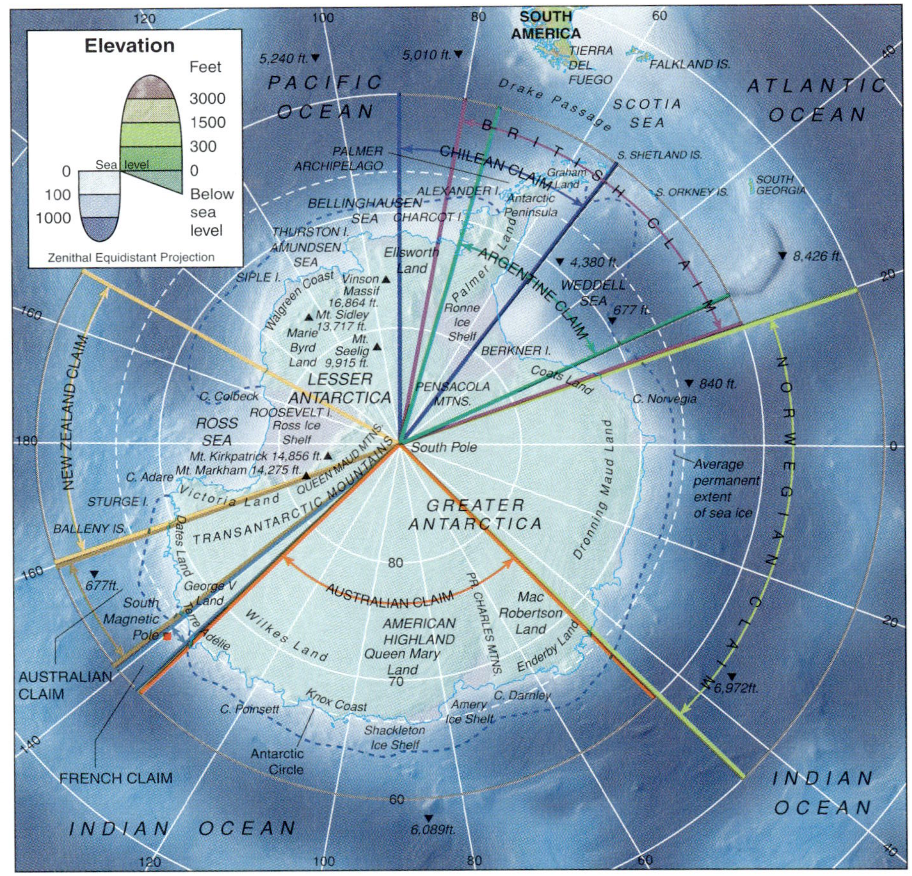

Map 102 Antarctica

Part VIII

World Countries: Data Tables

Table A

World Countries: Area, Population, and Population Density, 1998

COUNTRY	AREA		POPULATION	DENSITY	
	(Mi^2)	(Km^2)	(1998)[a]	(Pop/Mi^2)	(Pop/Km^2)
Afghanistan	251,826	652,229	23,738,085	94	36
Albania	11,100	28,749	3,293,252	297	115
Algeria	919,595	2,381,750	29,830,370	32	13
Andorra	175	453	74,839	428	165
Angola	481,354	1,246,706	10,523,994	22	8
Antigua and Barbuda	171	443	68,175	399	154
Argentina	1,073,400	2,780,104	35,797,536	33	13
Armenia	11,506	29,801	3,465,611	301	116
Australia	2,966,155	7,682,337	18,438,824	6	2
Austria	32,377	83,856	8,054,078	249	96
Azerbaijan	33,436	86,599	7,735,918	231	89
Bahamas	5,382	13,939	262,034	49	19
Bahrain	267	692	603,318	2,260	872
Bangladesh	55,598	143,999	125,340,261	2,254	870
Barbados	166	430	257,731	1,553	599
Belarus	80,155	207,601	10,439,916	130	50
Belgium	11,783	30,518	10,203,563	866	334
Belize	8,866	22,963	224,663	25	10
Benin	43,475	112,600	5,902,178	136	52
Bhutan	18,200	47,138	1,865,191	102	40
Bolivia	424,165	1,098,587	7,669,868	18	7
Bosnia-Herzegovina	19,741	51,129	2,607,734	132	51
Botswana	231,800	600,362	1,500,765	6	2
Brazil	3,286,488	8,511,999	164,611,355	50	19
Brunei Darussalam	2,226	5,765	307,616	138	53
Bulgaria	42,823	110,912	8,652,745	202	78
Burkina Faso	105,869	274,201	10,891,159	103	40
Burundi	10,745	27,830	6,052,614	563	217
Cambodia	69,898	181,036	11,164,861	160	62
Cameroon	183,569	475,443	14,877,510	81	31
Canada	3,849,674	9,970,650	29,123,194	8	3
Cape Verde	1,557	4,033	393,843	253	98
Central African Republic	240,535	622,985	3,342,051	14	5
Chad	495,755	1,284,005	7,166,023	14	6
Chile	292,135	756,629	14,508,168	50	19
China	3,689,631	9,556,139	1,210,004,956	328	127
Colombia	440,831	1,141,752	37,418,290	85	33
Comoros	863	2,235	589,797	683	264
Congo (Zaire)	905,446	2,345,104	47,440,362	52	20
Congo Republic	132,047	342,002	2,583,198	20	8
Costa Rica	19,730	51,101	3,353,174	170	66
Cote d'Ivoire	124,518	322,501	14,966,218	120	46
Croatia	21,829	56,537	5,026,995	230	89
Cuba	42,804	110,862	10,999,041	257	99
Cyprus	3,593	9,306	752,808	210	81
Czech Republic	30,613	79,288	10,318,958	337	130
Denmark	16,638	43,092	5,268,775	317	122
Djibouti	8,958	23,201	434,116	48	19
Dominica	305	790	83,226	273	105
Dominican Republic	18,704	48,443	828,151	44	17
Ecuador	109,484	283,563	11,690,535	107	41
Egypt	386,662	1,001,454	64,791,891	168	65
El Salvador	8,124	21,041	5,661,827	697	269
Equatorial Guinea	10,831	28,052	442,516	41	16
Eritrea	45,300	117,327	3,589,687	79	31
Estonia	17,413	45,100	1,444,721	83	32
Ethiopia	483,123	1,251,288	58,732,577	122	47
Fiji	7,078	18,332	792,441	112	43
Finland	130,559	338,148	5,109,148	39	15
France	211,208	547,028	58,040,230	275	106
Gabon	103,347	267,669	1,190,159	12	4
Gambia	4,127	10,689	1,248,085	302	117
Georgia	26,911	69,699	5,174,642	192	74
Germany	137,882	357,114	84,068,216	610	235
Ghana	92,098	238,534	18,100,703	197	76
Greece	50,962	131,992	10,583,126	208	80
Grenada	133	344	95,537	718	277
Guatemala	42,042	108,889	11,558,407	275	106
Guinea	94,926	245,858	7,405,375	78	30
Guinea-Bissau	13,948	36,125	1,178,584	84	33
Guyana	83,000	214,970	706,116	9	3
Haiti	10,714	27,749	6,611,407	617	238
Honduras	43,277	112,087	5,751,384	133	51
Hungary	35,920	93,033	9,935,774	277	107

(Continued on next page)

COUNTRY	AREA		POPULATION	DENSITY	
	(Mi²)	(Km²)	(1998)[a]	(Pop/Mi²)	(Pop/Km²)
Iceland	36,769	95,232	272,550	7	3
India	1,237,062	3,203,989	967,612,804	782	302
Indonesia	742,410	1,922,841	209,774,138	283	109
Iran	632,457	1,638,063	67,540,002	107	41
Iraq	169,235	438,318	22,219,289	131	51
Ireland	27,137	70,285	3,555,500	131	51
Israel[b]	8,019	20,769	5,534,872	690	266
Italy	116,234	301,046	57,534,088	495	191
Jamaica	4,244	10,992	2,615,582	616	238
Japan	145,870	377,803	125,716,637	862	333
Jordan	35,135	91,000	4,324,638	123	48
Kazakhstan	1,049,156	2,717,313	16,895,572	16	6
Kenya	224,961	582,649	28,803,085	128	49
Kiribati	280	725	82,449	294	114
Korea, North	46,540	120,539	24,317,004	522	202
Korea, South	38,230	99,016	45,948,811	1,202	464
Kuwait	6,880	17,819	2,076,805	302	117
Kyrgyzstan	76,641	198,500	4,540,185	59	23
Laos	91,429	236,801	5,116,959	56	22
Latvia	24,595	63,701	2,437,649	99	38
Lebanon	4,015	10,399	3,858,736	961	371
Lesotho	11,720	30,355	2,007,814	171	66
Liberia	38,250	99,067	2,602,068	68	26
Libya	679,362	1,759,547	5,648,359	8	3
Liechtenstein	62	161	31,461	507	196
Lithuania	25,174	65,201	3,635,932	144	56
Luxembourg	998	2,585	422,474	423	163
Macedonia	9,928	25,714	2,113,866	213	82
Madagascar	226,658	587,044	14,061,627	62	24
Malawi	45,747	118,485	9,609,081	210	81
Malaysia	129,251	334,760	20,376,235	158	61
Maldives	115	298	280,391	2,438	941
Mali	478,767	1,240,006	9,945,383	21	8
Malta	122	316	379,365	3,110	1,201
Marshall Islands	70	181	60,652	866	335
Mauritania	395,956	1,025,525	2,411,317	6	2
Mauritius	788	2,041	1,154,272	1,465	566
Mexico	756,066	1,958,210	97,563,374	129	50
Micronesia	271	702	127,616	471	182
Moldova	13,012	33,701	4,475,232	344	133
Monaco	1	2	31,892	43,688	16,868
Mongolia	604,829	1,566,506	2,538,211	4	2
Morocco	275,114	712,545	30,391,423	110	43
Mozambique	308,642	799,382	18,165,476	59	23
Myanmar (Burma)	261,228	676,580	46,821,943	179	69
Namibia	317,818	823,148	1,727,183	5	2
Nauru	8	21	10,390	1,267	489
Nepal	56,827	147,182	22,641,061	398	154
Netherlands	16,133	41,784	15,653,091	970	375
New Zealand	103,519	268,114	3,358,275	32	13
Nicaragua	50,054	129,640	4,386,399	88	34
Niger	489,191	1,267,004	9,388,859	19	7
Nigeria	356,669	923,772	107,129,469	300	116
Norway	125,050	323,879	4,404,456	35	14
Oman	82,030	212,458	2,264,590	28	11
Pakistan	310,432	804,018	132,185,299	426	164
Palau	177	458	17,240	97	38
Panama	29,157	75,517	2,693,417	92	36
Papua New Guinea	178,704	462,843	4,496,221	25	10
Paraguay	157,048	406,754	5,651,634	36	14
Peru	496,225	1,285,222	24,949,512	50	19
Philippines	115,831	300,002	76,103,564	657	254
Poland	120,728	312,685	38,700,291	321	124
Portugal	35,516	91,986	9,867,654	278	107
Qatar	4,416	11,437	665,485	151	58
Romania	91,699	237,500	21,399,114	233	90
Russian Federation	6,592,849	17,075,469	147,987,101	22	9
Rwanda	10,169	26,338	7,737,537	761	294
St. Kitts and Nevis	104	269	41,803	402	155
St. Lucia	238	616	159,639	671	259
St. Vincent/Grenadines	150	388	119,092	794	307
Samoa	1,093	2,831	219,509	201	78
San Marino	24	62	24,714	1,030	398
São Tomé and Principe	372	963	147,865	397	153
Saudi Arabia	830,000	2,149,699	20,087,965	24	9
Senegal	75,951	196,713	9,403,546	124	48
Seychelles	175	453	78,142	447	172
Sierra Leone	27,925	72,326	4,891,546	175	68
Singapore	246	637	3,461,929	14,073	5,434

(Continued on next page)

COUNTRY	AREA		POPULATION	DENSITY	
	(Mi^2)	(Km^2)	(1998)[a]	(Pop/Mi^2)	(Pop/Km^2)
Slovak Republic	18,933	49,036	5,393,016	285	110
Slovenia	7,819	20,251	1,945,998	0	0
Solomon Islands	10,594	28,371	426,855	39	15
Somalia	246,201	637,660	9,940,232	40	16
South Africa	433,680	1,123,231	42,327,458	98	38
Spain	194,885	504,752	39,244,195	201	78
Sri Lanka	24,962	64,652	18,762,075	752	290
Sudan	967,500	2,505,824	32,594,128	34	13
Suriname	63,251	163,820	443,446	7	3
Swaziland	6,704	17,363	1,031,600	154	59
Sweden	173,732	449,966	8,946,193	51	20
Switzerland	15,943	41,292	7,248,984	455	176
Syria	71,498	185,180	16,137,899	226	87
Taiwan	13,900	36,001	21,655,515	1,558	602
Tajikistan	55,251	143,100	6,013,855	109	42
Tanzania	364,900	945,090	29,460,753	81	31
Thailand	198,115	513,118	59,450,818	300	116
Togo	21,925	56,786	4,735,610	216	83
Tonga	290	751	107,335	370	143
Trinidad and Tobago	1,980	5,128	1,273,141	643	248
Tunisia	63,170	163,610	9,183,097	145	56
Turkey	300,948	779,455	63,528,225	211	82
Turkmenistan	188,456	488,101	4,225,351	22	9
Tuvalu	10	26	10,297	1,030	398
Uganda	93,104	241,139	20,604,874	221	85
Ukraine	233,090	603,703	50,684,635	217	84
United Arab Emirates	32,278	83,600	2,262,309	70	27
United Kingdom	94,248	244,102	58,610,182	622	240
United States	3,787,425	9,809,425	267,954,767	71	27
Uruguay	68,500	177,415	3,261,707	48	18
Uzbekistan	172,742	447,402	23,860,452	138	53
Vanatu	4,707	12,191	181,358	39	15
Venezuela	352,145	912,055	22,396,407	64	25
Vietnam	128,066	331,691	75,123,880	587	226
Yemen	205,356	531,872	13,972,477	68	26
Yugoslavia (Serbia-Montenegro)	26,913	69,705	10,655,317	396	153
Zambia	290,586	752,617	9,349,975	32	12
Zimbabwe	150,873	390,761	11,423,175	76	29

[a]Primary source for population figures: United Nations Population Division and International Labour Organisation.

[b]The figures for Israel do not include the West Bank and Gaza. The former has an area of approximately 2,300 square miles, a population of 1.8 million, and a density of about 780 persons per square mile; the latter has an area of 100 square miles, a population of nearly 900,000 persons, and an estimated population density of 8,700 persons per square mile.

Sources: The World Almanac and Book of Facts, 1998 (St. Martin's Press, New York, 1998); *The New York Times 1998 Almanac* (Penguin Putnam, Inc., New York, 1998); U.S. Census Bureau, *World Population Profile* (1998).

Table B

World Countries: Form of Government, Capital City, Major Languages

Notes: Unless indicated otherwise, republics are multi-party. "Theocratic" normally refers to fundamentalist Islamic rule. "Transitional" governments are those still in the process of change from a previous form (eg. single-party communist state to multi-party republic).

COUNTRY	GOVERNMENT	CAPITAL	MAJOR LANGUAGES
Afghanistan	Theocratic republic/transitional	Kabul	Dari, Pashton, Uzbek, Turkmen
Albania	Democratic	Tiranë	Albanian, Greek
Algeria	Military-transitional	Algiers	Arabic, Berber dialects, French
Andorra	Parliamentary democracy	Andorra	Catalán, French, Spanish
Angola	Multi-party democracy	Luanda	Portugese, indigenous
Antigua and Barbuda	Parliamentary democracy	St. John's	English, local dialects
Argentina	Federal republic	Buenos Aires	Spanish, English, Italian, German
Armenia	Republic	Yerevan	Armenian, Azerbaijani, Russian
Australia	Federal parliamentary	Canberra	English, indigenous
Austria	Federal republic	Vienna	German
Azerbaijan	Republic	Baku	Azerbaijani, Russian, Armenian
Bahamas	Independent commonwealth	Nassau	English
Bahrain	Traditional monarchy	Al Manamah	Arabic, English, Farsi, Urdu
Bangladesh	Republic	Dhaka	Bangla, English
Barbados	Parliamentary state	Bridgetown	English
Belarus	Republic	Minsk	Byelorussian, Russian
Belgium	Constitutional monarchy	Brussels	Dutch (Flemish), French, German
Belize	Parliamentary state	Belmopan	English, Spanish, Garifuna, Mayan
Benin	Multi-party republic	Porto-Novo	French, Fon, Adja, indigenous
Bhutan	Monarchy	Thimphu	Dzongha, Tibetan, Nepalese
Bolivia	Republic	La Paz	Spanish, Quechua, Aymara
Bosnia-Herzegovina	Republic/transitional	Sarajevo	Serb, Croat, Albanian
Botswana	Parliamentary republic	Gaborone	English, Tswania
Brazil	Federal republic	Brasília	Portugese, Spanish, English, French
Brunei	Constitutional monarchy	Bandar	Malay, English, Chinese
Bulgaria	Republic/transitional	Sofia	Bulgarian
Burkina Faso	Provisional military	Ouagadougou	French, indigenous
Burundi	Republic/transitional	Bujumbura	French, Kirundi, Swahili
Cambodia	Transitional UN management	Phnom Penh	Khmer, French
Cameroon	Multi-party republic	Yaoundé	English, French, indigenous
Canada	Federal parliamentary	Ottawa	English, French
Cape Verde	Republic	Praia	Portugese, Crioulu
Central African Republic	Republic	Bangui	French, Sango, Arabic, indigenous
Chad	Republic	N'Djamena	Arabic, French, indigenous
Chile	Republic	Santiago	Spanish
China	Single-party communist state	Beijing	Chinese dialects
Colombia	Republic	Bogotá	Spanish
Comoros	Republic	Moroni	Arabic, French, Shaafi Islam
Congo (Zaire)	Republic	Kinshasa	French, Lingala, Kingwana, Kikongo, Tshuliba
Congo Republic	Multi-party republic	Brazzaville	French, indigenous
Costa Rica	Republic	San José	Spanish
Côte d'Ivoire	Republic	Abidjan	French, indigenous
Croatia	Parliamentary democracy	Zaghreb	Croat, Serb
Cuba	Single-party communist state	Havana	Spanish
Cyprus	Republic	Nicosia	Greek, Turkish, English
Czech Republic	Federal republic	Prague	Czech, Slovak, Hungarian
Denmark	Constitutional monarchy	Copenhagen	Danish
Djibouti	Republic	Djibouti	French, Somali, Afar, Arabic
Dominica	Republic	Rosseau	English, French
Dominican Republic	Republic	Santo Domingo	Spanish
Ecuador	Republic	Quito	Spanish, Quechua, indigenous
Egypt	Republic	Cairo	Arabic
El Salvador	Republic	San Salvador	Spanish, Nahua
Equatorial Guinea	Republic	Malabo	Spanish, indigenous, English
Eritrea	Transitional government	Asmara	Afar, Bilen, Hadareb, Kunuama, Nara
Estonia	Republic	Tallinn	Estonian, Russian
Ethiopia	Republic/transitional	Addis Ababa	Amharic, Tigrinya, Orominga, Arabic
Fiji	Republic	Suva	English, Fijian, Hindustani
Finland	Republic	Helsinki	Finnish, Swedish
France	Republic	Paris	French
Gabon	Single-party republic	Libreville	French, Fang, indigenous
Gambia	Republic	Banjul	English, Malinke, Wolof, Fula
Georgia	Republic	Tbilisi	Georgian, Russian, Armenian
Germany	Federal republic	Berlin and Bonn	German
Ghana	Parliamentary democracy	Accra	English, Akan, indigenous

(Continued on next page)

COUNTRY	GOVERNMENT	CAPITAL	MAJOR LANGUAGES
Greece	Parliamentary democracy	Athens	Greek
Grenada	Parliamentary state	St. George's	English, French
Guatemala	Republic	Guatemala	Spanish, indigenous
Guinea	Republic/transitional	Conakry	French, indigenous
Guinea-Bissau	Single-party republic	Bissau	Portugese, Crioulo, indigenous
Guyana	Republic	Georgetown	English, indigenous
Haiti	Republic	Port-au-Prince	Creole, French
Honduras	Republic	Tegucigalpa	Spanish, indigenous
Hungary	Republic	Budapest	Hungarian
Iceland	Republic	Reykjavík	Icelandic
India	Federal republic	New Delhi	English, Hindi, Telugu, Bengali
Indonesia	Republic	Jakarta	Indonesian, Javanese, Sundanese
Iran	Theocratic republic	Tehran	Farsi, Turkish, Kurdish, Arabic, English
Iraq	Single-party republic	Baghdad	Arabic, Kurdish, Assyrian, Armenian
Ireland	Republic	Dublin	English, Irish Gaelic
Israel	Republic	Jerusalem	Hebrew, Arabic, Yiddish
Italy	Republic	Rome	Italian
Jamaica	Parliamentary state	Kingston	English, Creole
Japan	Constitutional monarchy	Tokyo	Japanese
Jordan	Constitutional monarchy	Amman	Arabic
Kazakhstan	Republic/transitional	Alma-Ata	Kazakh, Russian, German, Ukranian
Kenya	Republic	Nairobi	English, Swahili, indigenous
Kiribati	Republic	Tarawa	English, Gilbertese
Korea, North	Single-party communist state	Pyongyang	Korean
Korea, South	Republic	Seoul	Korean
Kuwait	Constitutional monarchy	Kuwait	Arabic, English
Kyrgyzstan	Republic/transitional	Bishkek	Kirghiz, Russian, Uzbek
Laos	Single-party communist state	Viangchan	Lao, French, Thai, indigenous
Latvia	Republic	Riga	Latvian, Russian
Lebanon	Republic	Beirut	Arabic, French, Armenian, English
Lesotho	Constitutional monarchy	Maseru	English, Sesotho, Zulu, Xhosa
Liberia	Republic	Monrovia	English, indigenous
Libya	Single-party parliamentary state	Tripoli	Arabic
Liechtenstein	Constitutional monarchy	Vaduz	German
Lithuania	Republic	Vilnius	Lithuanian, Russian, Polish
Luxembourg	Constitutional monarchy	Luxembourg	French, Luxembourgish, German
Macedonia	Republic/transitional	Skopje	Macedonian, Albanian
Madagascar	Military/transitional	Antananarivo	Malagasy, French
Malawi	Single-party republic	Lilongwe	Chichewa, English, Tombuka
Malaysia	Constitutional monarchy	Kuala Lumpur	Malay, Chinese, English
Maldives	Republic	Male	Divehi
Mali	Single-party republic	Bamako	French, Bambara, indigenous
Malta	Parliamentary democracy	Valletta	English, Maltese
Marshall Islands	Constitutional government	Majuro	English, Polynesian dialects, Japanese
Mauritania	Republic/transitional	Nouakchott	Arabic, French, indigenous
Mauritius	Parliamentary state	Port Louis	English, Creole, Bhojpun, Hindu
Mexico	Federal republic	Mexico City	Spanish, indigenous
Micronesia	Republic	Kolonia	English, Malay-Polynesian languages
Moldova	Republic	Kishinev	Moldavian, Russian, Ukrainian
Monaco	Constitutional monarchy	Monaco	French, English, Italian, Monegasque
Mongolia	Single-party communist state	Ulan Bator	Khalkha Mongol, Kazakh, Russian
Morocco	Constitutional monarchy	Rabat	Arabic, Berber dialects, French
Mozambique	Republic	Maputo	Portuguese, indigenous
Myanmar (Burma)	Provisional military	Rangoon	Burmese, indigenous
Namibia	Republic	Windhoek	Afrikaans, English, German, indigenous
Nauru	Republic	Yaren district	Nauruan, English
Nepal	Constitutional monarchy	Kathmandu	Nepali, Maithali, Bhojpuri, indigenous
Netherlands	Constitutional monarchy	Amsterdam	Dutch
New Zealand	Parliamentary state	Wellington	English, Maori
Nicaragua	Republic	Managua	Spanish, English, indigenous
Niger	Provisional military	Niamey	French, Hausa, Djerma, indigenous
Nigeria	Provisional military	Lagos/Abuja	English, Hausa, Fulani, Yorbua, Ibo
Norway	Constitutional monarchy	Oslo	Norwegian, Lapp
Oman	Traditional monarchy	Muscat	Arabic, English, Baluchi, Urdu
Pakistan	Federal Islamic republic	Islamabad	English, Urdu, Punjabi, Pashto, Sindhi
Palau	Republic	Koror state	English, Palauan
Panama	Republic	Panama	Spanish, English, indigenous
Papua New Guinea	Parliamentary state	Port Moresby	English, Motu, Pidgin, indigenous
Paraguay	Republic (authoritarian)	Asunción	Spanish, Guarani
Peru	Republic	Lima	Quechua, Spanish, Aymara
Philippines	Republic	Manila	English, Philipino, Tagalog
Poland	Republic	Warsaw	Polish

(Continued on next page)

COUNTRY	GOVERNMENT	CAPITAL	MAJOR LANGUAGES
Portugal	Republic	Lisbon	Portuguese
Qatar	Traditional monarchy	Doha	Arabic, English
Romania	Republic	Bucharest	Romanian, Hungarian, German
Russian Federation	Republic	Moscow	Russian, Tatar, Ukranian
Rwanda	Provisional military	Kigali	French, Kinyarwanda
St. Kitts and Nevis	Parliamentary state	Basseterre	English
St. Lucia	Parliamentary state	Castries	English, French
St. Vincent/Grenadines	Parliamentary state	Kingstown	English, French
Samoa	Constitutional monarchy	Apia	Samoan, English
San Marino	Republic	San Marino	Italian
São Tomé and Príncipe	Republic	São Tomé	Portuguese, Fang
Saudi Arabia	Islamic monarchy	Riyadh	Arabic
Senegal	Republic	Dakar	French, Wolof, indigenous
Seychelles	Republic	Victoria	English, French, Creole
Sierra Leone	Republic	Freetown	English, Krio, indigenous
Singapore	Republic	Singapore	Mandarin Chinese, English, Malay
Slovak Republic	Parliamentary democracy	Bratislava	Slovak, Hungarian, Polish
Slovenia	Republic/transitional	Ljubljana	Slovene
Solomon Islands	Parliamentary state	Honiara	English, Malay-Polynesian languages
Somalia	Provisional military	Mogadishu	Arabic, Somali, English, Italian
South Africa	Republic	Pretoria	Afrikaans, English, Zulu, Xhosa, other
Spain	Parliamentary monarchy	Madrid	Spanish, Catalán, Galician, Basque
Sri Lanka	Republic	Colombo	English, Sinhala, Tamil
Sudan	Islamic republic	Khartoum	Arabic, Dinka, Nubian
Suriname	Military/transitional	Paramaribo	Dutch, Sranan Tongo, English
Swaziland	Monarchy	Mbabane	English, Swahili
Sweden	Constitutional monarchy	Stockholm	Swedish
Switzerland	Federal republic	Bern	German, French, Italian, Romansch
Syria	Republic (authoritarian)	Damascus	Arabic, Kurdish, Armenian, Aramaic
Taiwan	Single-party republic	T'aipei	Chinese dialects
Tajikistan	Republic	Dushanbe	Tajik, Uzbek, Russian
Tanzania	Republic	Dar es Salaam	English, Swahili, indigenous
Thailand	Constitutional monarchy	Bangkok	Thai, indigenous
Togo	Single-party republic	Lomé	French, indigenous
Tonga	Constitutional monarchy	Nuku'alofa	Tongan, English
Trinidad and Tobago	Parliamentary democracy	Port of Spain	English, Hindi, French, Spanish
Tunisia	Republic	Tunis	Arabic, French
Turkey	Parliamentary democracy	Ankara	Turkish, Kurdish, Arabic
Turkmenistan	Republic	Ashkhabad	Turkmen, Russian, Uzbek, Kazakh
Tuvalu	Parliamentary democracy	Funafuti	Tuvaluan, English
Uganda	Republic	Kampala	English, Luganda, Swahili, indigenous
Ukraine	Republic	Kiev	Ukranian, Russian
United Arab Emirates	Federated monarchy	Abu Dhabi	Arabic, English, Farsi, Hindi, Urdu
United Kingdom	Constitutional monarchy	London	English, Welsh, Gaelic
United States	Federal republic	Washington	English, Spanish
Uruguay	Republic	Montevideo	Spanish
Uzbekistan	Republic	Tashkent	Uzbek, Russian, Kazakh, Tajik, Tatar
Vanatu	Republic	Port Vila	English, French, Bislama (pidgin)
Venezuela	Federal republic	Caracas	Spanish, indigenous
Vietnam	Single-party communist state	Hanoi	Vietnamese, French, Chinese, English
Yemen	Republic	San'a	Arabic
Yugoslavia (Serbia-Montenegro)	Republic	Belgrade	Serb, Albanian, Hungarian
Zambia	Single-party republic	Lusaka	English, Tonga, Lozi, other indigenous
Zimbabwe	Republic	Harare	English, ChiShona, SiNdebele

Sources: The World Almanac and Book of Facts, 2000 (St. Martin's Press, New York, 2000); *The New York Times 2000 Almanac* (Penguin Putnam, Inc., New York, 2000); U.S. Census Bureau, *World Population Profile* (2000).

Table C

World Countries: Basic Economic Indicators

COUNTRY	GROSS NATIONAL PRODUCT (GNP) 1998		GROSS DOMESTIC PRODUCT (GDP)1998		PURCHASING POWER PARITY (PPP) 1998		AVERAGE ANNUAL GROWTH RATE GDP 1980–1998 (percent)		DISTRIBUTION OF GDP, 1998 (percent)			
	Total (Billions $US)	Per Capita ($US)	Total (Millions $US)	Per Capita ($US)	Total (Billions $US)	Per Capita ($US)	1980–90	1990–98	Agriculture	Industry	Manufacturing	Services
AFRICA												
Algeria	46.5	1,550	49,585	1,662	131.4[c]	4,380[c]	2.7	1.2	12	47	9	41
Angola	4.1	340	6,648	632	10.1[c]	840[c]	3.7	-0.4	14	54	5	32
Benin	2.3	380	2,322	393	7.5	1,250	2.9	4.6	39	14	8	47
Botswana	5.6	3,600	5,690	3,791	13.0	8,310	10.3	4.8	4	46	5	51
Burkina Faso	2.6	240	2,581	237	11.0[c]	1,020[c]	3.6	3.5	32	28	21	40
Burundi	0.9	140	949	157	4.1[c]	620[c]	4.4	-3.2	49	19	11	32
Cameroon	8.7	610	8,736	587	25.9	1,810	3.4	0.6	42	22	11	36
Central African Republic	1.0	300	1,057	316	4.5[c]	1,290[c]	1.4	1.5	55	18	9	27
Chad	1.7	230	*1,603*	224	X	X	3.7	*4.6*	39	15	12	46
Congo (Zaire)	5.3	110	6,694	147	36.4[c]	750[c]	1.6	-5.1	*58*	17	X	25
Congo Republic	1.9	690	1,961	759	4.0	1,430	3.3	1.0	12	50	8	39
Côte d'Ivoire	10.1	700	11,041	738	25.0	1,730	0.7	3.5	25	23	19	52
Egypt	79.2	1,290	78,097	1,205	192.5	3,130	5.4	4.2	17	33	26	50
Equatorial Guinea	X	X	X	X	X	X	X	X	X	X	X	X
Eritrea	0.8	200	650	181	3.7	950	X	*5.2*	9	30	16	61
Ethiopia	6.1	100	6,568[a]	112	30.8	500	*1.1*[a]	4.9[a]	X[a]	X[a]	X[a]	X[a]
Gabon	X	X	X	X	X	X	X	X	X	X	X	X
Gambia	X	X	X	X	X	X	X	X	X	X	X	X
Ghana	7.2	390	7,501	414	29.8[c]	1,610[c]	3.0	4.2	37	25	8	38
Guinea	3.8	540	3,615	488	12.5	1,760	X	5.0	22	35	4	42
Guinea-Bissau	X	X	X	X	X	X	X	X	X	X	X	X
Kenya	9.7	330	11,083	385	33.1	1,130	4.2	2.2	29	16	10	55
Lesotho	1.2	570	792	394	4.8[c]	2,320[c]	4.4	7.2	*11*	42	17	47
Liberia	X	X	X	X	X	X	X	X	X	X	X	X
Libya	X	X	X	X	X	X	X	X	X	X	X	X
Madagascar	3.8	260	3,749	267	13.1	900	1.1	1.3	31	14	*11*	56
Malawi	2.1	200	1,643	171	7.7	730	2.5	3.9	39	19	15	41
Mali	2.6	250	2,695	271	7.7	720	0.9	3.7	45	21	6	34
Mauritania	1.0	410	971	403	4.2[c]	1,660[c]	1.8	4.2	24	30	9	45
Mauritius	X	X	X	X	X	X	X	X	X	X	X	X
Morocco	34.8	1,250	*33,514*	1,103	86.8	3,120	4.2	2.1	16	30	17	54
Mozambique	3.6	210	3,959	218	14.5[c]	850[c]	-0.1	5.7	*34*	18	10	48
Namibia	3.2	1,940	3,108	1,799	8.2[c]	4,950[c]	0.9	3.5	10	34	14	56
Niger	1.9	190	2,048	218	8.4	830	-0.1	1.9	41	17	6	42
Nigeria	36.4	300	41,353	386	99.7	820	1.6	2.6	32	41	5	27
Rwanda	1.9	230	2,082	269	5.6	690	2.2	-3.3	34	23	16	43
Senegal	4.8	530	4,836	514	15.4	1,710	3.1	3.0	17	23	15	59
Sierra Leone	0.7	140	647	132	1.9	390	0.3	-4.7	44	24	6	32
Somalia	X	X	X	X	X	X	X	X	X	X	X	X
South Africa	119.0	2,880	116,730	2,758	288.7[c]	6,990[c]	1.2	1.6	4	38	24	57
Sudan	X	X	X	X	X	X	X	X	X	X	X	X
Swaziland	X	X	X	X	X	X	X	X	X	X	X	X
Tanzania	6.7[b]	210[b]	7,917[b]	269	15.9	490	X	2.9[b]	46[b]	14[b]	7[b]	40[b]
Togo	1.5	330	1,510	319	6.2	1,390	1.7	2.3	42	21	9	37
Tunisia	19.2	2,050	22,041	X	48.3	5,160	3.3	4.4	14	28	18	58
Uganda	6.7	320	6,653	322	24.5[c]	1,170[c]	*3.2*	7.4	43	18	9	39

(Continued on next page)

COUNTRY	GROSS NATIONAL PRODUCT (GNP) 1998 Total (Billions $US)	GNP Per Capita ($US)	GROSS DOMESTIC PRODUCT (GDP)1998 Total (Millions $US)	GDP Per Capita ($US)	PURCHASING POWER PARITY (PPP) 1998 Total (Billions $US)	PPP Per Capita ($US)	AVERAGE ANNUAL GROWTH RATE GDP 1980–1998 (percent) 1980–90	1990–98	DISTRIBUTION OF GDP, 1998 (percent) Agriculture	Industry	Manufacturing	Services
Zambia	3.2	330	3,352	359	8.3	860	1.0	1.0	16	30	12	55
Zimbabwe	7.1	610	5,908	517	25.2	2,150	3.6	2.0	18	24	17	58
NORTH AND CENTRAL AMERICA												
Belize	X	X	X	X	X	X	X	X	X	X	X	X
Canada	612.2	20,020	598,847	20,563	735.6	24,050	3.3	2.2	X	X	X	X
Costa Rica	9.8	2,780	10,252	3,057	23.3	6,620	3.0	3.7	14	22	16	64
Cuba	X	X	X	X	X	X	X	X	X	X	X	X
Dominican Republic	14.6	1,770	15,489	18,703	38.8	4,700	3.1	5.5	12	33	17	56
El Salvador	11.2	1,850	12,148	2,146	17.3	2,850	0.2	5.3	13	28	22	59
Guatemala	17.7	1,640	19,281	1,668	44.0	4,070	0.8	4.2	21	19	13	60
Haiti	3.1	410	*2,815*	426	9.6[c]	1,250[c]	-0.2	*-2.5*	31	20	X	48
Honduras	4.5	730	*4,722*	821	13.2	2,140	2.7	3.6	23	30	18	47
Jamaica	4.3	1,680	6,607	X	8.3	3,210	2.0	0.1	7	35	16	58
Mexico	380.9	3,970	393,224	4,030	785.8[c]	8,190[c]	0.7	2.5	5	27	20	68
Nicaragua	X	X[f]	*1,971*	449	8.6[c]	1,790[c]	-2.0	*4.1*	34	22	16	44
Panama	8.5	3,080	9,218	3,422	19.2	6,940	0.5	4.3	7	17	9	76
Trinidad and Tobago	X	X	X	X	X	X	X	X	X	X	X	X
United States	7,921.3	29,340	8,210,600	30,642	7,922.6	29,340	3.0	2.9	*2*	27	18	71
SOUTH AMERICA												
Argentina	324.1	8,970	344,360	9,620	368.5	10,200	-0.4	5.3	7	37	25	56
Bolivia	7.9	1,000	8,558	1,116	22.4	2,820	-0.2	4.2	16	33	4	52
Brazil	758.0	4,570	778,292	4,728	1,021.4	6,160	2.7	3.3	8	36	23	56
Chile	71.3	4,810	78,025	5,378	191.1	12,890	4.2	7.9	8	35	17	57
Colombia	106.1	2,600	91,108	2,435	306.0	7,500	3.6	4.2	13	38	19	49
Ecuador	18.6	1,530	19,766	1,691	56.3	4,630	2.0	2.9	12	34	22	54
Guyana	X	X	X	X	X	X	X	X	X	X	X	X
Paraguay	9.2	1,760	8,571	1,517	19.0	3,650	2.5	2.8	25	22	15	53
Peru	61.1	2,460	64,122	2,570	X	X	-0.3	5.9	7	38	22	55
Suriname	X	X	X	X	X	X	X	X	X	X	X	X
Uruguay	20.3	6,180	20,155	6,179	31.2	9,480	0.4	3.9	8	27	18	64
Venezuela	81.3	3,500	105,756	4,722	190.4	8,190	1.1	2.0	4	43	17	52
ASIA												
Afghanistan	X	X	X	X	X	X	X	X	X	X	X	X
Armenia	1.8	480	*1,628*	470	X	X	X	-10.3	41	36	25	23
Azerbaijan	3.9	490	4,127	533	14.3	1,820	X	-10.5	19	44	9	36
Bangladesh	44.0	350	42,775	341	137.7	1,100	4.3	4.8	23	28	18	49
Bhutan	X	X	X	X	X	X	X	X	X	X	X	X
Cambodia	3.0	280	*3,089*	277	13.3	1,240	X	5.5	51	15	6	34
China	928.9	750	960,924	794	3,983.6	3,220	10.2	11.1	18	49	37	33
Georgia	5.1	930	*5,244*	1,013	X	X	0.4	-16.3	32	23	18	45
India	421.3	430	383,429	396	1,660.9	1,700	5.8	6.1	25	30	19	45
Indonesia	138.5	680	96,265	459	568.9	2,790	6.1	5.8	16	43	26	41
Iran	109.6	1,770	X	X	X	X	1.7	*4.0*	X	X	X	X
Iraq	X	X	X	X	X	X	X	X	X	X	X	X
Israel	95.2	15,940	100,031	18,073	103.4	17,310	3.5	5.4	X	X	X	X
Japan	4,089.9	32,380	3,783,140	30,093	2,928.4	23,180	4.0	1.3	X	X	X	X
Jordan	6.9	1,520	*7,015*	1,622	14.8	3,230	2.5	5.4	3	25	13	72
Kazakhstan	20.6	1,310	21,029	1,245	53.4	3.400	X	-6.9	10	27	12	63

(Continued on next page)

COUNTRY	GROSS NATIONAL PRODUCT (GNP) 1998 Total (Billions $US)	GNP Per Capita ($US)	GROSS DOMESTIC PRODUCT (GDP)1998 Total (Millions $US)	GDP Per Capita ($US)	PURCHASING POWER PARITY (PPP) 1998 Total (Billions $US)	PPP Per Capita ($US)	AVERAGE ANNUAL GROWTH RATE GDP 1980–1998 (percent) 1980–90	1990–98	DISTRIBUTION OF GDP, 1998 (percent) Agriculture	Industry	Manufacturing	Services
Korea, North	X	X	X	X	X	X	X	X	X	X	X	X
Korea, South	369.9	7,970	297,900	X	569.3	12,270	9.4	6.2	*6*	43	26	51
Kuwait	X	X[e]	*30,373*	14,625	X	X	1.3	X	X	X	X	X
Kyrgyzstan	1.6	350	1,704	375	10.3	2,200	X	-7.3	46	24	18	30
Laos	1.6	330	*1,753*	X	6.5[c]	1,300[c]	X	*6.7*	*52*	*21*	*16*	*27*
Lebanon	15.0	3,560	17,073	4,425	25.9	6,150	X	7.7	12	27	17	61
Malaysia	79.8	3,600	71,302	3,499	155.1[c]	6,990[c]	5.3	7.7	*12*	48	34	40
Mongolia	1.0	400	1,043	X	3.9	1,520	*5.4*	0.1	33	28	X	40
Myanmar (Burma)	X	X[f]	X	X	X	X	0.6	*6.3*	59	10	7	31
Nepal	4.8	210	4,479	198	24.9	1,090	4.6	4.8	40	22	10	38
Oman	X	X	X	X	X	X	X	X	X	X	X	X
Pakistan	63.2	480	63,895	483	204.9	1,560	6.3	4.1	25	25	17	50
Phillippines	78.9	1,050	65,096	3,241	265.6	3,540	1.0	3.3	17	32	22	52
Saudi Arabia	X	X[g]	125,840	76,085	X	X	0.0	1.6	*6*	45	10	49
Singapore	95.1	30,060	85,424	24,676	90.5	28,620	6.6	8.0	0	*35*	24	65
Sri Lanka	15.2	810	*15,093*	804	X	X	4.0	5.3	22	26	17	52
Syria	15.6	1,020	*17,899*	1,109	45.8	3,000	1.5	5.9	X	X	X	X
Tajikistan	2.1	350	*1,990*	331	X	X	X	-16.4	X	X	X	X
Thailand	134.4	2,200	*153,909*	2,572	357.1	5,840	7.6	7.4	11	40	29	49
Turkey	200.5	3,160	*189,878*	2,989	X	X	5.4	4.1	15	28	18	57
Turkmenistan	X	X[f]	*4,397*	1,041	X	X	X	-9.6	X	X	X	X
United Arab Emirates	X	X	X	X	X	X	X	X	X	X	X	X
Uzbekistan	20.9	870	14,194	595	69.8	2,900	X	-1.9	28	30	13	42
Vietnam	25.6	330	*24,848*	331	131.0	1,690	*4.6*	*8.6*	*26*	*31*	X	*43*
Yemen	4.9	300	4,318	309	12.1	740	X	3.8	18	49	11	34
EUROPE												
Albania	2.7	810	*2,460*	747	X	X	1.5	1.8	63	18	X	19
Austria	217.2	26,850	212,069	26,331	183.9	22,740	2.2	2.0	*1*	30	20	68
Belarus	22.5	2,200	*22,629*	2,168	X	X	X	-6.1	14	44	37	42
Belguim	259.0	25,380	247,076	24,215	239.7	23,480	2.0	1.6	*1*	27	18	72
Bosnia-Herzegovina	X	X	X	X	X	X	X	X	X	X	X	X
Bulgaria	10.1	1,230	*10,085*	1,166	X	X	3.4	-3.3	23	26	18	50
Croatia	20.7	4,520	*19,081*	3,796	X	X	X	-1.0	X	X	X	X
Czech Republic	51.8	5,040	*52,035*	5,043	X	X	1.7	-0.2	X	X	X	X
Denmark	176.4	33,260	174,272	33,076	126.4	23,830	2.3	2.8	X	X	X	X
Estonia	4.9	3,390	5,462	3,781	X	X	2.2	-2.1	5	27	17	67
Finland	124.3	24,110	125,673	24,598	104.5	20,270	3.3	2.0	4	24	25	62
France	1,466.2	24,940	1,432,902	24,688	1,312.0	22,320	2.3	1.5	2	26	19	72
Germany	2,122.7	25,850	2,142,018	25,480	1,708.5	20,810	2.2[d]	1.6[D]	*1*	X	24	44
Greece	122.9	11,650	120,304	11,368	137.2	13,010	1.8	2.0	X	X	X	X
Hungary	45.6	4,510	*45,725*	4,602	X	X	1.3	-0.2	6	34	25	60
Iceland	X	X	X	X	X	X	X	X	X	X	X	X
Ireland	67.5	18,340	80,880	22,748	67.5	18,340	3.2	7.5	X	X	X	X
Italy	1,166.2	20,250	1,171,044	20,354	1,163.4	20,200	2.4	1.2	*3*	31	20	66
Latvia	5.9	2,430	5,527	2,267	X	X	3.5	*-8.5*	7	31	21	62
Lithuania	9.0	2,440	10,517	2,893	15.9	4,310	X	*-5.2*	14	40	26	46
Macedonia	2.6	1,290	*2,201*	1,041	7.4	3,660	X	*-0.1*	12	27	0	61
Moldova	1.8	410	*1,872*	418	X	X	3.0	-14.1	31	35	28	34
Netherlands	388.7	24,760	382,487	24,435	339.3	21,620	2.3	2.6	X	X	X	X
Norway	152.1	34,330	145,896	33,125	107.6	24,290	2.8	3.9	*2*	32	11	66
Poland	150.8	3,900	148,863	3,847	260.7	6,740	1.8	4.5	4	26	17	70

(Continued on next page)

COUNTRY	GROSS NATIONAL PRODUCT (GNP) 1998		GROSS DOMESTIC PRODUCT (GDP)1998		PURCHASING POWER PARITY (PPP) 1998		AVERAGE ANNUAL GROWTH RATE GDP 1980–1998 (percent)		DISTRIBUTION OF GDP, 1998 (percent)			
	Total (Billions $US)	Per Capita ($US)	Total (Millions $US)	Per Capita ($US)	Total (Billions $US)	Per Capita ($US)	1980–90	1990–98	Agriculture	Industry	Manufacturing	Services
Portugal	106.4	10,690	106,650	10,808	143.1	14,380	3.1	2.3	X	X	X	X
Romania	31.3	1,390	*34,843*	1,628	89.3	3,970	0.5	-0.6	15	36	25	48
Russian Federation	337.9	2,300	*446,982*	3,020	579.8	3,950	X	-7.0	9	42	X	49
Slovak Republic	20.0	3,700	*19,461*	3,609	X	X	2.0	0.6	5	33	X	62
Slovenia	19.4	9,760	*18,201*	9,353	X	X	X	1.4	5	39	29	57
Spain	553.7	14,080	551,923	14,064	631.5	16,060	3.0	1.9	*3*	X	18	X
Sweden	226.9	25,620	224,953	25,145	172.5	19,480	2.3	1.2	X	X	X	X
Switzerland	284.8	40,080	264,352	36,467	189.1	26,620	2.0	0.4	X	X	X	X
Ukraine	42.7	850	*49,677*	980	X	X	X	-13.1	12	40	6	48
United Kingdom	1,263.8	21,400	1,357,429	23,160	1,218.6	20,640	3.2	2.2	*2*	31	21	67
Yugoslavia (Serbia-Montenegro)	X	X	X	X	X	X	X	X	X	X	X	X
OCEANIA												
Australia	380.6	20,300	364,247	19,754	377.5	20,130	3.4	3.6	*3*	26	14	71
Fiji	X	X	X	X	X	X	X	X	X	X	X	X
New Zealand	55.8	14,700	54,093	16,107	60.1	15,840	1.8	3.2	X	X	X	X
Papua New Guinea	4.1	890	*4,639*	1,044	12.4[c]	2,700[c]	1.9	*5.7*	28	36	9	36
Solomon Islands	X	X	X	X	X	X	X	X	X	X	X	X

Figures in italics are for years other than those specified.
[a]Data prior to 1992 include Eritrea.
[b]Data cover mainland Tanzania only.
[c]Estimate based on regression; others are extrapolated from the latest International Comparison Programme Benchmark estimates.
[d]Data prior to 1990 refer to the Federal Republic of Germany before unification.
[e]Estimated to be high income ($9,361 or more).
[f]Estimated to be low income ($760 or less).
[g]Estimated to be upper middle income ($3,031 to $9,360).

Source: Entering the 21st Century: World Development Report 1999/2000 (Oxford University Press, World Bank, 2000).

Table D

World Countries: Population Growth, 1950–2050

	POPULATION (thousands)				AVERAGE ANNUAL POPULATION CHANGE (percent)			AVERAGE ANNUAL INCREMENT TO THE POPULATION (thousands)		
COUNTRY	1950	1998	2025	2050	1985–90	1995–00	2005–10	1985–90	1995–00	2005–10
WORLD	**2,513,878**	**5,929,839**	**8,039,130**	**9,366,724**	**1.7**	1.4	**1.2**	**86,966**	**80,848**	**80,011**
AFRICA	**223,974**	778,484	**1,453,899**	**2,046,401**	**2.8**	**2.6**	**2.5**	**16,330**	**20,063**	**24,232**
Algeria	8,753	30,175	47,322	58,991	2.6	2.3	1.9	610	698	690
Angola	4,131	11,967	25,547	38,897	2.9	3.3	2.9	245	393	461
Benin	2,046	5,681	12,276	18,095	3.0	2.8	2.9	132	163	227
Botswana	389	1,551	2,576	3,320	3.3	2.2	2.0	39	34	39
Burkina Faso	3,654	11,402	23,451	35,419	2.8	2.8	2.8	240	316	414
Burundi	2,456	6,589	12,341	16,937	2.9	2.8	2.4	148	182	205
Cameroon	4,466	14,323	28,521	41,951	2.8	2.7	2.7	301	387	496
Central African Republic	1,314	3,489	6,006	8,215	2.4	2.1	2.1	66	73	89
Chad	2,658	6,892	12,648	18,004	2.0	2.8	2.3	106	187	200
Congo (Zaire)	12,184	49,208	105,925	164,635	3.3	2.6	3.0	1,142	1,259	1,943
Congo Republic	808	2,822	5,747	8,729	3.0	2.8	2.7	62	78	99
Cote d'Ivoire	2,776	14,567	24,397	31,706	3.3	2.0	2.2	349	290	395
Egypt	21,834	65,675	96,766	115,480	2.5	1.9	1.6	1,313	1,205	1,197
Equatorial Guinea	226	430	798	1,144	2.4	2.5	2.4	8	10	13
Eritrea	1,140	3,548	6,504	8,808	1.3	3.7	2.3	37	128	104
Ethiopia	18,434	62,111	136,288	212,732	3.1	3.2	3.0	1,401	1,954	2,480
Gabon	469	1,170	2,118	2,952	3.1	2.8	2.3	26	32	34
Gambia	294	1,194	1,984	2,604	4.2	2.3	2.0	34	27	29
Ghana	4,900	18,857	36,341	51,205	3.1	2.8	2.6	436	518	636
Guinea	2,550	7,673	15,286	22,914	2.9	1.4	2.8	154	102	272
Guinea-Bissau	505	1,134	1,921	2,674	2.0	2.0	2.0	18	22	28
Kenya	6,265	29,020	50,202	66,054	3.3	2.2	2.4	721	638	880
Lesotho	734	2,184	4,031	5,643	2.6	2.5	2.4	44	53	67
Liberia	824	2,748	6,573	9,955	3.2	8.6	3.0	75	227	123
Libya	1,029	5,980	12,885	19,109	3.7	3.3	3.0	152	196	246
Madagascar	4,229	16,348	34,476	50,807	3.4	3.1	3.0	395	504	643
Malawi	2,881	10,377	20,391	39,825	5.1	2.4	2.6	417	262	341
Mali	3,520	11,832	24,575	36,817	3.0	3.0	2.8	259	353	441
Mauritania	825	2,453	4,443	6,007	2.5	2.5	2.4	47	62	73
Mauritius	493	1,154	1,481	1,654	0.8	1.1	1.0	8	12	13
Morocco	8,953	28,012	39,925	47,276	2.1	1.8	1.4	479	492	437
Mozambique	6,198	18,691	35,444	51,774	0.9	2.5	2.5	128	461	582
Namibia	511	1,653	2,999	4,167	2.7	2.4	2.3	35	39	48
Niger	2,400	10,119	22,385	24,576	3.1	3.3	3.1	225	331	418
Nigeria	21,935	121,773	238,397	338,510	2.9	2.8	2.6	2,617	3,413	4,152
Rwanda	2,120	6,528	12,981	16,937	2.8	7.9	2.4	180	498	215
Senegal	2,500	9,001	16,896	23,442	2.8	2.7	2.5	190	237	286
Sierra Leone	1,944	4,577	8,200	11,368	2.2	3.0	2.2	82	134	125
Somalia	3,072	10,653	23,669	36,408	1.8	3.9	3.1	150	408	445
South Africa	13,683	44,295	71,621	91,466	2.3	2.2	2.0	805	958	1,050
Sudan	9,190	28,526	46,850	59,947	2.3	2.2	2.1	520	623	721
Swaziland	264	931	1,675	2,228	2.7	2.8	2.4	19	25	28
Tanzania	7,886	32,189	62,436	88,963	3.1	2.3	2.6	740	732	1,088
Togo	1,329	4,434	8,762	12,655	3.0	2.7	2.6	99	118	150
Tunisia	3,530	9,497	13,524	15,907	2.1	1.8	1.4	166	170	151
Uganda	4,762	21,318	44,983	66,305	2.4	2.6	2.9	377	554	821
Zambia	2,440	8,690	16,163	21,965	2.4	2.5	2.5	163	210	275
Zimbabwe	2,730	11,924	19,347	24,904	3.2	2.1	2.0	293	237	293
NORTH AND CENTRAL AMERICA										
Belize	69	230	375	480	2.4	2.5	2.0	4	6	6
Canada	13,737	30,194	36,385	36,352	1.4	0.9	0.7	370	255	231
Costa Rica	862	3,650	5,608	6,902	2.8	2.1	1.7	79	75	74
Cuba	5,850	11,115	11,798	13,141	1.0	0.4	0.3	103	47	29
Dominican Republic	2,353	8,232	11,164	13,141	2.2	1.7	1.2	147	134	117
El Salvador	1,951	6,059	9,221	11,364	1.5	2.2	1.7	71	131	121
Guatemala	2,969	11,562	21,668	29,353	2.9	2.8	2.5	247	320	371
Haiti	3,261	7,534	12,513	17,524	2.0	1.9	1.9	122	139	169
Honduras	1,380	6,147	10,656	13,920	3.1	2.8	2.2	139	166	171
Jamaica	1,403	2,539	3,370	3,886	0.5	0.9	1.2	11	24	32
Mexico	27,727	95,831	130,196	154,120	2.0	1.6	1.2	1,552	1,547	1,349
Nicaragua	1,098	4,464	7,639	9,922	2.2	2.6	2.2	73	114	123
Panama	860	2,767	3,779	4,365	2.0	1.6	1.3	46	45	40
Trinidad and Tobago	636	1,318	1,692	1,899	1.0	0.8	1.1	12	11	15
United States	157,813	273,754	332,481	347,543	1.0	0.8	0.8	2,450	2,142	2,204

(Continued on next page)

	POPULATION (thousands)				AVERAGE ANNUAL POPULATION CHANGE (percent)			AVERAGE ANNUAL INCREMENT TO THE POPULATION (thousands)		
COUNTRY	**1950**	**1998**	**2025**	**2050**	**1985–90**	**1995–00**	**2005–10**	**1985–90**	**1995–00**	**2005–10**
SOUTH AMERICA										
Argentina	17,150	36,123	47,160	54,522	1.4	1.3	1.1	444	453	434
Bolivia	2,714	7,957	13,131	16,956	2.2	2.3	2.0	136	183	191
Brazil	53,975	165,158	216,596	243,259	1.8	1.2	1.1	2,548	2,037	2,067
Chile	6,082	14,824	19,548	22,215	1.7	1.4	1.1	210	200	175
Colombia	11,945	37,685	52,668	62,284	2.1	1.7	1.3	636	618	579
Ecuador	3,387	12,175	17,796	21,290	2.4	2.0	1.5	233	237	220
Guyana	423	856	1,114	1,239	0.1	1.0	1.0	0	9	10
Paraguay	1,488	5,222	9,355	12,565	3.1	2.6	2.3	122	134	153
Peru	7,632	24,797	35,518	42,292	2.0	1.7	1.4	415	426	416
Suriname	215	442	605	711	1.2	1.2	1.3	5	5	6
Uruguay	2,239	3,239	3,692	4,027	0.6	0.6	0.5	17	18	18
Venezuela	5,094	23,242	34,775	42,152	2.6	2.0	1.6	473	465	450
ASIA										
Afghanistan	8,958	23,364	45,262	61,373	0.3	5.3	2.4	47	1,186	737
Armenia	1,354	3,646	4,185	4,376	1.2	0.2	0.7	41	6	25
Azerbaijan	2,896	7,714	9,714	10,881	1.4	0.8	0.9	98	59	72
Bangladesh	41,783	124,043	179,980	218,188	2.0	1.6	1.6	2,091	2,016	2,396
Bhutan	734	1,917	3,646	5,184	2.5	2.8	2.5	39	52	60
Cambodia	4,346	10,751	16,990	21,394	3.2	2.2	1.8	255	237	226
China	554,760	1,255,091	1,480,430	1,516,664	1.5	0.9	0.7	17,026	11,215	8,676
Georgia	3,527	5,428	5,762	6,028	0.6	(0.1)	0.2	35	(6)	11
India	357,561	975,772	1,330,201	1,532,674	2.1	1.6	1.3	16,571	15,553	14,020
Indonesia	79,538	206,522	275,245	318,264	1.8	1.5	1.1	3,096	3,021	2,488
Iran	16,913	73,057	128,251	170,269	3.8	2.2	2.4	2,061	1,613	2,250
Iraq	5,158	21,795	41,600	56,129	3.3	2.8	2.6	552	603	751
Israel	1,258	5,883	7,977	9,144	1.9	1.9	1.2	85	110	83
Japan	83,625	125,920	121,348	109,546	0.4	0.2	(0.0)	540	272	(30)
Jordan	1,237	5,956	11,894	16,671	2.1	3.3	2.8	85	191	217
Kazakhstan	6,703	16,854	20,047	22,260	1.1	0.1	0.7	183	22	121
Korea, North	9,488	23,206	30,046	32,873	1.5	1.6	0.9	284	363	232
Korea, South	20,357	46,115	52,533	52,146	1.0	0.9	0.6	413	395	288
Kuwait	152	1,809	2,904	3,406	4.4	3.0	1.7	85	55	40
Kyrgyzstan	1,740	4,497	5,950	7,182	1.8	0.4	1.1	76	17	51
Laos	1,755	5,358	10,202	13,889	3.1	3.1	2.6	122	162	181
Lebanon	1,443	3,194	4,424	5,189	(0.9)	1.8	1.1	(23)	56	41
Malaysia	6,110	21,450	32,577	38,089	2.6	2.0	1.5	443	432	382
Mongolia	761	2,624	4,052	4,986	3.0	2.1	1.8	61	55	58
Myanmar (Burma)	17,832	47,625	67,654	80,896	1.9	1.8	1.4	762	847	796
Nepal	7,862	23,168	40,554	53,621	2.6	2.5	2.3	454	578	657
Oman	456	2,504	6,538	10,930	4.5	4.2	3.8	72	102	137
Pakistan	39,513	147,811	268,904	357,353	3.3	2.7	2.4	3,589	3,950	4,606
Philippines	20,988	72,164	105,194	130,511	2.1	2.0	1.6	122	1,440	1,342
Saudi Arabia	3,201	20,207	43,363	59,812	4.8	2.4	2.9	680	681	793
Singapore	1,022	3,491	4,212	4,190	2.2	1.5	0.7	61	52	27
Sri Lanka	7,678	18,450	23,934	26,995	1.2	1.0	1.1	199	179	224
Syria	3,495	15,335	26,303	34,463	3.5	2.5	2.3	398	385	446
Tajikistan	1,532	6,161	9,747	12,366	3.0	1.9	1.9	147	114	141
Thailand	20,010	59,612	69,089	72,969	1.7	0.8	0.6	890	451	391
Turkey	20,809	63,763	85,791	97,911	2.2	1.6	1.2	1,151	979	834
Turkmenistan	1,211	4,316	6,470	7,916	2.6	1.9	1.7	88	81	85
United Arab Emirates	70	2,354	3,297	3,668	4.3	2.0	1.5	74	47	42
Uzbekistan	6,314	24,105	36,500	45,094	2.4	1.9	1.7	468	451	495
Vietnam	29,954	77,896	110,107	129,763	2.2	1.8	1.2	1,358	1,351	1,083
Yemen	4,316	16,891	39,589	61,129	3.6	3.7	3.3	379	618	775
EUROPE										
Albania	1,230	3,445	4,295	4,747	2.1	0.6	0.8	65	22	28
Austria	6,935	8,210	8,305	7,430	0.4	0.6	0.1	29	49	9
Belarus	7,745	10,323	9,641	8,726	0.5	(0.1)	(0.2)	52	(14)	(22)
Belgium	8,639	10,213	10,271	9,763	0.2	0.3	0.0	19	26	4
Bosnia-Herzegovina	2,661	3,994	4,303	3,789	0.9	3.9	0.0	37	154	1
Bulgaria	7,251	8,387	7,453	6,690	(0.6)	(0.5)	(0.4)	(48)	(41)	(31)
Croatia	3,850	4,494	4,243	3,991	0.2	(0.1)	(0.2)	9	(4)	(8)
Czech Republic	8,925	10,223	9,627	8,572	0.0	(0.1)	(0.2)	0	(14)	(16)
Denmark	4,271	5,258	5,324	5,234	0.1	0.2	0.0	5	10	1
Estonia	1,101	1,442	1,256	1,084	0.7	(1.0)	(0.4)	10	(14)	(6)
Finland	4,009	5,156	5,294	5,172	0.3	0.3	0.1	17	14	5
France	41,829	58,733	60,393	58,370	0.6	0.3	0.1	310	191	67
Germany	68,376	82,401	80,877	69,542	0.4	0.3	(0.1)	339	219	(57)
Greece	7,566	10,551	10,074	9,013	0.6	0.3	(0.2)	57	29	(17)
Hungary	9,338	9,930	8,667	7,715	(0.4)	(0.6)	(0.5)	(43)	(59)	(48)
Iceland	143	277	336	363	1.1	1.0	0.8	3	3	2

(Continued on next page)

COUNTRY	POPULATION (thousands) 1950	1998	2025	2050	AVERAGE ANNUAL POPULATION CHANGE (percent) 1985–90	1995–00	2005–10	AVERAGE ANNUAL INCREMENT TO THE POPULATION (thousands) 1985–90	1995–00	2005–10
Ireland	2,969	3,564	3,723	3,809	(0.3)	0.2	0.3	(10)	6	11
Italy	47,104	57,244	51,774	42,092	0.1	0.0	(0.3)	50	(2)	(175)
Latvia	1,949	2,447	2,108	1,891	0.7	(1.1)	(0.5)	18	(28)	(12)
Lithuania	2,567	3,710	3,521	3,297	1.0	(0.3)	(0.2)	36	(9)	(6)
Macedonia	1,230	2,205	2,541	2,646	1.2	0.7	0.6	25	15	14
Moldova	2,341	4,451	4,869	5,138	0.7	0.1	0.4	30	4	18
Netherlands	10,114	15,739	16,141	14,956	0.6	0.5	0.1	92	78	20
Norway	3,265	4,379	4,662	4,696	0.4	0.4	0.2	18	15	10
Poland	24,824	38,664	39,973	39,725	0.5	0.1	0.2	183	34	77
Portugal	8,405	9,798	9,438	8,701	(0.1)	(0.1)	(0.1)	(7)	(5)	(8)
Romania	16,311	22,573	21,098	19,009	0.4	(0.2)	(0.2)	96	(45)	(47)
Russian Federation	102,192	147,231	131,995	114,318	0.7	(0.3)	(0.4)	993	(453)	(513)
Slovak Republic	3,463	5,360	5,469	5,260	0.5	0.1	0.2	23	7	8
Slovenia	1,473	1,919	1,738	1,471	0.4	(0.1)	(0.3)	7	(2)	(5)
Spain	28,009	39,754	37,500	31,755	0.4	0.1	(0.1)	160	35	(57)
Sweden	7,014	8,863	9,511	9,574	0.5	0.3	0.2	42	22	22
Switzerland	4,694	7,325	7,581	6,935	0.9	0.7	0.2	60	49	15
Ukraine	37,906	51,218	45,979	40,802	0.4	(0.4)	(0.4)	190	(191)	(175)
United Kingdom	50,616	58,249	59,535	58,733	0.3	0.1	0.1	189	51	37
Yugoslavia (Serbia-Montenegro)	7,131	10,410	10,679	10,979	0.6	0.5	(0.0)	62	50	(1)
OCEANIA										
Australia	8,219	18,445	29,931	25,286	1.5	1.1	1.0	249	194	201
Fiji	289	822	1,170	1,393	0.8	1.6	1.5	5	13	14
New Zealand	1,908	3,680	4,878	5,271	0.7	1.1	1.1	23	40	43
Papua New Guinea	1,613	4,602	7,546	9,637	2.2	2.2	2.0	79	102	113
Solomon Islands	90	417	844	1,192	3.4	3.2	2.8	10	13	16
DEVELOPING COUNTRIES	**1,711,191**	**4,783,310**	**6,818,880**	**8,204,983**	**2.0**	**1.7**	**1.4**	**80,235**	**77,726**	**78,204**
DEVELOPED COUNTRIES	**812,687**	**1,181,530**	**1,220,250**	**1,161,741**	**0.5**	**0.3**	**0.2**	**6,761**	**3,121**	**1,806**

Source: United Nations Population Division and International Labour Organisation. World Resources Institute, *World Resources 1998–99.*

Table E

World Countries: Basic Demographic Data, 1975–2000

COUNTRY	CRUDE BIRTH RATE (births per 1,000 population)		LIFE EXPECTANCY AT BIRTH (years)		LIFE EXPECTANCY OF FEMALES AS A PERCENTAGE OF MALES (years)		TOTAL FERTILITY RATE		PERCENTAGE OF POPULATION IN SPECIFIC AGE GROUPS					
									1980			2000		
	1975–1980	1995–00	1975–80	1995–00	1975–80	1995–00	1975–80	1995–00	<15	15–65	>65	<15	15–65	>65
WORLD	**28.3**	**22.6**	**59.7**	**65.6**	**106.0**	**106.8**	**3.9**	**2.8**	**35.2**	**58.9**	**5.9**	**30.0**	**63.2**	**6.8**
AFRICA	**46.0**	**39.2**	**47.9**	**53.8**	**106.7**	**105.7**	**6.5**	**5.3**	**44.7**	**52.2**	**3.1**	**43.0**	**53.8**	**3.2**
Algeria	45.0	29.2	57.5	68.9	103.5	104.1	7.2	3.8	46.5	49.6	3.9	36.6	59.6	3.8
Angola	50.2	47.7	40.0	46.5	108.1	107.1	6.8	6.7	44.7	52.4	2.9	47.4	49.8	2.8
Benin	51.4	42.0	47.0	54.8	108.2	109.2	7.1	5.8	45.1	50.8	4.1	46.5	50.7	2.8
Botswana	46.6	235.0	56.5	50.4	106.6	105.7	6.4	4.5	48.7	49.3	2.0	41.9	55.6	2.4
Burkina Faso	50.8	45.9	42.9	46.0	106.0	104.2	7.8	6.6	47.4	49.8	2.8	47.0	50.3	2.7
Burundi	44.7	42.5	46.0	47.2	107.2	107.3	6.8	6.3	44.7	51.8	3.4	45.0	52.3	2.7
Cameroon	45.5	39.3	48.5	55.9	106.4	105.0	6.5	5.3	44.4	52.0	3.6	43.5	52.9	3.6
Central African Republic	44.1	37.6	44.5	48.6	111.9	109.9	5.9	5.0	41.7	54.4	4.0	41.6	54.4	4.0
Chad	44.1	41.6	41.0	47.7	108.1	106.5	5.9	5.5	41.9	54.5	3.6	43.0	53.4	3.6
Congo (Zaire)	47.8	44.9	48.0	52.9	107.1	106.2	6.5	6.2	46.0	51.1	2.8	48.0	49.1	2.9
Congo Republic	45.8	42.5	48.7	50.9	111.3	109.9	6.3	5.9	45.1	51.5	3.4	45.7	51.1	3.3
Cote d'Ivoire	50.7	37.2	47.9	51.0	107.1	104.4	7.4	5.1	46.6	51.0	2.5	43.0	54.0	3.0
Egypt	38.9	26.1	54.1	66.0	104.5	104.0	5.3	3.4	39.5	56.5	4.0	35.0	60.5	4.5
Equatorial Guinea	42.7	40.8	42.0	50.0	107.9	106.6	5.7	5.5	41.0	54.8	4.1	43.1	52.9	4.0
Eritrea	45.1	39.8	45.3	50.6	106.8	106.1	6.1	5.3	44.2	53.1	2.6	43.6	53.3	3.1
Ethiopia	49.0	48.2	42.0	49.9	107.9	106.6	6.8	7.0	46.1	51.2	2.7	47.1	50.2	2.8
Gabon	32.9	37.6	47.0	55.5	107.3	106.3	4.4	5.4	34.4	59.5	6.1	39.8	54.6	5.7
Gambia	48.8	39.9	39.0	47.0	108.3	107.3	6.5	5.2	42.6	54.4	2.8	41.2	55.5	3.1
Ghana	45.1	38.2	51.0	58.0	106.9	106.6	6.5	5.3	44.9	52.3	2.8	43.4	53.6	3.0
Guinea	51.6	48.2	38.8	46.5	102.6	102.2	7.0	6.6	45.8	51.6	2.6	47.0	50.4	2.6
Guinea-Bissau	42.4	40.3	37.5	43.8	108.6	106.6	5.6	5.4	39.0	57.0	4.0	41.7	54.2	4.2
Kenya	53.6	36.9	53.4	54.5	107.8	106.5	8.1	4.9	50.1	46.5	3.4	43.4	53.7	2.9
Lesotho	41.9	35.4	51.8	58.6	107.0	104.5	5.7	4.9	41.9	53.9	4.2	41.0	55.0	4.1
Liberia	47.4	47.5	49.5	51.5	106.3	106.0	6.8	6.3	44.3	52.0	3.7	43.7	52.7	3.6
Libya	47.3	40.0	55.8	65.5	106.3	105.6	7.4	5.9	46.7	51.1	2.2	44.7	52.4	2.9
Madagascar	46.9	41.1	49.5	58.5	106.3	105.3	6.6	5.7	45.9	51.4	2.7	45.8	51.6	2.6
Malawi	57.2	47.7	43.1	40.7	103.3	102.0	7.6	6.7	47.5	50.3	2.3	46.4	50.9	2.7
Mali	50.7	47.4	40.0	48.0	108.1	107.1	7.1	6.6	46.8	50.7	2.5	47.2	50.2	2.5
Mauritania	44.7	38.3	45.5	53.5	107.3	106.2	6.5	5.0	43.7	53.3	3.0	41.5	55.2	3.3
Mauritius	26.7	19.3	64.9	71.6	108.3	109.8	3.1	2.3	35.6	60.8	3.6	26.6	67.3	6.0
Morocco	39.4	25.8	55.8	66.7	106.3	105.7	5.9	3.1	43.2	52.7	4.1	33.8	61.9	4.3
Mozambique	45.4	42.5	43.5	46.9	107.6	106.4	6.5	6.1	43.4	53.4	3.2	44.7	52.1	3.2
Namibia	41.9	35.9	51.3	55.5	105.0	103.5	6.0	4.9	43.1	53.4	3.5	41.6	54.6	3.8
Niger	59.7	50.2	40.5	48.5	108.2	107.0	8.1	7.1	46.8	50.8	2.5	48.6	49.0	2.4
Nigeria	46.6	42.3	45.0	52.4	107.4	106.3	6.5	6.0	44.3	53.1	2.6	45.0	52.1	2.9
Rwanda	52.8	42.8	45.0	42.1	107.4	106.4	8.5	6.0	48.8	48.8	2.4	44.7	53.0	2.4
Senegal	49.3	41.1	42.8	51.3	104.8	104.0	7.0	5.6	45.3	51.8	2.8	43.6	53.4	3.0
Sierra Leone	48.8	46.5	35.2	37.5	108.9	108.6	6.5	6.1	43.0	53.9	3.1	43.9	53.1	3.0
Somalia	50.4	50.0	42.0	49.0	107.9	106.8	7.0	7.0	46.0	51.0	3.0	48.0	49.5	2.6
South Africa	37.3	29.7	55.9	65.2	111.3	109.6	5.1	3.8	40.3	55.9	3.9	36.2	59.3	4.5
Sudan	47.1	33.7	46.7	55.0	106.2	105.2	6.7	4.6	44.9	52.4	2.7	38.7	58.1	3.2

(Continued on next page)

COUNTRY	CRUDE BIRTH RATE (births per 1,000 population)		LIFE EXPECTANCY AT BIRTH (years)		LIFE EXPECTANCY OF FEMALES AS A PERCENTAGE OF MALES (years)		TOTAL FERTILITY RATE		PERCENTAGE OF POPULATION IN SPECIFIC AGE GROUPS					
									1980			2000		
	1975–1980	1995–00	1975–80	1995–00	1975–80	1995–00	1975–80	1995–00	<15	15–65	>65	<15	15–65	>65
Swaziland	46.2	36.8	49.9	60.0	109.9	108.0	6.5	4.5	45.9	51.3	2.9	41.7	55.6	2.7
Tanzania	47.5	41.2	49.0	51.4	107.2	105.6	6.8	5.5	47.6	50.1	2.3	45.1	52.3	2.6
Togo	45.2	41.9	48.0	50.1	107.1	105.5	6.6	6.1	44.6	52.3	3.2	45.6	51.3	3.1
Tunisia	36.4	23.9	60.0	69.6	101.7	103.4	5.7	2.9	41.6	54.6	3.8	32.2	62.9	4.9
Uganda	50.3	51.1	47.0	41.4	107.0	104.7	6.9	7.1	47.8	49.7	2.5	49.1	48.6	2.2
Zambia	51.6	42.4	49.3	43.0	106.9	103.6	7.2	5.5	49.4	48.2	2.4	46.3	51.4	2.3
Zimbabwe	44.2	37.1	53.8	48.5	106.9	103.8	6.6	4.7	47.9	49.5	2.6	43.6	53.7	2.7
NORTH AMERICA	**15.1**	**13.6**	**73.3**	**76.9**	**111.2**	**109.1**	**1.8**	**1.9**	**22.5**	**66.4**	**11.0**	**21.2**	**66.4**	**12.4**
Canada	15.4	11.9	74.2	78.9	110.8	107.5	1.8	1.6	22.7	67.9	9.4	19.3	68.1	12.6
United States	15.1	13.8	73.2	76.7	111.2	109.1	1.8	2.0	22.5	66.3	11.2	21.4	66.2	12.4
CENTRAL AMERICA	**38.2**	**26.5**	**63.7**	**71.7**	**110.2**	**108.4**	**5.4**	**3.0**	**45.1**	**51.2**	**3.6**	**34.8**	**60.7**	**4.5**
Belize	40.9	31.3	69.7	74.7	102.5	103.7	6.2	3.7	47.2	48.6	4.8	39.7	55.8	4.1
Costa Rica	31.7	24.0	71.0	76.8	106.4	106.3	3.9	3.0	38.9	57.5	3.6	33.1	61.8	5.1
Cuba	17.2	13.1	73.0	76.0	104.8	105.1	2.1	1.6	32.9	60.5	7.6	21.2	69.2	9.6
Dominican Republic	34.9	24.1	62.0	70.9	106.1	106.1	4.7	2.8	42.3	54.6	3.1	33.1	62.5	4.5
El Salvador	41.5	27.9	57.2	69.5	119.5	109.0	5.7	3.1	46.1	50.8	3.1	35.6	59.7	4.7
Guatemala	44.3	36.3	56.4	67.2	107.2	107.9	6.4	4.9	45.9	51.3	2.8	42.9	53.3	3.7
Haiti	36.8	34.1	50.7	54.5	106.3	106.1	5.4	4.6	40.7	54.8	4.4	40.0	56.2	3.8
Honduras	44.9	33.5	57.7	69.8	107.7	107.1	6.6	4.3	47.2	50.1	2.7	41.6	54.9	3.4
Jamaica	28.8	21.7	70.1	74.6	106.3	106.1	4.0	2.4	40.2	53.0	6.8	30.2	53.4	6.4
Mexico	37.1	24.6	65.3	72.5	110.3	108.6	5.3	2.8	45.1	51.1	3.8	33.1	62.1	4.7
Nicaragua	45.7	33.5	57.6	68.2	108.5	107.3	6.4	3.9	47.7	49.8	2.5	40.8	56.0	3.2
Panama	31.0	22.5	69.0	73.9	105.8	106.4	4.1	2.6	40.5	55.0	4.5	31.3	63.7	5.5
Trinidad and Tobago	29.3	16.6	68.3	73.7	107.6	106.6	3.4	2.1	34.2	60.2	5.5	26.1	67.4	6.5
SOUTH AMERICA	**32.0**	**21.5**	**62.9**	**69.0**	**108.8**	**110.7**	**4.3**	**2.5**	**37.8**	**57.6**	**4.6**	**30.2**	**64.2**	**5.6**
Argentina	25.7	19.9	68.7	73.2	110.4	110.3	3.4	2.6	30.5	61.4	8.1	27.7	62.6	9.7
Bolivia	41.0	33.2	50.1	61.5	108.8	105.7	5.8	4.4	42.6	53.9	3.5	30.5	56.4	4.0
Brazil	32.6	10.6	61.8	67.1	108.1	112.3	4.3	2.2	38.1	57.8	4.2	28.4	66.4	5.2
Chile	24.0	19.9	67.2	75.3	110.5	108.3	3.0	2.4	33.5	60.9	5.6	28.5	64.4	7.2
Colombia	31.7	23.4	64.0	70.9	107.3	108.1	4.1	2.7	40.0	56.2	3.7	32.5	62.8	4.6
Ecuador	38.2	25.6	61.4	69.8	105.9	107.7	5.4	3.1	42.8	53.2	4.0	33.8	61.5	4.7
Guyana	31.5	21.9	60.7	64.4	108.4	111.1	3.9	2.3	40.8	55.2	4.0	29.9	65.9	4.2
Paraguay	35.9	32.3	66.6	69.7	106.7	106.7	5.2	4.2	42.2	53.3	4.5	39.5	57.0	3.5
Peru	38.0	24.9	58.5	68.3	106.7	107.6	5.4	3.0	41.9	54.5	3.6	33.4	61.8	4.8
Suriname	29.5	21.8	65.1	71.5	107.8	107.2	4.2	2.4	39.7	55.8	4.5	32.3	62.4	5.5
Uruguay	20.3	16.8	69.6	72.9	110.2	109.3	2.9	2.3	26.9	62.5	10.5	23.9	63.5	12.7
Venezuela	34.2	24.9	67.6	72.8	109.1	108.1	4.5	3.0	40.7	56.1	3.2	34.0	61.5	4.4
ASIA	**29.6**	**22.3**	**58.5**	**66.2**	**102.6**	**104.5**	**4.2**	**2.7**	**37.6**	**58.0**	**4.4**	**30.1**	**64.1**	**5.8**
Afghanistan	50.8	53.4	40.0	45.5	100.0	102.2	7.2	6.9	43.0	54.5	2.5	41.7	55.6	2.7
Armenia	20.9	13.3	72.3	70.6	109.0	110.1	2.5	1.7	30.4	63.6	6.0	24.5	66.8	8.7
Azerbaijan	24.7	19.2	68.5	70.6	112.1	112.0	3.6	2.3	34.5	60.0	5.4	29.5	63.6	6.9
Bangladesh	47.2	26.8	46.6	58.1	97.9	100.2	6.7	3.1	46.0	50.5	3.4	35.6	61.2	3.3
Bhutan	42.8	41.3	42.6	53.2	104.8	106.4	5.9	5.9	41.3	55.6	3.1	43.0	53.8	3.2
Cambodia	30.0	33.7	31.2	54.1	108.3	105.3	4.1	4.5	39.2	57.9	2.9	40.4	56.6	3.0

(Continued on next page)

COUNTRY	CRUDE BIRTH RATE (births per 1,000 population)		LIFE EXPECTANCY AT BIRTH (years)		LIFE EXPECTANCY OF FEMALES AS A PERCENTAGE OF MALES (years)		TOTAL FERTILITY RATE		PERCENTAGE OF POPULATION IN SPECIFIC AGE GROUPS					
									1980			2000		
	1975–1980	1995–00	1975–80	1995–00	1975–80	1995–00	1975–80	1995–00	<15	15–65	>65	<15	15–65	>65
China	21.5	16.2	65.3	69.9	103.0	105.1	3.3	1.8	35.5	59.7	4.7	24.9	68.4	6.7
Georgia	18.1	13.8	70.7	72.7	111.9	112.0	2.4	1.9	25.7	65.1	9.1	22.0	65.4	12.6
India	34.7	25.2	52.9	62.4	96.3	101.0	4.8	3.1	38.5	57.4	4.0	32.7	62.3	5.0
Indonesia	35.4	23.1	52.8	65.1	104.9	105.8	4.7	2.6	41.0	55.6	3.3	30.8	64.6	4.7
Iran	44.7	34.0	58.6	69.2	101.4	102.2	6.5	4.8	44.9	51.8	3.3	43.1	52.8	4.1
Iraq	41.9	36.4	61.4	62.4	103.0	104.9	6.6	5.3	46.0	51.3	2.7	41.4	55.5	3.1
Israel	26.0	20.3	73.1	77.7	104.9	105.0	3.4	2.8	33.2	58.2	8.6	28.1	62.4	9.5
Japan	15.2	10.3	75.5	80.0	107.4	107.8	1.8	1.5	23.6	67.4	9.0	15.2	68.3	16.5
Jordan	45.0	37.5	61.2	69.7	106.1	106.1	7.4	5.1	49.4	47.5	3.1	43.3	53.8	2.9
Kazakhstan	24.9	18.1	65.4	67.6	117.1	115.4	3.1	2.3	32.4	61.5	6.1	27.5	65.4	7.1
Korea, North	22.2	21.3	65.8	72.2	110.3	109.0	3.3	2.1	39.5	57.0	3.5	27.3	57.4	5.3
Korea, South	23.9	15.0	64.8	72.4	111.6	110.5	2.9	1.7	34.0	62.2	3.8	21.4	72.0	6.7
Kuwait	40.1	21.3	69.6	76.0	106.2	105.5	5.9	2.8	40.2	58.3	1.4	33.2	64.8	2.0
Kyrgyzstan	29.9	25.5	64.2	67.6	114.2	113.4	4.1	3.2	37.1	57.1	5.8	35.0	59.0	6.0
Laos	45.1	44.2	43.5	53.5	106.9	105.8	6.7	6.7	42.0	55.2	2.8	45.4	51.7	3.0
Lebanon	30.1	24.2	65.0	69.9	106.2	105.3	4.3	2.8	40.1	54.5	5.4	32.9	61.3	5.8
Malaysia	30.4	25.2	65.3	72.0	105.7	106.3	4.2	3.2	39.3	57.0	3.7	35.3	60.6	4.1
Mongolia	39.2	27.8	56.3	65.8	104.5	104.7	6.7	3.3	43.2	53.9	2.9	36.4	59.8	3.8
Myanmar (Burma)	37.5	27.2	51.2	60.1	106.4	105.6	5.3	3.3	39.6	56.4	4.0	34.0	61.4	4.6
Nepal	43.4	36.3	46.2	57.3	96.6	99.1	6.2	5.0	42.9	54.1	3.0	42.0	54.5	3.5
Oman	46.1	44.1	54.9	70.8	104.3	106.4	7.2	7.2	44.6	52.8	2.6	47.7	49.9	2.3
Pakistan	47.3	36.1	53.4	63.9	101.3	103.5	7.0	5.0	44.4	52.7	2.9	41.8	55.0	3.2
Philippines	35.9	28.4	59.9	68.3	105.5	105.4	5.0	3.6	41.9	55.3	2.8	36.7	59.7	3.6
Saudi Arabia	45.9	34.3	58.8	71.4	104.0	105.0	7.3	5.9	44.3	52.9	2.8	40.7	56.4	2.9
Singapore	17.2	15.7	70.8	77.3	106.6	105.9	1.9	1.8	27.0	68.2	4.7	22.6	70.3	7.1
Sri Lanka	28.5	17.8	66.8	73.1	105.4	106.3	3.8	2.1	35.3	60.4	4.3	26.2	67.2	6.6
Syria	46.0	30.4	60.1	68.9	106.2	106.7	7.4	4.0	48.5	48.3	3.2	40.8	56.1	3.1
Tajikistan	37.2	30.4	64.5	67.2	108.3	109.3	5.9	3.9	42.9	52.5	4.6	36.5	55.9	4.6
Thailand	31.6	16.7	61.2	69.3	106.6	109.0	4.3	1.7	40.0	56.5	3.5	25.2	69.1	5.8
Turkey	32.0	21.9	60.3	69.0	107.8	107.8	4.5	2.5	39.2	56.0	4.7	28.3	65.7	5.9
Turkmenistan	35.3	28.6	61.6	64.6	11.20	111.1	5.3	3.6	41.3	54.4	4.3	37.4	58.3	4.2
United Arab Emirates	30.5	18.7	66.8	74.8	106.5	103.5	5.7	3.5	28.6	70.1	1.3	28.1	69.4	2.5
Uzbekistan	34.4	28.2	65.1	67.5	111.0	110.0	5.1	3.5	40.9	54.0	5.1	37.5	57.9	4.6
Vietnam	38.3	25.1	55.8	67.4	108.2	107.2	5.6	3.0	42.5	52.7	4.8	34.3	60.5	5.2
Yemen	53.7	47.7	44.1	58.0	101.1	101.7	7.6	7.6	50.2	47.2	2.6	48.3	49.3	2.3
EUROPE	**14.8**	**10.5**	**71.3**	**72.6**	**111.4**	**112.7**	**2.0**	**1.5**	**22.2**	**65.5**	**12.3**	**17.5**	**67.9**	**14.6**
Albania	30.3	21.4	68.9	70.9	106.6	106.8	4.2	2.6	35.9	58.9	5.2	29.7	64.4	6.0
Austria	11.5	10.3	72.0	77.0	110.4	108.7	1.7	1.4	20.4	64.2	15.4	17.1	68.5	14.4
Belarus	16.1	10.0	71.1	69.6	114.7	116.1	2.1	1.4	22.9	66.4	10.7	18.8	67.3	13.8
Belgium	12.4	11.2	72.3	77.3	109.6	109.1	1.7	1.6	20.2	65.5	14.3	17.4	66.2	16.4
Bosnia-Herzegovina	19.6	10.8	69.9	73.2	107.0	107.7	2.2	1.4	27.3	66.7	6.1	18.9	71.2	9.8
Bulgaria	15.8	10.3	71.3	71.3	107.9	110.5	2.2	1.5	22.1	66.0	11.9	16.9	67.2	15.8
Croatia	15.6	10.8	70.6	72.2	110.4	112.3	2.0	1.6	21.2	67.2	11.7	17.3	68.0	14.6
Czech Republic	17.4	10.7	70.6	72.9	110.4	108.9	2.3	1.4	23.5	63.2	13.4	17.6	69.8	12.6
Denmark	12.3	13.0	74.2	75.6	108.4	107.3	1.7	1.8	20.8	64.7	14.4	18.6	66.7	14.7
Estonia	15.0	9.0	69.7	69.4	115.3	117.4	2.1	1.3	21.7	65.8	12.5	17.6	68.5	13.9
Finland	13.6	12.0	72.7	76.6	112.6	109.7	1.6	1.8	20.3	67.7	12.0	18.4	67.1	14.6

(Continued on next page)

COUNTRY	CRUDE BIRTH RATE (births per 1,000 population)		LIFE EXPECTANCY AT BIRTH (years)		LIFE EXPECTANCY OF FEMALES AS A PERCENTAGE OF MALES (years)		TOTAL FERTILITY RATE		PERCENTAGE OF POPULATION IN SPECIFIC AGE GROUPS					
									1980			2000		
	1975–1980	1995–00	1975–80	1995–00	1975–80	1995–00	1975–80	1995–00	<15	15–65	>65	<15	15–65	>65
France	14.0	11.6	73.7	76.8	111.6	111.1	1.9	1.6	22.3	63.8	14.0	18.3	65.4	16.2
Germany	10.4	9.3	72.5	76.7	109.4	108.9	1.5	1.3	18.5	65.9	15.6	15.4	68.8	15.9
Greece	15.6	10.0	73.7	78.1	105.7	106.8	2.3	1.4	22.8	64.0	13.1	15.3	66.9	17.8
Hungary	16.2	10.2	69.4	69.0	109.8	114.4	2.1	14	21.9	64.6	13.4	17.0	68.5	14.5
Iceland	19.2	16.5	76.3	79.3	108.0	104.9	2.3	2.2	27.6	62.7	10.1	23.8	64.9	11.3
Ireland	21.2	13.0	72.0	76.6	107.2	107.3	3.5	1.8	30.6	58.7	10.7	21.2	67.5	11.4
Italy	13.0	9.1	73.6	78.3	109.2	108.4	1.9	1.2	22.3	64.6	13.1	14.2	68.1	17.7
Latvia	14.0	9.8	69.2	68.4	115.6	118.9	2.0	1.4	20.4	66.5	13.0	18.2	67.5	14.4
Lithuania	15.4	10.8	70.8	70.4	114.2	117.1	2.1	1.5	23.6	65.1	11.3	19.5	67.0	13.5
Macedonia	22.6	14.5	69.6	72.5	105.2	106.3	2.7	1.9	28.6	64.5	6.9	22.3	68.3	9.4
Moldova	19.6	13.6	64.8	67.5	111.2	112.6	2.4	1.8	26.7	65.5	7.8	23.4	66.8	9.8
Netherlands	12.7	11.9	75.3	77.9	109.0	107.5	1.6	1.6	22.3	66.2	11.5	18.2	68.2	13.6
Norway	12.9	13.4	75.3	77.6	108.9	107.8	1.8	1.9	22.2	63.1	14.8	19.8	65.1	15.0
Poland	19.2	11.9	70.9	71.1	111.9	113.5	2.3	1.7	24.3	65.6	10.1	19.8	68.4	11.8
Portugal	18.2	11.2	70.2	75.4	110.6	109.9	2.4	1.5	25.9	63.6	10.5	16.7	67.5	15.7
Romania	19.1	11.0	69.6	69.5	107.0	110.9	2.6	1.4	26.7	63.1	10.3	18.5	68.4	13.2
Russian Federation	15.8	9.6	67.4	64.4	118.1	123.3	1.9	1.4	21.6	68.1	10.2	18.0	69.3	12.7
Slovak Republic	20.6	11.7	70.4	71.3	110.9	113.1	2.5	1.5	26.1	63.5	10.4	20.0	68.8	11.1
Slovenia	16.6	9.5	71.0	73.5	111.6	112.4	2.2	1.3	23.4	65.3	11.4	15.7	70.2	14.2
Spain	17.4	9.7	74.3	78.0	108.4	109.4	2.6	1.2	26.6	62.7	10.7	15.0	68.4	16.5
Sweden	11.7	11.9	75.2	78.5	109.3	106.0	1.7	1.8	19.6	64.1	16.3	19.2	64.3	16.7
Switzerland	11.6	10.9	75.2	78.6	109.2	108.6	1.5	1.5	19.7	66.4	13.8	17.2	68.1	14.7
Ukraine	14.9	9.7	69.3	68.8	114.8	116.4	2.0	1.4	21.4	66.7	11.9	17.8	67.9	14.3
United Kingdom	12.4	11.9	72.8	77.1	109.0	107.1	1.7	1.7	20.9	64.0	15.1	18.9	65.5	15.8
Yugoslavia (Serbia-Montenegro)	18.4	12.6	70.3	72.5	106.5	107.9	2.4	1.8	24.1	66.1	9.8	19.8	66.9	13.3
OCEANIA	**20.9**	**18.4**	**68.2**	**73.9**	**108.7**	**106.9**	**2.8**	**2.5**	**29.3**	**62.7**	**8.0**	**25.5**	**64.9**	**9.7**
Australia	16.0	14.3	73.4	78.3	109.8	107.7	2.1	1.9	25.3	65.1	9.6	21.0	67.1	11.9
Fiji	33.2	22.6	67.1	72.6	105.3	106.1	4.0	2.8	39.1	58.0	2.8	31.3	64.3	4.5
New Zealand	17.2	15.4	72.4	77.2	109.2	106.7	2.2	2.0	26.7	63.3	10.0	23.0	65.6	11.3
Papua New Guinea	39.6	32.3	49.7	57.9	101.0	102.6	5.9	4.7	43.0	55.5	1.6	38.7	58.3	3.0
Solomon Islands	45.0	36.1	65.3	71.6	106.2	106.2	7.1	5.0	47.6	49.3	3.1	43.0	54.1	2.9
DEVELOPING COUNTRIES	**32.8**	**25.4**	**56.7**	**63.6**	**103.8**	**105.0**	**4.7**	**3.1**	**39.3**	**56.6**	**4.1**	**32.8**	**62.2**	**5.0**
DEVELOPED COUNTRIES	**14.9**	**11.4**	**72.2**	**74.5**	**110.8**	**111.0**	**1.9**	**1.6**	**22.5**	**65.9**	**11.6**	**18.3**	**67.5**	**14.2**

Source: United Nations Population Division, *World Resources 1998–99*.

Table F

World Countries: Mortality, Health, and Nutrition, 1970–1997

COUNTRY	MORTALITY									HEALTH					NUTRITION
	Crude Death Rate per 1,000 of the Population			Infant Mortality Rate per 1,000 Live Births			Under-5 Mortality per 1,000 Live Births			Population per Physician		Population per Nursing Person		Total Expenditure on Health as a % of GDP	Calories Available as a Percent of Need
	1975–80	1995–00	2015–20	1975–80	1995–00	2015–20	1960	1980	1995	1970	1994	1970	1994	1997	1995
AFRICA	17.7	12.9	8.4	120	85	55	X	X	X	X	X	X	X	X	X
Algeria	13.4	5.6	4.6	112	44	21	243	134	61	8100	X	X	X	3.3	123
Angola	24.4	18.7	11.1	160	124	79	345	261	292	X	X	X	X	3.9	8
Benin	21.1	12.4	6.9	122	84	46	210	176	142	28,960	X	2,610	X	1.7	104
Botswana	11.3	13.0	7.5	76	56	33	170	94	52	15,540	X	1,920	X	1.8	97
Burkina Faso	21.9	17.7	10.7	127	97	63	318	218	164	95,690	X	X	X	4.7	94
Burundi	18.8	17.0	10.8	127	114	78	255	193	176	58,570	17,240	6,910	4,800	1.0	84
Cameroon	17.6	11.9	6.5	102	58	34	264	173	106	29,390	12,000	2,610	2,000	1.0	95
Central African Republic	20.6	16.4	10.3	122	96	60	294	202	165	44,020	X	2,480	X	2.0	82
Chad	23.1	17.3	11.3	154	115	79	325	254	152	61,900	29,410	8,020	X	1.6	73
Congo (Zaire)	17.5	13.5	8.0117	89	53	X	286	204	185	X	X	X	X	0.2	96
Congo	17.4	14.6	8.5	91	90	55	220	125	108	9,940	X	810	X	1.8	103
Cote d'Ivoire	17.5	13.8	8.7	117	86	54	300	180	150	15,540	X	1,930	X	1.4	111
Egypt	14.2	7.1	6.0	131	54	25	258	180	51	2,030	1,340	2,480	500	1.7	132
Equatorial Guinea	22.7	16.2	10.7	149	107	73	316	243	X	X	X	X	X	X	X
Eritrea	18.9	14.7	9.0	130	98	57	X	X	195	X	X	X	X	1.1	X
Ethiopia	22.1	16.2	9.4	149	107	65	260	260	195	85,690	X	X	X	1.6	73
Gabon	19.2	14.3	9.3	122	85	47	194	194	148	5,520	X	570	X	X	104
Gambia	24.9	17.4	12.3	167	122	85	276	X	110	24,420	X	X	X	X	X
Ghana	15.3	10.4	6.9	103	73	43	157	170	130	12,910	X	690	X	2.9	93
Guinea	25.4	18.4	12.1	167	124	87	337	278	219	50,650	X	3,370	X	1.2	97
Guinea-Bissau	26.2	20.6	14.0	176	132	94	336	290	227	17,500	X	2,860	X	X	97
Kenya	15.5	11.3	6.2	88	65	37	202	112	90	8,000	X	2,520	X	1.9	89
Lesotho	16.5	10.6	6.6	121	72	37	204	173	154	30,400	X	3,860	X	3.7	93
Liberia	18.1	15.3	8.0	167	153	67	288	235	216	X	X	X	X	X	98
Libya	12.7	6.9	4.5	107	56	25	269	150	63	X	X	X	X	X	140
Madagascar	16.1	9.9	6.0	150	77	42	364	216	164	10,310	X	2,500	X	1.4	95
Malawi	24.0	22.4	12.6	177	142	93	365	290	219	76,580	50,360	5,330	1,980	2.3	88
Mali	24.1	17.1	11.1	191	149	107	400	210	210	45,320	21,180	2,670	2,050	2.0	96
Mauritania	20.0	13.1	8.8	125	92	59	321	249	195	17,960	X	3,750	X	1.8	106
Mauritius	6.3	6.5	6.9	38	15	8	84	42	23	4,170	X	610	X	X	128
Morocco	13.0	6.7	5.8	110	51	24	215	145	75	13,090	X	X	X	1.2	125
Mozambique	20.8	17.5	11.1	160	110	74	331	269	275	18,870	X	4,280	X	4.6	77
Namibia	15.1	11.8	7.4	98	60	36	206	114	78	X	4,320	X	X	4.1	X
Niger	23.8	17.1	10.9	157	114	79	320	320	320	60,360	35,140	5,690	660	1.6	95
Nigeria	19.2	13.9	9.2	105	77	51	204	196	191	20,530	X	4,370	X	0.2	93
Rwanda	20.2	19.7	11.7	133	125	84	191	222	139	60,130	X	5,630	X	1.9	82
Senegal	21.7	14.5	9.6	97	62	39	303	221	110	15,810	X	1,670	X	1.2	98
Sierra Leone	29.0	25.7	16.1	192	169	114	385	301	284	17,830	X	2,700	X	1.6	83
Somalia	22.7	16.9	10.7	149	112	77	294	246	211	X	X	X	X	X	81
South Africa	12.4	7.9	6.0	72	48	27	91	91	67	X	X	300	X	3.6	126
Sudan	17.8	11.7	8.4	97	71	45	292	210	115	X	X	X	X	X	87
Swaziland	16.0	9.2	5.7	108	65	34	233	151	X	X	X	X	X	X	X
Tanzania	16.4	13.5	8.0	113	80	51	249	202	160	22,900	3,400	X	X	1.1	X
Togo	17.4	14.9	8.5	117	86	52	164	175	128	28,860	X	1,590	X	1.6	99
Tunisia	10.0	5.9	5.5	88	37	18	244	102	37	5,930	1,540	940	300	3.0	131

(Continued on next page)

COUNTRY	MORTALITY									HEALTH					NUTRITION
	Crude Death Rate per 1,000 of the Population			Infant Mortality Rate per 1,000 Live Births			Under-5 Mortality per 1,000 Live Births			Population per Physician		Population per Nursing Person		Total Expenditure on Health as a % of GDP	Calories Available as a Percent of Need
	1975–80	1995–00	2015–20	1975–80	1995–00	2015–20	1960	1980	1995	1970	1994	1970	1994	1997	1995
Uganda	17.6	21.0	10.7	114	113	72	218	181	185	9,210	X	X	X	1.9	93
Zambia	16.5	18.0	9.3	94	103	55	220	160	203	13,640	11,430	1,730	610	2.9	87
Zimbabwe	13.1	14.6	8.0	86	68	39	181	125	74	6,310	X	650	X	1.7	94
NORTH AMERICA	8.5	8.6	8.8	14	7	5	X	X	X	X	X	X	X	X	X
Canada	7.2	7.4	8.7	12	6	5	33	13	8	680	X	140	X	6.3	122
United States	8.6	8.7	8.8	14	7	5	30	15	10	630	X	160	X	6.6	138
CENTRAL AMERICA	8.3	5.3	5.5	62	33	22	X	X	X	X	X	X	X	X	X
Belize	6.5	4.3	3.6	45	30	21	X	X	X	X	X	X	X	X	X
Costa Rica	4.8	3.8	4.7	30	12	8	112	29	16	1,620	X	460	X	6.0	121
Cuba	6.0	7.0	8.9	X	22	9	650	26	10	X	X	X	X	X	135
Dominican Republic	8.4	5.3	5.6	84	34	19	152	94	44	X	X	1,400	X	1.8	102
El Salvador	11.2	6.0	5.6	87	39	25	210	120	40	4,100	X	890	X	2.4	102
Guatemala	12.0	6.7	5.2	82	40	25	205	136	67	3,660	X	X	X	1.7	103
Haiti	16.0	12.8	8.8	121	82	51	270	195	124	X	X	X	X	1.2	89
Honduras	11.0	5.4	4.8	81	35	21	203	100	38	X	X	X	X	2.8	96
Jamaica	7.4	5.8	5.3	26	12	7	76	39	13	2,630	X	530	X	2.5	114
Mexico	7.7	5.1	5.6	57	31	21	141	81	32	1,480	X	1,620	X	2.8	X
Nicaragua	11.3	5.8	4.8	90	44	28	209	143	60	2,150	1,490	X	X	5.3	99
Panama	6.3	5.1	5.8	35	21	13	104	31	20	1,630	X	1,540	X	4.7	98
Trinidad and Tobago	7.1	6.0	6.4	32	14	7	73	40	18	2,250	X	150	X	X	114
SOUTH AMERICA	8.9	6.8	6.8	72	36	23	X	X	X	X	X	X	X	X	X
Argentina	8.9	7.9	7.5	39	22	14	68	41	27	530	X	960	X	4.3	131
Bolivia	16.0	9.1	6.4	131	66	33	252	170	105	1,970	X	2,990	X	3.8	84
Brazil	9.1	7.1	7.4	79	42	26	181	93	60	2,030	X	4,140	X	1.9	114
Chile	7.5	5.6	6.6	45	13	9	138	35	15	2,160	2,150	460	330	2.3	102
Colombia	7.6	5.6	5.9	59	24	21	132	59	36	2,260	X	X	X	2.9	106
Ecuador	9.8	6.0	6.0	82	46	29	180	101	40	2,870	960	2,640	600	2.0	105
Guyana	9.2	7.4	7.0	67	58	37	128	86	X	X	X	X	X	X	X
Paraguay	7.8	5.4	4.7	51	39	27	90	61	34	2,300	1,260	2,210	X	1.8	116
Peru	10.9	6.4	6.1	99	45	24	236	130	55	1,920	940	X	X	2.2	87
Suriname	7.3	5.5	5.4	44	24	12	96	52	X	X	X	X	X	X	X
Uruguay	10.1	10.4	10.3	42	17	14	47	42	21	910	X	X	X	1.9	101
Venezuela	5.8	4.7	5.2	39	21	14	70	42	24	1,130	640	450	330	1.0	99
ASIA	10.5	7.9	7.4	94	56	32	X	X	X	X	X	X	X	X	X
Afghanistan	24.0	20.8	12.8	183	154	118	360	280	257	X	X	X	X	X	72
Armenia	5.9	7.5	9.0	22	25	19	X	X	31	350	260	140	100	3.1	X
Azerbaijan	7.0	6.6	7.3	41	33	24	X	X	50	390	260	130	110	1.1	X
Bangladesh	18.9	9.7	6.7	137	78	38	247	211	115	8,450	5,220	65,810	11,350	1.2	88
Bhutan	21.2	13.7	8.0	165	104	56	324	249	189	X	X	X	X	X	128
Cambodia	40.0	12.2	8.1	263	102	55	217	330	174	X	X	X	X	0.7	96
China	6.7	7.1	8.2	52	38	20	209	65	47	1,500	1,060	2,500	1,490	2.1	112
Georgia	8.7	9.5	10.7	36	23	18	X	X	26	280	180	110	80	0.6	X
India	13.9	9.0	7.6	129	72	45	236	177	115	4,950	X	3,760	X	0.7	101
Indonesia	15.1	7.6	7.0	105	48	23	216	128	75	27,440	X	4,910	X	0.7	121
Iran	11.8	6.0	4.4	100	39	20	233	126	40	3,270	X	1,780	X	1.7	125

(Continued on next page)

COUNTRY	MORTALITY									HEALTH					NUTRITION
	Crude Death Rate per 1,000 of the Population			Infant Mortality Rate per 1,000 Live Births			Under-5 Mortality per 1,000 Live Births			Population per Physician		Population per Nursing Person		Total Expenditure on Health as a % of GDP	Calories Available as a Percent of Need
	1975–80	1995–00	2015–20	1975–80	1995–00	2015–20	1960	1980	1995	1970	1994	1970	1994	1997	1995
Iraq	8.8	8.5	4.5	84	95	23	171	83	71	X	X	X	X	X	128
Israel	6.8	6.4	6.5	18	7	5	39	19	9	410	X	X	X	0.3	125
Japan	6.1	8.2	12.1	9	4	4	40	11	6	890	X	310	X	5.7	125
Jordan	9.6	4.8	3.7	65	30	15	149	66	25	2,480	770	870	500	3.7	110
Kazakhstan	8.8	8.5	8.7	45	34	24	X	X	47	460	250	120	90	2.5	X
Korea, North	6.2	5.5	6.7	38	22	13	120	43	30	X	X	X	X	X	121
Korea, South	7.1	6.4	8.4	30	9	6	124	18	9	2,220	950	1,190	450	2.3	120
Kuwait	4.2	2.2	4.0	34	14	7	128	35	14	1,050	X	260	X	3.5	X
Kyrgyzstan	9.6	7.4	6.5	55	39	27	X	X	54	480	310	140	110	2.9	X
Laos	20.7	13.5	7.5	135	86	49	233	190	134	15,160	4,450	1,380	490	1.3	111
Lebanon	8.7	6.4	6.0	48	29	17	91	52	40	X	X	X	X	3.0	X
Malaysia	7.2	4.8	5.1	34	11	7	105	42	13	4,310	2,410	1,270	470	1.4	120
Mongolia	11.4	6.8	5.2	88	52	33	185	112	74	580	360	250	X	4.3	97
Myanmar (Burma)	14.9	9.8	7.1	114	78	33	237	146	150	8,820	12,900	3,050	1,240	0.4	114
Nepal	18.4	11.0	6.6	142	82	40	279	177	114	52,050	16,110	17,970	2,300	1.2	100
Oman	12.4	4.3	3.2	95	25	12	300	95	25	9,270	X	3,820	X	X	X
Pakistan	15.4	7.8	5.2	130	74	45	221	151	137	4,670	X	7,020	X	0.8	99
Philippines	9.0	5.7	5.3	62	35	18	102	70	53	9,270	X	2,680	X	1.3	104
Saudi Arabia	10.7	4.2	3.7	75	23	10	292	90	34	7,460	710	2,080	460	6.4	120
Singapore	5.1	5.0	7.1	13	5	5	40	13	6	1,520	X	280	X	1.5	136
Sri Lanka	7.1	5.9	6.6	44	15	8	130	52	19	5,900	X	1,290	X	1.4	101
Syria	8.9	4.9	4.0	67	33	17	201	73	36	X	X	X	X	X	126
Tajikistan	8.9	6.9	5.5	69	56	38	X	X	79	630	430	190	140	2.4	X
Thailand	8.3	6.6	7.4	56	30	13	146	61	32	8,290	4,420	1,170	910	2.0	103
Turkey	10.2	6.5	6.7	120	44	22	217	141	50	2,230	980	1,000	1,110	2.7	127
Turkmenistan	9.6	7.6	6.0	73	57	38	X	X	85	460	280	140	90	1.2	X
United Arab Emirates	7.4	2.9	6.0	38	15	6	240	64	19	1,120	1,100	X	580	X	X
Uzbekistan	8.5	6.6	5.7	58	43	30	X	X	62	490	280	150	90	3.3	X
Vietnam	11.4	7.0	5.8	82	37	21	219	105	X	X	2,300	4,310	400	1.1	103
Yemen	20.7	10.4	5.2	158	80	38	X	X	110	34,790	X	X	X	1.3	X
EUROPE	10.5	11.5	12.4	22	12	8	X	X	X	X	X	X	X	X	X
Albania	6.4	6.2	7.1	50	32	20	151	57	40	1,070	X	230	X	2.5	107
Austria	12.4	10.0	10.7	17	6	5	43	17	7	550	230	300	X	5.7	133
Belarus	9.4	12.1	13.3	22	15	10	X	X	20	390	230	120	90	5.2	X
Belgium	11.7	10.5	11.3	14	7	5	35	15	10	640	X	X	X	6.7	149
Bosnia-Herzegovina	6.5	7.3	10.9	36	13	9	X	X	17	X	X	X	X	X	X
Bulgaria	10.5	13.3	13.9	22	16	10	70	25	19	540	X	240	X	3.5	148
Croatia	10.8	11.7	13.4	21	10	7	X	X	14	X	X	X	X	8.4	X
Czech Republic	13.2	12.0	12.3	18	9	6	X	X	10	X	270	X	X	6.4	X
Denmark	10.4	11.8	11.8	9	7	5	25	10	7	690	X	X	X	5.1	135
Estonia	12.1	13.1	13.9	22	12	6	X	X	22	300	260	110	130	5.8	X
Finland	9.3	10.2	11.3	9	5	5	28	9	5	960	X	130	X	5.7	113
France	10.3	9.1	10.5	11	7	6	34	13	9	750	X	270	X	7.7	143
Germany	12.2	10.9	12.6	15	6	5	40	16	7	580	X	X	X	8.1	X
Greece	8.8	9.9	12.3	25	8	7	64	23	10	620	X	990	X	5.3	151
Hungary	12.8	14.6	14.5	27	14	9	57	26	14	510	X	210	X	4.5	137
Iceland	6.4	6.8	7.4	9	5	5	22	9	X	X	X	X	X	X	X

(Continued on next page)

COUNTRY	MORTALITY									HEALTH					NUTRITION
	Crude Death Rate per 1,000 of the Population			Infant Mortality Rate per 1,000 Live Births			Under-5 Mortality per 1,000 Live Births			Population per Physician		Population per Nursing Person		Total Expenditure on Health as a % of GDP	Calories Available as a Percent of Need
	1975–80	1995–00	2015–20	1975–80	1995–00	2015–20	1960	1980	1995	1970	1994	1970	1994	1997	1995
Ireland	10.2	8.6	8.9	15	6	5	36	14	7	980	X	160	X	5.1	157
Italy	9.8	9.9	12.4	18	7	6	50	17	8	550	X	X	X	5.3	139
Latvia	12.4	13.8	14.6	23	16	11	X	X	26	X	280	X	120	3.5	X
Lithuania	9.9	11.6	12.9	22	13	7	X	X	19	360	230	130	90	5.0	X
Macedonia	7.1	7.4	9.3	57	23	13	X	X	31	X	430	X	X	6.2	X
Moldova	10.6	10.8	10.6	46	26	19	X	X	34	490	250	X	X	6.2	X
Netherlands	8.1	8.8	10.3	10	6	5	22	11	8	800	X	300	X	6.2	114
Norway	10.0	10.7	10.3	9	5	5	23	11	8	720	X	160	X	6.2	120
Poland	9.2	10.7	11.1	23	13	8	70	24	16	700	450	260	190	4.8	131
Portugal	10.3	10.9	11.7	30	8	5	112	31	11	1,110	X	860	X	4.9	136
Romania	9.7	11.6	12.8	31	24	14	82	36	29	840	540	430	X	2.9	116
Russian Federation	10.3	14.5	14.8	30	19	12	X	X	30	340	220	110	90	4.1	X
Slovak Republic	10.4	10.5	10.8	22	12	8	X	X	15	X	290	X	110	6.1	X
Slovenia	10.4	10.7	13.3	17	7	5	X	X	8	X	X	X	X	7.1	X
Spain	8.1	9.4	11.3	16	7	6	57	16	9	750	X	X	X	5.8	141
Sweden	10.9	11.2	10.4	8	5	5	20	9	5	730	X	140	X	7.2	111
Switzerland	9.0	9.1	10.4	10	5	5	27	11	7	700	X	X	X	7.1	136
Ukraine	11.0	13.8	14.4	23	18	10	X	X	24	360	220	110	90	3.9	X
United Kingdom	11.9	11.1	11.0	14	6	5	27	14	7	810	X	240	X	5.7	130
Yugoslavia Serbia-Montenegro)	9.2	9.7	11.6	38	19	12	X	X	23	X	X	X	X	X	X
OCEANIA	8.7	7.7	7.6	35	24	15	X	X	X	X	X	X	X	X	X
Australia	7.7	7.5	8.1	13	6	5	24	13	8	840	X	X	X	5.8	124
Fiji	5.8	4.6	5.5	37	20	10	97	42	X	X	X	X	X	X	X
New Zealand	8.2	7.9	8.0	14	7	5	26	16	9	870	X	150	X	5.9	131
Papua New Guinea	15.0	9.9	7.0	77	61	37	248	95	95	11,640	12,750	1,710	1,160	2.8	114
Solomon Islands	7.4	4.1	3.4	47	23	12	X	X	X	X	X	X	X	X	X
DEVELOPING COUNTRIES	11.5	8.5	7.4	98	6	2	38	X	X	X	X	X	X	X	X
DEVELOPED COUNTRIES	9.5	10.3	11.2	18	9	7	X	X	X	X	X	X	X	X	X

Sources: United Nations Children's Fund, United Nations Development Programme, UNESCO; World Resources Institute, *World Resource 1998–1999, World Almanac and Book of Facts 1998.*

Table G

World Countries: Illiteracy and Education

COUNTRY	ILLITERACY				EDUCATION											
	ADULT MALE ILLITERACY (% of above age 15)		ADULT FEMALE ILLITERACY (% of above age 15)										FEMALE ENROLEMENT as a % of the Total			
					Preprimary	Primary % of Relevant Age Group		Secondary % of Relevant Age Group		HIgher Ed. % of Relevant Age Group		Primary		Secondary	
	1970	1995	1970	1995	1995	1980	1995	1980	1995	1980	1995	1980	1995	1980	1995
AFRICA															
Algeria	61	26	88	51	2	94	107	33	62	6	11	42	46	59	54
Angola	84	X	93	X	68	174	88	21	14	0	1	47	X	33	X
Benin	83	51	96	74	3	67	72	16	16	1	3	32	X	26	X
Botswana	40	20	69	40	X	91	115	19	56	1	4	55	50	56	53
Burkina Faso	87	71	98	91	X	17	38	3	8	0	1	37	39	33	34
Burundi	70	51	93	78	X	26	70	3	7	1	1	39	45	25	38
Cameroon	53	25	82	48	11	98	88	18	27	2	X	45	47	34	40
Central African Republic	79	32	95	48	71	58	14	10	1	1	X	37	X	25	X
Chad	64	38	88	65	1	X	55	X	9	X	1	X	32	X	17
Congo (Zaire)	39	13	72	32	1	80	72	24	26	1	2	42	43	X	30
Congo Republic	51	17	79	33	1	141	114	74	53	5	X	48	48	40	41
Cote d'Ivoire	75	50	94	70	2	75	69	19	23	3	4	40	43	28	34
Egypt	53	36	82	61	9	73	100	50	74	16	18	40	45	36	44
Equatorial Guinea	35	X	71	X	X	X	X	X	X	X	X	X	X	X	X
Eritrea	X	X	X	X	X	X	X	X	X	X	X	X	44	X	42
Ethiopia	76	55	91	75	1	36	31	9	11	0	1	35	38	36	46
Gabon	61	26	86	47	X	X	142	X	X	X	X	49	50	42	X
Gambia	72	47	93	75	24	53	73	11	22	X	2	35	41	30	X
Ghana	55	24	83	47	X	79	76	41	37	2	X	44	46	38	X
Guinea	75	50	94	78	9	36	48	17	12	5	X	33	33	28	24
Guinea-Bissau	57	32	83	58	X	68	64	6	X	X	X	32	X	22	X
Kenya	41	14	73	30	36	115	85	20	24	1	X	47	49	42	44
Lesotho	38	19	66	38	X	102	99	18	28	1	2	59	53	60	59
Liberia	73	X	93	X	X	X	X	X	X	X	X	X	X	X	X
Libya	43	12	89	37	X	125	110	76	97	8	16	47	49	39	X
Madagascar	34	X	57	X	X	133	72	X	14	3	3	49	49	X	50
Malawi	42	28	80	58	X	60	135	3	98	1	2	41	47	29	39
Mali	89	61	96	77	3	26	34	8	9	1	X	36	39	29	34
Mauritania	63	50	83	74	0	37	78	11	15	X	4	35	45	21	36
Mauritius	24	13	45	21	85	93	107	50	62	1	6	49	49	48	51
Morocco	67	43	91	69	63	83	83	26	39	6	11	37	42	38	42
Mozambique	74	42	94	77	X	99	60	5	7	0	1	43	42	29	40
Namibia	X	X	X	X	11	X	133	X	62	X	8	X	50	X	55
Niger	89	79	99	93	1	25	29	5	7	0	X	35	38	29	33
Nigeria	68	33	89	53	X	105	89	16	30	2	4	43	44	36	X
Rwanda	55	30	82	48	X	63	82	3	11	0	X	48	50	28	X
Senegal	76	57	93	77	2	46	65	11	16	3	3	40	43	34	35
Sierra Leone	78	55	95	82	X	52	X	14	X	1	X	42	X	30	X
Somalia	95	X	99	X	X	X	X	X	X	X	X	X	X	X	X
South Africa	28	18	32	18	28	85	117	X	84	X	17	X	49	X	53
Sudan	67	42	91	65	37	50	54	16	13	2	X	40	44	37	X

(Continued on next page)

COUNTRY	ILLITERACY				EDUCATION										
	ADULT MALE ILLITERACY (% of above age 15)		ADULT FEMALE ILLITERACY (% of above age 15)									FEMALE ENROLEMENT as a % of the Total			
					Preprimary	Primary % of Relevant Age Group		Secondary % of Relevant Age Group		Higher Ed. % of Relevant Age Group		Primary		Secondary	
	1970	1995	1970	1995	1995	1980	1995	1980	1995	1980	1995	1980	1995	1980	1995
Swaziland	47	X	56	X	X	X	X	X	X	X	X	X	X	X	X
Tanzania	45	21	79	43	0	93	67	3	5	X	1	47	49	33	43
Togo	64	33	90	63	3	118	118	33	27	2	3	38	40	24	26
Tunisia	58	21	83	45	X	102	116	27	61	5	13	42	47	39	47
Uganda	47	26	78	50	X	50	73	5	12	1	2	43	44	29	38
Zambia	36	14	68	29	X	90	89	16	28	2	3	47	48	35	38
Zimbabwe	25	10	62	20	X	85	116	8	47	1	7	48	48	42	44
NORTH AMERICA AND CENTRAL AMERICA															
Belize	X	X	X	X	X	X	X	X	X	X	X	X	X	X	X
Canada	X	X	X	X	63	99	102	88	106	57	103	49	48	49	49
Costa Rica	12	5	13	5	70	105	107	48	50	21	32	49	49	54	52
Cuba	15	4	22	5	89	106	105	81	80	17	14	48	49	51	54
Dominican Republic	30	18	34	18	20	118	103	42	41	X	X	40	50	X	57
El Salvador	39	27	48	30	31	74	88	25	32	13	18	49	49	43	48
Guatemala	49	38	64	51	32	71	84	18	25	8	8	45	46	43	X
Haiti	72	52	80	58	X	76	X	14	X	1	X	46	X	47	X
Honduras	43	27	49	27	14	98	111	30	32	8	10	50	50	50	X
Jamaica	34	19	27	11	81	103	109	67	66	7	6	50	49	52	X
Mexico	20	8	30	13	71	120	115	49	58	14	14	49	48	43	48
Nicaragua	42	35	44	33	20	98	110	43	47	13	9	51	50	52	53
Panama	20	9	22	10	76	106	106	61	68	21	30	48	X	51	X
Trinidad and Tobago	5	1	11	3	10	99	96	70	72	4	8	50	49	50	51
United States	1	X	1	X	68	99	102	91	97	56	81	49	49	49	49
SOUTH AMERICA															
Argentina	7	4	8	4	50	106	108	56	72	22	38	49	X	64	X
Bolivia	29	10	54	24	X	87	X	37	X	16	X	47	X	X	X
Brazil	28	17	35	27	56	98	112	33	45	11	11	49	X	X	X
Chile	11	5	13	5	96	109	99	53	69	12	28	49	49	55	54
Colombia	18	9	21	9	28	124	114	41	67	9	17	50	50	50	X
Ecuador	21	8	30	12	49	117	109	53	50	35	X	49	49	48	47
Guyana	6	X	12	X	X	X	X	X	X	X	X	X	X	X	X
Paraguay	14	7	24	9	38	106	109	27	38	9	10	X	X	X	X
Peru	17	6	40	17	36	114	123	59	70	17	31	X	X	X	X
Suriname	12	X	24	X	X	X	X	X	X	X	X	X	X	X	X
Uruguay	8	3	7	2	33	107	111	62	82	17	27	49	49	58	55
Venezuela	20	8	27	10	43	93	94	21	35	21	29	50	50	X	58
ASIA															
Afghanistan	75	X	97	X	X	X	X	X	X	X	X	X	X	X	X
Armenia	X	X	X	X	22	X	82	X	79	30	49	X	50	X	X
Azerbaijan	X	X	X	X	20	115	104	93	74	24	20	X	47	X	48
Bangladesh	64	51	88	74	X	61	92	18	X	3	X	37	X	24	X

(Co

(Continued on next page)

COUNTRY	ILLITERACY				EDUCATION										
	ADULT MALE ILLITERACY (% of above age 15)		ADULT FEMALE ILLITERACY (% of above age 15)									FEMALE ENROLEMENT as a % of the Total			
					Preprimary	Primary % of Relevant Age Group		Secondary % of Relevant Age Group		Higher Ed. % of Relevant Age Group		Primary		Secondary	
	1970	1995	1970	1995	1995	1980	1995	1980	1995	1980	1995	1980	1995	1980	1995
Bhutan	69	X	91	X	X	X	X	X	X	X	X	X	X	X	X
Cambodia	X	20	77	47	5	X	122	32	27	1	2	X	44	X	38
China	33	10	64	27	29	113	118	46	67	2	5	45	47	40	44
Georgia	X	X	X	X	32	X	82	X	73	30	38	X	X	X	X
India	52	35	82	62	5	83	100	30	49	5	6	39	43	32	38
Indonesia	31	10	56	22	19	107	114	29	48	4	11	46	48	36	46
Iran	X	22	X	34	7	87	99	42	69	X	15	40	47	39	45
Iraq	56	29	85	55	8	113	90	57	44	9	X	46	45	32	39
Israel	X	X	X	X	71	95	99	73	89	29	41	49	49	56	53
Japan	1	X	1	X	49	101	102	93	99	31	40	49	49	50	50
Jordan	27	7	66	21	25	104	94	75	X	27	X	48	49	46	55
Kazakhstan	X	X	X	X	29	84	96	93	83	34	33	X	49	X	52
Korea, North	X	1	X	3	X	X	X	X	X	X	X	X	X	X	X
Korea, South	6	1	20	3	85	110	101	78	101	15	52	49	48	46	47
Kuwait	35	18	55	25	52	102	73	80	64	11	25	48	49	46	49
Kyrgyzstan	X	X	X	X	8	116	107	110	81	16	14	49	50	49	51
Laos	55	31	82	56	7	113	107	21	25	0	2	45	43	38	39
Lebanon	13	10	27	20	74	111	109	59	81	30	27	48	48	51	53
Malaysia	31	11	56	22	X	93	91	48	61	4	11	49	49	48	51
Mongolia	25	X	48	X	23	107	88	91	59	X	15	49	51	52	58
Myanmar (Burma)	16	11	40	22	X	91	100	22	32	5	5	48	48	45	X
Nepal	76	59	96	86	X	86	110	22	38	3	5	28	39	X	X
Oman	X	X	X	X	3	51	80	12	66	X	5	34	48	25	48
Pakistan	69	50	91	76	X	39	74	14	26	X	3	33	31	26	X
Philippines	14	5	17	6	13	112	116	64	79	24	27	49	50	53	X
Saudi Arabia	51	29	79	50	8	61	78	29	58	7	15	39	47	37	44
Singapore	13	4	39	14	X	108	104	58	62	8	34	48	X	51	X
Sri Lanka	12	7	29	13	X	103	113	55	75	3	5	48	48	51	51
Syria	39	14	79	44	7	100	101	46	44	17	18	43	47	37	44
Tajikistan	X	X	X	X	10	X	89	X	82	24	20	X	49	X	47
Thailand	14	4	30	8	58	99	87	29	55	15	20	48	49	46	50
Turkey	27	8	60	28	6	96	105	35	56	5	18	45	47	35	39
Turkmenistan	X	X	X	X	X	X	X	X	X	23	X	X	X	X	X
United Arab Emirates	39	21	60	20	57	89	95	52	78	3	9	48	48	45	51
Uzbekistan	X	X	X	X	54	81	77	105	93	29	32	49	49	46	48
Vietnam	18	X	35	X	35	109	114	42	47	2	4	47	X	47	X
Yemen	X	X	X	X	1	X	79	X	23	X	4	X	28	X	X
EUROPE															
Albania	X	X	X	X	38	113	87	67	35	8	19	47	48	59	54
Austria	X	X	X	X	76	99	101	99	104	26	45	49	49	49	49
Belarus	X	X	X	X	80	104	97	98	X	39	X	X	48	X	50
Belgium	1	X	1	X	116	104	103	91	144	26	49	49	49	X	X
Bosnia-Herzegovina	X	X	X	X	X	X	X	X	X	X	X	X	X	X	X
Bulgaria	6	X	X	X	62	98	94	84	78	16	39	49	48	68	67
Croatia	X	X	X	X	31	X	86	X	82	19	28	49	49	X	65

(Continued on next page)

COUNTRY	ILLITERACY				EDUCATION										
	ADULT MALE ILLITERACY (% of above age 15)		ADULT FEMALE ILLITERACY (% of above age 15)									FEMALE ENROLEMENT as a % of the Total			
					Preprimary	Primary % of Relevant Age Group		Secondary % of Relevant Age Group		HIgher Ed. % of Relevant Age Group		Primary		Secondary	
	1970	1995	1970	1995	1995	1980	1995	1980	1995	1980	1995	1980	1995	1980	1995
Czech Republic	X	X	X	X	91	X	96	X	96	18	21	X	49	X	52
Denmark	X	X	X	X	81	996	99	105	118	28	45	49	49	51	52
Estonia	X	X	X	X	56	98	91	X	86	25	38	49	48	X	53
Finland	X	X	X	X	39	56	100	100	116	32	67	49	49	53	53
France	1	X	2	X	84	111	106	85	111	25	50	48	48	49	51
Germany	X	X	X	X	84	X	102	98	103	34	43	X	49	X	50
Greece	7	X	24	X	61	103	X	81	95	17	38	48	48	50	50
Hungary	2	X	2	X	86	96	97	70	81	14	19	49	49	65	63
Iceland	X	X	X	X	X	X	X	X	X	X	X	X	X	X	X
Ireland	X	X	X	X	107	100	104	90	114	18	37	49	49	51	50
Italy	1	X	1	X	96	100	98	72	74	27	41	49	49	48	50
Latvia	X	X	X	X	44	78	89	100	85	24	26	49	48	X	52
Lithuania	X	X	X	X	36	79	96	114	84	35	28	49	48	X	52
Macedonia	X	X	X	X	24	100	89	61	57	28	18	X	48	X	60
Moldova	X	X	X	X	45	83	94	78	80	30	25	49	49	51	51
Netherlands	X	X	X	X	100	100	107	93	139	29	49	49	50	52	52
Norway	X	X	X	X	98	100	99	94	92	26	55	49	49	51	51
Poland	1	X	3	X	45	100	98	77	96	18	27	49	48	71	68
Portugal	22	X	35	X	58	123	128	37	102	11	34	48	X	48	X
Romania	4	X	X	X	53	102	100	71	66	12	18	49	49	65	53
Russian Federation	X	X	X	X	63	102	108	96	87	46	43	49	49	51	52
Slovak Republic	X	X	X	X	71	X	97	X	91	X	20	X	49	X	51
Slovenia	X	X	X	X	66	X	98	X	91	X	32	X	49	X	52
Spain	6	X	14	X	69	109	105	87	118	23	46	49	48	51	51
Sweden	X	X	X	X	60	97	105	88	132	31	43	49	49	51	51
Switzerland	X	X	X	X	94	X	107	X	91	18	32	49	49	49	50
Ukraine	X	X	X	X	54	102	87	94	91	42	41	49	49	X	51
United Kingdom	X	X	X	X	29	103	115	83	134	19	48	49	49	49	49
Yugoslavia (Serbia-Montenegro)	X	X	X	X	31	29	72	X	65	X	21	X	49	X	51
OCEANIA															
Australia	X	X	X	X	73	112	108	71	147	25	72	49	49	50	49
Fiji	21	X	33	X	X	X	X	X	X	X	X	X	X	X	X
New Zealand	X	X	X	X	77	111	104	83	117	27	58	49	49	49	50
Papua New Guinea	40	19	67	37	1	59	80	12	14	2	3	41	45	32	41
Solomon Islands	X	X	X	X	X	X	X	X	X	X	X	X	X	X	X

Sources: World Development Indicators (World Bank, 1998); *Human Development Report* (World Bank, 1995); *World Resources 1998–99* (World Resources Institute, 1999); United Nations Children's Fund; UNESCO; the World Health Organization.

Table H

Land Use and Agricultural Productivity, 1998

Country	Land Under Permanent Crops % of land area		Irrigated Land % of cropland		Arable land Hectares per capita		Agricultural Machinery Tractors per thousand agricultural workers		Agricultural Productivity Agr. value added per agricultural worker 1995 dollars		Food Production Index 1989–91 = 100	
	1980	1996	1979–81	1994–96	1979–81	1994–96	1979–81	1994–96	1979–81	1995–97	1979–81	1995–97
AFRICA												
Algeria	0.3	0.2	3.4	6.9	0.37	0.27	27	43	1,411	1,903	69.7	118.2
Angola	0.4	0.4	2.2	2.1	0.41	0.27	4	3	X	117	91.9	130.1
Benin	4.0	4.1	0.3	0.5	0.39	0.26	0	0	302	504	63.4	129.5
Botswana	*0.0*	*0.0*	0.5	*0.3*	0.44	0.25	9	21	619	647	87.6	104.2
Burkina Faso	0.1	0.1	0.4	0.7	0.39	0.34	0	0	134	159	62.6	122.4
Burundi	10.1	12.9	0.7	1.3	0.22	0.13	0	0	177	139	80.5	96.4
Cameroon	2.2	2.3	0.2	0.3	0.68	0.45	0	0	834	958	83.2	118.7
Central African Republic	0.1	0.1	X	X	0.81	0.59	0	0	396	439	79.9	122.7
Chad	0.0	0.0	0.2	0.4	0.70	0.48	0	0	155	212	90.6	117.5
Congo (Zaire)	0.3	0.4	0.1	0.1	0.25	0.16	0	0	270	285	71.9	104.9
Congo Republic	0.1	0.1	0.7	0.6	0.07	0.05	2	1	391	470	80.3	114.5
Côte d'Ivoire	7.2	13.5	1.0	1.0	0.24	0.21	1	1	1,074	1,005	70.9	119.2
Egypt	0.2	0.5	100.0	100.0	0.06	0.05	4	10	721	1,163	68.4	129.8
Equatorial Guinea	X	X	X	X	X	X	X	X	X	X	X	X
Eritrea	X	0.8	X	5.4	X	0.12	X	1	X	X	X	102.3
Ethiopia	X	0.6	X	1.6	X	0.20	X	0	X	X	90.2	X
Gabon	X	X	X	X	X	X	X	X	X	X	X	X
Gambia	X	X	X	X	X	X	X	X	X	X	X	X
Ghana	7.5	7.5	0.2	0.1	0.18	0.16	1	1	663	533	73.5	147.7
Guinea	0.9	1.2	12.8	10.9	0.11	0.09	0	0	X	262	96.5	129.2
Guinea-Bissau	X	X	X	X	X	X	X	X	X	X	X	X
Kenya	0.8	0.9	0.9	1.5	0.23	0.15	1	1	262	230	67.7	102.9
Lesotho	X	X	X	X	0.22	0.17	6	6	498	319	89.4	104.4
Liberia	X	X	X	X	X	X	X	X	X	X	X	X
Libya	X	X	X	X	X	X	X	X	X	X	X	X
Madagascar	X	X	X	X	X	X	X	X	X	X	X	X
Malawi	0.9	1.1	1.3	1.6	0.20	0.16	0	0	100	122	91.2	105.3
Mali	0.0	0.0	2.9	2.3	0.31	0.37	0	1	225	241	79.7	118.7
Mauritania	0.0	0.0	22.8	10.3	0.14	0.20	1	1	301	439	86.1	103.2
Mauritius	X	X	X	X	X	X	X	X	X	X	X	X
Morocco	1.1	1.9	15.2	13.0	0.38	0.33	7	10	1,117	1,593	55.9	94.9
Mozambique	0.3	0.3	2.1	3.4	0.24	0.19	1	1	X	76	99.2	119.5
Namibia	0.0	0.0	0.6	0.8	0.64	0.51	10	11	876	1,235	107.4	118.8
Niger	0.0	0.0	0.7	1.4	0.62	0.53	0	0	222	190	101.4	118.4
Nigeria	2.8	2.8	0.7	0.7	0.39	0.27	1	1	370	541	57.7	134.2
Rwanda	10.3	12.2	0.4	0.3	0.15	0.13	0	0	307	201	89.7	76.9
Senegal	0.0	0.1	2.6	3.1	0.42	0.27	0	0	341	321	74.5	109.1
Sierra Leone	0.7	0.8	4.1	5.4	0.14	0.11	0	1	368	404	84.5	94.7
Somalia	X	X	X	X	X	X	X	X	X	X	X	X
South Africa	0.7	0.7	8.4	8.1	0.45	0.38	90	69	2,465	3,355	92.8	97.5
Sudan	X	X	X	X	X	X	X	X	X	X	X	X
Swaziland	X	X	X	X	X	X	X	X	X	X	X	X
Tanzania	1.0	1.0	3.8	4.6	0.12	0.10	1	1	X	159	76.8	97.2
Togo	6.6	6.6	0.3	0.3	0.76	0.50	0	0	345	510	77.0	129.9
Tunisia	9.7	13.1	4.9	7.5	0.51	0.32	30	39	1,743	2,750	67.6	108.3
Uganda	8.0	8.8	0.1	0.1	0.32	0.26	0	1	X	326	70.5	107.7
Zambia	0.0	0.0	0.4	0.9	0.89	0.59	3	2	331	226	74.2	95.6
Zimbabwe	0.3	0.3	3.1	4.6	0.36	0.27	7	7	307	316	82.1	94.8
NORTH AMERICA												
Canada	0.0	0.0	1.3	1.6	1.86	1.53	824	1,683	X	X	79.9	112.7
United States	0.2	0.2	10.8	12.0	0.83	0.67	1,230	1,452	X	34,727	94.7	113.7
CENTRAL AMERICA												
Belize	X	X	X	X	X	X	X	X	X	X	X	X
Costa Rica	4.4	4.8	12.1	23.8	0.12	0.08	22	23	3,159	4,627	73.0	128.4
Cuba	X	X	X	X	X	X	X	X	X	X	X	X
Dominican Republic	7.2	11.4	11.7	13.7	0.19	0.17	3	3	1,839	2,454	85.1	109.1
El Salvador	8.0	10.5	14.8	14.2	0.12	0.11	5	5	2,013	1,705	90.8	109.5
Guatemala	4.4	5.1	5.0	6.5	0.19	0.14	3	2	2,110	1,902	69.9	114.0
Haiti	12.5	12.7	7.9	9.7	0.10	0.08	0	0	578	407	105.5	90.5
Honduras	1.8	3.1	4.1	3.6	0.44	0.30	5	7	697	1,018	88.2	104.7
Jamaica	5.5	6.1	13.6	14.0	0.08	0.07	9	11	892	1,294	86.0	117.9
Mexico	0.8	1.1	20.3	23.1	0.34	0.27	16	20	1,482	1,690	84.9	120.6
Nicaragua	1.5	2.4	6.0	3.3	0.39	0.54	6	7	1,334	1,407	117.9	123.7
Panama	1.6	2.1	5.0	4.9	0.22	0.19	27	20	2,122	2,463	85.6	102.5
Trinidad and Tobago	X	X	X	X	X	X	X	X	X	X	X	X

(Continued on next page)

	Land Under Permanent Crops % of land area		Irrigated Land % of cropland		Arable land Hectares per capita		Agricultural Machinery Tractors per thousand agricultural workers		Agricultural Productivity Agr. value added per agricultural worker 1995 dollars		Food Production Index 1989–91 = 100	
Country	**1980**	**1996**	**1979–81**	**1994–96**	**1979–81**	**1994–96**	**1979–81**	**1994–96**	**1979–81**	**1995–97**	**1979–81**	**1995–97**
SOUTH AMERICA												
Argentina	0.8	0.8	5.8	6.3	0.89	0.72	132	190	12,195	13,833	94.9	121.9
Bolivia	0.2	0.2	6.6	3.7	0.35	0.27	4	4	X	X	71.0	126.7
Brazil	1.2	1.4	3.3	4.9	0.32	0.32	31	51	2,047	3,931	69.5	122.2
Chile	0.3	0.4	29.6	32.6	0.36	0.25	43	44	2,612	5,211	71.5	128.7
Colombia	1.4	2.4	7.7	23.4	0.13	0.05	8	7	1,926	2,890	76.0	110.8
Ecuador	3.3	5.2	19.4	8.1	0.20	0.14	6	7	1,206	1,764	76.6	136.9
Guyana	X	X	X	X	X	X	X	X	X	X	X	X
Paraguay	0.3	0.2	3.4	3.0	0.52	0.45	14	25	2,506	3,295	60.6	116.7
Peru	0.3	0.4	32.8	41.8	0.19	0.16	5	3	1,349	1,619	78.4	131.5
Suriname	X	X	X	X	X	X	X	X	X	X	X	X
Uruguay	0.3	0.3	5.4	10.7	0.48	0.39	171	172	6,822	9,384	86.8	128.8
Venezuela	0.9	1.0	3.6	5.2	0.19	0.12	50	58	4,041	4,931	79.6	114.0
ASIA												
Afghanistan	X	X	X	X	X	X	X	X	X	X	X	X
Armenia	X	3.5	X	43.7	X	0.15	X	64	X	4,477	X	82.3
Azerbaijan	X	4.6	X	50.0	X	0.21	X	31	X	847	X	55.6
Bangladesh	2.0	2.5	17.1	39.1	0.10	0.07	0	0	181	221	79.2	106.0
Bhutan	X	X	X	X	X	X	X	X	X	X	X	X
Cambodia	0.4	0.6	4.9	4.5	0.30	0.37	0	0	X	407	51.1	124.8
China	0.4	1.2	45.1	37.0	0.10	0.10	2	1	162	296	61.0	155.8
Hong Kong, China	*1.0*	1.0	43.8	28.6	0.00	0.00	0	0	X	X	97.4	56.7
Georgia	X	4.7	X	42.2	X	0.14	X	28	X	1,838	X	74.6
India	1.8	2.4	22.8	32.0	0.24	0.17	2	5	253	343	68.4	117.1
Indonesia	4.4	7.2	16.2	15.0	0.12	0.09	0	1	610	745	63.5	122.4
Iran	0.5	1.0	35.5	38.0	0.36	0.30	17	39	2,533	3,831	60.9	136.8
Iraq	X	X	X	X	X	X	X	X	X	X	X	X
Israel	4.3	4.2	49.3	45.3	0.08	0.06	294	336	X	X	85.7	114.1
Japan	1.6	1.0	62.6	62.7	0.04	0.03	209	593	15,698	28,665	94.2	96.9
Jordan	0.4	1.0	11.0	18.2	0.14	0.08	48	42	1,447	1,634	55.3	157.3
Kazakhstan	X	0.1	X	6.9	X	2.04	X	106	X	1,477	X	68.5
Korea, South	1.4	2.0	59.6	60.7	0.05	0.04	1	34	3,957	10,962	77.9	119.1
Kuwait	X	X	X	X	0.00	0.00	3	14	X	X	98.9	139.3
Kyrgyzstan	X	2.7	X	76.8	X	0.23	X	44	X	2,917	X	123.8
Laos	0.1	0.2	15.4	20.3	0.21	0.17	0	0	X	526	71.2	112.4
Lebanon	8.9	12.5	28.3	28.4	0.07	0.05	28	77	X	X	57.8	117.6
Malaysia	11.6	17.6	6.7	4.5	0.07	0.09	4	23	3,279	6,267	55.4	124.0
Mongolia	*0.0*	0.0	3.0	6.1	0.71	0.54	32	22	*727*	1,085	88.2	81.6
Myanmar (Burma)	0.7	0.9	10.4	15.9	0.28	0.22	1	1	X	X	87.8	133.5
Nepal	0.2	0.4	22.5	30.6	0.16	0.13	0	0	162	187	65.1	113.5
Oman	X	X	X	X	X	X	X	X	X	X	X	X
Pakistan	0.4	0.7	72.7	80.2	0.24	0.17	5	12	392	585	66.4	130.5
Philippines	14.8	14.4	14.0	16.7	0.09	0.07	1	1	1,348	1,379	86.4	120.6
Saudi Arabia	0.0	0.1	28.9	38.7	0.20	0.20	2	11	2,167	10,507	31.0	90.8
Singapore	9.8	*0.0*	X	X	0.00	0.00	3	16	13,937	39,851	154.3	37.9
Sri Lanka	15.9	15.5	28.3	29.2	0.06	0.05	8	9	648	732	98.4	113.0
Syria	2.5	3.9	9.6	20.4	0.60	0.33	29	65	X	X	94.5	136.7
Tajikistan	X	0.5	X	80.6	X	0.14	X	37	X	X	X	67.9
Thailand	3.5	6.6	16.4	23.2	0.35	0.29	1	7	630	928	79.9	107.2
Turkey	4.1	3.2	9.6	15.4	0.57	0.40	38	57	1,852	1,835	75.8	106.3
Turkmenistan	X	0.1	X	87.8	X	0.32	X	83	X	X	X	108.7
United Arab Emirates	X	X	X	X	X	X	X	X	X	X	X	X
Uzbekistan	X	0.9	X	81.6	X	0.20	X	59	X	2,085	X	100.7
Vietnam	1.9	3.8	24.1	29.6	0.11	0.07	1	4	X	226	64.0	132.7
Yemen	0.2	0.2	19.9	31.3	0.16	0.09	3	2	X	305	75.0	115.5
EUROPE												
Albania	4.3	4.6	53.0	48.4	0.22	0.18	15	10	1,193	1,717	X	X
Austria	1.2	1.1	0.2	0.3	0.20	0.18	945	1,492	9,761	15,474	92.3	100.0
Belarus	X	0.7	X	1.9	X	0.60	X	131	X	3,461	X	58.9
Belgium	0.4	0.5	0.1	0.1	X	X	917	1,130	X	X	88.4	114.4
Bosnia-Herzegovina	X	X	X	X	X	X	X	X	X	X	X	X
Bulgaria	3.2	1.8	28.3	18.7	0.43	0.48	66	61	2,754	4,351	105.3	68.3
Croatia	X	2.2	X	0.2	X	0.24	X	14	X	7,144	X	57.7
Czech Republic	X	3.1	X	0.7	X	0.30	X	148	X	X	X	81.9
Denmark	0.3	0.2	14.5	20.3	0.52	0.45	973	1,088	21,321	46,621	83.2	102.5
Estonia	X	0.4	X	X	X	0.76	X	475	X	3,342	X	49.3
Finland	X	X	X	X	0.54	0.49	721	1,301	16,995	28,296	92.8	92.4
France	2.5	2.1	4.6	8.2	0.32	0.31	737	1,189	14,956	34,760	93.7	103.6
Germany	1.4	0.7	3.7	3.9	0.15	0.14	624	954	X	19,930	91.0	90.9
Greece	7.9	8.4	24.2	33.8	0.30	0.28	120	267	8,804	12,611	91.2	98.4
Hungary	3.3	2.4	3.6	4.2	0.47	0.47	59	54	3,389	4,655	91.0	76.8
Iceland	X	X	X	X	X	X	X	X	X	X	X	X
Ireland	0.0	0.0	X	X	0.33	0.37	606	978	X	X	83.3	106.2

(Continued on next page)

	Land Under Permanent Crops % of land area		Irrigated Land % of cropland		Arable land Hectares per capita		Agricultural Machinery Tractors per thousand agricultural workers		Agricultural Productivity Agr. value added per agricultural worker 1995 dollars		Food Production Index 1989–91 = 100	
Country	**1980**	**1996**	**1979–81**	**1994–96**	**1979–81**	**1994–96**	**1979–81**	**1994–96**	**1979–81**	**1995–97**	**1979–81**	**1995–97**
Italy	10.0	9.1	19.3	24.9	0.17	0.14	370	867	9,994	19,001	101.5	99.7
Latvia	X	0.5	X	X	X	0.68	X	284	X	3,125	X	49.8
Lithuania	X	0.9	X	X	X	0.79	X	239	X	2,907	X	69.8
Macedonia	X	1.9	X	9.4	X	0.31	X	323	X	1,528	X	95.9
Madagascar	0.9	0.9	21.5	35.0	0.28	0.19	1	1	198	180	82.1	105.3
Moldova	X	12.5	X	14.1	X	0.41	X	82	X	1,473	X	58.3
Netherlands	0.9	1.0	58.5	61.5	0.06	0.06	561	646	21,663	43,836	87.0	106.1
Norway	X	X	X	X	0.20	0.22	824	1,251	17,044	31,577	91.8	99.7
Poland	1.1	1.2	0.7	0.7	0.41	0.37	112	277	X	1,647	87.9	84.8
Portugal	7.8	8.2	20.1	21.7	0.25	0.22	72	203	X	5,574	71.9	99.8
Romania	2.9	2.4	21.9	31.4	0.44	0.41	39	80	X	3,170	112.7	100.5
Russian Federation	X	0.1	X	4.0	X	0.88	X	122	X	2,540	X	69.5
Slovak Republic	X	2.7	X	13.4	X	0.28	X	100	X	3,347	X	74.4
Slovenia	X	2.7	X	0.7	X	0.12	X	2,762	X	26,006	X	100.9
Spain	9.9	9.8	14.8	17.7	0.42	0.39	200	513	X	12,022	82.1	99.4
Sweden	X	X	X	X	0.36	0.32	715	931	X	X	100.2	95.1
Switzerland	0.5	0.6	6.2	5.9	0.06	0.06	494	616	X	X	95.8	96.2
Ukraine	X	1.8	X	7.5	X	0.65	X	92	X	2,259	X	69.9
United Kingdom	0.3	0.2	2.0	1.8	0.12	0.10	726	871	X	X	91.6	100.5
Yugoslavia (Serbia-Montenegro)	X	X	X	X	X	X	X	X	X	X	X	X
OCEANIA												
Australia	0.0	0.0	3.5	4.8	2.97	2.68	751	698	20,880	29,044	91.5	126.9
Fiji	X	X	X	X	X	X	X	X	X	X	X	X
New Zealand	3.7	6.4	5.2	8.9	0.80	0.43	619	451	X	X	90.8	120.3
Papua New Guinea	0.9	1.1	X	X	0.01	0.01	1	1	717	827	86.1	106.8
Solomon Islands	X	X	X	X	X	X	X	X	X	X	X	X
WORLD	0.9w	**1.0w**	**17.8w**	**18.8w**	**0.24w**	**0.24w**	**19w**	**20w**	**X w**	**X w**	**76.0w**	**128.2w**
Low income	0.9	1.3	25.5	28.9	0.18	0.15	2	3	X	339	69.3	137.5
Excl. China & India	1.0	1.3	16.2	19.4	0.23	0.18	X	X	X	X	74.9	123.1
Middle income	1.2	1.0	15.8	14.1	0.23	0.36	25	46	X	X	80.1	118.4
Lower middle income	1.3	0.8	22.9	14.9	0.16	0.39	17	34	X	X	X	X
Upper middle income	1.1	1.3	10.3	12.4	0.34	0.30	37	71	X	X	78.6	116.7
Low and middle income	1.0	1.1	21.9	21.5	0.20	0.21	5	8	X	601	72.0	132.6
East Asia & Pacific	1.5	2.6	37.0	35.5	0.11	0.11	2	2	X	X	67.1	152.9
Europe & Central Asia	3.2	0.4	11.6	9.9	0.14	0.61	X	102	X	2,272	X	X
Latin America & Carib.	1.1	1.3	11.6	13.3	0.33	0.28	25	34	X	X	80.7	121.0
Middle East & N. Africa	0.4	0.7	25.8	35.0	0.29	0.21	12	24	X	X	70.5	128.5
South Asia	1.5	1.9	28.7	38.9	0.23	0.16	2	5	189	380	70.8	119.1
Sub-Saharan Africa	0.7	0.8	4.0	4.3	0.32	0.26	3	2	269	355	80.2	119.6
High income	0.5	0.5	9.8	11.1	0.46	0.41	520	877	X	X	93.1	105.2

Note: Figures in italics are for years other than those specified.

Table I

World Countries: Energy Production and Consumption

COUNTRY	COMMERCIAL ENERGY								TRADITIONAL ENERGY % of total energy use		CARBON DIOXIDE EMISSIONS				
	TOTAL PRODUCTION (1000 metric tons of oil equivalent)		TOTAL CONSUMPTION (1000 metric tons of oil equivalent)			PER CAPITA CONSUMPTION (Kilogram of oil equivalent)					Total Millions of Metric Tons		Per Capita Metric Tons (Kilogram of oil equivalent)		Kg of CO_2 per US$ of Gross Domestic Product
	1980	1995	1980	1995	Average Annual % Growth	1980	1995	Average Annual % Growth	1980	1995	1980	1995	1980	1995	1995
WORLD	6,273,572	8,385,643	6,325,980	8,244,516	3.2	1,456	1,474	3.3	7.1	6.8	13,585.7	22,700	3.4	4.1	1.2
AFRICA															
Algeria	66,730	109,257	12,078	24,346	4.2	647	866	1.4	12.3	8.6	4.8	1.8	1.9	0.6	1.0
Angola	7,700	26,189	937	959	0.5	133	89	(2.3)	47.2	59.5	5.3	4.6	0.8	0.4	1.4
Benin	X	232	149	107	(3.3)	43	20	(6.2)	84.9	92.5	0.5	0.6	0.1	0.1	0.3
Botswana	260	250	384	555	2.5	426	383	(0.8)	35.7	X	1.0	2.2	1.1	1.5	0.8
Burkina Faso	0	0	144	162	1.1	21	16	(1.5)	91.4	93.3	0.4	1.0	0.1	0.1	0.4
Burundi	1	5	58	144	6.4	14	23	3.5	92.7	88.8	0.1	0.2	0.0	0.0	0.2
Cameroon	2,885	5,380	774	1,556	3.3	89	117	0.4	69.4	77.3	3.9	4.1	0.4	0.3	0.4
Central African Republic	17	24	59	94	2.6	26	29	0.2	90.8	89.0	0.1	0.2	0.0	0.1	0.2
Chad	0	0	93	101	0.6	21	16	(1.8)	87.4	90.2	0.2	0.1	0.0	0.0	0.1
Congo (Zaire)	1,478	1,948	1,487	2,058	2.2	55	47	(1.1)	79.5	83.9	3.5	2.1	0.1	0.0	0.4
Congo Republic	3,387	9,031	262	367	2.6	157	139	(0.5)	55.9	61.0	0.4	1.3	0.2	0.5	0.5
Cote d'Ivoire	192	435	1,535	1,362	1.2	175	97	(2.4)	53.5	67.2	4.7	10.4	0.6	0.7	0.9
Egypt	33,374	59,287	15,178	34,678	5.4	371	596	2.9	5.0	3.3	45.2	91.7	1.1	1.6	1.6
Equatorial Guinea	X	X	X	X	X	X	X	X	X	X	X	X	X	X	X
Eritrea	X	X	X	X	X	X	X	X	X	X	X	X	X	X	X
Ethiopia	55	158	624	1,178	4.9	17	21	21.0	92.4	90.1	1.8	3.5	0.0	0.1	0.9
Gabon	9,090	18,703	831	644	(4.3)	1,203	587	(7.2)	33.6	51.8	4.8	3.5	6.9	3.2	0.7
Gambia	0	0	53	61	0.9	83	55	(2.9)	79.7	81.2	0.2	0.2	0.2	0.8	
Ghana	554	526	1,303	1,564	2.7	121	92	(0.5)	68.2	79.0	2.4	4.0	0.2	0.2	0.6
Guinea	38	58	356	422	1.3	80	64	(1.4)	68.4	69.9	0.9	1.1	0.2	0.2	0.4
Guinea-Bissau	0	0	31	40	2.1	38	37	0.3	76.1	70.5	0.1	0.2	0.2	0.2	1.0
Kenya	91	518	1,991	2,907	3.5	120	109	0.3	75.4	76.1	6.2	6.7	0.4	0.3	0.7
Lesotho	X	X	X	X	X	X	X	X	X	X	X	X	X	X	X
Liberia	X	X	X	X	X	X	X	X	X	X	X	X	X	X	X
Libya	96,537	77,825	7,048	15,781	4.5	2,316	3,129	1.1	1.7	0.8	26.9	39.4	8.8	7.8	X
Madagascar	38	84	391	484	1.6	45	36	(1.2)	77.1	83.8	1.6	1.1	0.2	0.1	0.4
Malawi	99	154	334	374	1.6	54	38	(1.6)	89.1	86.8	0.7	0.7	0.1	0.1	0.5
Mali	21	42	164	207	1.7	25	21	(0.9)	85.2	87.4	0.4	0.5	0.1	0.0	0.2
Mauritania	0	0	214	231	0.5	138	102	(2.0)	0.7	X	0.6	3.1	0.4	1.3	2.7
Mauritius	21	34	339	435	2.8	351	388	1.7	44.1	41.6	0.6	1.5	0.6	1.3	0.5
Morocco	617	440	4,518	8,253	4.4	233	311	2.2	5.4	4.7	15.9	29.3	0.8	1.1	1.3
Mozambique	1,293	160	1,123	662	(1.6)	93	38	(3.5)	72.6	86.0	3.2	1.0	0.3	0.1	0.4
Namibia	X	X	X	X	X	X	X	X	X	X	X	X	X	X	X
Niger	14	56	210	330	2.0	38	38	(1.2)	78.0	79.6	0.6	1.1	0.1	0.1	0.5
Nigeria	105,512	104,475	9,879	18,393	3.4	139	165	0.4	63.7	56.6	68.1	90.7	1.0	0.8	2.7
Rwanda	29	46	190	211	(0.7)	37	33	(2.6)	84.8	85.7	0.3	0.5	0.1	0.1	0.4
Senegal	0	46	875	866	(0.3)	158	104	(3.0)	48.6	55.9	2.8	3.1	0.5	0.4	0.6
Sierra Leone	0	0	310	326	0.5	96	72	(1.7)	63.5	69.4	0.6	0.4	0.2	0.1	0.6

(Continued on next page)

COUNTRY	COMMERCIAL ENERGY								TRADITIONAL ENERGY % of total energy use		CARBON DIOXIDE EMISSIONS				
	TOTAL PRODUCTION (1000 metric tons of oil equivalent)		TOTAL CONSUMPTION (1000 metric tons of oil equivalent)			PER CAPITA CONSUMPTION (Kilogram of oil equivalent)					Total Millions of Metric Tons		Per Capita Metric Tons (Kilogram of oil equivalent)		Kg of CO_2 per US$ of Gross Domestic Product
	1980	1995	1980	1995	Average Annual % Growth	1980	1995	Average Annual % Growth	1980	1995	1980	1995	1980	1995	1995
Somalia	X	X	X	X	X	X	X	X	X	X	X	X	X	X	X
South Africa	66,740	116,160	59,051	88,882	1.8	2,175	2,405	(0.2)	4.5	3.9	211.3	305.8	7.8	8.3	3.4
Sudan	58	81	1,140	1,745	3.3	61	65	0.9	76.4	76.4	3.3	3.5	0.2	0.1	0.2
Swaziland	X	X	X	X	X	X	X	X	X	X	X	X	X	X	X
Tanzania	86	135	1,023	947	0.8	55	32	(2.3)	83.7	89.6	1.9	2.4	0.1	0.1	X
Togo	1	0	195	185	0.9	75	45	(2.1)	38.3	73.1	0.6	0.7	0.2	0.2	0.6
Tunisia	6,149	4,579	3,083	5,314	4.0	483	591	1.7	15.4	12.9	9.4	15.3	1.5	1.7	1.2
Uganda	153	185	320	430	2.8	25	22	0.0	87.2	89.2	0.6	1.0	0.1	0.1	0.1
Zambia	1,146	898	1,685	1,302	(2.1)	294	145	(5.0)	54.6	71.2	3.5	2.4	0.6	0.3	1.1
Zimbabwe	2,024	3,567	2,797	4,673	4.4	399	424	1.3	33.6	27.4	9.6	9.7	1.4	0.9	1.5
NORTH AMERICA															
Canada	207,359	350,629	192,942	233,328	1.6	7,845	7,879	0.3	0.6	0.6	420.9	435.7	17.1	14.7	0.9
United States	1,546,307	1,655,644	1,801,406	2,078,265	1.3	7,928	7,905	0.3	1.2	4.2	4,515.3	5,468.6	19.9	20.8	1.0
CENTRAL AMERICA															
Belize	X	X	X	X	X	X	X	X	X	X	X	X	X	X	X
Costa Rica	181	380	949	1,971	6.0	415	584	3.3	40.4	12.7	2.5	5.2	1.1	1.6	0.6
Cuba	293	1,223	9,645	10,437	0.1	992	949	(0.9)	28.1	19.7	30.7	29.1	3.2	2.6	X
Dominican Republic	50	171	2,211	3,801	4.3	388	486	2.1	28.3	12.1	6.4	22.8	1.1	1.5	1.6
El Salvador	407	703	1,004	2,332	5.7	221	410	4.2	50.3	42.9	2.1	5.2	0.5	0.9	0.9
Guatemala	230	589	1,443	2,191	3.6	209	206	0.6	53.1	59.9	4.5	7.2	0.6	0.7	0.7
Haiti	19	32	241	357	0.1	45	50	(1.8)	82.4	80.3	0.8	0.6	0.1	0.1	0.5
Honduras	67	235	636	1,401	5.1	174	236	1.9	61.2	49.3	2.1	3.9	0.6	0.7	0.7
Jamaica	10	10	2,164	3,003	2.7	1,015	1,191	1.6	6.2	8.0	8.4	9.1	4.0	3.6	2.4
Mexico	149,365	201,957	98,904	133,371	2.2	1,486	1,456	0.0	4.4	4.4	255.0	357.8	3.8	3.9	2.1
Nicaragua	44	302	696	1,159	3.4	248	265	0.3	50.4	45.8	2.0	2.7	0.7	0.6	0.7
Panama	83	202	1,419	1,783	1.6	725	678	(0.4)	26.4	19.4	3.5	6.9	1.8	2.6	1.0
Trinidad and Tobago	13,127	12,991	3,860	6,925	4.0	3,567	5,381	2.8	1.8	1.0	16.7	17.1	15.4	13.3	3.5
SOUTH AMERICA															
Argentina	36,661	66,055	39,716	53,016	1.9	1,413	1,525	0.5	6.5	4.0	107.5	129.5	3.8	3.7	1.0
Bolivia	3,553	4,478	1,599	2,939	3.2	299	396	1.0	19.8	12.8	4.5	10.5	0.8	1.4	1.8
Brazil	25,777	73,172	73,041	122,928	4.2	602	772	2.3	41.2	27.5	183.4	249.2	1.5	1.6	0.8
Chile	3,871	4,361	7,732	15,131	5.4	694	1,065	3.6	14.5	13.3	27.9	44.1	2.5	3.1	1.2
Colombia	13,047	54,361	13,962	24,120	3.5	501	655	1.6	21.4	21.1	39.8	67.5	1.4	1.8	1.3
Ecuador	10,774	20,967	4,209	6,343	2.6	529	553	0.1	26.5	14.8	13.4	22.6	1.7	2.0	1.6
Guyana	X	X	X	X	X	X	X	X	X	X	X	X	X	X	X
Paraguay	58	3,578	544	1,487	7.1	173	308	4.1	66.1	51.5	1.5	3.8	0.5	0.8	0.7
Peru	11,188	8,388	8,233	10,035	0.6	476	421	(1.5)	18.7	22.9	23.5	30.6	1.4	1.3	1.3
Suriname	X	X	X	X	X	X	X	X	X	X	X	X	X	X	X
Uruguay	233	477	2,206	2,035	0.7	757	639	0.1	20.4	26.7	5.8	5.4	2.0	1.7	0.6
Venezuela	132,919	187,498	35,011	47,140	1.7	2,354	2,158	(0.9)	1.0	1.2	89.6	180.2	6.0	8.3	3.1

(Continued on next page)

COUNTRY	Commercial Energy: Total Production (1000 metric tons of oil equivalent) 1980	Total Production 1995	Total Consumption (1000 metric tons of oil equivalent) 1980	Total Consumption 1995	Total Consumption Average Annual % Growth	Per Capita Consumption (Kilogram of oil equivalent) 1980	Per Capita Consumption 1995	Per Capita Consumption Average Annual % Growth	Traditional Energy % of total energy use 1980	Traditional Energy 1995	Carbon Dioxide Emissions: Total Millions of Metric Tons 1980	Total Millions of Metric Tons 1995	Per Capita Metric Tons (Kilogram of oil equivalent) 1980	Per Capita Metric Tons 1995	Kg of CO_2 per US$ of Gross Domestic Product 1995
ASIA															
Afghanistan	X	X	X	X	X	X	X	X	X	X	X	X	X	X	X
Armenia	1,263	244	1,070	1,671	(1.8)	346	444	(3.1)	X	X	X	3.6	X	1.0	3.4
Azerbaijan	14,821	14,719	15,001	13,033	(3.9)	2,433	1,735	(5.1)	X	X	X	42.6	X	5.7	14.6
Bangladesh	1,113	5,962	2,809	8,061	7.4	32	67	5.1	67.8	49.9	7.6	20.9	0.1	0.2	0.9
Bhutan	X	X	X	X	X	X	X	X	X	X	X	X	X	X	X
Cambodia	13	22	393	517	2.1	60	52	(1.0)	71.2	75.3	0.3	0.5	0.0	0.0	0.4
China	428,693	866,556	413,176	860,520	5.1	421	707	3.7	8.0	5.6	1,476.8	3,192.5	1.5	2.7	5.5
Georgia	4,706	478	4,474	1,850	(3.3)	882	342	(3.7)	X	1.3	X	7.7	X	1.4	X
India	73,760	196,941	93,897	241,291	6.5	137	260	4.4	34.7	23.3	347.3	908.7	0.5	1.0	2.2
Indonesia	94,717	169,325	25,904	85,785	8.9	175	442	7.0	51.6	29.9	94.6	296.1	0.6	1.5	2.1
Iran	83,430	216,406	38,347	84,069	6.3	980	1,374	3.2	1.6	0.8	116.1	263.8	3.0	4.3	1.4
Iraq	136,616	31,100	12,003	25,061	4.1	923	1,206	0.8	0.2	0.1	44.0	99.0	3.4	4.8	X
Israel	151	562	8,607	16,650	5.0	2,219	3,003	2.6	X	X	21.1	46.3	5.4	8.4	0.8
Japan	43,247	99,468	346,567	497,231	2.8	2,968	3,964	2.3	0.1	0.5	907.4	1,126.8	7.8	9.0	0.4
Jordan	0	192	1,713	4,323	5.2	785	1,031	0.7	X	X	4.7	13.3	2.2	3.2	1.7
Kazakhstan	76,799	64,354	75,799	55,432	(3.1)	5,153	3,337	(3.8)	X	0.1	X	221.5	X	13.3	13.8
Korea, North	28,275	21,538	30,932	24,600	(1.2)	1,751	1,113	(2.6)	2.7	3.9	124.9	257.0	7.1	11.6	X
Korea, South	9,644	20,570	41,426	145,099	9.6	1,087	3,225	8.4	5.7	0.7	125.2	373.6	3.3	8.3	1.5
Kuwait	94,084	111,227	9,561	14,494	0.3	6,953	9,381	0.2	X	X	24.7	48.7	18.0	31.5	1.7
Kyrgyzstan	2,190	1,377	1,938	2,315	5.0	534	513	3.4	X	X	X	5.5	X	1.2	4.9
Laos	236	220	107	184	2.6	33	40	0.1	86.6	85.1	0.2	0.3	0.1	0.1	0.2
Lebanon	73	69	2,376	4,486	3.2	791	1,120	1.2	4.3	2.6	6.2	13.3	2.1	3.3	2.4
Malaysia	15,049	62,385	9,522	33,252	9.8	692	1,655	7.0	14.4	6.6	28.0	106.60	2.0	5.3	1.7
Mongolia	1,195	2,190	1,943	2,576	1.8	1,168	1,045	(0.9)	14.0	3.6	6.8	8.5	4.1	3.4	X
Myanmar (Burma)	1,940	2,167	1,858	2,234	0.2	55	50	(1.7)	66.5	69.4	4.8	7.0	0.1	0.2	X
Nepal	15	97	174	700	9.3	12	33	6.5	94.8	88.9	0.5	1.5	0.0	0.1	0.3
Oman	14,756	45,403	1,010	4,013	9.2	917	1,880	4.6	X	X	5.9	11.4	5.3	5.3	0.9
Pakistan	6,970	18,612	11,451	31,536	7.0	139	243	3.8	27.2	20.2	31.6	85.4	0.4	0.7	1.7
Philippines	2,789	6,006	13,357	21,542	3.6	276	307	0.9	35.8	30.5	36.5	61.2	0.8	0.9	1.4
Saudi Arabia	533,071	469,820	35,355	82,742	5.2	3,772	4,360	0.3	X	X	130.7	254.3	14.0	13.4	2.6
Singapore	0	0	6,049	21,389	10.0	2,651	7,162	8.1	0.0	0.0	30.1	63.7	13.2	21.3	1.5
Sri Lanka	127	383	1,411	2,469	2.7	96	136	1.3	54.3	48.4	3.4	5.9	0.2	0.3	0.6
Syria	9,495	34,287	5,343	14,121	5.9	614	1,001	2.5	0.1	0.0	19.3	46.0	2.2	3.3	2.6
Tajikistan	1,986	1,325	1,650	3,283	8.9	416	563	6.1	X	X	X	3.7	X	0.6	2.5
Thailand	535	19,430	12,093	52,125	11.1	259	878	9.4	48.3	32.7	40.1	175.0	0.9	2.9	1.6
Turkey	17,190	26,079	31,314	62,187	4.9	704	1,009	2.6	18.0	3.1	76.3	165.9	1.7	2.7	1.5
Turkmenistan	8,034	32,589	7,948	13,737	X	2,778	3,047	(9.8)	X	X	X	28.3	X	6.3	X
United Arab Emirates	93,915	138,821	8,576	28,454	7.5	8,222	11,567	1.6	X	X	36.3	68.3	34.8	27.8	X
Uzbekistan	4,615	49,135	4,821	46,543	11.6	302	2,043	8.9	X	X	X	98.9	X	4.3	7.3
Vietnam	2,728	13,808	4,024	7,694	4.1	75	104	1.8	53.5	49.1	16.8	31.7	0.3	0.4	0.5
Yemen	X	17,394	1,364	2,933	5.3	160	192	1.2	X	X	1.2	X	0.1	X	X
EUROPE															
Albania	3,053	940	2,674	1,020	(6.4)	1,001	324	(7.7)	12.3	8.6	4.8	1.8	1.8	0.6	1.0

(Continued on next page)

COUNTRY	COMMERCIAL ENERGY								TRADITIONAL ENERGY % of total energy use		CARBON DIOXIDE EMISSIONS				
	TOTAL PRODUCTION (1000 metric tons of oil equivalent)		TOTAL CONSUMPTION (1000 metric tons of oil equivalent)			PER CAPITA CONSUMPTION (Kilogram of oil equivalent)					Total Millions of Metric Tons		Per Capita Metric Tons (Kilogram of oil equivalent)		Kg of CO_2 per US$ of Gross Domestic Product
	1980	1995	1980	1995	Average Annual % Growth	1980	1995	Average Annual % Growth	1980	1995	1980	1995	1980	1995	1995
Austria	7,654	8,481	23,449	26,383	1.3	3,105	3,279	0.9	1.4	2.8	52.2	59.3	6.9	7.4	0.4
Belarus	2,566	2,793	2,385	23,808	10.3	247	2,305	9.7	X	0.8	X	59.3	X	5.7	3.4
Belgium	7,986	11,628	46,100	52,378	1.6	4,682	5,167	1.3	0.2	0.9	127.2	103.8	12.9	10.2	0.6
Bosnia-Herzegovina	X	470	X	1,595	X	X	364	X	X	9.9	X	1.8	X	0.4	X
Bulgaria	7,541	9.810	28,476	22,878	(2.5)	3,213	2,724	(2.1)	0.7	0.8	75.3	56.7	8.5	6.7	2.5
Croatia	X	3,917	X	6,852	X	X	1,435	X	X	3.0	X	17.0	X	3.6	X
Czech Republic	40,002	20,448	45,766	39,013	(1.2)	4,473	3,776	(1.2)	X	0.5	X	112.0	X	10.8	3.4
Denmark	896	15,497	19,734	20,481	0.7	3,852	3,918	0.6	0.3	3.3	62.9	54.9	12.3	10.5	0.5
Estonia	X	3,117	X	5,126	X	X	3,454	X	X	2.3	X	16.4	X	11.1	4.3
Finland	6,912	12,911	25,002	28,670	1.5	5,235	5,613	1.1	3.8	5.1	54.9	51.0	11.5	10.0	0.5
France	46,829	126,868	190,109	241,322	2.1	3,528	4,150	1.6	1.3	1.0	482.7	340.1	9.0	5.8	0.3
Germany	184,238	142,712	358,995	339,287	(0.2)	4,585	4,156	(0.5)	X	0.7	X	835.1	X	10.2	X
Greece	3,696	9,053	15,960	23,698	3.2	1,655	2,266	2.7	2.8	1.5	51.7	76.3	5.4	7.3	1.5
Hungary	14,442	13,295	28,556	25,103	(1.0)	2,667	2,454	(0.7)	2.1	1.8	82.5	55.9	7.7	5.5	2.3
Iceland	X	X	X	X	X	X	X	X	X	X	X	X	X	X	X
Ireland	1,894	3,601	8,484	11,461	2.2	2,495	3,196	2.0	0.1	0.2	25.2	32.2	7.4	9.0	0.7
Italy	19,644	28,645	138,629	161,360	1.4	2,456	2,821	1.3	0.7	1.9	371.9	410.0	6.6	7.2	0.5
Latvia	261	322	566	3,702	22.9	222	1,471	22.9	X	18.0	X	9.3	X	3.7	1.9
Lithuania	186	3,316	11,353	8,510	(3.2)	3,326	2,291	(3.8)	X	5.6	X	14.8	X	4.0	2.1
Macedonia	X	1,621	X	2,572	X	X	1,308	X	X	6.9	X	X	X	X	X
Moldova	35	24	X	4,177	X	X	963	X	X	0.5	X	10.8	X	2.5	X
Netherlands	71,830	65,705	65,000	73,292	1.4	4,594	4,741	0.8	0.0	0.5	152.6	135.9	10.8	8.8	0.5
Norway	55,743	182,428	18,819	23,715	1.8	4,600	5,439	1.4	0.8	1.1	90.4	72.5	22.1	16.6	0.7
Poland	120.774	94,666	124,557	94,472	(2.0)	3,501	2,448	(2.5)	0.4	1.1	456.2	338.0	12.8	8.8	5.1
Portugal	1,481	1,870	10,291	19,245	4.6	1,054	1,939	4.6	1.1	0.7	27.1	51.9	2.8	5.2	1.0
Romania	51,631	30,008	63,751	44,026	(2.9)	2,872	1,941	(3.1)	1.5	21.5	191.8	121.1	8.6	5.3	3.9
Russian Federation	749,289	928,870	764,349	604,461	(3.0)	5,499	4,079	(3.4)	X	1.1	X	1,818.0	X	12.3	6.1
Slovak Republic	3,251	4,846	20,648	17,447	(1.3)	4,142	3,272	(1.7)	X	0.5	X	38.0	X	7.1	2.3
Slovenia	1,623	2,578	4,269	5,583	0.7	2,245	2,806	0.4	X	0.8	X	11.7	X	5.9	X
Spain	15,781	31,422	68,583	103,491	3.2	1,834	2,639	2.9	0.5	0.6	200.0	231.6	5.3	5.9	0.6
Sweden	16,133	31,549	40,984	50,658	1.3	4,932	5,736	0.9	3.9	2.5	71.4	44.6	8.6	5.0	0.3
Switzerland	7,030	10,961	20,814	25,142	1.7	3,294	3,571	0.9	1.1	2.1	40.9	38.9	6.5	5.5	0.2
Ukraine	109,708	80,700	97,893	161,586	2.1	1,956	3,136	1.9	X	0.4	X	438.2	X	8.5	X
United Kingdom	197,738	254,967	102,268	221,911	1.0	3,571	3,786	0.7	0.0	1.1	585.1	542.1	10.4	9.3	0.7
Yugoslavia (Serbia-Montenegro)	X	11,295	X	11,865	X	X	1,125	X	X	X	X	33.0	x	3.1	X
OCEANIA															
Australia	86,096	186,625	70,372	94,200	2.2	4,790	5,215	0.7	2.1	3.8	202.8	289.8	13.8	16.0	1.1
Fiji	X	X	X	X	X	X	X	X	X	X	X	X	X	X	X
New Zealand	5,592	12,436	9,190	15,409	3.9	2,952	4,290	3.1	0.2	X	17.6	27.4	5.6	7.6	0.6
Papua New Guinea	80	2,500	705	1,000	2.4	228	232	0.2	64.1	58.9	1.8	2.5	0.6	0.6	0.5
Solomon Islands	X	X	X	X	X	X	X	X	X	X	X	X	X	X	X

(Continued on next page)

COUNTRY	COMMERCIAL ENERGY								TRADITIONAL ENERGY % of total energy use		CARBON DIOXIDE EMISSIONS				
	TOTAL PRODUCTION (1000 metric tons of oil equivalent)		TOTAL CONSUMPTION (1000 metric tons of oil equivalent)			PER CAPITA CONSUMPTION (Kilogram of oil equivalent)					Total Millions of Metric Tons		Per Capita Metric Tons (Kilogram of oil equivalent)		Kg of CO_2 per US$ of Gross Domestic Product
	1980	1995	1980	1995	Average Annual % Growth	1980	1995	Average Annual % Growth	1980	1995	1980	1995	1980	1995	1995
DEVELOPING COUNTRIES	3,488,398	4,811,025	2,522,195	3,569,396	5.9	1,665	1,415	2.3	34.3	31.7	4,813.6	11,577.5	2.7	3.1	2.6
DEVELOPED COUNTRIES	2,785,174	3,574,618	3,803,785	4,675,120	1.7	4,611	5,123	1.1	1.1	2.5	8,772.1	11,122.7	12.0	12.5	0.7

Sources: United Nations Statistical Division: *World Development Indicators* (World Bank, 1998); *World Resources 1998–1999* (World Resources Institute, 1998).

Table J

World Countries: Land Use and Change

COUNTRY	Domestic and Forested Land: Domestic Land as a % of Land Area 1994	Forests as a % of Original Forest: Current Forests	Forests as a % of Original Forest: Frontier Forests	Percent Frontier Forests Threatened 1994	Land Use (in Thousands of Hectares): Cropland 1992–94	Cropland % Change Since 1982–84	Permanent Pasture 1992–94	Permanent Pasture % Change Since 1982–84	Forest and Woodland 1992–94	Forest and Woodland % Change Since 1982–94	Other Land 1992–94	Other Land % Change Since 1982–84
WORLD	37	53.4	2.17	39.5	1,465,814	2.0	3,419,203	3.2	4,177,088	(2.2)	3,992,533	(1.0)
AFRICA	36	33.9	7.8	76.8	189,803	6.5	889,350	0.0	713,405	(0.3)	1,171,024	(0.8)
Algeria	17	12.0	0.0	0.0	8,088	9.1	32,014	(2.8)	3,949	(10.0)	195,197	0.4
Angola	46	15.3	0.0	0.0	3,500	2.9	54,000	0.0	23,000	(0.9)	44,170	0.2
Benin	21	3.5	0.0	0.0	1,880	3.9	42	0.0	3,400	(11.0)	5,340	7.0
Botswana	46	100.0	0.0	0.0	420	5.0	25,600	0.0	26,500	0.0	4,153	(0.5)
Burkina Faso	34	0.0	0.0	0.0	3,465	18.0	6,000	0.0	13,800	0.0	4,082	(11.7)
Burundi	86	3.5	0.0	0.0	1,120	(5.1)	1,080	9.1	325	0.0	43	(41.1)
Cameroon	19	42.4	7.9	97.4	7,040	1.2	2,000	0.0	35,900	0.0	1,600	(4.9)
Central African Republic	8	15.9	4.4	100.0	2,020	2.5	3,000	0.0	46,700	0.0	10,578	(0.5)
Chad	38	0.0	0.0	0.0	3,256	3.4	45,000	0.0	32,400	0.0	45,264	(0.2)
Congo (Zaire)	30	60.4	15.6	70.4	170	9.9	10,000	0.0	19,900	0.0	4,080	(0.4)
Congo Republic	10	67.8	28.7	64.6	7,900	2.5	15,000	0.0	166,000	0.0	37,805	(0.5)
Cote d'Ivoire	54	9.9	2.2	100.0	4,031	22.5	13,000	0.0	9,600	(5.9)	5,149	(3.0)
Egypt	3	0.0	0.0	0.0	3,137	26.5	X	X	34	9.7	96,374	(0.7)
Equatorial Guinea	12	38.4	0.0	0.0	230	0.0	104	0.0	1,830	0.0	641	0.0
Eritrea	75	X	X	X	366	X	4,622	X	523	X	1,155	X
Ethiopia	31	17.3	0.0	0.0	12,197	X	28,267	X	13,633	X	49,269	X
Gabon	20	90.4	32.4	100.0	460	1.8	4,700	0.0	19.900	(0.4)	707	11.3
Gambia	37	61.9	0.0	0.0	165	(10.6)	194	2.1	94	(6.0)	547	4.1
Ghana	57	8.6	0.0	0.0	4,407	15.0	8,400	0.0	9,300	(3.1)	647	(29.7)
Guinea	47	5.0	0.0	0.0	787	10.2	10,700	0.0	6,700	0.0	6,385	(1.1)
Guinea-Bissau	50	33.7	0.0	0.0	340	10.3	1,080	0.0	1,070	0.0	322	(9.0)
Kenya	45	18.5	0.0	0.0	4,520	5.6	21,300	0.0	16,800	0.0	14,294	(1.6)
Lesotho	76	0.0	0.0	0.0	320	10.6	2,000	0.0	X	X	715	(4.1)
Liberia	25	44.2	0.0	0.0	371	(0.1)	2,000	0.0	4,600	0.0	2,661	0.0
Libya	9	0.0	0.0	0.0	2,170	3.1	13,300	0.3	840	33.0	159,644	(0.2)
Madagascar	47	13.1	0.0	0.0	3,105	3.1	24,000	0.0	23,200	0.0	7,849	(1.2)
Malawi	38	0.0	0.0	0.0	1,700	19.9	1,840	0.0	3,700	(1.1)	2,168	(10.0)
Mali	27	0.0	0.0	0.0	2,569	25.1	30,000	0.0	11,800	(1.7)	77,650	(0.4)
Mauritania	38	0.0	0.0	0.0	208	6.7	39,250	0.0	4,410	(2.0)	58,654	0.1
Mauritius	56	X	X	X	106	(0.9)	7	0.0	44	(24.1)	46	48.4
Morocco	68	7.3	0.0	0.0	9,686	13.9	20,933	0.2	8,613	9.9	5,397	(28.8)
Mozambique	60	13.6	0.0	0.0	3,180	3.2	44,000	0.0	17,300	0.0	13,929	(0.7)
Namibia	47	95.3	0.0	0.0	704	6.6	38,000	0.0	12,500	0.0	31,125	(0.1)
Niger	12	0.0	0.0	0.0	4,035	13.9	10,400	13.1	2,500	0.0	109,695	(1.5)
Nigeria	80	10.7	0.6	100.0	32,579	6.1	40,000	0.0	14,300	(10.6)	4,198	(3.9)
Rwanda	75	16.1	0.0	0.0	1,150	5.4	695	(0.7)	250	0.0	372	(12.7)
Senegal	42	16.0	0.0	0.0	2,355	0.2	5,700	0.0	7,467	(1.8)	3,731	3.6
Sierra Leone	38	9.7	0.0	0.0	540	4.4	2,201	(0.1)	1,947	2.5	2,474	(2.6)
Somalia	70	0.0	0.0	0.0	1,026	1.1	43,000	0.0	16,000	6.7	2,708	(27.2)
South Africa	79	0.2	0.0	0.0	15,200	15.4	81,433	0.1	8,200	0.0	17,271	(10.8)
Sudan	52	0.0	0.0	0.0	12,975	3.3	110,000	12.2	42,367	(1.5)	2,258	(14.0)

(Continued on next page)

COUNTRY	Domestic and Forested Land: Domestic Land as a % of Land Area	Forests as a % of Original Forest		Percent Frontier Forests Threatened	Land Use (in Thousands of Hectares): Cropland		Permanent Pasture		Forest and Woodland		Other Land	
	1994	Current Forests	Frontier Forests	1994	1992–94	% Change Since 1982–84	1992–94	% Change Since 1982–84	1992–94	% Change Since 1982–94	1992–94	% Change Since 1982–84
Swaziland	73	0.0	0.0	0.0	191	24.3	1,070	(5.1)	119	16.6	340	0.9
Tanzania	44	9.1	0.0	0.0	3,660	23.7	35,000	0.0	33,067	(1.9)	16,632	(0.4)
Togo	48	7.0	0.0	0.0	2,420	2.5	200	0.0	900	(11.8)	1,919	3.2
Tunisia	51	4.7	0.0	0.0	4,882	(0.1)	3,416	1.8	666	17.1	6,602	(1.8)
Uganda	43	4.4	0.0	0.0	6,780	9.1	1,800	0.0	6,300	5.0	5,085	(14.6)
Zambia	47	70.1	0.0	0.0	5,273	2.2	30,000	0.0	32,000	6.7	7,066	(23.0)
Zimbabwe	52	67.3	0.0	0.0	2,876	2.5	17,190	0.5	8,800	(7.4)	9,819	5.8
NORTH AMERICA	27	28.2	5.3	63.1	233,276	(1.1)	267,072	(1.2)	749,290	2.9	588,371	(2.6)
Canada	8	91.2	56.5	20.9	45,500	(1.3)	27,900	(3.1)	453,300	3.9	395,397	(3.8)
United States	47	60.2	6.3	84.7	187,776	(1.1)	239,172	(1.0)	295,990	1.5	192,974	(0.0)
CENTRAL AMERICA	53	54.5	9.7	87.0	40,053	5.4	98,503	6.2	74,524	1.2	85,910	(9.2)
Belize	6	95.7	35.5	66.1	81	52.2	49	11.4	2,100	0.0	50	(39.4)
Costa Rica	56	34.9	9.5	100.0	530	2.9	2,340	6.9	1,570	(3.4)	666	(14.4)
Cuba	61	28.8	0.0	0.0	3,745	12.4	2,705	0.8	2,505	(6.2)	2,027	(11.8)
Dominican Republic	81	25.1	0.0	0.0	1,743	21.9	2,090	(0.1)	603	(4.1)	401	(41.6)
El Salvador	65	9.9	0.0	0.0	742	2.3	600	(1.6)	105	(13.9)	625	1.7
Guatemala	42	46.2	2.2	100.0	1,858	4.1	2,568	65.5	5,212	15.8	1,171	(60.9)
Haiti	51	0.8	0.0	0.0	910	1.2	495	(2.2)	140	0.0	1,211	0.0
Honduras	32	51.6	16.0	100.0	1,967	11.0	1,524	1.6	6,000	0.0	1,698	(11.4)
Jamaica	44	35.6	0.0	0.0	219	(1.9)	257	0.0	185	(3.8)	422	2.8
Mexico	55	63.4	8.1	77.0	24,370	0.2	79,000	6.0	48,700	4.3	38,439	(14.6)
Nicaragua	61	44.3	21.6	100.0	2,480	55.6	4,815	0.0	3,200	(22.9)	1,645	4.0
Panama	29	62.0	34.8	100.0	662	14.0	1,483	9.1	3,260	(16.0)	2,038	25.6
Trinidad and Tobago	26	35.5	0.0	0.0	122	3.4	11	0.0	235	3.5	145	(7.6)
SOUTH AMERICA	35	69.1	45.6	54.0	113,116	9.0	495,341	3.0	934,860	0.6	209,471	(12.3)
Argentina	62	59.5	6.3	99.9	27,200	0.0	142,000	(0.6)	50,900	0.0	53,569	1.7
Bolivia	27	77.2	43.6	96.9	2,370	8.9	26,500	(1.7)	58,000	0.0	21,565	1.2
Brazil	29	66.4	42.2	47.8	58,667	15.0	185,600	5.9	557,667	0.8	43,718	(34.1)
Chile	23	40.6	54.5	76.0	4,216	(2.0)	13,100	(0.4)	16,500	0.0	41,030	0.3
Colombia	45	53.5	36.4	18.7	6,073	15.7	40,083	(0.0)	53,167	(3.3)	4,547	29.1
Ecuador	29	66.4	36.9	99.5	3,010	20.8	5,009	11.1	15,600	0.6	4,065	(21.6)
Guyana	9	97.4	81.8	41.1	496	0.2	1,230	0.3	16,456	0.5	1,503	(5.7)
Paraguay	60	44.5	0.0	0.0	2,270	17.6	21,700	27.6	12,850	(31.6)	2,910	43.6
Peru	24	86.6	56.7	99.6	3,767	3.3	27,120	0.0	84,800	(0.1)	12,213	(1.4)
Suriname	1	95.6	92.2	21.7	68	19.3	21	12.5	15,000	0.8	511	(21.3)
Uruguay	85	0.0	0.0	0.0	1,304	(5.0)	13,520	(0.5)	930	0.0	1,727	8.8
Venezuela	25	83.6	59.3	37.3	3,663	(3.0)	18,742	2.7	45,000	22.3	21,300	(28.7)
ASIA	51	28.2	5.3	63.1	520,175	X	1,051,311	X	556,996	X	956,913	X
Afghanistan	58	6.5	0.0	0.0	8,054	0.0	30,000	0.0	1,700	(10.5)	25,455	0.8
Armenia	46	21.1	0.0	0.0	582	X	688	X	413	X	1,137	X
Azerbaijan	48	32.0	0.0	0.0	1,967	X	2,200	X	950	X	3,543	X
Bangladesh	71	7.9	3.8	100.0	8,849	(3.1)	600	0.0	1,891	(11.3)	1,677	45.2
Bhutan	9	61.8	24.0	100.0	136	7.7	273	2.5	3,100	14.2	1,191	(25.2)
Cambodia	30	65.1	10.3	100.0	3,832	81.9	1,500	158.5	12,200	(7.3)	120	(93.4)
China	53	21.6	1.8	92.8	95,145	(3.6)	400,000	12.5	128,630	(1.1)	305,324	(11.4)

(Continued on next page)

COUNTRY	Domestic Land as a % of Land Area	Forests as a % of Original Forest		Percent Frontier Forests Threatened	Cropland		Permanent Pasture		Forest and Woodland		Other Land	
	1994	Current Forests	Frontier Forests	1994	1992–94	% Change Since 1982–84	1992–94	% Change Since 1982–84	1992–94	% Change Since 1982–94	1992–94	% Change Since 1982–84
Georgia	43	57.3	0.0	0.0	1,036	X	1,962	X	2,988	X	984	X
India	61	20.5	1.3	57.2	169,569	0.5	11,424	(4.8)	68,173	1.2	48,136	(2.1)
Indonesia	23	64.5	28.5	53.8	31,146	19.9	11,800	1.2	111,516	(2.6)	26,695	(8.1)
Iran	39	3.3	0.0	0.0	18,500	21.7	44,000	0.0	11,400	0.0	88,300	(3.6)
Iraq	22	0.0	0.0	0.0	5,550	1.9	4,000	0.0	192	0.0	33,995	(0.3)
Israel	28	0.0	0.0	0.0	434	4.6	145	5.8	126	16.7	1,357	(3.2)
Japan	13	58.2	0.0	0.0	4,467	(7.0)	660	8.9	25,110	(0.2)	7,416	4.8
Jordan	13	0.0	0.0	0.0	405	17.1	791	0.0	70	5.5	7,627	(0.8)
Kazakhstan	83	22.9	2.9	100.0	35,239	X	186,549	X	9,600	X	35,685	X
Korea, North	17	38.7	0.0	0.0	2,007	2.7	50	0.0	7,370	0.0	2,614	(2.7)
Korea, South	22	16.5	0.0	0.0	2,053	(5.3)	91	30.8	6,450	(1.3)	1,270	(6.5)
Kuwait	8	0.0	0.0	0.0	5	114.3	137	2.2	2	0.0	1,638	(0.3)
Kyrgyzstan	54	14.0	0.0	0.0	1,387	X	8,900	X	730	X	8,163	X
Laos	7	30.00	2.1	100.0	900	18.5	800	0.0	12,560	(4.1)	8,820	4.7
Lebanon	31	0.7	0.0	0.0	306	2.7	14	40.0	80	(3.6)	623	(1.5)
Malaysia	24	63.8	14.5	48.5	7,535	46.6	281	8.9	22,248	0.0	2,790	(46.4)
Mongolia	76	49.6	8.2	0,0	1,357	4.4	117,983	(4.4)	13,750	(9.4)	23,560	40.5
Myanmar (Burma)	16	40.6	0.0	0.0	10,067	(0.1)	354	(1.8)	32,398	0.8	22,935	(1.0)
Nepal	31	22.4	0,0	0.0	2,556	10.0	1,757	(9.4)	5,750	4.7	4,237	(6.8)
Oman	5	0.0	0.0	0.0	63	44.3	1,000	0.0	X	X	20,193	(0.1)
Pakistan	34	5.8	0.0	0.0	21,323	4.7	5,000	0.0	3,477	15.1	47,288	(2.9)
Philippines	36	6.0	0.0	0.0	9,320	5.0	1,280	14.3	13,600	15.6	5,617	(30.3)
Saudi Arabia	58	0.0	0.0	0.0	3,777	67.6	120,000	38.5	1,800	33.3	89,392	(28.3)
Singapore	2	3.1	0.0	0.0	1	(83.3)	X	X	3	0.0	57	9.6
Sri Lanka	36	18.1	11.9	76.2	1,889	1.3	440	0.2	2,100	20.2	2,034	(15.6)
Syria	78	0.0	0.0	0.0	5,985	5.2	8,191	(1.8)	484	(2.4)	3,718	(3.6)
Tajikistan	31	4.2	0.0	0.0	846	X	3,533	X	537	X	9,144	X
Thailand	42	22.2	4.9	100.0	20,488	6.7	800	14.3	14,833	(3.7)	14,968	(5.1)
Turkey	52	11.3	0.0	0.0	27,611	2.1	2,378	22.2	20,199	0.0	16,775	(14.4)
Turkmenistan	67	4.1	0.0	0.0	1,471	X	33,202	X	4,000	X	8,320	X
United Arab Emirates	4	0.0	0.0	0.0	75	148.4	280	40.0	3	0.0	8,002	(1.5)
Uzbekistan	61	10.2	0.0	0.0	4,618	X	21,490	X	1,311	X	14,005	X
Vietnam	22	17.2	1.9	100.0	6,738	2.3	328	5.1	9,650	(3.9)	15,883	1.4
Yemen	33	0.0	0.0	0.0	1,520	3.8	16,065	0.0	2,000	(25.0)	33,212	1.9
EUROPE	22	58.4	21.3	18.7	317,837	X	178,549	X	947,761	X	816,036	X
Albania	41	37.3	0.0	0.0	702	(1.2)	424	5.6	1,049	1.7	565	(5.2)
Austria	43	52.8	0.0	0.0	1,506	(3.3)	1,985	(1.0)	3,233	(0.3)	1,550	5.4
Belarus	44	27.2	0.0	0.0	6,245	X	3,070	X	7,109	X	4,324	X
Belgium	45	21.0	0.0	0.0	790	2.4	687	(9.0)	709	2.0	1,095	3.4
Bosnia-Herzegovina	39	X	0.0	0.0	893	X	1,200	X	2,033	X	973	X
Bulgaria	54	31.7	0.0	0.0	4,286	3.5	1,811	(11.0)	3,348	0.1	1,609	5.0
Croatia	41	X	X	0.0	1,242	X	1,088	X	2,075	X	1,187	X
Czech Republic	55	X	X	0.0	2,265	X	588	X	173	X	547	X
Denmark	63	0.8	0.0	0.0	2,488	(5.3)	241	2.1	417	(13.8)	1,097	23.1
Estonia	34	29.4	0.0	0.0	1,145	X	311	X	2,018	X	753	X
Finland	9	82.3	1.1	100.0	2,585	4.5	112	(21.7)	23,186	(0.6)	4,575	1.2
France	55	16.5	0.0	0.0	19,387	1.7	10,830	(13.4)	14,938	2.3	9,854	11.5
Germany	50	26.3	0.0	0.0	11,885	(4.5)	5,255	(10.8)	10,700	4.0	7,087	12.5

Domestic and Forested Land; Land Use (in Thousands of Hectares)

(Continued on next page)

COUNTRY	Domestic Land as a % of Land Area	Forests as a % of Original Forest		Percent Frontier Forests Threatened	Cropland		Permanent Pasture		Forest and Woodland		Other Land	
	1994	Current Forests	Frontier Forests	1994	1992–94	% Change Since 1982–84	1992–94	% Change Since 1982–84	1992–94	% Change Since 1982–94	1992–94	% Change Since 1982–84
Greece	68	17.0	0.0	0.0	3,502	(11.3)	5,252	(0.1)	2,620	0.0	1,516	42.2
Hungary	66	8.2	0.0	0.0	4,973	(6.1)	1,156	(9.4)	1,717	5.1	1,388	34.5
Iceland	23	X	0.0	0.0	6	(21.7)	2,274	0.0	120	0.0	7,625	0.0
Ireland	64	3.6	0.0	0.0	1,266	21.6	3,137	(32.8)	570	14.0	1,916	181.8
Italy	53	20.4	0.0	0.0	11,594	(5.8)	4,479	(11.2)	6,794	6.4	6,519	14.9
Latvia	41	19.8	0.0	0.0	1,720	X	808	X	2,841	X	836	X
Lithuania	54	16.0	0.0	0.0	3,041	X	472	X	1,983	X	984	X
Macedonia	51	X	0.0	0.0	662	X	638	X	1,035	X	227	X
Moldova	78	3.7	0.0	0.0	2,195	X	363	X	358	X	381	X
Netherlands	58	4.8	0.0	0.0	922	10.8	1,060	(10.0)	334	12.6	1,076	(0.9)
Norway	3	90.4	0.0	0.0	891	5.1	124	25.7	8,330	0.0	21,338	(0.3)
Poland	61	22.2	0.0	0.0	14,673	(1.0)	4,049	(0.7)	8,732	0.7	2,988	3.9
Portugal	43	9.4	0.0	0.0	3,057	(3.0)	900	7.4	3,102	4.6	2,091	(4.7)
Romania	64	41.5	0.0	0.0	9,942	(5.8)	4,851	9.6	6,681	1.8	1,559	4.6
Russian Federation	13	68.7	29.3	18.6	133,072	X	86,858	X	767,347	X	701,573	X
Slovak Republic	51	X	0.0	0.0	1,074	X	557	X	1,326	X	249	X
Slovenia	39	X	0.0	0.0	296	X	540	X	1,077	X	98	X
Spain	62	15.1	0.0	0.0	19,910	(2.9)	10,416	0.5	16,063	3.1	3,555	1.7
Sweden	8	86.0	2.9	100.0	2,776	(5.6)	576	(17.0)	28,025	0.1	9,653	1.3
Switzerland	40	44.8	0.0	0.0	433	5.1	1,148	(28.6)	1,186	12.7	1,187	34.6
Ukraine	72	20.4	0.0	0.0	34,410	X	7,483	X	9,239	X	6,803	X
United Kingdom	71	6.0	0.0	0.0	6,224	(10.9)	11,090	(1.4)	2,390	8.2	4,456	19.7
Yugoslavia (Serbia-Montenegro)	61	X	0.0	0.0	4,080	X	2,119	X	1,769	X	2,233	X
OCEANIA	57	64.9	22.3	76.3	51,553	1.4	430,077	(2.8)	200,252	(0.2)	164,807	6.3
Australia	60	64.3	17.8	62.8	47,023	1.7	415,700	(2.8)	145,000	(0.4)	158,057	6.4
Fiji	24	49.9	0.0	0.0	260	40.5	174	29.1	1,185	0.0	208	(35.5)
New Zealand	62	29.2	8.9	100.0	3,307	(5.5)	13,774	(2.2)	7,667	2.6	2,051	17.2
Papua New Guinea	1	85.4	39.6	83.5	423	13.4	90	(4.6)	42,000	0.0	2,776	(1.5)
Solomon Islands	3	93.9	0.0	0.0	57	6.9	39	0.0	2,450	(2.8)	253	35.5

Header groups: Domestic and Forested Land (Domestic Land as a % of Land Area; Forests as a % of Original Forest; Percent Frontier Forests Threatened); Land Use (in Thousands of Hectares) (Cropland; Permanent Pasture; Forest and Woodland; Other Land).

Source: World Resources Institute, *World Resources 1998–1999.*

Table K

Power and Transportation

	Electric power										
	Consumption per capita Kilowatt-hours		Transmission and distribution losses % of output		Paved Roads % of total		Goods transported by road Millions of ton-km hauled		Goods transported by rail Ton-km per $ million of GDP (PPP)		Air passengers carried Thousands
Country	**1980**	**1996**	**1980**	**1996**	**1990**	**1997**	**1990**	**1997**	**1990**	**1997**	**1996**
AFRICA											
Algeria	265	524	11	18	67	*69*	14,000	X	25,161	X	3,494
Angola	67	61	25	28	*25*	25	X	X	X	X	585
Benin	36	48	220	87	20	*20*	X	X	X	X	75
Botswana	X	X	X	X	32	*24*	X	X	X	X	104
Burkina Faso	X	X	X	X	17	*16*	X	X	X	X	138
Burundi	X	X	X	X	18	*7*	X	X	X	X	9
Cameroon	167	171	7	20	11	*13*	X	X	33,209	34,023	362
Central African Republic	X	X	X	X	X	X	144	*60*	X	X	75
Chad	X	X	X	X	1	*1*	X	X	X	X	93
Congo (Zaire)	147	130	8	3	X	X	X	X	32,198	X	178
Congo Republic	94	207	1	0	10	*10*	X	X	144,851	X	253
Côte d'Ivoire	192	174	7	16	9	*10*	X	X	15,791	13,486	179
Egypt	380	924	13	0	72	*78*	31,400	31,500	23,310	X	4,282
Equatorial Guinea	X	X	X	X	X	X	X	X	X	X	X
Eritrea	X	X	X	X	19	*22*	X	X	X	X	X
Ethiopia	16	18	8	1	15	*15*	X	X	2,467	X	743
Gabon	X	X	X	X	X	X	X	X	X	X	X
Gambia	X	X	X	X	X	X	X	X	X	X	X
Ghana	X	X	X	X	X	X	X	X	X	X	X
Guinea	X	X	X	X	15	*17*	X	X	X	X	36
Guinea-Bissau	X	X	X	X	X	X	X	X	X	X	X
Kenya	92	126	16	16	13	*14*	X	X	75,496	X	779
Lesotho	X	X	X	X	18	*18*	X	X	X	X	17
Liberia	X	X	X	X	X	X	X	X	X	X	X
Libya	X	X	X	X	X	X	X	X	X	X	X
Madagascar	X	X	X	X	15	*12*	X	X	X	X	542
Malawi	X	X	X	X	22	19	X	X	14,881	*10,003*	153
Mali	X	X	X	X	11	*12*	X	X	53,882	X	75
Mauritania	X	X	X	X	11	*11*	X	X	X	X	235
Mauritius	X	X	X	X	X	X	X	X	X	X	X
Morocco	223	408	10	4	49	52	2,638	*2,086*	72,108	55,523	2,301
Mozambique	370	76	*0*	0	17	19	X	*110*	X	X	163
Namibia	X	X	X	X	11	8	X	X	308,833	*139,137*	237
Niger	X	X	X	X	29	*8*	X	X	X	X	75
Nigeria	68	85	36	32	30	*19*	X	X	3,009	X	221
Rwanda	X	X	X	X	9	*9*	X	X	X	X	9
Senegal	97	103	11	16	27	*29*	X	X	51,209	X	155
Sierra Leone	X	X	X	X	11	8	X	X	X	X	15
Somalia	X	X	X	X	X	X	X	X	X	X	X
South Africa	3,213	3,719	8	8	30	*42*	X	X	430,594	337,153	7,183
Sudan	X	X	X	X	X	X	X	X	X	X	X
Swaziland	X	X	X	X	X	X	X	X	X	X	X
Tanzania	50	59	14	12	37	*4*	X	X	77,466	*91,623*	224
Togo	X	X	X	X	21	*32*	X	X	X	X	75
Tunisia	379	674	12	11	76	*79*	X	X	58,795	53,343	1,371

(Continued on next page)

	Electric power										
	Consumption per capita Kilowatt-hours		Transmission and distribution losses % of output		Paved Roads % of total		Goods transported by road Millions of ton-km hauled		Goods transported by rail Ton-km per $ million of GDP (PPP)		Air passengers carried Thousands
Country	1980	1996	1980	1996	1990	1997	1990	1997	1990	1997	1996
Uganda	X	X	X	X	X	X	X	X	12,582	*11,567*	100
Zambia	1,016	560	7	11	17	X	X	X	73,728	*56,426*	235
Zimbabwe	990	765	14	7	14	*47*	X	X	274,759	196,429	654
NORTH AMERICA											
Canada	12,329	15,129	9	7	35	*35*	54,700	71,473	433,765	X	22,856
United States	8,914	11,796	9	7	58	*61*	1,073,100	1,439,532	360,699	*361,911*	571,072
CENTRAL AMERICA											
Belize	X	X	X	X	X	X	X	X	X	X	X
Costa Rica	860	1,349	*0*	12	15	17	2,243	3,070	X	X	918
Cuba	X	X	X	X	X	X	X	X	X	X	X
Dominican Republic	433	608	21	25	45	*49*	X	X	X	X	30
El Salvador	293	516	13	13	14	20	X	X	X	X	1,800
Guatemala	212	364	6	13	25	*28*	X	X	X	X	300
Haiti	41	34	26	54	22	*24*	X	X	X	X	X
Honduras	225	350	14	27	21	*20*	X	X	X	X	X
Jamaica	482	2,108	17	11	64	*71*	X	X	X	X	1,388
Mexico	846	1,381	11	15	35	*37*	108,884	165,000	64,884	*53,917*	14,678
Nicaragua	303	256	14	28	11	*10*	X	X	X	X	51
Panama	828	1,140	13	18	32	*34*	X	X	X	X	689
Trinidad and Tobago	X	X	X	X	X	X	X	X	X	X	X
SOUTH AMERICA											
Argentina	1,170	1,541	13	18	29	*29*	X	X	36,412	X	7,913
Bolivia	226	371	10	12	4	*6*	X	X	37,118	X	1,784
Brazil	974	1,660	12	17	10	*9*	X	X	56,068	X	22,012
Chile	876	1,864	12	9	14	*14*	X	X	15,882	5,998	3,622
Colombia	561	922	16	22	12	12	6,227	X	2,400	X	8,342
Ecuador	361	616	14	21	13	19	2,638	*3,558*	X	X	1,925
Guyana	X	X	X	X	X	X	X	X	X	X	X
Paraguay	233	914	6	7	9	*10*	X	X	X	X	261
Peru	502	598	13	15	10	*10*	X	X	7,486	X	2,328
Suriname	X	X	X	X	X	X	X	X	X	X	X
Uruguay	977	1,605	15	20	74	*90*	X	X	10,455	16,125	504
Venezuela	2,037	2,498	12	20	36	*39*	X	X	X	X	4,487
ASIA											
Afghanistan	X	X	X	X	X	X	X	X	X	X	X
Armenia	2,729	905	10	38	99	*100*	1,533	479	X	X	X
Azerbaijan	2,440	1,822	14	22	X	X	3,287	497	X	X	1,233
Bangladesh	16	97	35	30	*7*	12	X	X	8,032	X	1,252
Bhutan	X	X	X	X	X	X	X	X	X	X	X
Cambodia	X	X	X	X	8	8	X	*1,200*	X	X	X
China	253	687	8	7	X	X	X	X	671,824	*364,633*	51,770
Hong Kong, China	2,167	5,013	11	14	100	*100*	X	X	X	X	X
Georgia	1,910	1,020	16	23	94	*94*	7,370	98	X	X	152
India	130	347	18	18	*47*	46	X	X	248,469	*176,217*	13,395
Indonesia	44	296	19	12	46	46	X	X	8,619	X	17,139

(Continued on next page)

Country	Electric power: Consumption per capita Kilowatt-hours		Electric power: Transmission and distribution losses % of output		Paved Roads % of total		Goods transported by road Millions of ton-km hauled		Goods transported by rail Ton-km per $ million of GDP (PPP)		Air passengers carried Thousands
	1980	1996	1980	1996	1990	1997	1990	1997	1990	1997	1996
Iran	491	1,142	10	20	X	*50*	X	X	40,223	X	7,610
Iraq	X	X	X	X	X	X	X	X	X	X	X
Israel	2,826	5,081	5	4	100	100	X	X	16,663	*11,947*	3,695
Japan	4,395	7,083	4	4	69	*74*	274,444	305,510	11,603	*8,664*	95,914
Jordan	387	1,187	19	10	100	*100*	X	X	78,625	47,242	1,299
Kazakhstan	0	2,865	X	15	55	83	44,775	6,481	5,042,201	X	568
Korea, North	X	X	X	X	X	X	X	X	X	X	X
Korea, South	841	4,453	6	5	72	74	31,841	74,504	40,875	*24,826*	33,033
Kuwait	4,749	12,808	10	0	73	*81*	X	X	X	X	2,133
Kyrgyzstan	1,556	1,479	6	33	90	*91*	5,627	350	X	X	488
Laos	X	X	X	X	24	*14*	120	X	X	X	125
Lebanon	789	1,651	10	13	95	*95*	X	X	X	X	775
Malaysia	630	2,078	9	11	70	*75*	X	X	16,313	9,416	15,118
Mongolia	X	X	X	X	10	3	1,871	X	1,324,119	X	X
Myanmar (Burma)	31	58	22	36	11	*12*	X	X	X	X	335
Nepal	13	39	29	28	38	*42*	X	X	X	X	755
Oman	X	X	X	X	X	X	X	X	X	X	X
Pakistan	125	333	29	23	54	58	352	84,174	43,586	*26,582*	5,375
Philippines	353	405	2	17	*0*	0	X	X	X	X	7,263
Saudi Arabia	1,356	3,980	9	8	41	*43*	X	X	4,634	4,206	11,706
Singapore	2,412	7,196	5	4	97	97	X	X	X	X	11,841
Sri Lanka	96	203	15	17	*32*	40	*19*	*30*	5,926	X	1,171
Syria	345	755	18	0	*72*	23	X	X	48,075	29,655	599
Tajikistan	2,217	2,292	7	12	72	*83*	X	X	X	X	594
Thailand	279	1,289	10	9	55	*98*	X	X	14,869	X	14,078
Turkey	439	1,161	12	17	X	25	X	139,789	30,838	*17,747*	8,464
Turkmenistan	1,720	1,020	12	11	74	*81*	X	X	X	X	523
United Arab Emirates	X	X	X	X	X	X	X	X	X	X	X
Uzbekistan	2,085	1,657	9	9	79	*87*	X	X	X	X	1,566
Vietnam	50	177	18	19	24	*25*	X	X	13,526	16,352	2,108
Yemen	59	99	*6*	26	9	8	X	X	X	X	X
EUROPE											
Albania	1,083	904	4	52	X	*30*	1,195	*80*	85,396	*5,523*	13
Austria	4,371	5,952	6	6	100	100	13,300	*16,600*	89,362	78,423	4,719
Belarus	2,455	2,476	9	16	*96*	98	22,128	9,065	1,297,626	*624,045*	843
Belgium	4,402	6,878	5	5	*81*	80	32,100	*42,800*	46,189	*31,976*	5,174
Bosnia-Herzegovina	X	X	X	X	X	X	X	X	X	X	X
Bulgaria	3,349	3,577	10	13	92	92	13,823	483	360,291	*210,161*	718
Croatia	0	2,291	X	16	80	*82*	2,458	470	190,170	*86,593*	727
Czech Republic	3,595	4,875	7	8	100	*100*	X	43,088	X	207,099	1,394
Denmark	4,245	6,113	7	5	100	*100*	9,400	9,400	19,119	*14,518*	5,892
Estonia	3,433	3,293	5	19	52	51	4,510	2,773	*516,391*	536,100	149
Finland	7,779	12,979	6	4	61	64	26,300	*24,100*	99,052	68,994	5,598
France	3,881	6,091	7	6	X	100	137,000	*158,200*	49,908	39,109	41,253
Germany	5,005	5,596	4	5	99	*99*	245,700	*281,300*	X	*39,350*	40,118
Greece	2,064	3,395	7	7	92	*92*	12,600	12,800	6,395	*1,913*	6,396
Hungary	2,335	2,814	10	13	50	43	1,836	770	247,428	*104,327*	1,563
Ireland	2,528	4,363	10	9	94	*94*	5,100	5,500	14,322	9,132	7,677

(Continued on next page)

	Electric power										
	Consumption per capita Kilowatt-hours		**Transmission and distribution losses % of output**		**Paved Roads % of total**		**Goods transported by road Millions of ton-km hauled**		**Goods transported by rail Ton-km per $ million of GDP (PPP)**		**Air passengers carried Thousands**
Country	**1980**	**1996**	**1980**	**1996**	**1990**	**1997**	**1990**	**1997**	**1990**	**1997**	**1996**
Italy	2,831	4,196	9	7	100	*100*	177,900	197,600	20,795	*18,420*	25,839
Latvia	2,664	1,783	26	47	13	38	5,853	*800*	1,209,517	1,114,210	276
Lithuania	2,715	1,785	12	11	82	89	*7,019*	8,622	915,522	545,100	214
Macedonia	0	*2,443*	X	X	59	64	*1,708*	*1,210*	X	X	287
Moldova	1,495	1,314	8	23	87	*87*	6,305	780	X	X	190
Netherlands	4,057	5,555	4	4	88	90	22,900	*27,600*	12,779	9,751	17,114
New Zealand	6,269	8,420	13	11	57	*58*	X	X	51,927	X	9,597
Norway	18,289	23,487	9	8	69	74	7,940	11,838	X	X	12,727
Poland	2,470	2,420	10	13	62	66	49,800	95,500	475,103	*284,381*	1,806
Portugal	1,469	3,044	12	10	X	X	10,900	*11,200*	13,976	13,598	4,806
Romania	2,434	1,757	6	12	*51*	51	13,800	22,400	507,379	*231,838*	913
Russian Federation	4,706	4,165	8	9	74	X	*300*	138	2,725,816	X	22,117
Slovak Republic	3,817	4,450	8	6	99	99	4,180	3,779	X	*297,426*	63
Slovenia	4,089	4,766	8	6	72	83	3,440	1,775	*142,879*	112,529	393
Spain	2,401	3,749	9	9	74	99	151,000	186,700	22,427	*15,984*	27,759
Sweden	10,216	14,239	9	7	71	77	26,500	*31,200*	127,826	103,299	9,879
Switzerland	5,579	6,919	7	7	X	X	10,400	13,000	X	X	10,468
Ukraine	3,598	2,640	8	10	94	95	79,668	20,532	2,109,937	*1,411,737*	1,151
United Kingdom	4,160	5,198	8	9	100	100	136,300	*153,900*	17,191	X	64,209
Yugoslavia (Serbia-Montenegro)	X	X	X	X	X	X	X	X	X	X	X
OCEANIA											
Australia	5,393	8,086	10	7	35	*39*	X	X	82,122	X	30,075
Fiji	X	X	X	X	X	X	X	X	X	X	X
New Zealand	6,269	8,420	13	11	57	*58*	X	X	51,927	X	9,597
Papua New Guinea	X	X	X	X	3	*4*	X	X	X	X	970
Solomon Islands	X	X	X	X	X	X	X	X	X	X	X
World	1,576w	**2,027w**	**8w**	**8w**	**39m**	**44m**					**1,389,943s**
Low income	188	433	12	12	17	*19*					103,110
Excl. China & India	155	218	14	19	17	*18*					37,945
Middle income	1,585	1,902	9	12	52	*51*					238,360
Lower middle income	1,835	1,771	8	11	54	*51*					102,609
Upper middle income	1,188	2,106	10	13	52	*47*					135,751
Low and middle income	633	886	9	12	29	*30*					341,470
East Asia & Pacific	260	724	8	9	24	*12*					143,204
Europe & Central Asia	2,925	2,795	8	11	77	*83*					46,014
Latin America & Carib.	854	1,347	12	16	22	*26*					76,275
Middle East & N. Africa	483	1,162	10	9	67	*50*					37,484
South Asia	116	313	19	19	38	*41*					22,445
Sub-Saharan Africa	444	439	9	10	17	*16*					16,049
High income	5,783	8,121	8	6	86	*92*					1,048,473

Note: Figures in italics are for years other than those specified.

Source: Entering the 21st Century: World Development Report 1999/2000 (Oxford University Press, World Bank, 2000).

Table L

Communications, Information, and Science and Technology

Country	Daily newspapers (Per 1,000 People) 1996	Radios (Per 1,000 People) 1996	Television sets (Per 1,000 People) 1997	Telephone main lines (Per 1,000 People) 1997	Mobile telephones (Per 1,000 People) 1997	Personal computers (Per 1,000 People) 1997	Internet hosts Per 10,000 people January 1999	Scientists and engineers in R&D Per million people 1985–95	High-technology exports % of mfg. exports 1997	No. of patent applications filed[a] Residents	No. of patent applications filed[a] Nonresidents
AFRICA											
Algeria	38	239	*67*	48	1	4.2	0.01	X	22	48	150
Angola	12	54	91	5	1	0.7	0.00	X	X	X	X
Benin	2	108	*91*	6	1	0.9	0.02	177	X	X	X
Botswana	27	155	*27*	56	0	13.4	4.18	X	X	5	56
Burkina Faso	1	32	*6*	3	0	0.7	0.16	X	X	X	X
Burundi	3	68	10	3	0	X	0.00	32	X	1	4
Cameroon	7	162	*81*	5	0	1.5	0.00	X	3	X	X
Central African Republic	2	84	*5*	3	0	X	0.00	55	0	X	X
Chad	0	249	*2*	1	0	X	0.00	X	X	X	X
Congo (Zaire)	3	98	*43*	1	0	X	0.00	X	X	2	27
Congo Republic	*8*	124	8	8	0	X	0.00	X	16	X	X
Côte d'Ivoire	16	157	61	9	2	3.3	0.16	X	X	X	X
Egypt	38	316	*127*	56	0	7.3	0.31	458	7	504	706
Equatorial Guinea	X	X	X	X	X	X	X	X	X	X	X
Eritrea	X	101	11	6	0	X	0.00	X	X	X	X
Ethiopia	2	194	*5*	3	0	X	0.01	X	0	3	X
Gabon	X	X	X	X	X	X	X	X	X	X	X
Gambia	X	X	X	X	X	X	X	X	X	X	X
Ghana	14	238	109	6	1	1.6	0.10	X	X	X	33
Guinea	X	47	41	3	0	0.3	0.00	X	X	X	X
Guinea-Bissau	X	X	X	X	X	X	X	X	X	X	X
Kenya	9	108	19	8	0	2.3	0.23	X	11	15	39,034
Lesotho	7	48	*24*	10	1	X	0.09	X	X	2	37,043
Liberia	X	X	X	X	X	X	X	X	X	X	X
Libya	X	X	X	X	X	X	X	X	X	X	X
Madagascar	4	192	*45*	3	0	1.3	0.04	11	2	7	20,800
Malawi	*3*	256	2	4	0	X	0.00	X	3	3	39,031
Mali	1	49	10	2	0	0.6	0.00	X	X	X	X
Mauritania	*1*	150	89	5	0	5.3	0.06	X	X	X	X
Mauritius	X	X	X	X	X	X	X	X	X	X	X
Morocco	26	241	160	50	3	2.5	0.20	X	27	90	237
Mozambique	3	39	*4*	4	0	1.6	0.08	X	8	X	X
Namibia	19	143	*32*	58	8	18.6	15.79	X	X	X	X
Niger	0	69	*26*	2	0	0.2	0.02	X	X	X	X
Nigeria	24	197	*61*	4	0	5.1	0.03	15	X	X	X
Rwanda	*0*	102	X	3	0	X	0.00	24	X	X	X
Senegal	5	141	*41*	13	1	11.4	0.21	X	55	X	X
Sierra Leone	5	251	20	4	0	X	0.03	X	X	X	X
Somalia	X	X	X	X	X	X	X	X	X	X	X
South Africa	30	316	125	107	37	41.6	34.67	938	X	X	X
Sudan	X	X	X	X	X	X	X	X	X	X	X
Swaziland	X	X	X	X	X	X	X	X	X	X	X
Tanzania	4	278	21	3	1	1.6	0.04	X	X	X	X
Togo	4	217	19	6	1	5.8	0.24	X	X	X	X
Tunisia	31	218	182	70	1	8.6	0.07	388	11	46	128

(Continued on next page)

Country	Daily newspapers (Per 1,000 People)	Radios (Per 1,000 People)	Television sets (Per 1,000 People)	Telephone main lines (Per 1,000 People)	Mobile telephones (Per 1,000 People)	Personal computers (Per 1,000 People)	Internet hosts Per 10,000 people	Scientists and engineers in R&D Per million people	High-technology exports % of mfg. exports	No. of patent applications filed[a]	
	1996	1996	1997	1997	1997	1997	January 1999	1985–95	1997	Residents	Nonresidents
Uganda	2	123	*26*	2	0	1.4	0.05	X	X	X	38,497
Zambia	14	121	*80*	9	0	X	0.31	X	X	6	93
Zimbabwe	18	96	*29*	17	1	9.0	0.87	X	6	30	181
NORTH AMERICA											
Canada	159	1,078	708	609	139	270.6	364.25	2,656	25	3,316	45,938
United States	212	2,115	847	644	206	406.7	1,131.52	3,732	*44*	111,883	111,536
CENTRAL AMERICA											
Belize	X	X	X	X	X	X	X	X	X	X	X
Costa Rica	91	271	403	169	19	X	9.20	X	*14*	X	X
Cuba	X	X	X	X	X	X	X	X	X	X	X
Dominican Republic	52	177	*84*	88	16	X	5.79	X	23	X	X
El Salvador	48	461	*250*	56	7	X	1.33	19	16	3	64
Guatemala	31	73	126	41	6	*3.0*	0.83	99	13	2	102
Haiti	3	55	*5*	8	0	X	0.00	X	X	3	6
Honduras	55	409	*90*	37	2	X	0.16	X	4	10	126
Jamaica	64	482	*323*	140	22	4.6	1.24	8	67	X	X
Mexico	97	324	251	96	18	37.3	11.64	213	33	389	30,305
Nicaragua	32	283	190	29	2	X	1.47	214	38	X	X
Panama	62	299	*187*	134	6	X	2.66	X	14	31	142
Trinidad and Tobago	X	X	X	X	X	X	X	X	X	X	X
SOUTH AMERICA											
Argentina	123	677	289	191	56	39.2	18.28	671	15	X	X
Bolivia	55	672	*115*	69	15	X	0.78	250	9	17	106
Brazil	40	435	316	107	28	26.3	12.88	168	18	2,655	29,451
Chile	*99*	354	233	180	28	54.1	20.18	X	19	189	1,771
Colombia	49	565	217	148	35	33.4	3.93	X	20	87	1,172
Ecuador	70	342	294	75	13	*13.0*	1.26	169	12	7	354
Guyana	X	X	X	X	X	X	X	X	X	X	X
Paraguay	50	182	*101*	43	17	X	2.18	X	4	X	X
Peru	43	271	143	68	18	12.3	1.91	625	10	52	565
Suriname	X	X	X	X	X	X	X	X	X	X	X
Uruguay	116	610	*242*	232	46	21.9	46.61	688	8	25	182
Venezuela	206	471	172	116	46	36.6	3.37	208	10	182	1,822
ASIA											
Afghanistan	X	X	X	X	X	X	X	X	X	X	X
Armenia	*23*	5	218	150	2	X	1.01	X	X	162	20,268
Azerbaijan	*28*	20	211	87	5	X	0.21	X	X	165	16,470
Bangladesh	9	50	*7*	3	0	X	X	X	0	70	156
Bhutan	X	X	X	X	X	X	X	X	X	X	X
Cambodia	X	127	124	2	3	0.9	0.06	X	X	X	X
China	X	195	270	56	10	6.0	0.14	350	21	11,698	41,016
Hong Kong, China	800	695	412	565	343	230.8	122.71	98	29	41	2,059
Georgia	X	553	*473*	114	6	X	1.27	X	X	289	21,124
India	X	105	69	19	1	2.1	0.13	149	*11*	1,660	6,632
Indonesia	23	155	134	25	5	8.0	0.75	X	20	40	3,957

(Continued on next page)

Country	Daily newspapers (Per 1,000 People)	Radios (Per 1,000 People)	Television sets (Per 1,000 People)	Telephone main lines (Per 1,000 People)	Mobile telephones (Per 1,000 People)	Personal computers (Per 1,000 People)	Internet hosts Per 10,000 people	Scientists and engineers in R&D Per million people	High-technology exports % of mfg. exports	No. of patent applications filed[a]	
	1996	1996	1997	1997	1997	1997	January 1999	1985–95	1997	Residents	Nonresidents
Iran	24	237	148	107	4	*32.7*	0.04	521	X	X	X
Iraq	X	X	X	X	X	X	X	X	X	X	X
Israel	291	530	321	450	283	186.1	161.96	X	33	1,363	12,172
Japan	580	957	708	479	304	202.4	133.53	6,309	38	340,861	60,390
Jordan	45	287	43	70	*2*	8.7	0.80	106	26	X	X
Kazakhstan	30	384	*234*	108	1	X	0.94	X	X	1,024	20,064
Korea, North	X	X	X	X	X	X	X	X	X	X	X
Korea, South	394	1,037	341	444	150	150.7	40.00	2,636	39	68,446	45,548
Kuwait	376	688	*491*	227	116	82.9	32.80	X	4	X	X
Kyrgyzstan	13	115	44	76	*0*	X	4.04	703	24	126	20,179
Laos	4	139	4	5	1	*1.1*	0.00	X	X	X	X
Lebanon	141	892	354	179	135	31.8	5.56	X	X	X	X
Malaysia	163	432	166	195	113	46.1	21.36	87	*67*	X	X
Mongolia	27	139	63	37	1	5.4	0.08	943	*2*	114	20,882
Myanmar (Burma)	10	89	*7*	5	0	X	0.00	X	X	X	X
Nepal	11	*37*	4	8	0	X	0.07	X	0	X	X
Oman	X	X	X	X	X	X	X	X	X	X	X
Pakistan	*21*	92	65	19	1	4.5	0.23	54	4	16	782
Philippines	82	159	109	29	18	13.6	1.21	157	56	163	2,634
Saudi Arabia	59	319	*260*	117	17	43.6	0.15	X	29	27	810
Singapore	324	739	354	543	273	399.5	210.02	2,728	71	215	38,403
Sri Lanka	29	210	91	17	6	4.1	0.29	173	X	50	21,138
Syria	20	274	*68*	88	0	1.7	0.00	X	1	X	X
Tajikistan	20	X	281	38	0	X	0.12	709	X	32	19,570
Thailand	65	204	234	80	33	19.8	3.35	119	43	203	4,355
Turkey	111	178	286	250	26	20.7	*4.30*	261	9	367	19,668
Turkmenistan	X	96	*175*	78	0	X	0.55	X	X	66	18,948
United Arab Emirates	X	X	X	X	X	X	X	X	X	X	X
Uzbekistan	3	452	*273*	63	0	X	0.10	1,760	X	914	21,088
Vietnam	4	106	*180*	21	2	4.6	0.00	308	X	37	22,206
Yemen	15	64	*273*	13	1	1.2	0.01	X	0	X	X
EUROPE											
Albania	34	235	*161*	23	1	X	0.30	X	1	1	18,761
Austria	294	740	496	492	144	210.7	176.79	1,631	*24*	2,506	75,985
Belarus	*174*	290	314	227	1	X	0.70	2,339	X	701	20,347
Belgium	160	792	510	468	95	235.3	162.39	1,814	23	1,356	59,099
Bosnia-Herzegovina	X	X	X	X	X	X	X	X	X	X	X
Bulgaria	253	531	*366*	323	8	29.7	9.05	X	X	318	22,235
Croatia	114	333	*267*	335	27	22.0	12.84	1,978	19	259	356
Czech Republic	256	806	447	318	51	82.5	71.79	1,159	13	623	24,856
Denmark	311	1,146	568	633	273	360.2	526.77	2,647	27	2,452	72,151
Estonia	173	680	479	321	99	15.1	152.98	2,018	24	12	21,144
Finland	455	1,385	534	556	417	310.7	1,058.13	2,812	26	3,262	61,556
France	218	943	606	575	99	174.4	82.91	2,584	*31*	17,090	81,418
Germany	311	946	570	550	99	255.5	160.23	2,843	26	56,757	98,338
Greece	*153*	477	466	516	89	44.8	48.81	774	12	434	52,371
Hungary	189	697	436	304	69	49.0	82.74	1,033	39	832	24,147
Ireland	153	703	*455*	411	146	241.3	148.70	1,871	62	925	52,407

(Continued on next page)

Country	Daily newspapers	Radios	Television sets	Telephone main lines	Mobile telephones	Personal computers	Internet hosts Per 10,000 people	Scientists and engineers in R&D Per million people	High-technology exports % of mfg. exports	No. of patent applications filed[a]	
	Per 1,000 People										
	1996	1996	1997	1997	1997	1997	January 1999	1985–95	1997	Residents	Nonresidents
Italy	104	874	483	447	204	113.0	58.80	1,325	15	8,860	71,992
Latvia	246	699	*592*	302	31	7.9	42.59	1,189	15	197	21,498
Lithuania	92	292	*377*	283	41	6.5	27.48	X	21	101	21,249
Macedonia	19	184	*252*	204	6	X	2.56	X	X	53	18,934
Moldova	59	720	302	145	1	3.8	1.17	1,539	*9*	290	20,245
Netherlands	305	963	541	564	110	280.3	358.51	2,656	44	4,884	61,958
Norway	593	920	579	621	381	360.8	717.53	3,678	*24*	1,550	25,638
Poland	113	518	413	194	22	36.2	28.07	1,299	12	2,414	24,902
Portugal	75	306	523	402	152	74.4	50.01	1,185	11	105	71,544
Romania	X	317	*226*	167	9	8.9	7.42	1,382	7	1,831	22,139
Russian Federation	105	344	390	183	3	32.0	10.04	3,520	19	18,138	28,149
Slovak Republic	185	580	401	259	37	241.6	33.27	1,821	15	201	22,865
Slovenia	206	416	353	364	47	188.9	89.83	2,544	16	301	21,686
Spain	99	328	506	403	110	122.1	67.21	1,210	*17*	2,689	81,294
Sweden	446	907	531	679	358	350.3	487.13	3,714	34	7,077	76,364
Switzerland	330	969	536	661	147	394.9	315.52	X	28	2,699	75,576
Ukraine	54	872	493	186	1	*5.6*	3.13	3,173	X	3,640	22,862
United Kingdom	332	1,445	641	540	151	242.4	240.99	2,417	41	25,269	104,084
Yugoslavia (Serbia-Montenegro)	X	X	X	X	X	X	X	X	X	X	X
OCEANIA											
Australia	297	1,385	638	505	264	362.2	420.57	3,166	39	9,196	34,125
Fiji	X	X	X	X	X	X	X	X	X	X	X
New Zealand	223	1,027	*501*	486	149	263.9	360.44	1,778	11	1,421	26,947
Papua New Guinea	15	91	24	*11*	1	X	0.25	X	X	X	X
Solomon Islands	X	X	X	X	X	X	X	X	X	X	X
WORLD	X w	380w	280w	144w	40w	58.4w	75.22w				
Low income	X	147	162	32	5	4.4	0.17				
Excl. China & India	13	133	*59*	16	1	X	0.23				
Middle income	75	383	272	136	24	32.4	10.15				
Lower middle income	63	327	247	108	11	*12.2*	4.91				
Upper middle income	95	469	302	179	43	45.5	19.01				
Low and middle income	X	218	194	65	11	12.3	3.08				
East Asia & Pacific	X	206	237	60	15	11.3	1.66				
Europe & Central Asia	99	412	380	189	13	*17.7*	13.00				
Latin America & Carib.	71	414	263	110	26	31.6	9.64				
Middle East & N. Africa	33	265	*140*	71	6	9.8	0.25				
South Asia	X	99	69	18	1	2.1	0.14				
Sub-Saharan Africa	12	172	*44*	16	4	7.2	2.39				
High income	286	1,300	664	552	188	269.4	470.12				

Note: Figures in italics are for years other than those specified.

a. Other patent applications filed in 1996 include those filed under the auspices of the African Intellectual Property Organization (75 by residents, 20,863 by nonresidents), the African Regional Industrial Property Organization (10 by residents, 20,347 by nonresidents), the European Patent Office (38,546 by residents, 48,068 by nonresidents), and the Eurasian Patent Organization (39 by residents, 18,055 by nonresidents). The original information was provided by the World Intellectual Property Organization (WIPO). The International Bureau of WIPO assumes no liability or responsibility with regard to the transformation of these data.

Source: Entering the 21st Century: World Development Report 1999/2000 (Oxford University Press, World Bank, 2000).

Table M

World Countries: Globally Threatened Plant and Animal Species–1996

COUNTRY	Mammals: Threatened Species	Mammals: Number of Species per 10,000 km²	Birds: Threatened Species	Birds: Number of Species per 10,000 km²	Repitles: Threatened Species	Repitles: Number of Species per 10,000 km²	Amphibians: Threatened Species	Amphibians: Number of Species per 10,000 km²	Freshwater Fish: Threatened Species	Plants: Rare and Threatened Species	Plants: Number of Species per 10,000 km²
AFRICA											
Algeria	15	15	8	32	1	X	0	X	1	145	509
Angola	17	56	13	156	5	X	0	X	0	25	1,017
Benin	9	85	1	138	2	X	0	X	0	3	899
Botswana	5	43	7	101	0	41	0	X	0	4	X
Burkina Faso	6	49	1	112	1	X	0	10	0	0	369
Burundi	5	76	6	322	0	X	0	X	0	1	1,783
Cameroon	32	83	14	193	3	X	1	X	26	74	2,237
Central African Republic	11	53	2	137	1	X	0	X	0	0	921
Chad	14	27	3	75	1	X	0	X	0	12	322
Congo (Zaire)	38	69	26	153	3	X	0	X	1	7	1,817
Congo Republic	10	62	3	140	2	X	0	X	0	3	1,356
Cote d'Ivoire	16	73	12	170	4	X	1	X	0	66	1,118
Egypt	15	21	11	33	6	18	0	1	0	84	452
Equatorial Guinea	12	131	4	194	2	X	1	X	0	9	2,135
Eritrea	6	49	3	140	3	X	0	X	0	X	X
Ethiopia	35	54	20	133	1	X	0	X	0	153	1,378
Gabon	12	64	4	157	3	X	0	X	0	78	2,197
Gambia	4	104	1	269	1	X	0	X	0	0	928
Ghana	13	78	10	186	4	X	0	X	0	32	1,264
Guinea	11	66	12	142	3	X	1	X	0	35	1,043
Guinea-Bissau	4	71	1	159	3	X	0	X	0	0	655
Kenya	43	94	24	221	5	49	0	23	20	158	1,571
Lesotho	2	23	5	40	0	X	0	X	1	7	1,093
Liberia	11	87	13	168	3	28	1	17	0	1	1,037
Libya	11	14	2	17	3	X	0	X	0	57	327
Madagascar	46	27	28	53	17	66	2	38	13	189	2,347
Malawi	7	86	9	230	0	55	0	31	0	61	1,592
Mali	13	28	6	81	1	3	0	X	0	14	355
Mauritania	14	13	3	59	3	X	0	X	0	3	239
Mauritius	4	7	10	46	6	19	0	0	0	222	1,183
Morocco	18	30	11	60	2	X	0	X	1	195	1,028
Mozambique	13	42	14	117	5	X	0	15	2	92	1,294
Namibia	11	36	8	109	3	X	1	7	3	23	729
Niger	11	27	2	60	1	X	0	X	0	0	237
Nigeria	26	62	9	153	4	X	0	X	0	9	1,036
Rwanda	9	110	6	373	0	X	0	X	0	0	1,662
Senegal	13	58	6	144	7	X	0	X	0	32	771
Sierra Leone	9	77	12	243	3	X	0	X	0	12	1,091
Somalia	18	43	8	107	2	49	0	7	3	57	761
South Africa	33	51	16	122	19	61	9	19	27	953	4,711
Sudan	21	43	9	110	3	X	0	X	0	8	506
Swaziland	5	37	6	303	0	85	0	33	0	41	2,197
Tanzania	33	70	30	183	4	63	0	28	19	406	229
Togo	8	110	1	220	3	X	0	X	0	0	1,128
Tunisia	11	31	6	69	2	X	0	X	0	24	855
Uganda	18	118	10	290	1	52	0	17	28	6	1,762

(Continued on next page)

COUNTRY	Mammals		Birds		Repitles		Amphibians		Freshwater Fish	Plants	
	Threatened Species	Number of Species per 10,000 km^2	Threatened Species	Number of Species per 10,000 km^2	Threatened Species	Number of Species per 10,000 km^2	Threatened Species	Number of Species per 10,000 km^2	Threatened Species	Rare and Threatened Species	Number of Species per 10,000 km^2
Zambia	11	55	10	145	0	X	0	20	0	9	1,105
Zimbabwe	9	81	9	159	0	46	0	36	0	94	1,253
NORTH AMERICA											
Canada	7	20	5	44	3	4	1	4	13	649	299
United States	35	45	50	68	28	29	24	24	123	1,845	1,679
CENTRAL AMERICA											
Belize	5	95	1	271	5	81	0	24	0	41	2,090
Costa Rica	14	120	13	350	7	125	1	95	0	456	6,421
Cuba	9	14	13	62	7	46	0	19	4	811	2,714
Dominican Republic	4	12	11	81	10	62	1	21	0	73	2,965
El Salvador	2	106	0	196	6	57	0	18	0	35	1,956
Guatemala	8	114	4	208	9	105	0	45	0	315	3,638
Haiti	4	2	11	54	6	73	1	33	0	28	3,345
Honduras	7	78	4	190	7	68	0	25	0	55	2,252
Jamaica	4	23	7	110	8	35	4	20	0	371	2,662
Mexico	64	79	36	135	18	120	3	50	86	1,048	4,382
Nicaragua	4	86	3	207	7	69	0	25	0	78	3,003
Panama	17	112	10	376	7	116	0	84	1	561	4,618
Trinidad and Tobago	1	125	3	324	5	87	0	32	0	16	2,470
SOUTH AMERICA											
Argentina	27	50	41	140	5	34	5	23	1	170	1,407
Bolivia	23	67	27	X	3	44	0	24	0	49	3,500
Brazil	71	43	103	161	15	51	5	54	12	463	5,935
Chile	16	22	18	71	1	17	3	10	4	292	1,229
Colombia	35	75	64	355	15	122	0	123	5	376	10,479
Ecuador	28	100	53	460	12	124	0	133	1	375	6,052
Guyana	10	70	3	246	8	X	0	X	0	47	2,180
Paraguay	10	90	26	164	3	35	0	25	0	12	2,208
Peru	46	69	64	310	9	60	1	63	0	377	3,448
Suriname	10	72	2	240	6	60	0	38	0	48	1,870
Uruguay	5	31	11	92	0	X	0	X	0	11	845
Venezuela	24	69	22	266	14	58	0	45	5	107	4,510
ASIA											
Afghanistan	11	31	13	59	1	26	1	2	0	6	882
Armenia	4	X	5	X	3	32	0	4	0	0	X
Azerbaijan	11	X	8	X	3	26	0	4	5	1	X
Bangladesh	18	45	30	122	13	49	0	8	0	24	2,074
Bhutan	20	59	14	269	1	11	0	14	0	20	3,268
Cambodia	23	47	18	118	9	32	0	11	5	7	X
China	75	41	90	114	15	35	1	27	28	343	3,112
Georgia	10	X	5	X	7	24	0	6	3	1	X
India	75	47	73	136	16	57	3	29	4	1,256	2,216
Indonesia	128	77	104	269	19	90	0	48	60	281	4,864
Iran	20	26	14	60	8	30	2	2	7	1	X
Iraq	7	23	12	49	2	23	0	2	2	2	X
Israel	13	72	8	141	5	X	0	X	0	38	X
Japan	29	40	33	X	8	20	10	16	7	704	1,418

(Continued on next page)

COUNTRY	Mammals: Threatened Species	Mammals: Number of Species per 10,000 km²	Birds: Threatened Species	Birds: Number of Species per 10,000 km²	Repitles: Threatened Species	Repitles: Number of Species per 10,000 km²	Amphibians: Threatened Species	Amphibians: Number of Species per 10,000 km²	Freshwater Fish: Threatened Species	Plants: Rare and Threatened Species	Plants: Number of Species per 10,000 km²
Jordan	7	34	4	68	1	X	0	X	0	10	1,069
Kazakhstan	15	X	15	X	1	6	1	2	5	0	X
Korea, North	7	X	19	51	0	8	0	6	0	7	1,274
Korea, South	6	23	19	53	0	12	0	7	0	69	1,360
Kuwait	1	17	3	17	2	24	0	2	0	0	193
Kyrgyzstan	6	X	5	X	1	9	0	1	0	1	X
Laos	30	61	27	171	7	23	0	13	4	5	X
Lebanon	5	53	5	152	2	X	0	X	0	4	X
Malaysia	42	90	34	158	14	85	0	50	14	510	4,732
Mongolia	12	25	14	X	0	4	0	2	0	1	429
Myanmar (Burma)	31	62	44	216	20	51	0	19	1	29	1,742
Nepal	28	70	27	255	5	33	0	15	0	21	2,716
Oman	9	20	5	39	4	23	0	X	3	4	371
Pakistan	13	36	25	88	6	41	0	4	1	12	1,163
Philippines	49	50	86	129	7	62	2	21	26	371	2,604
Saudi Arabia	9	13	11	26	2	14	0	X	0	6	294
Singapore	6	113	9	295	1	X	0	X	1	14	5,007
Sri Lanka	14	47	11	134	8	77	0	21	8	436	1,613
Syria	4	24	7	78	3	X	0	X	0	10	X
Tajikistan	5	X	9	X	1	16	0	1	1	0	X
Thailand	34	72	45	168	16	81	0	29	14	382	2,999
Turkey	15	28	14	72	12	24	2	4	18	1827	2,012
Turkmenistan	11	X	12	X	2	22	0	1	5	1	X
United Arab Emirates	3	12	4	33	2	18	0	X	1	0	X
Uzbekistan	7	X	11	X	0	15	0	1	3	5	X
Vietnam	38	67	47	168	12	57	1	25	3	350	X
Yemen	5	18	13	39	2	21	0	X	0	X	X
EUROPE											
Albania	2	48	7	162	1	22	0	9	7	50	2,093
Austria	7	41	5	106	1	7	0	10	7	22	1,462
Belarus	4	X	4	81	0	3	0	4	0	0	X
Belgium	6	40	3	125	0	6	0	12	1	3	969
Bosnia-Herzegovina	10	X	2	X	X	X	1	X	6	0	X
Bulgaria	13	37	12	108	1	15	0	8	8	94	1,584
Croatia	10	X	4	126	X	X	1	X	20	0	X
Czech Republic	7	X	6	101	X	X	X	X	6	X	X
Denmark	3	27	2	121	0	3	0	9	0	6	741
Estonia	4	40	2	130	0	3	0	7	1	2	992
Finland	4	18	4	78	0	2	0	2	1	11	325
France	13	25	7	72	3	9	2	9	3	117	1,198
Germany	8	23	5	73	0	4	0	6	7	X	X
Greece	13	41	10	107	6	22	1	6	16	539	2,091
Hungary	8	34	10	98	1	7	0	8	11	24	1,029
Iceland	1	5	0	41	0	0	0	0	0	1	157
Ireland	2	13	1	75	0	1	0	2	1	9	469
Italy	10	29	7	76	4	13	4	11	9	273	1,776
Latvia	4	45	6	117	0	4	0	7	1	0	623
Lithuania	5	37	4	109	0	4	0	7	1	0	646
Macedonia	10	X	3	X	1	X	X	X	4	X	X
Moldova	2	46	7	119	1	6	0	9	9	1	X

(Continued on next page)

COUNTRY	Mammals		Birds		Repitles		Amphibians		Freshwater Fish	Plants	
	Threatened Species	Number of Species per 10,000 km²	Threatened Species	Number of Species per 10,000 km²	Threatened Species	Number of Species per 10,000 km²	Threatened Species	Number of Species per 10,000 km²	Threatened Species	Rare and Threatened Species	Number of Species per 10,000 km²
Netherlands	6	35	3	120	0	4	0	10	1	1	758
Norway	4	17	3	77	0	2	0	2	1	20	524
Poland	10	27	6	72	0	3	0	6	2	27	738
Portugal	13	30	7	99	0	14	1	8	9	240	1,200
Romania	16	29	11	87	2	9	0	7	11	122	1,116
Russian Federation	31	23	38	54	5	5	0	2	13	127	X
Slovak Republic	8	X	4	124	0	X	0	X	7	X	X
Slovenia	10	55	3	164	0	17	1	X	5	11	X
Spain	19	22	10	76	6	15	3	7	10	896	X
Sweden	5	17	4	71	0	2	0	4	1	19	1,400
Switzerland	6	47	4	121	0	9	0	11	4	9	1,033
Ukraine	15	X	10	85	2	6	0	5	12	16	756
United Kingdom	4	17	2	80	0	3	0	2	1	28	539
Yugoslavia (Serbia-Montenegro)	12	X	8	X	1	X	X	X	13	X	X
OCEANIA											
Australia	58	28	45	72	37	83	25	23	37	1,597	1,672
Fiji	4	3	9	61	6	20	1	2	0	72	1,071
New Zealand	3	3	44	51	11	13	1	1	8	236	727
Papua New Guinea	57	60	31	182	10	79	0	56	13	95	2,821
Solomon Islands	20	37	18	115	4	43	0	12	0	43	1,959

Source: World Conservation Monitoring Centre and World Conservation Union; World Resources Institute, *World Resources 1998–99, 1998.*

Table N

World Countries: Water Resources

COUNTRY	Annual Renewable Water Resources[a]		Annual Average Groundwater Resources[b]		Sectoral Withdrawals (%)[c]					
	Supply Per Capita (cubic meters) 1998 est.	Withdrawal Per Capita (cubic meters) 1988	Recharge Per Capita (cubic meters) 1988 est.	Withdrawal Per Capita (cubic meters) 1998	Domestic		Industry		Agriculture	
WORLD	6,918	645	X	X	8	X	23	X	69	X
AFRICA	5,133	202	X	X	7	X	5	X	88	X
Algeria	460	180	56	91	25	X	15	X	60	X
Angola	15,376	57	6,017	X	14	X	10	X	76	X
Benin	1,751	28	306	X	23	X	10	X	67	X
Botswana	1,870	84	1,096	X	32	X	20	X	48	X
Burkina Faso	1,535	39	833	X	19	X	0	X	81	X
Burundi	546	20	319	X	36	X	0	X	64	X
Cameroon	18,711	38	6,982	X	46	X	19	X	35	X
Central African Republic	40,413	26	16,050	X	21	X	5	X	74	X
Chad	2,176	34	1,669	15.3	16	29.4	2	0.0	82	70.6
Congo (Zaire)	19,001	10	149,185	X	61	X	16	X	23	X
Congo Republic	78,668	20	70,163	X	62	X	27	X	11	10.00
Cote d'Ivoire	5,265	67	2,588	X	22	X	11	X	67	X
Egypt	43	921	20	68.3	6	X	8	X	86	X
Equatorial Guinea	69,767	15	24,256	X	81	X	13	X	6	X
Eritrea	789	X	X	X	X	X	X	X	X	X
Ethiopia	1,771	51	708	X	11	X	3	X	86	X
Gabon	140,171	70	52,991	0.36	72	100.0	22	0.0	6	0.0
Gambia	2,513	29	419	X	7	X	2	X	91	X
Ghana	1,607	35	1,326	X	35	X	13	X	52	X
Guinea	29,454	142	4,952	X	10	X	3	X	87	X
Guinea-Bissau	14,109	17	142,346	X	60	X	4	X	36	X
Kenya	696	87	103	X	20	X	4	X	76	X
Lesotho	2,395	30	229	X	22	X	22	X	56	X
Liberia	72,780	54	21,834	X	27	X	13	X	60	X
Libya	100	880	84	554.7	11	13.3	2	4.3	87	82.5
Madagascar	20,614	1,579	3,364	461.2	1	100.0	0	0.0	99	0.0
Malawi	1,690	98	135	X	10	X	3	X	86	X
Mali	5,071	162	1,690	11.2	2	7.1	1	0.0	97	92.9
Mauritania	163	923	122	498.3	6	X	2	X	92	X
Mauritius	1,915	410	589	X	16	X	7	X	77	X
Morocco	1,071	433	268	138.6	5	X	3	X	92	X
Mozambique	5,350	40	910	X	9	X	2	X	89	X
Namibia	3,751	179	1,270	X	29	X	3	X	68	X
Niger	346	69	247	17.9	16	57.7	2	3.8	82	38.5
Nigeria	1,815	41	714	X	31	X	15	X	54	X
Rwanda	965	135	551	X	5	X	2	X	94	X
Senegal	2,933	202	844	39.2	5	25.0	3	0.0	92	75.0
Sierra Leone	34,957	98	10,924	X	7	X	4	X	89	X
Somalia	563	99	310	38.1	3	X	0	X	97	X
South Africa	1,011	359	108	61.4	17	10.6	11	5.6	72	83.8
Sudan	1,227	666	245	13.0	4	X	1	X	94	X
Swaziland	2,836	1,171	X	X	2	X	2	X	96	X
Tanzania	2,485	40	932	X	9	X	2	X	89	X
Togo	2,594	28	1,286	X	62	X	16	X	25	X

(Continued on next page)

COUNTRY	Annual Renewable Water Resources[a]		Annual Average Groundwater Resources[b]		Sectoral Withdrawals (%)[c]					
	Supply Per Capita (cubic meters) 1998 est.	Withdrawal Per Capita (cubic meters) 1988	Recharge Per Capita (cubic meters) 1988 est.	Withdrawal Per Capita (cubic meters) 1998	Domestic		Industry		Agriculture	
Tunisia	371	376	127	167.7	9	13.6	6	0.0	89	86.4
Uganda	1,829	20	1,360	X	32	X	8	X	60	X
Zambia	9,229	216	5,420	X	16	X	7	X	77	X
Zimbabwe	1,182	136	419	X	14	X	7	X	79	X
NORTH AMERICA	17,458	1,798	X	X	13	X	47	X	39	X
Canada	94,373	1,602	12,241	38.8	18	43.3	70	14.2	12	42.5
United States	8,983	1,839	5,531	432.9	13	22.7	45	6.1	42	71.1
CENTRAL AMERICA	8,084	916	X	X	6	X	8	X	86	X
Belize	69,565	109	X	X	10	X	0	X	90	X
Costa Rica	26,027	780	5,753	X	4	X	7	X	89	X
Cuba	3,104	870	720	408.3	9	X	2	X	89	X
Dominican Republic	2,430	446	364	X	5	X	6	X	89	X
El Salvador	3,128	244	X	X	7	X	4	X	89	X
Guatemala	10,033	139	2,681	X	9	X	17	X	74	X
Haiti	1,460	7	382	X	24	X	8	X	68	X
Honduras	9,015	294	6,345	X	4	X	5	X	91	X
Jamaica	3,269	159	X	X	7	X	7	X	86	X
Mexico	3,729	915	1,450	311.4	6	13.2	8	23.0	86	63.8
Nicaragua	39,203	368	13,217	X	25	X	21	X	54	X
Panama	52,042	754	15,179	X	12	X	11	X	77	X
Trinidad and Tobago	3,869	148	X	X	27	X	38	X	35	X
SOUTH AMERICA	28,072	335	X	X	18	X	23	X	59	X
Argentina	19,212	1,043	3,543	180.4	9	10.6	18	19.1	73	70.2
Bolivia	37,703	201	16,338	X	10	X	5	X	85	X
Brazil	31,424	246	11,347	X	22	X	19	X	59	X
Chile	31,570	1,625	9,444	X	6	X	5	X	89	X
Colombia	28,393	174	13,533	X	41	X	16	X	43	X
Ecuador	25,791	581	11,006	X	7	X	3	X	90	X
Guyana	281,542	1,819	120,327	X	1	X	0	X	99	X
Paraguay	18,001	112	7,851	X	15	X	7	X	78	X
Peru	1,613	300	12,219	139.4	19	25.0	9	15.0	72	60.0
Suriname	452,489	1,192	180,995	X	6	X	5	X	89	X
Uruguay	18,215	241	7,101	X	6	X	3	X	91	X
Venezuela	36,830	382	9,767	X	43	X	11	X	46	X
ASIA	3,680	542	X	X	6	X	9	X	85	X
Afghanistan	2,354	1,825	1,241	X	1	X	0	X	99	X
Armenia	2,493	804	1,154	X	30	X	4	X	66	X]
Azerbaijan	1,069	2,177	856	X	5	X	25	X	70	X
Bangladesh	10,940	217	274	39.6	3	12.9	1	0.9	96	86.2
Bhutan	49,557	13	X	X	36	X	10	X	54	X
Cambodia	8,195	66	2,790	X	5	X	1	X	94	X
China	2,231	461	693	69.7	6	X	7	46.4	87	53.6
Georgia	10,682	637	3,166	X	21	X	20	X	59	X
India	1,896	612	359	222.4	3	3.1	4	1.3	93	95.7
Indonesia	12,251	96	1,094	X	13	X	11	X	76	X
Iran	1,755	1,079	671	738.8	6	X	2	X	92	X
Iraq	1,615	2,368	55	13.1	3	55.6	5	44.4	92	0.0

(Continued on next page)

COUNTRY	Annual Renewable Water Resources[a]		Annual Average Groundwater Resources[b]		Sectoral Withdrawals (%)[c]					
	Supply Per Capita (cubic meters) 1998 est.	Withdrawal Per Capita (cubic meters) 1988	Recharge Per Capita (cubic meters) 1988 est.	Withdrawal Per Capita (cubic meters) 1998	Domestic		Industry		Agriculture	
Israel	289	407	187	279.1	16	X	5	X	79	X
Japan	4,344	735	1,469	104.3	17	29.3	33	40.7	50	30.1
Jordan	114	201	97	107.0	22	X	3	X	75	X
Kazakhstan	4,484	2,002	2,133	X	2	X	17	X	81	X
Korea, North	2,887	727	X	X	11	X	16	X	73	X
Korea, South	1,434	632	X	29.4	19	0.0	35	83.3	46	16.7
Kuwait	11	307	X	X	37	X	2	X	60	X
Kyrgyzstan	10,394	2,257	3,043	X	3	X	3	X	94	X
Laos	50,392	259	9,332	X	8	X	10	X	82	X
Lebanon	1,315	444	1,002	224.9	28	X	4	X	68	X
Malaysia	21,259	768	3,310	X	23	X	30	X	47	X
Mongolia	9,375	271	8,765	X	11	X	27	X	62	X
Myanmar (Burma)	22,719	101	3,276	X	7	X	3	X	90	X
Nepal	7,338	154	X	X	4	X	1	X	95	X
Oman	393	656	381	280.7	5	X	2	X	94	X
Pakistan	1,678	1,269	372	527.6	2	X	2	11.1	97	88.9
Philippines	4,476	686	2,494	82.8	18	0.0	21	50.0	61	50.0
Saudi Arabia	119	1,003	109	587.4	9	5.4	1	8.1	90	86.5
Singapore	172	84	X	X	45	X	51	X	4	X
Sri Lanka	2,341	503	921	X	2	X	2	X	96	X
Syria	456	1,069	280	353.0	4	X	2	X	94	X
Tajikistan	11,171	2,001	1,011	X	3	X	4	X	92	X
Thailand	1,845	602	721	15.0	4	60.0	6	25.7	90	14.3
Turkey	3,074	544	314	112.3	16	42.9	11	0.0	72	57.1
Turkmenistan	232	5,723	778	X	1	X	1	X	98	X
United Arab Emirates	64	954	51	251.3	7	X	1	X	62	X
Uzbekistan	704	2,501	848	X	4	X	5	X	94	X
Vietnam	4,827	416	1,078	X	13	X	9	X	78	X
Yemen	243	253	89	139.2	7	X	1	X	92	X
EUROPE	8,547	625	X	X	14	X	55	X	31	X
Albania	2,903	94	2,032	X	6	X	18	X	76	X
Austria	6,857	304	2,716	144.7	33	52.1	58	42.7	9	5.1
Belarus	3,595	264	1,740	106.0	22	55.6	43	14.1	35	30.3
Belgium	822	917	84	79.2	11	68.3	85	27.0	4	4.8
Bosnia-Herzegovina	X	X	X	X	X	X	X	X	X	X
Bulgaria	2,146	1,574	1,598	566.0	3	X	76	X	22	X
Croatia	13,663	X	X	X	X	X	X	X	X	X
Czech Republic	5,694	266	X	77.9	41	X	57	X	2	X
Denmark	2,092	233	5,706	215.1	30	40.2	27	22.0	43	37.9
Estonia	8,642	107	2,718	X	56	X	39	X	5	X
Finland	21,334	440	369	47.3	12	64.9	85	10.8	3	24.3
France	3,065	665	1,703	109.5	16	52.5	69	30.2	15	17.3
Germany	1,165	580	555	97.4	11	48.6	70	47.5	20	3.9
Greece	4,279	523	237	193.9	8	12.8	29	2.7	63	84.5
Hungary	604	660	685	99.1	9	35.0	55	47.5	36	17.5
Iceland	606,498	636	86,643	394.2	31	X	63	X	6	X
Ireland	13,187	233	971	50.0	16	34.5	74	36.8	10	28.7
Italy	2,785	986	524	211.4	14	53.1	27	13.3	59	33.7
Latvia	6,685	114	879	X	55	X	32	X	13	X
Lithuania	4,174	68	322	X	81	X	16	X	3	X

(Continued on next page)

COUNTRY	Annual Renewable Water Resources[a]		Annual Average Groundwater Resources[b]		Sectoral Withdrawals (%)[c]					
	Supply Per Capita (cubic meters) 1998 est.	Withdrawal Per Capita (cubic meters) 1988	Recharge Per Capita (cubic meters) 1988 est.	Withdrawal Per Capita (cubic meters) 1998	Domestic		Industry		Agriculture	
Macedonia	X	X	X	X	X	X	X	X	X	X
Moldova	225	667	90	X	9	X	65	X	26	X
Netherlands	635	518	286	78.7	5	32.0	61	44.5	34	23.4
Norway	87,691	488	21,923	26.5	20	27.3	72	72.7	8	0.0
Poland	1,278	321	931	63.2	13	70.0	76	30.0	11	0.0
Portugal	3,878	738	521	210.6	15	38.6	37	22.8	48	38.6
Romania	1,639	1,139	368	55.5	8	61.0	33	38.1	59	0.8
Russian Federation	29,115	521	5,320	X	19	X	62	X	20	X
Slovak Republic	5,745	337	X	142.5	X	X	X	X	X	X
Slovenia	X	X	X	X	X	X	X	X	X	X
Spain	2,775	781	521	140.0	12	X	26	22.2	62	77.8
Sweden	19,858	340	2,257	69.8	36	91.7	55	8.3	9	0.0
Switzerland	5,802	173	369	138.6	23	94.7	73	5.3	4	0.0
Ukraine	1,029	504	388	82.8	18	30.3	52	17.5	30	52.1
United Kingdom	1,219	204	168	47.1	20	51.3	77	46.6	3	2.1
Yugoslavia (Serbia-Montenegro)	X	X	X	X	X	X	X	X	X	X
OCEANIA	54,795	591	X	X	64	X	2	X	34	X
Australia	18,596	933	X	162.2	65	X	2	22.6	33	77.4
Fiji	34,732	42	87,591	X	20	X	20	X	60	X
New Zealand	88,859	589	53,804	X	46	X	10	X	44	X
Papua New Guinea	174,055	28	X	X	29	X	22	X	49	X
Solomon Islands	107,194	0	X	X	40	X	20	X	40	X

[a]Annual renewal water resources usually include river flows from other countries.
[b]Withdrawal data from most recent year available; varies by country from 1987 to 1995.
[c]Total withdrawals may exceed 100% because of groundwater withdrawals or river inflows.

Source: World Resources 1998–99 (World Resources Institute).

Part IX

Geographic Index

The geographic index contains approximately 1500 names of cities, states, countries, rivers, lakes, mountain ranges, oceans, capes, bays, and other geographic features. The name of each geographical feature in the index is accompanied by a geographical coordinate (latitude and longitude) in degrees and by the page number of the primary map on which the geographical feature appears. Where the geographical coordinates are for specific places or *points,* such as a city or a mountain peak, then the latitude and longitude figures give the location of the map symbol denoting that point. Thus, Los Angeles, California, is at 34N and 118W and the location of Mt. Everest is 28N and 87E. The coordinates for political features (countries or states) or physical features (oceans, deserts) that are *areas* rather than *points* are given according to the location of the name of the feature on the map, except in those cases where the name of the feature is separated from the feature (a country's name appearing over an adjacent ocean area because of space requirements). In such cases, the feature's coordinates will indicate the location of the center of the feature. The coordinates for the Sahara Desert will lead the reader to the place name "Sahara Desert" on the map; the coordinates for North Carolina will show the center location of the state since the name appears over the adjacent Atlantic Ocean. Finally, the coordinates for geographical features that are *lines* rather than *points* or *areas* will also appear near the center of the text identifying the geographical feature. Alphabetizing follows general conventions; the names of physical features such as lakes, rivers, mountains are given as: proper name, followed by the generic name. Thus "Mount Everest" is listed as "Everest, Mt." Where an article such as "the," "le," or "al" appears in a geographic name, the name is alphabetized according to the article. Hence, "La Paz" is found under "L" and not under "P."

Name/Description	Latitude & Longitude	Page
Herat, Afghanistan *(city)*	34N 62E	116
Hermosillo, Sonora *(city, st. cap., Mex.)*	29N 111W	88
Hidalgo *(st., Mex.)*	20N 98W	88
Himalayas	26N 80E	117
Hindu Kush	30N 70E	117
Ho Chi Minh City, Vietnam *(city)*	11N 107E	116
Hobart, Tasmania *(city, st. cap., Aust.)*	43S 147E	125
Hokkaido *(island)*	43N 142E	117
Honduras *(country)*	16N 87W	88
Honduras, Gulf of	15N 88W	89
Honiara, Solomon Islands *(city, nat. cap.)*	9S 160E	125
Honolulu, Hawaii *(city, st. cap., US)*	21N 158W	88 inset
Honshu *(island)*	38N 140E	117
Hormuz, Strait of	25N 58E	117
Horn, Cape	55S 70W	97
Houston, TX *(city)*	30N 95W	88
Howe, Cape	37S 150E	126
Huambo, Angola *(city)*	13S 16E	110
Huang *(riv., Asia)*	30N 105E	117
Huascaran, Mt. 22,133	8N 79W	97
Hudson *(riv., N.Am.)*	42N 76W	88
Hudson Bay	60N 90W	89
Hudson Strait	63N 70W	89
Hue, Vietnam *(city)*	15N 110E	116
Hughes, Aust. *(city)*	30S 130E	125
Hungary *(country)*	48N 20E	102
Huron *(lake, N.Am.)*	45N 85W	89
Hyderabad, India *(city)*	17N 79E	116
Ibadan, Nigeria *(city)*	7N 4E	110
Iceland *(country)*	64N 20W	102
Idaho *(st., US)*	43N 113W	88
Iguassu Falls	25S 55W	97
Illimani, Mt. 20,741	16S 67W	97
Illinois *(riv., N.Am.)*	40N 90W	89
Illinois *(st., US)*	44N 90W	88
India *(country)*	23N 80E	116
Indiana *(st., US)*	46N 88W	88
Indianapolis, Indiana *(city, st. cap., US)*	40N 86W	88
Indigirka *(riv., Asia)*	70N 145E	117
Indonesia *(country)*	2S 120E	116
Indus *(riv., Asia)*	25N 70E	117
Ionian Sea	38N 19E	103
Iowa *(st., US)*	43N 95W	88
Iquitos, Peru *(city)*	4S 74W	96
Iran *(country)*	30N 55E	116
Iraq *(country)*	30N 50E	116
Ireland *(country)*	54N 8W	102
Irish Sea	54N 5W	102
Irkutsk, Russia *(city)*	52N 104E	116
Irrawaddy *(riv., Asia)*	25N 95E	117
Irtysh *(riv., Asia)*	50N 70E	117
Ishim *(riv., Asia)*	48N 70E	117
Isla de los Estados *(island)*	55S 60W	97
Islamabad, Pakistan *(city, nat. cap.)*	34N 73E	116
Isles of Scilly	50N 8W	103
Israel *(country)*	31N 36E	102
Istanbul, Turkey *(city)*	41N 29E	102
Italy *(country)*	42N 12E	102
Jabal Marrah, 10,131	10N 23E	111
Jackson, Mississippi *(city, st. cap., US)*	32N 84W	88
Jacksonville, FL *(city)*	30N 82W	88
Jakarta, Indonesia *(city, nat. cap.)*	6S 107E	116 inset
Jalisco *(st., Mex.)*	20N 105W	88
Jamaica *(country)*	18N 78W	88
James Bay	54N 81W	89
Japan *(country)*	35N 138E	116
Japan, Sea of	40N 135E	117
Japura, Rio *(riv., S.Am.)*	3S 65W	97
Java *(island)*	6N 110E	117 inset
Jaya Peak 16,503	4S 136W	126
Jayapura, New Guinea (Indon.) *(city)*	3S 141E	116 inset
Jebel Toubkal 13,665	31N 8W	111
Jefferson City, Missouri *(city, st. cap., US)*	39N 92W	88
Jerusalem, Israel *(city, nat. cap.)*	32N 35E	102
Joao Pessoa, Paraiba *(city, st. cap., Braz.)*	7S 35W	96
Johannesburg, South Africa *(city)*	26S 27E	110
Jordan *(country)*	32N 36E	102
Juan Fernandez *(island)*	33S 80W	97
Jubba *(riv., Africa)*	3N 43E	111
Jujuy *(st., Argentina)*	23S 67W	96
Jujuy, Jujuy *(city, st. cap., Argen.)*	23S 66W	96
Juneau, Alaska *(city, st. cap., US)*	58N 134W	88
Jura Mountains	46N 5E	103
Jurua, Rio *(riv., S.Am.)*	6S 70W	97
Kabul, Afghanistan *(city, nat. cap.)*	35N 69E	116
Kalahari Desert	25S 20E	111
Kalgourie-Boulder, Australia *(city)*	31S 121E	125
Kaliningrad, Russia *(city)*	55N 21E	102
Kamchatka Range	55N 159E	117

Sources

After the storm. (1991, August). *National Geographic,* 180.

Alaska's big spill. (1990, January). *National Geographic,* 177.

Amazonia [map]. (1994). *National Geographic,* 186.

An atmosphere of uncertainty. (1987, April). *National Geographic,* 171.

Crabb, C. (1993, January). Soiling the planet. *Discover, 14*(1), 74–75.

DeBlij, H. J., & Muller, P. (1998). *Geography: Realms, regions and concepts* (8th ed., revised). New York: John Wiley & Sons.

Department of Geography, Pennsylvania State University. (1996). Unpublished computer model output. State College, PA: Pennsylvania State University.

Domke, K. (1988). *War and the changing global system.* New Haven, CT: Yale University Press.

Eastern Europe's dark dawn. (1991, June). *National Geographic,* 179.

Economic consequences of the accident at Chernobyl nuclear plant. (1987). PlanEcon Reports, 3.

Environmental Protection Agency. (1996). Unpublished data [Online]. Available: http://www.epa.gov.

Fellman, J., Getis, A., & Getis, J. (1995). *Human geography: Landscapes of human activities* (4th ed.). Dubuque, IA: Wm. C. Brown Publishers.

Fuller, Harold. (Ed.). (1971). *World patterns: The Aldine college atlas.* Chicago: Aldine Publishing Co.

Johnson, D. (1977). *Population, society, and desertification.* New York: United Nations Conference on Desertification, United Nations Environment Programme.

Kuchler, A. W. (1949). Natural vegetation. *Annals of the Association of American Geographers,* 39.

Köppen, W., & Geiger, R. (1954). *Klima der erde* [Climate of the earth]. Darmstadt, Germany: Justus Perthes.

Lindeman, M. (1990). *The United States and the Soviet Union: Choices for the 21st century.* Guilford, CT: McGraw-Hill/Dushkin.

Mather, J. R. (1974). *Climatology: Fundamentals and applications.* New York: McGraw-Hill.

Miller, G. T. (1992). *Living in the environment* (7th ed.). Belmont, CA: Wadsworth.

Murphy, R. E. (1968). Landforms of the world [Map supplement No. 91]. *Annals of the Association of American Geographers, 58*(1), 198–200.

National Aeronautics and Space Administration. (1996–1999). Unpublished data and images [Online]. Available: http://www.nasa.gov.

National Geographic Society. (2000). *Atlas of the world,* 7th edition. Washington, DC: National Geographic Society.

National Oceanic and Atmospheric Administration. (1999). Unpublished data [Online]. Available: http://www.noaa.gov.

The Oglalla Aquifer. (1993, March). *National Geographic,* 183.

Population Reference Bureau. (1999). *1999 world population data sheet.* New York: Population Reference Bureau.

Rand McNally. (1996). *Goode's world atlas* (19th ed.). Chicago: Rand McNally and Co.

Rand McNally answer atlas. (1996). Chicago: Rand McNally and Co.

Rondonia: Brazil's imperiled rainforest. (1988, December). *National Geographic,* 174.

Rourke, J. T. (1997). *International politics on the world stage* (7th ed). Guilford, CT: McGraw-Hill/Dushkin.

Shelley, F., & Clarke, A. (1994). *Human and cultural geography: A global perspective,* Dubuque, IA: Wm. C. Brown Publishers.

Smith, Dan (1997). *The state of war and peace atlas,* 3rd edition. Penguin Books: New York.

Soiling the planet. (1993, January). *Discover,* 14.

Spector, L. S., & Smith, J. R. (1990). *Nuclear ambitions: The spread of nuclear weapons.* Boulder, CO: Westview Press.

This fragile earth [map]. (1988. December). *National Geographic,* 174.

Thornthwaite, C. W., & Mather, J. R. (1955). *The water balance* [Publications in Climatology No. 8]. Centerton, NJ: Drexel Institute of Technology, Laboratory of Climatology.

Times atlas of world history. (1978). Maplewood, NJ: Hammond.

United Nations Food and Agriculture Organization (FAO). (1995). *Forest resources assessment 1990: Global synthesis* [FAO Forestry Paper No. 124]. Rome: FAO.

United Nations Population Fund. (1998). *The state of the world's population.* New York: United Nations Population Fund.

United Nations Population Reference Bureau. (1998). *1998 world population data sheet.* New York: Oxford University Press.

United Nations Population Reference Bureau. (1999). *World development report.* New York: Oxford University Press.

U.S. Census Bureau. (1994). *World population profile.* Washington, DC: U.S. Government Printing Office.

U.S. Central Intelligence Agency. (1998). *World factbook 1997–98.* Washington, DC: Brassey.

U.S. Central Intelligence Agency. (1998). *World factbook 1998.* Available: http://www.odci.gov/cia/pub1ications/95fact/jndex html.

U.S. Central Intelligence Agency. (1999). Unpublished data [Online]. Available: http://www.odci.gov/cia/publications.

U.S. Committee for Refugees. *World refugee survey* (Washington, DC, 1996).

U.S. Department of Energy. (1996). *U.S.–Canada memorandum of intent on transboundary air pollution.* Washington, DC: U.S. Government Printing Office.

U.S. Department of State. (1999). *Statesman's year-book, 1998–99.* Washington: U.S. Goverment Printing Office.

U.S. Forest Service. (1989). *Ecoregions of the continents.* Washington, DC: U.S. Government Printing Office.

U.S. Soil Conservation Service [now the U.S. Natural Resources Conservation Service]. (1996). *World soils.* Washington, DC: U.S. Soil Conversation Service.

The World Almanac and Book of Facts 2000, Millennium Edition. (2000). Mahwah, NJ: World Almanac Books.

The World Bank. (1995). *World development report 1995.* Geneva: World Bank.

The World Bank. (1998). *1998 world development indicators* (Washington, World Bank).

The World Bank. (2000). *Entering the 21st century: World development report 1999/2000.* New York: Oxford University Press.

World Conservation Monitoring Centre. (1996). Unpublished data. Cambridge. England: World Conservation Monitoring Centre.

World Health Organization. (1998). *World health statistics annual.* Geneva: World Health Organization.

World Resources Institute. *World resources 1998–99: A guide to the global environment.* New York: Oxford University Press.

Worldwatch Institute. (1987). *Reassessing nuclear power: The fallout from Chernobyl* [Worldwatch paper no. 75]. New York: Worldwatch Institute.

Wright, John W. (Ed.). (2000). *The New York Times 2000 Almanac.* New York: Penguin Reference Books.